FIRST JIHAD?! FIRST GENOCIDE?!

A CENTENNIAL RE-INTRODUCTION TO

THE ARMENIAN HOLOCAUST OF 1915

First Jihad?! First Genocide?!

A Centennial Re-Introduction to the Armenian Holocaust of 1915

W. Colin Marris

CIRCUIT RIDER MINISTRIES, Inc.
P. O. Box 313
Oconomowoc, WI 53066

ISBN: 0692383131
ISBN 13: 9780692383131
Library of Congress Control Number: 2015904211
Circuit Rider Ministries, Oconomowoc, WI

To Garbo, with deepest gratitude for pointing the way!

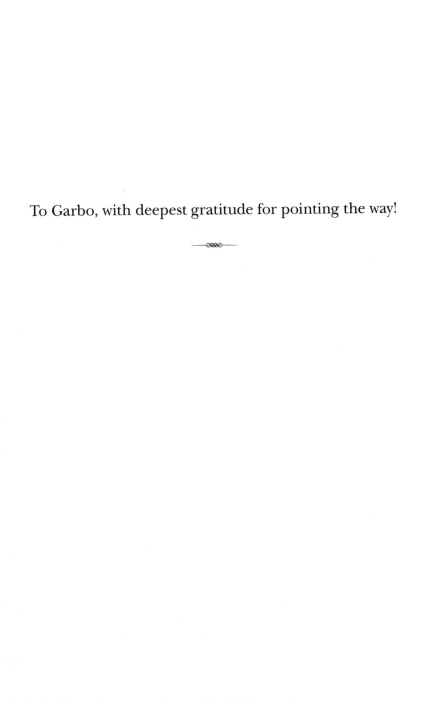

ACKNOWLEDGEMENTS

THE AUTHOR WISHES to thank the following individuals, without whom, the writing of this book would not have been possible.

The distinguished panel of professors that presided over my Master's Thesis defense: Ellen Amster, Ph.D., Neal Pease Ph.D., and especially my Thesis Advisor, friend, and mentor, Philip Shashko, Ph.D.

My appreciation also goes out to Levon Saryan, Ph.D., for his valuable advice, and guidance in the preparation of this text.

Special thanks to my close friend and associate Daniel D'Amore for his technical assistance, and constant moral support.

Most importantly, I wish to extend deepest appreciation to Dr. Charles Hajinian, who inspired the project from beginning to end.

Finally, with love and heartfelt thanks to my wonderful wife Lynne, who patiently endured the whole process.

TABLE OF CONTENTS

ILLUSTRATIONS

1) Sultan Abdul Hamid II
   From the George Grantham Bain collection, of the Library of Congress. Wikimedia (Public Domain {PD-US})
2) "DEEDS—NOT WORDS!"
   John Bull: *"Look here,—we've had enough of your palaver! Are you going to let the girl go, or have we got to make you?"*
   Great Britain, France, and Russia protest the Turkish treatment of the Armenians. British Political Cartoon from *PUNCH*, June 15, 1895 (Public Domain {PD-US})
3) French Political Cartoon portraying Sultan Abdul Hamid as a butcher for his treatment of the Armenians
   Wikimedia (Public Domain {PD-US})
4) Kurdish *Hamidiye* Cavalry
   Author: Harry Finnis Blosse Lynch, London, 1901. Wikimedia (Public Domain {PD-US})
5) An Armenian woman and her children who had sought help from missionaries, after fleeing the *Hamidiye* that had killed her husband
   Author: Bain News Service, 1899. From the George Grantham Bain collection, of the Library of Congress. Wikimedia (Public Domain {PD-US})
6) The paranoid Sultan Abdul Hamid II on a rare public excursion beyond the safety of the *Yildiz Palace*
   Photo by Bilinmiyor, 1880-1909 Wikimedia (Public Domain {PD-US})

7) "The Three Pashas" The Young Turk Ruling Triumvirate
Enver Pasha
Talaat Pasha
Djemal Pasha
Wikimedia (All Three Photos in the Public Domain {PD-US})

8) Kaiser Wilhelm II
By Court Photographer T. H. Voigt of Frankfurt, 1902. Photograph HU 68367 from the collections of the Imperial War Museum. Wikimedia (Public Domain {PD-US})

9) British Political Cartoon of the "Muslim Kaiser" Wilhelm II, dressed as the 9th century Islamic Caliph, riding the Berlin-to-Baghdad Railway
From *PUNCH*, January 25, 1911. Wikimedia (Public Domain {PD-US})

10) The "Red Sultan" near the end of his life in forced but luxurious retirement
Author Unknown. Wikimedia (Public Domain {PD-US})

11) The Battlecruiser *SMS Goeben*
Author Unkown, Deutsches Bundesarchiv. Wikimedia (Public Domain {PD-US})

12) Sir Winston Churchill, 1912
His actions as Lord of the Admiralty helped to push the hesitant Turkish Government into the welcoming arms of the German Kaiser
Bibliothèque nationale de France (Agence Rol). Wikimedia (Public Domain {PD-US})

13) "His Master's Voice"
The Ottoman Empire rashly follows Germany into the First World War
Cartoon by Leonard Raven-Hill
From *Punch*, November 11, 1914.
Wikimedia (Public Domain {PD-US})

14) The Turkish Trenches at Gallipoli

   Lt. Col. Mustafa Kemal (Atatürk) leads a brilliant defense as Commander of the Ottoman 19th Division...The Turkish victory would later have terrible consequences for the Armenians Author Unknown. Wikimedia (Public Domain {PD-US})

15) Kaiser Wilhelm II, Sultan Mehmet V, and Enver Pasha during the German monarch's visit to the Sublime Porte in 1917

   Photograph HU 57202 from the collections of the Imperial War Museum. Wikimedia (Public Domain {PD-US})

16) Death March, Kharpert, Western Armenia, Ottoman Empire, April, 1915

   Photo by anonymous German traveler. Wikimedia (Public Domain {PD-US})

17) The Armenians were packed into the concentration camp bound cattle-cars, *"after having been compelled to pay their railway fare."*

   --- Eyewitness Dr. William Dodd

   Author unknown, Historical Institute of German Bunk, Eastern office record, 1704. Wikimedia (Public Domain{PD-US})

18) The *Yildiz* Palace in 1905

   Unknown photographer. Wikimedia (Public Domain {PD-US})

19) Ambassador Henry Morgenthau, Sr.

   This is a photograph from the Harris & Ewing Collection at the Library of Congress.

   Wikimedia (Public Domain{PD-US})

20) "[We] began to see bodies by the roadside...There were between five and ten thousand all entirely naked, nearly all women and children."

   ---Eyewitness Dr. Tacy Atkinson

   Image taken from *Ambassador Morgenthau's Story*, by Henry Morgenthau, Sr. (Doubleday, 1918). Wikimedia (Public Domain {PD-US})

21) The Lucky Ones?!?

"A group of Armenian girls who escaped from the Turks and sought refuge in Russia. Some of them are the only remaining members of their family."
Chicago Examiner (December 19, 1915)

One can only guess their ultimate fate---living later under the severe repression of Lenin and Stalin!
Chicago Examiner, from the collection of Dr. Charles Hajinian (Public Domain {PD-US})

22) Mustafa Kemal Atatürk, Founder of the Turkish Republic
Foto raflarla Atatürk (*Images Atatürk*) collection of the Republic of Turkey Ministry of National Education (MEB) Wikimedia (Public Domain{PD-US})

23) Soghomon Tehlirian
Depending upon one's viewpoint, either the cold-blooded assassin, or the justly avenging executioner of Talaat Pasha
Photo by permission of Levon A. Saryan, Ph.D.

24) The "Loyal Millet"
A prosperous Armenian family... The young girl and mother holding her were both slain in the genocide. The boy nearly starved but survived and eventually lived in Beirut. The father had earlier emigrated from Turkey to America in the hopes of later sending for the rest of the family.
The Grandmother, (seated) knit her own burial cloth as she marched through the desert with her daughter-in-law. She was later wrapped in her shroud and left at the side of the road as the survivors did not have time to bury anyone.
All were peaceful citizens of the Ottoman Empire victimized by their own government.
Photo by permission of Dr. Charles Hajinian

25) *"Der Voorghmia, Der Voorghmia"* ("Lord have mercy, Lord have mercy")
An Armenian woman mourning over her dead child

Author: American Committee for Relief in the Near East
(Between 1915-1919)
Wikimedia (Public Domain {PD-US})

Please note that every effort has been made to properly trace the copyright holders of the individual photographs. Each one selected is believed to be in the Public Domain (PD-US) unless otherwise indicated

"The punishment of those who wage war against Allah and His Messenger, and spread disorders in the land, is execution, or crucifixion...or exile from the land."

---The Koran, Sura 5:33

"And they cried with a loud voice, saying, 'How long, O Lord, holy and true, wilt thou refrain from judging and avenging our blood on those who dwell on the land?'"

---Revelation 6:10

FOREWARD

"GET OVER IT!"

THE YEAR 2015 will mark the 100ᵗʰ Anniversary of what has become known as the "Armenian Genocide."

Although this terrible chapter in history witnessed the death of nearly two million human beings it is still relatively unknown to average Americans. Far overshadowed by the Jewish Holocaust of the 1930's and '40's, the tragedy that had taken place two decades earlier in eastern Turkey, remains largely ignored by the public.

Ironically, the Armenian Holocaust was both the very <u>first</u> **genocide**, and the very <u>first</u> *jihad* of the Twentieth Century!

Remaining a much disputed and very contentious topic to contemporary Turks and Armenians alike, the horrors of 1915 are vividly emblazoned on the national consciousness of both peoples. This despite the fact that all of the perpetrators, and all but the very youngest victims, have since died long ago.

At the core of the century-old debate is the abject refusal of the Turkish Government to admit to any culpability or responsibility, and the Armenians' often obsessive demand that they do so. It is impossible, however, to deny the fact that after 1915, the Armenian population of the Ottoman Empire virtually ceased to exist.

Those that perished deserve answers.

Still very timely, the issue of the Ottoman Empire's alleged complicity in the Armenian holocaust has recently been used as a reason for excluding Turkey from membership in the European Union, and was even the subject of controversy during President Barack Obama's visit to Ankara shortly after first taking office. In recent years, various nations in the EU led by France have expressed opposition to Turkey's admittance into membership without a prior *admission* of guilt for the genocide. Some observers have seen this as just an excuse masking the true economic reasons for denying Turkey acceptance, but it is still a compelling issue for many nonetheless.

Most alarmingly, the Jihadist and genocidal persecution of relatively defenseless ethnic and religious minorities is again being perpetrated in the Middle East. The brutal onslaught of the Muslim terrorist "Islamic State of Iraq and ash Sham" (ISIS) that is now being visited upon the Yazidis and minority Christians of Syria and Iraq is an eerie reminder of the horrors of 1915.

Just as it was a century ago, through man's unquenchable depravity the sands of the Levant are again being stained with the ravaged blood of innocent women and children.

"KILLING MORE TREES?!"

One might reasonably ask, "Why write another genocide book?"

After all, much has been written by historians and sociologists regarding this grisly episode. Do we really need to kill more trees and further waste the paper on this long-ago event?

Indeed, hundreds of scholarly texts have been produced that describe the alleged atrocities of 1915 but the simple answer is that despite the huge body of literature that exists on the topic, the American public still knows very little about the Armenian Holocaust with most people having never heard about it all. This is despite the fact that after one hundred years it still remains a highly contentious and controversial subject to the descendants of those who were involved.

Even lack of public awareness notwithstanding, that which has been previously published is typically either too scholarly for casual reading or is so biased as to attract only the already interested advocates of either position. Unfortunately the overwhelming majority of written material is the product of either Turkish or Armenian apologists, and is often presented with very suspect subjectivity, or is intended to further advance a large-scale agenda.

American scholars are also sharply divided. At times many of them have been accused of allowing personal prejudices, or even the lure of financial incentives to taint their objectivity. Perhaps it is high time that the American public is finally offered a basic understanding of the Armenian Holocaust, presented without ethnic or academic bias.

Now it is obvious to anyone reading the title of this text that the author refers to the Armenian plight as both a *Jihad*, and *Genocide*. (Note also the "Question Marks" indicating that the matter is yet to be finally settled). Nonetheless, it is reasonable to assume that this writer has already chosen sides and already lost all sense of fairness and balance.

All I ask is that you please hear me out, before you throw me out (and the book as well)!

Consider the simple fact that in April, 1915 the virtual destruction of the Armenian population of the Ottoman Empire began in earnest. Regardless of the reason, it happened <u>within</u> the borders of their own country and with at least the tacit knowledge of their own government.

One must suspect therefore that the century-old claims of genocide may truly be valid. When coupled with the additional fact that the victims were minority, *infidel* Christians, and the Ottoman majority were Muslim Turks who had answered the call to "Holy War" as proclaimed by their Caliph; Islamic *Jihad* is also indicated.

What yet remains to be explored together is the question of motive and intent, in as objective a fashion as possible. Then the gentle readers may decide these questions for themselves. Before that can happen, however, one must know for certain that a crime was actually committed. The American public is virtually unaware of one of the most compelling chapters in modern history, and it occurred <u>exactly</u> a century ago.

The purpose of this book, therefore, is to explore the political, moral, religious and cultural climate that precipitated what is now called the Armenian Genocide, and to attempt to reintroduce it to the American public at large. Beyond just a glimpse at a century-old crime-scene, the lessons that may be gleaned from the tragedy of Anatolia are also important for the present. With the realization that history often "repeats itself," it is no coincidence that very similar hatreds are now still converging in the Middle East.

As the twentieth century's first genocide and it's first Muslim *Jihad;* the study of the holocaust may actually help to explain the sinister forces that are still so prevalent in the same part of the world today.

"DRILLING" FOR TREASURE

My own interest in the subject began by random chance. As a student of the First World War, I had a vague notion of the Turkish Government's forced deportation of its Armenian population, but thought of it as little more than an obscure side-show. It was only after a visit to Israel that the horrors of racial and ethnic genocide first became vivid to me. Strangely, that included an introduction to the Armenian as well as the Jewish holocaust.

Visiting the Armenian quarter of Jerusalem, I became immediately aware of the seething hostility and visceral emotional attachment that the Christian minority still held for the alleged perpetrators of that long-ago event. Ninety years later the doors, walls, and lamp posts were everywhere adorned with handbills denouncing the Muslim Turks who were yet being blamed for the Armenian Holocaust.

Five years after my first trip to Jerusalem, I retired from business at the age of forty-nine and returned to the university. As a Graduate Student pursuing a Masters Degree in History, I was in the process of deciding upon the topic for my thesis when, per chance, late in 2002 it was time for my routine annual visit to the dentist.

A longtime personal friend, Dr. Charles Hajinian began the customary examination of my oral cavity in search of smaller examples of the same name. Discovering just such an object, it was decided that necessity and my year-end dental insurance benefits, prompted his immediate action. With careful skill, and a sense of professional *elan*, the good doctor proceeded to drill. During his assault on my hapless tooth, "Garbo" (the Armenian sobriquet for "Charles") began a prolonged and oft-repeated discourse on the 1915 disaster known to many as the Armenian Genocide.

Waxing eloquently and passionately on the alleged massacre of more than one million of his ancestors by the Turkish government, my second generation Armenian dentist again reminded me, as he had done so many times before, of the atrocities and depredations suffered so long ago. As soon as I was able to come up for air, during a brief respite from the depredations being committed in my mouth, I simply responded, "Garbo, it's been nearly ninety years...Get over it!"

Woe to the malefactor that provokes a dentist who currently has a high-speed drill aimed at his teeth!

Dr. Garbo now felt it his mission to not only provide for my dental hygiene, but to also convert me to the Armenian position in this decades-long debate. In the succeeding forty-five minutes, I sustained a revelation. Suffice it to say, that I later left the office with numbed lips and a clear idea for my Master's Thesis.

During the subsequent two years I immersed myself in the horrific events of 1915.

NATURAL ENEMIES?

On a later visit to Chicago during the annual April commemoration of the Armenian Holocaust, I travelled from Milwaukee on a charter bus occupied exclusively by Armenian-Americans. Invited to come along by my Armenian dentist, I soon discovered the seriousness of the pilgrimage. One elderly lady seated next to me casually enquired my name. Upon hearing it pronounced she recoiled loudly, "What are you doing on this bus? You are not Armenian!"

People around us immediately ceased their conversations and glared suspiciously in my direction. Before I could explain my research project, my friend Dr. Garbo came to my aid and announced authoritatively, "He's OK, he's Greek!"

To this, the agitated lady proclaimed with relief, "Oh that is good; Greeks hate the Turks too!"

Now in fairness, I don't personally know any Turks and was very courteously treated on a visit to Turkey. My paternal third generation Greek heritage in no way influences my feelings nor causes me to "hate" anyone. (I'm not even Greek Orthodox!) In fact, if my objectivity is questioned because of my Greek descent, it should also be noted that my maternal grandfather was German, and my grandmother was born in Austria-Hungary. As both of those vanished empires were allied to Turkey during the First World War; that should square any reason for my "taking sides" one way or another.

Seriously, my sole purpose is to attempt to render the facts as they appear from the sources in as unbiased and dispassionate a way as one can ever reasonably hope to convey. Unfortunately, however, that has not always been the case.

OPPOSING SCHOOLS

Embarking upon my new quest, I immediately ascertained that the vast majority of commentaries written on the events in question fall into two very subjective and opposing schools. On the one hand, much has been written by Armenian apologists who almost universally express a virulence and hostility towards the Turks that forbids any attempt at objectivity. This becomes somewhat understandable when one learns that each Armenian family has its own personal recollections of family members that suffered in the holocaust.

This became graphically available to me through the intervention of a friend who personally introduced me to the last Wisconsin surviving Armenian member of the 1915 "Death March." Shortly before her own death in 2004, the sweet and ingratiating ninety-seven year old recounted her horrifying experience as a little girl clinging to her mother's skirt while the latter was being sexually assaulted. To hear such a vivid and electrifying account from one so aged and feeble, gave credence to the very real connection that contemporary Armenians have to something that happened so long ago. Objectivity, by human nature, is sometimes strained to the maximum.

On the other side we discover Turkish attempts to totally discredit the allegations of government sponsored genocide and to minimize or even deny any responsibility for the well-attested destruction of the Armenian people. The usual reasons given for the undeniable demise of Turkey's Armenian population are that they fell, the unintended victims of the excesses of modern warfare; were often in armed revolt while being guilty of aiding the invading Russians; and finally noting that numerous Muslims died in the war as well.

Unquestionably, all of these answers are true.

Still they fail to address the myriad number of eyewitness accounts testifying to the mass starvation, torture, rape, and murder of an entire civilian population. The localized individual crimes and atrocities that were committed were so widespread and so numerous that they included virtually every person in the Armenian population. The same types of crimes occurred throughout Turkey, targeting the same victims and at the same point in time. That cannot just be random coincidence!

In virtual disregard for the overwhelming body of evidence, the position of Turkish apologists and their supporting scholars often falls closely to the absurd ravings of those who also deny the Jewish holocaust, the Moon landing, and the very notion that the world is round.

Into this arena, I submit that originally my own humble efforts were relatively free of personal bias. Of course it is impossible to have no subjectivity whatsoever, but my own position was neutral at the outset. I harbor no animosity to either side, and somewhat ruefully remind the reader that everyone who had perpetrated a purported crime has long ago faced the ultimate judge. The present contentious debate is alone between the heirs of the victims, and deceased participants of both sides.

As such, my ultimate purpose is to introduce the Armenian Holocaust, in this centennial year, to those in the American public who have yet to hear of its tragic circumstances. In order to give the reader an opportunity to differentiate between the opposing schools of thought, I have endeavored to specifically name the distinguished scholars most frequently quoted herein as well as to dutifully cite their work in the endnotes. This will hopefully provide the person who is newly introduced to the topic the ability to further explore it in much greater detail by consulting the wealth of scholarly manuscripts that have already been written.

As a result of my study, I was able to detect a pattern which did not *excuse* the alleged Turkish actions of 1915, but might perhaps help to *explain* them. It is high time that after one hundred years the ghosts are at last allowed to rest and that the living heirs move on, and finally do "get over it."

What follows therefore, is the result of my modest efforts and hopefully it will fairly and adequately help introduce the reader to the catastrophic events of 1915.

In any event, it will likely save you a trip to the Dentist.

W. Colin Marris
Oconomowoc,
WI
November 2014

1

A QUESTION OF INTENT: LIES, DAMNED LIES, OR GENOCIDE?

DURING THE SPRING of 1915, an alleged crime was committed on the plains of Asia Minor. Its alleged perpetrator was a government and its victim was a people. Later that year, *The New York Times* exclaimed, "the deliberate murder of a nation is taking place in the twentieth century. Turkey is now in the act of murdering Armenia and she has almost completed her work."[1]

A WOUND THAT NEVER HEALS

In early 1999, on a trip to Jerusalem's "Armenian Quarter," I was personally struck by the ubiquitous display of defamatory broadsides and posters that adorned nearly all of the myriad doors, walls, and lampposts. They told of Armenian grievances against the present Turkish government and demanded justice, reparations and an official public apology. What surprised me, however, was that this plethora of handbills and notices described an event that had occurred nearly ninety years before.

Back in 1915, during the early stages of the First World War, the plaintiffs allege that the Ottoman Turkish government systematically executed hundreds of thousands of men, women and children in what they now call "the Armenian Holocaust." I was told that the final number of Armenian dead has been calculated to total as many as two million civilian non-combatants.

As horrible as that seemed, I was still perplexed by the vehemence and the passion that was clearly exhibited by the alleged victims' descendants, so many decades later. I wondered, what could perpetuate such anger and frustration while causing it to endure beyond the conclusion of two World Wars, the Cold War, and finally the subsequent establishment of an independent Armenian Republic? It soon became certain, however, that there still exists a seething and unhealed animosity between Armenians and Turks that is as real and efficacious today, as it was in 1915.

Perhaps more remarkably, there also persists to this day a total denial of any responsibility by the official Turkish government, and even the complete rejection of the notion that such a holocaust ever in fact, took place. It is also fairly apparent that various Turkish historians (as well as a select group of their American colleagues) are determined to combat the Armenian allegations and portray the events of 1915 in a widely different light.

Both sides do agree, however, that many thousands perished. They only differ regarding the cause. Whatever the reason or responsibility, the overwhelming historical evidence testifies to the inescapable record of the mass destruction of Turkey's Armenian population. The wealth of eyewitness accounts, government documents, contemporary newspaper dispatches, and the subsequent actions of the participants speak loudly and appear to corroborate the claims for the holocaust. What is remarkable, however, is that the alleged events of 1915 were virtually unprecedented in modern times. Never before had such a thing happened for at least the previous five centuries.

The Armenian Holocaust was the starting point for a century of horror. It shocked the post-Victorian sensibilities of Western observers, and ushered the modern world into an era of genocide and Muslim *jihad*.

BRIDGING THE CHASM

In the subsequent decades since the events of 1915, open hostility and heated dispute have ensued unabated. At present there are two basic positions regarding the Armenian Genocide of 1915.

The Turkish position is one of denial and explains away the well-documented destruction of the Armenian population as an unfortunate result of the horrors of modern warfare. Advocates of the Turkish position tend to fully excuse the actions of the Ottoman government and deny that there was any premeditation or genocidal intent. They blame the Armenians as revolutionaries and point to Muslim deaths as proof.

The opposing viewpoint held by the Armenians, depicts the events of 1915 as the calculated and willful mass murder of their people by the Ottoman Empire. They contend that the government of the "Young Turks" (the popular name for the political leadership) planned to settle the Armenian Question by extermination and see the subsequent denials as a large, orchestrated cover-up.

It is possible, however, to explain the alleged genocide from a third position. Contrary to the arguments of the opposing factions, the evidence strongly indicates a shared responsibility for the initiation of the events in question. My study also convinces me that, as stipulated by the Armenians, a government-sponsored genocide did in fact take place. It challenges, however, their widely held view that the Young Turks intentionally embarked on such a policy, but rather finds on the contrary that they were originally rather well-intentioned and fairly enlightened in their treatment of the Armenians.

The genocide of 1915 was unprecedented in modern times, and was so horrible in its consequences, as to logically defy any simple explanation. Now virtually overshadowed by the later Jewish Holocaust, the Armenian affair actually helped to set the stage for it. Unlike the Nazis, however, the Young Turks came to power without a pre-arranged commitment to persecute their minority victims. In fact, the new Turkish leadership was enthusiastically received by the Armenian population. The question of motive and the apparent Turkish government shift from a policy of fraternity to one of fratricide must therefore be re-visited.

As a consequence, I hope to offer a balanced, approach to the topic, and suggest at least ten separate, but interconnected reasons for the alleged genocide.

EXPLANATIONS WITHOUT EXCUSES

As the historical evidence is overwhelming for the mass destruction of Turkey's Armenian population, it is essential to look for any indications of government sponsorship, and to study all possible reasons that such a policy would be undertaken. The intention is not to exonerate or excuse the actions, but rather to offer a plausible explanation.

In order to build the case, one needs to examine the cultural, political, economic and religious dynamics within the Ottoman Empire of the late-nineteenth and early twentieth century and search for clues to the causes of the alleged genocide. In order to provide a fair and reasoned analysis of the events of 1915, a number of steps must be taken.

First, the concept of genocide as a general topic needs be discussed so to fully assess whether the events of 1915 should be thusly classified. In addition, the lack of precedence for genocide should be considered in order to understand how such a policy could have actually been designed and inaugurated without a prior modern example.

In order to ascertain possible motives, and to understand the traditional interaction between the Turks and Armenians, the domestic, cultural, and political situation in 19th century Turkey must also be re-visited. The *Tanzimat* period and the reign of Turkish Sultan Abdul

Hamid II need to be searched for clues as to the historical status and treatment of the Armenian subjects in the decades prior to the alleged genocide.

The focus must then shift to the rise of the "Young Turks," a highly nationalistic group that took political control of Turkey in the early 20th century. We will examine what influenced their rise to power and the internal and external forces that later shaped, impacted, and even altered the new leadership's initial policies and intentions. Originally, the new government professed an enlightened and benevolent program of equality and justice towards the Christian minorities. It is therefore essential to attempt to analyze why, and how, the Young Turks stated policy of inclusion and protection for all peoples within the Ottoman Empire could eventually lead to persecution and genocide.

Next, the extent of Armenian nationalism and its historical and traditional foundations must also be explored to determine the efficacy of their claims to statehood, and whether a dangerous threat actually existed to the stability and security of the Turkish Empire. It is certain that the Armenians had inhabited the area of eastern Turkey for many centuries. Did this long-standing presence justify claims to an independent national homeland? If so, to what extant if any, did the Armenians actually intend to challenge the hegemony of their Turkish overlords?

Interestingly, the answer to that question has great relevance to the present day. It may be argued that the present Turkish policy of denial is directly tied to a persistent fear that any subsequent admission might result in financial and even territorial demands for restitution.

Of course any book on the Armenian Holocaust must include a graphic account of what actually transpired. The primary evidence for the holocaust must also be examined, but only relying on as impartial a set of witnesses as possible. Rather than rehash the much reported and possibly subjective evidence of the Armenian or Turkish participants; we will concentrate on the presumably impartial testimony of foreign missionaries, medical personnel, and diplomats that witnessed the events in question.

Although no testimony can be deemed totally free of personal bias, it is reasonable to accept the words of those that have little or no partiality or motive to take sides one way or the other. In fact, the accounts herein are primarily the reports of individuals whose sole desire was to remain within the good graces of the Turkish authorities in order to maintain and continue their individual missions within the country.

Finally, the aftermath to the tragic affair and the subsequent decades of charge, countercharge and denial need to be evaluated, in order to ascertain why this smoldering issue remains so volatile to the present day, and why it continues to be an international political concern.

I believe it is most desirable, that after one hundred years this festering demon is exorcised at last, and that the un-avenged ghosts of eastern Anatolia be finally laid to rest.

"Two Wrongs..."

After studying the claims and counter-claims of both sides, one finds that there is certainly ample shared responsibility for the mutual distrust and animosity that ultimately led to the Armenian massacres of 1915. While one might understand the explanations for Turkish concerns, it can in no way excuse either the severity or the totality of the Armenian civilian persecution.

At the risk of being branded an Armenian apologist, what has perplexed me is the total Turkish denial of any wrong-doing whatsoever. Their defense is that many thousands of Muslims also died during the same period, often at the blood-stained hands of Armenian revolutionaries. Professor Justin McCarthy has painstakingly described the persecution and atrocities that had been visited upon Ottoman

Muslims during the nineteenth and early twentieth century. He described the long prelude to the 1915 massacres as a century old "Intercommunal War," fought triangularly between three opposing foes: Turks, Armenians, and Muslim Kurds (who were at odds with both of the other groups). In explaining his intention to primarily reference "the murders of Muslims," McCarthy states that, "The effect of this on the Armenian population was great and has been long discussed."[2]

While it is certainly true that the Turks suffered harsh depredations at the hands of Christians, particularly in the Balkans; it fails to explain how that matters when considering the virtual annihilation of the Ottoman Armenian civilian population. Terrible crimes were committed by perpetrators on both sides, and both Muslim and Christian apologists have little difficulty in finding evidence of the unspeakable horrors that were visited upon their people.

In pointing justifiably to the terrible plight of Turkish refugees, McCarthy and others fail to explain how that in any way negates or justifies the well-attested crimes that were committed by Muslims against Christians in Eastern Anatolia. The adage of "two wrongs not making a right" could have easily been coined for just this debate.

The question is not whether innocent Turks died at the hands of Armenians...they certainly did. It is even possible, if unlikely, that more Turkish civilians died than Armenians. What is important to understand, however, is that the Turkish government was still fully in charge. When thousands of Muslims died, they were the victims of a myriad of individual crimes. When the Ottoman Armenians were slaughtered, however, regardless of the number; they were killed on Ottoman soil with the alleged consent of the Ottoman government... their government!

As a consequence, <u>no</u> charge of government sponsored genocide can ever be made against the Armenians. Can the same be said of the Turks?

MOTIVES FOR MAYHEM

What is not easily ascertained or proven is the charge of premeditated government sponsored genocide. Nonetheless, the Armenian population certainly ceased to exist and something had to be the cause. I believe that it was actually the result of a number of converging influences some of which were random but others were not. As will be explained, it is my conclusion that the possible Turkish motive for deporting and effectively exterminating the Armenians encompassed no less than ten separate factors. These will be examined in the following pages and include:

(1) A Turkish fear of the potential for an Armenian uprising, or "fifth-column," in association with threatened Russian military incursions into the Caucasus;

(2) The ample contemporary evidence for the existence of Armenian revolutionary activities similar to those previously exhibited against the Turks by other Christian nationalities in the Balkans;

(3) Pent-up "vengeance" focused against Europeans, and unleashed on undefended Christian minorities as an aftermath of the decades of Great Power intimidation, and the cumulative Turkish defeats previously inflicted upon them by the British, French, Russians, Greeks, Serbs, Rumanians, Italians, Bulgarians, Albanians and others, during both of the Balkan Wars and other hostilities that ultimately led up to the First World War;

(4) Traditional ethnic hatreds between Turks, Kurds and Armenians as a continuation of centuries of "blood feuds" and animosities caused and exacerbated by the conflicting hereditary racial, social, economic, and religious relationships of "Asian/European," "master/ servant," "poor/affluent," and "Muslim/ Christian;"

(5) As a result of the call for Muslim *Jihad* (or Holy War) against Christian "infidels" and to further the goals of "Pan-Islam" (The <u>first</u> jihad of the 20th century!);

(6) The local promise of plunder and material spoils often seen as tacit government "payment" to Turkish troops, paramilitary gendarmes, and civilian perpetrators;

(7) The systematic subjugation of the male Armenian population for forced labor and the females for sexual bondage;

(8) Elimination of the perceived physical barrier that the Armenian lands geographically posed to the realization of "Pan-Turkish" expansion into the Caucasus and Central Asia;

(9) As a backlash against the well-documented racial discrimination and contempt by which Europeans had traditionally characterized the Turks as inferiors;

(10) As a direct result of the growing personal paranoia, pride, or perfidy exhibited by the individual members of the Turkish leadership. In this final premise, we will explore the apparent personality flaws of the individual ruling government members themselves in search of a further possible cause for genocide.

Although much of this has been previously explored in great detail, the compilation of this list is intended to exhibit the uniquely varied yet inter-dependent causes that are embodied together beneath the one overarching heading of "Holocaust."

While each of these separate motives is individually important to a varying degree, and might help to explain the events; it is when this list is taken in its entirety as a comprehensive and corporate result, that the evidence for the holocaust becomes overwhelming.

RUSH TO JUDGMENT

As a result, it certainly appears that the Turkish Government did indeed willfully and knowingly participate in a policy that resulted in the deportation and mass extermination of the Armenian population. How else does a whole people, virtually disappear from its homeland? We shall see that any subsequent denial or continued Turkish failure to recognize the existence of the holocaust simply defies the historical facts. Countless individual robberies, rapes, torture, and murders were perpetrated against the Armenians. That remains undeniably true even acknowledging that many Turks suffered the same fate. The question remains, however, whether a host of separate crimes against individual Armenians proves the government's responsibility for the large national crime of the sponsored extermination of their entire people.

Even if it can be reasonably demonstrated that the Ottoman Empire was responsible for the Armenian Holocaust, what is so not easy to corroborate is the allegation that the Turkish actions were part of a long-standing, premeditated and intentional government program.

As we shall discuss, much of the documentary "evidence" that has been used to prove the claims of pre-meditation are suspect at best. Time and again the very same "proof" is accepted wholeheartedly by one side and summarily rejected by the other. Of course when two sides disagree, both can be wrong but they cannot both be right. In some of the matters at hand we will discover that the latter is sometimes the case.

After considering both sides, it is my belief that the Young Turks were originally genuine in their stated policy of inclusion for all ethnic groups within the Ottoman Empire, but eventually changed their beliefs as a result of both internal and external threats to their rule. Much of what later happened was due to the fact that the Turkish government was itself a victim of circumstances.

My contention is that the Young Turks never really had a chance to succeed with their original plan of inclusion due to the almost immediate challenges that faced them upon taking power. In fact, much of the blame for their shift from a relatively benevolent policy to one of hostility toward the Armenians was initially beyond their control and can actually be laid at the door of the Great Powers.

A combination of factors ultimately led to a growing paranoia and unfortunately drove the members of the Turkish government to take drastic and deadly measures. As a consequence they permitted the violent unleashing of centuries-old destructive forces that were either long dormant, or intentionally suppressed, and which subsequently erupted with catastrophic results. For this they are guilty of the near annihilation of the Ottoman Armenian population...but was it premeditated murder or involuntary man-slaughter?

LIES, DAMNED LIES, OR GENOCIDE?

In 1915 the word "genocide" was not yet in existence and is not listed in dictionaries of the time.

That is not to say, however, that the practice of government sponsored racial or national extermination is of recent vintage. The Bible tells of such practices, as do other ancient texts. As Leo Kuper observed, "the word is new, the crime ancient."[3] The actual term is originally credited to Raphael Lemkin, who first defined genocide in 1944.[4] He combined the Greek word for "race" (*genos*) with the Latin suffix for "murder" (*cide*). Lemkin's coining of the word "genocide" was first used to describe the then current Nazi atrocities against the Jewish people, and to explain that the German government had, in fact, orchestrated racial murder.

After the Second World War, The United Nations borrowed Lemkin's semantic invention and in 1948, formally adopted the "Convention on the Prevention and Punishment of the Crime of Genocide" (commonly called the Genocide Convention).[5] Although the convention itemized a number of so-called "crimes against humanity"[6] what typically separated genocide from other random acts of mass violence was the question of government intent.

Although modern history is replete with reports of massacres, pogroms, and large-scale atrocities against ethnic groups, actual government sponsored genocide was virtually dormant since ancient times, and is a reprised product of the Twentieth Century. Eric Weitz notes that from the ancient world, the Bible describes the genocidal policy that Joshua inflicted on the Canaanites under direct orders from the Hebrew God, and he also reminds us of the complete Roman destruction of Carthage, as two early examples of government sponsored holocaust.[7] Similarly, it was nearly six hundred years since Tamerlane annihilated countless civilians during his unprecedented reign of terror. Since then, however, no actual government sponsored *intentional* genocide had occurred until the Armenian holocaust of 1915.

It has been argued that the near annihilation of the Native American peoples in the United States would qualify as genocide. The centuries of warfare and contest over Indian lands resulted in the destruction of Native American tribes through a combination of combat attrition, newly acquired contagious diseases, and starvation due to the exhaustion of staple Indian resources such as the buffalo. Nonetheless, it was not the result of Federal plans to actually exterminate the indigenous peoples, many of whom were forcibly placed on federal reservations.

Some scholars have suggested that on at least one occasion the American army willfully provided small-pox infected blankets to unwary Native Americans with the ultimate intention of exterminating them. This rather unsubstantiated claim runs counter with the fact that the United States Government, under the direct auspices of Pres. Thomas Jefferson, actually introduced a program for Indian small-pox vaccination as early as 1801.[8]

The United States is not without blame for what at times was the shameful treatment of the indigenous population. It is certain that the American government often followed policies of deportation and the forced re-location of Indian populations, as evidenced by the Jackson Administration's expulsion of Cherokees along the infamous "way of tears." In addition, the indiscriminate slaughter of Sioux men, women and children at Wounded Knee, was the direct result of Army orders, (whether confused or not) which were derived from a Federal policy of brutal subjugation.[9] It is not apparent, however, that the United States Government actually conceived and perpetrated a policy of willful and intentional extermination.

Genocide scholar Guenter Lewy explains that, "The United States did not wage biological warfare against the Indians; neither can the large number of deaths as a result of disease be considered the result of a genocidal design...As for the larger society, even if some elements in the white population, mainly in the West, at times advocated extermination, no official of the U.S. government ever seriously proposed it. Genocide was never American policy, nor was it the result of policy."[10]

Similarly, the "Black Holocaust" of American slavery was the cause of untold misery and death. It was not, however, a program of intentional extermination. The black population in the South was actually perceived to be an economic asset of great value, and slave-masters sought to increase their holdings through the continued breeding of human beings. That many perished from inhumane conditions, disease, and ill-treatment is undeniable, but barbaric as American slavery was, it does not qualify as genocide.

Leo Kuper has argued that the American bombing of Hiroshima and Nagasaki were acts of genocide as they intentionally targeted civilians and killed them in huge numbers.[11] Many have countered, however, that the attacks were actually designed to shorten the war and were directed at an enemy nation, and not calculated to destroy a people. George Andreopoulos correctly contends that "had Japan capitulated before 1945, neither Hiroshima or Nagasaki would have been bombed."[12]

It was estimated that the full-scale invasion of Japan might have cost upwards of one million American deaths; a number nearly triple that which had been lost in the war thus far. The Japanese population would have been fighting for their "divine" Emperor, as well as defending their homes and families for the first time. There is no doubt that the Atom Bomb saved many thousands of American lives.

(As a personal aside, my father was an eighteen year-old United States Marine preparing for the initial landings on the Japanese mainland. It is quite possible that the implementation of the atom bomb actually saved him and consequently permitted the birth of his future sons as well).

The sad truth is that due to the acts of war, conquest, or imperialist expansion, countless millions have been displaced or slain. Whether the victims' deaths were the result of intentional government extermination or the random and unfortunate result of the horrors of modern warfare, determines the charge of genocide.

What then, is the case of the Armenians?

DISTINCTLY DIFFERENT

Whether the Armenians were merely the random victims of the "fog of war," or systematically exterminated by their government, is still hotly debated. What is distinctly different, however, is that unlike any previously recorded mass mortality caused by wars or conquests of enemy or alien peoples; all the targeted fatalities of the Armenian holocaust were *Ottoman* citizens living on *Ottoman* lands.

That is far contrary to the deadly actions waged against Hereros in Namibia[13] or Apaches in Arizona, where however deplorable, the clear cause was colonial or territorial expansion. The murderous events of 1915 were not the result of imperialist foreign designs, or the "manifest destiny" of pioneer expansionists, but rather were specifically targeted at a large segment of the nation's own *internal population*.

The discovery of the motives of the alleged perpetrators and what consequently precipitated the Turkish policy will ultimately help determine the fairness of the charge of genocide. This can be accomplished by first exploring the political, moral, religious, cultural, and military situation, and thereby finding if any justification existed for such a desperate action.

The charge that the alleged massacre of 1915 was "the first of the modern ideologically-motivated genocides"[14] has been claimed by a host of historians and sociologists. Whether viewed as a government inaugurated "strategic necessity,"[15] or simply disguised as random acts begotten of centuries of racial, religious, or class hatreds;[16] all agree that the final result was the extermination of between 600,000[17] and 2,000,000[18] human beings.

Numerous scholars affixed their signatures to "The Armenian Genocide Resolution," that was submitted and unanimously passed at the 1997 Association of Genocide Scholars (AGS) conference in Montreal.[19] It can also be argued that the United Nations Genocide Convention of 1948 would indicate that the Armenian holocaust should be considered genocide, as defined under Article II.[20]

Many compare the lesser-known Armenian genocide with the Jewish Holocaust of the 1930's-40's. George Bournoutian suggests that "in both instances a dictatorial party was in control of the state and obedience to the state was an essential part of the national culture. Nationalism and racial homogeneity was advocated and the preparations for the elimination of specific minorities were coordinated, made in advance, and in secret."[21]

Robert Melson further notes that, "under the old regimes of the Ottoman Empire and Germany, Armenians and Jews were ethno religious minorities of inferior status that had experienced rapid social progress and mobilization in the nineteenth century. These circumstances helped to create what were known as the 'Armenian Question' and the 'Jewish Problem,' respectively."[22]

It is somewhat paradoxical, however, that U.S. President Jimmy Carter's 1979 "Commission on the Holocaust" patently ignored the Armenian genocide when it stated that the Jewish Holocaust was unique and "unprecedented." The final report claimed that "never before in human history had genocide been an all-pervasive government policy unaffected by territorial or economic advantage and unchecked by moral or religious constraints."[23] Nonetheless, a plethora of comparisons exist relating the two events. Some have even suggested that the leader of Nazi Germany had actually been influenced by the Armenian massacres.

TRIAL RUN FOR HOLOCAUST

Just prior to the 1939 invasion of Poland, Adolf Hitler was reportedly queried by his generals as to the efficacy and legality of the proposed wholesale deportation or slaughter of civilians. In notes taken at the meeting by Admiral Wilhelm Canaris, chief of the *Abwher* (German Intelligence), Hitler has been quoted as saying, "...the aim of war is not to reach definite lines but to annihilate the opponent physically. It is by this means that we shall obtain the vital living space that we need. Who today still speaks of the massacre of the Armenians?"[24]

Coded as Document "L3" and placed as evidence at the 1945 Nuremberg Trials, it was reportedly given by Admiral Canaris to Louis Lochner, the Bureau Chief of the Associated Press in Berlin.[25] The notes were first published in England in 1942, and used by the Allies for propaganda purposes. Today there is widespread debate over the authenticity of Document L3 with many believing it to be specious, and in fairness, it should be noted that such an eminent observer as William Shirer, and others either ignore or dispute the validity of the quote.[26] The fact that it was formally entered as evidence in the post-war tribunal, certainly gives it added credence, however.

History Professor Margaret Lavinia Anderson asserts that there is "no reason to doubt the remark is genuine." Regardless of its authenticity, however, she correctly observes that "the Armenians and their extermination *had* once excited considerable 'talk'...the ubiquity of [which]...offers a fortiori proof that the extermination occurred."[27]

Whether or not Admiral Canaris' notes are authentic in no way affects the ultimate question as to the truth of the charges of Armenian genocide. Whether Hitler truly believed the reports of an Armenian genocide or not is immaterial. It merely indicates that there was a belief by some within the Third Reich that such an event actually took place, and that the Nazi Fuhrer may have borrowed the comparison for his own purposes. Regardless of the accuracy of Document L3, it is fairly certain that Adolf Hitler was familiar with, and impressed by the alleged Turkish actions of 1915. It is even quite likely that he would have been personally briefed on the matter.[28]

One of the Fuhrer's closest early associates, and a man to whom Hitler actually dedicated his autobiography <u>Mein Kampf</u>, was Dr. Max Erwin von Scheubner-Richter. A German envoy stationed in Turkey in 1915, Scheubner-Richter was an eyewitness to the events then taking place in the country, and certainly was aware of the Armenian holocaust.[29] As Vahakn Dadrian suggests, it is not hard to imagine that Hitler discussed the Armenian genocide with his close friend. It is similarly intriguing that the anti-Semitic Scheubner-Richter actually described Armenians as the "Jews of the Orient."[30]

The Nazis certainly cast degrading aspersions on the Armenian people and the racial theories of Alfred Rosenberg, Hitler's architect of "Aryan supremacy," classified them alongside Jews and Greeks as inferior "merchants."[31]

After the First World War, German General Major Fritz Bronsart von Schellendorf, the former Chief of Staff at the Ottoman General Headquarters, unwittingly presaged the later racial categorization of the Nazi Holocaust. In a haunting postwar dismissal of the 1915 genocide, Bronsart scornfully asserted that, "the Armenian is just like the Jew, a parasite outside the confines of his homeland, sucking off the marrow of the people of the host country...Hence the hatred which, in a medieval form, has unleashed itself against them as an unpleasant people, entailing their murder."[32]

That such a cold-blooded comparison was offered as early as 1919 certainly suggests that a blueprint model for the subsequent Jewish Holocaust was not only conceived but also readily available for copy. Eric Weitz even posits that both Hitler and Stalin personally used the lessons learned during the 1915 deportations, and the Armenians' subsequent national betrayal in the 1923 Lausanne Treaty, as a model for the later Nazi and Soviet depredations of the Second World War.[33]

In 1933, Raphael Lemkin, a young Jewish lawyer, drafted a paper that prophetically compared the rise of German Nazism with the

Ottoman slaughter of the Armenians, and even eerily suggested, "...if it happened once...it would happen again."[34]

Whatever the grounds for comparison, it does appear that classifying the events of 1915 as a genocidal holocaust is generally accepted as fact by a host of scholars. Not all agree with this characterization, however.

IMPLAUSIBLE DENIAL

The Turkish Government has consistently denied that the events in question ever actually occurred. One might fairly ask why, after so many decades, is this still their public policy?

Perhaps the fear of losing geographic territory to the formation of an Armenian homeland, or the potential payment of reparations to victim's families, have influenced Turkish thinking. Roger W. Smith attributes the official Turkish denials to a growing paranoia resulting from the post-war German response to the Jewish Holocaust. He detects a Turkish concern that "after the defeat of the Nazis, and Germany's offer to pay reparations to the victims of the Holocaust or their heirs...[that] Armenians might make claims to similar treatment."[35] This fear became further exacerbated when with the "renewed claims to self-determination that followed the close of World War II, there was the further danger that Armenians might claim not only reparations but territory as well."[36]

In the 1980's "the Turkish Government went on the offensive," and hired a public relations firm, a lobbying organization and established an Institute of Turkish Studies in Washington, D.C. Dennis Papazian concluded that those steps were taken "for the purpose of influencing the United States Administration, the State Department, the Congress, and opinion makers in the apparent hope...that either the Turkish version of history would be accepted or, at least the reality of the genocide would be considered debatable."[37]

That the Armenian genocide has scant current awareness in the American public consciousness cannot be overstated. Amazingly, even the United States Holocaust Museum, in Washington, D.C. virtually ignores the Armenian question. Aside from an occasional lecture, often as part of a broader series on genocide, the 1915 Anatolian tragedy is little ever mentioned or addressed.[38]

In the 1979 report of the "President's Commission on the Holocaust," no less an expert than the Nobel Laureate and concentration camp survivor Elie Wiesel stated that "with the Nazi genocide... the concept of the annihilation of an entire people, as distinguished from their subjugation, was unprecedented."[39]

Indeed, if those are the words of such a tireless champion of human rights, "who today still speaks of the massacre of the Armenians?"

ACADEMIC DISSENT

The matter of Turkish denials will be revisited later, but it is appropriate to point out that a group of respected, non-Turkish historians have also questioned the issue of an Armenian holocaust. Justin McCarthy prefers to depict the events as the result of an "Armenian revolt,"[40] while Heath Lowry defends the historical treatment of minorities in the Ottoman Empire, tracing what he regards as their fairly benevolent rule all the way back to the fifteenth century.[41]

A.L. MacFie presents a somewhat balanced portrayal of the events of 1915 stating that "Ottoman responsibility for the deportation and massacre of the Armenians in the eastern provinces is not in doubt... but the precise extent of Ottoman culpability remains in doubt."[42] The author then explains both the Turkish and the Armenian positions, while also discussing the merits of the contemporary belief expressed by the Entente Powers, that Germany was behind the deportations, a notion that he rejects.[43]

Harvard's William L. Langer was less reserved in his judgment, believing that Turkish actions were the understandable result of provocations that were the product of a decades-old Armenian plan to usher in Great Power intervention.[44] His assessment of the history of Ottoman-Armenian relations is decidedly partial to the Turks.[45] Similarly, Bernard Lewis described the Armenian-Turkish conflict as "a struggle between two nations for the possession of a single homeland."[46]

One of the most notable Western apologists for the Turkish position, however, was the late Stanford Shaw. His consideration of the Armenian question includes a conviction that the1915 population and fatality statistics were nothing more than exaggerated "Entente propaganda."[47] He further submits a defense of Turkish practices by actually suggesting the existence of benevolent government safeguarding of minorities after "the long years of Armenian terrorism."[48]

The present-day Turkish lobby quotes extensively from these scholars[49] while Armenian-American apologists, such as Richard Hovannisian, often denounce them as "deniers and rationalizers,"[50] or what Bournoutian calls "revisionist historians."[51] It is even felt by some that Turkish scholarship grants and access to financial incentives have unduly influenced the thinking of certain academics. What does remain quite clear, however, is the dearth of public knowledge that presently exists in this country about the Armenian question, and the apparent success of the Turkish lobby in suppressing adverse information.

Often as not, what is commonly depicted will be decidedly pro-Turkish and will fault or dismiss the Armenian position. One example is a recently published text aimed at a juvenile elementary school audience that explained the 1915 massacres as the justifiable result of Turkish "revenge for Armenian atrocities."[52]

It is not only those on the Turkish side that have exhibited subjectivity regarding the century-old debate. The defenders of the Armenian position have all but ignored the fact that hundreds of thousands of Turkish civilians also perished during the same period. It is only Ottoman atrocities that are ever considered but evidence suggests that there was a large share of Christian depredations against of Turkish victims as well.

Some have gone so far as to bring a civil-suit against Bernard Lewis for "causing very grievous prejudice to truthful memory, to the respect and to the compassion due to the survivors and to their families."[53] The verdict, in a Paris court found that "Bernard Lewis has not fulfilled his responsibilities as a conscientious historian."[54] In the resulting judgment, "a token fine was imposed." More seriously, Professor Stanford Shaw has been harassed by extremists who allegedly bombed his home, ransacked his university office, and have threatened him with other acts of violence.[55]

TRASH TALK

It is apparent to this humble observer that the debate has clearly gotten out of hand as evidenced by the name-calling and charges that scholars on both sides of the argument regularly hurl at each other. At times the debate has even turned quite ugly. One particularly vitriolic web-site labeled (libeled?!) respected opposing professors as being "incompetent," "sleaze," "racist," "criminal,""shameful," "unethical," "unscrupulous," and "kooky." One was called a "village idiot," and another professor was described as being "mentally inadequate." A certain *New York Times* best-selling author was even depicted with his photograph altered to show him sporting a "Pinocchio" nose.[56]

There is certainly no room for this type of character assassination particularly as it is leveled <u>not</u> at the alleged perpetrators themselves, but rather against modern academics with opposing views. It is even more remarkable when one considers that the alleged crimes occurred one hundred years ago.

How can the topic stir such venom amongst those that merely study it? It is as if scholars debating the real identity of "Jack the Ripper," heatedly resorted to a fist fight to settle the question!

The debate is clearly passionate some one hundred years later. It also appears that many scholars have convinced themselves that only the evidence which supports their own position is truly acceptable.

This writer hopes to provide the reader with a balanced basic introduction of the case both for and against genocide, while crediting the work of those distinguished scholars on both sides. The interested reader can then navigate the great body of solid scholarship that exists, and ultimately gain a deeper understanding of this great tragedy. With no preconceived position or personal grievance, I hope to maintain a dispassionate fairness.

"ONE PICTURE IS WORTH..."

Perhaps one of the reasons that the American public has not fully embraced the Armenian claims of genocide is the relative paucity of visual imagery when compared to the significantly greater volume of graphic material that has emerged from the Jewish Holocaust. One might point to the more advanced photographic capabilities of the 1930's and 1940's when compared with the available technology of the First World War as a logical reason for the vastly greater quality and abundance of pictures and film. What is important to note, however, is the difference in the Nazi approach to genocide.

Irving Louis Horowitz suggests that "in Germany, the genocide was highly systematic and rationalized; whereas in Turkey, genocide was random, sporadic, and episodic in character."[57] Whereas the Turks denied any government sponsored genocide, the Germans were methodically recording each heinous detail for National Socialist posterity.

The Nazis, with unbelievably cold and barbaric efficiency, documented, filmed, categorized, and indelibly preserved for future generations, the most intricate details of the extermination of millions of human beings. By contrast, the majority of images that have survived from the Armenian genocide are the result at times, of secret photographs often taken by foreign missionaries or other random witnesses, as opposed to production for official government records. Nonetheless, a large body of photographic evidence does exist and points forcefully to the claims of massacre and genocide.[58]

The debate between Turks, Armenians, and scholars identified with both sides, continues unabated, and after a century of vitriolic polemic is no closer to resolution. To judge the competing discourse, one can only attempt to individually weigh the claims and counter-claims; sift through the mounds of eyewitness testimony; and finally to independently judge the merits of the arguments.

One fact that is undeniable, however, is that where once an Armenian population flourished, it now no longer exists. Like the once large Jewish populations of Poland and Germany that are barely identified in those lands today; the Armenian population of Turkey numbered upwards of two million in 1915 and now accounts for less than 100,000 out of a Turkish national population of nearly fifty million. Horowitz shares the notion that the Turks wished to purge their Armenian subjects and he wryly observes that, "it is evident that the results have been successful."[59]

In 1983, the editorial page of *The Wall Street Journal*, felt by some to be often sympathetic to the Turkish lobby, enlisted the services of journalist, Dr. James Ring Adams, and commissioned him to fully investigate the charges. After weeks of exhaustive study, he finally concluded that, "humane opinion has the duty to judge whether we're dealing with a monstrous crime or a colossal fraud. Three months of extensive research leave little doubt that a horrible crime certainly did occur...and that Talaat and Company probably did plan a genocide."[60]

HELL IN FOUR OR FIVE PART HARMONY

Genocide scholar Helen Fein has distinguished at least "four separate types of genocide, based on the predominant motive: ideological, retributive, developmental, and despotic genocide."[61]

The "Retributive" form of genocide is used when the group in power perceives a potential threat and is fearful of a revolt from the minority.

"Developmental" genocide occurs when a group physically stands in the way of the government's planned economic expansion and exploitation of resources. This form might be either intentional or unintentional.[62]

In the case of "Despotic" genocide the perpetrator is attempting to eliminate the real or potential threat of opposition.

Finally, "Ideological" genocide is perpetrated against persons deemed as enemies of the state, and those who fail to share the same beliefs or are unlike those in the majority.

Helen Fein suggests that the Armenian massacres were of the last type, similar to the Nazi Holocaust and the Cambodian genocide of Pol Pot; while seemingly dismissing the notion that the Turkish actions were the result of attempts to eliminate an Armenian threat to their power (the retributive form).[63] If her conclusions were correct, the indications would therefore to point to the pre-meditated, systematic extermination of the Armenian population, and not just to a reaction against revolt, as the Turks contend.

The premier Armenian holocaust scholar, Vahakn Dadrian posits five types of genocide.

In the first case, "Cultural" genocide, the perpetrator attempts to forcefully assimilate and incorporate the minority group into the whole. Such a case is the Red Chinese destruction of the culture and "Sinicization" of Tibet.

Next, there is "Latent" genocide in which any human loss is due to accidental or unintended means. Collateral civilian fatalities suffered as a result of the "fog of war," or by means of the unintended and unforeseen spread of deadly disease would fall under this heading. One might place the purported Native American "holocaust," and the civilian bombing victims of Dresden, and Hiroshima, in this category.

The third, form is also identified as "Retributive," and Dadrian agrees that this is the result of the dominant group's desire to punish and suppress a potentially rebellious minority. This is the Turkish position regarding the Armenians.

"Utilitarian" genocide is the fourth and corresponds to Fein's "Developmental" type, in which the aim is the take-over and exploitation of a group's economic resources. This was often the classic by-product of European colonialism in Africa, Asia, and in the Western Hemisphere.

Finally, Dadrian suggests what he titles "Optimal" genocide in which the primary goal is the complete annihilation of the targeted group. In his opinion, this would include both the Jewish and the Armenian Holocausts.

James Waller identifies what he calls "the procedure for annihilation."[64] In his analysis of the Armenian holocaust, he exposes a pattern of extermination "set by the central government. First writers, poets, jurists, educators, clergy, and community leaders were sent to their deaths. Next, able-bodied men who appeared to be between fourteen and sixty were drafted into special 'labor battalions' [and]... worked to death, or murdered. Last women, children, and the aged, on pretext of 'relocation,' were set [out] on...death marches."[65]

To an impartial observer the charge of willful annihilation or sponsored genocide appears to be merited. That being the case, an important question remains to be answered. If the Turkish Government of 1915, actually perpetrated genocide and deliberately caused the murder of hundreds of thousands of people; what drove them to such a heinous policy?

Before we can attempt to answer that question, one first needs to examine the historical background, and the rise of the leadership itself.

—⊷⊶—

2

Tanzimat and "The Red Sultan"

O n July 24, 1908, Ottoman Sultan Abdul Hamid II, a monarch whose main preoccupation was his own survival, "bowed to the inevitable and announced to his people that the constitution of 1876...was now in effect once more."[1] From his *Yildiz* palace, in Constantinople, the Sultan received great praise and thanksgiving from his Ottoman subjects for an act that he was grudgingly forced to perform.

The Western-style legal instrument was the result of liberal calls for government tolerance and democratic reforms. What had forced the autocratic sultan to reinstate the document which he had so deliberately suppressed for decades was the bloodless coup, led by a faction of military leaders and liberal intellectuals, known to history as "The Young Turks."

What is singularly amazing, considering subsequent events, was the general euphoria and optimism that the successful revolution spawned in the Armenian population. One diarist noted how it was "impossible to describe the joy of all the Armenians."[2] Another observer wrote that, "in Istanbul, a city tense with excitement, Muslims walked the streets arm in arm with Christians; the old order and the new mingled; and high hopes were held for the future."[3]

The correspondent for *The London Times* noted that "the words 'liberty,' 'nation,' 'fraternity,' have acted like a charm on the peoples...and the response has been unanimous, enthusiastic, and overwhelming."[4]

Even the slain Armenians of Abdul Hamid's deadly 1896 repression were remembered and honored. A witness described how, "...in an Armenian cemetery a procession of Turks and Armenians listened to prayers, offered up by their respective priests, for the victims of the Armenian massacres."[5]

It appeared to many foreign observers that the Ottoman Empire was finally in the process of transforming from a feudal despotic society into a modern state with western style ideals and a commitment to human rights.

"BEDROS THE ARMENIAN"

History has cast a dim view of Abdul Hamid II. Seen as a bloody butcher, and villainous autocrat, he was often called the "Red Sultan" in the western press. France's Georges Clemenceau denounced Abdul Hamid as the *"Monstre de Yildiz et le Sultan Rouge."*[6] British Prime Minister William Gladstone referred to the Turkish monarch as "The Great Assassin."[7]

Strangely, the physically diminutive Abdul Hamid was often disparagingly called "the Armenian" or "Bedros" (Peter in Armenian) because of his appearance. Lord Kinross even suggested that the Sultan's mother might have been an Armenian.[8] It is more likely that Abdul Hamid's mother was in fact, a Circassian; a blonde slave girl from the sultan's harem who died when Abdul Hamid was still an adolescent.[9] Andrew Wheatcroft concurred that the sultan's mother was a Circassian but regarding Abdul Hamid's appearance also offers the more intriguing variant that "others more crudely questioned his paternity by suggesting that it was his father from whom he inherited an Armenian cast."[10]

Given his later "reputation as oppressor of the Armenian People,"[11] one can only marvel at the irony. Or is there possibly a deeper and more sinister lesson? Was Abdul Hamid's persecution of Armenian's partially the product of his own desire to distance himself from any direct physical descent? It is my suspicion that Abdul Hamid may have developed and exhibited a pathological loathing of the Armenians partially as *proof* of his racial "purity." Some have even proposed the seemingly outlandish theory that Adolf Hitler, and other Nazi elites, suppressed a similar fear of past Jewish blood lurking deep within their ancestries, and covered their concerns with vehement protestations of Aryan supremacy.[12]

Quoting Shakespeare, perhaps they "...doth protest too much?"[13]

(Oddly enough, a similar question of suspected Armenian parentage "diluting" pure Turkish blood is currently causing a stir in present-day Turkey. Recently allegations have been made, amidst death threats, that Kemal Ataturk's adopted daughter, Sabiha Gokcen, a heroine of the Republic, and Turkey's first female airplane pilot, is also Armenian by birth.)[14]

Abdul Hamid's ethnic ancestry was apparently "tainted" with non-Turkish blood; perhaps even that of his hated Christian minority. Whatever his reasons may have been, soon after ascending to the Turkish throne, the Sultan embarked upon a program of Armenian repression. It was to be a grisly prelude to the genocide of 1915.

"IF I WAS A CARPENTER..."

Interestingly, the Ottoman Sultan was not always regarded with derision. Initially viewed with nearly universal favor, Abdul Hamid II began his reign with great promise. In fact, it was clear in the beginning that "foreign observers were almost unanimous in their praise of the new Sultan."[15] Great Britain's Benjamin Disraeli admiringly wrote to Lord Salisbury, "The new Sultan really promises. Will he be a Solyman the Great?"[16]

The German Ambassador to the Ottoman Empire was particularly lavish with praise for both the foreign and domestic policy acumen of the Turkish monarch. In an apparent jibe at their shared European rivals, Baron Marschall von Biberstein wrote to the Austrian Prime Minister Hohenlohe that the Sultan, "...has a fine understanding for the great political questions that are bound to the existence of His Empire. With great skill He knows how to position His figures on the chessboard of Oriental politics and masterfully understands how to play the greed of certain powers against one another. But also in the realm of domestic politics He has great merits."[17]

Even those with ample reason to suspect the Ottoman throne were hopeful with the rise of the new monarch. Technically representing a semi-autonomous part of the Ottoman Empire, the Bulgarian Prime Minister Stambuloff offered personal congratulations to the Sultan on a visit to Constantinople. In September 1890, it was reported in the American Press that, "The Journal of Bulgars in an article on the anniversary of the accession of Abdul Hamid II to the Turkish throne, glowingly praises the sultan's wise and far seeing policy, which, it says, had the effect of uniting the Bulgarians and their Suzerain by bonds of gratitude."[18]

William Stearns Davis noted that, "the world at first looked on the new sultan as a man likely to bring a real regeneration to Turkey."[19]

Similarly, contemporary Western writer Elizabeth Wormeley Latimer said of him, "His rare industry, his unexampled economy, his steadfastness of purpose, and his moral courage, have won for him the affection of his subjects, and the commendation of foreigners who visit his capital."[20]

Unfortunately, the world, and his subjects, would soon discover that Abdul Hamid's "steadfastness of purpose" pertained exclusively to his own survival.

Truly a man of conflicting images, Abdul Hamid was seen as cowardly and craven by his enemies, yet the Sultan was an avid wrestler and often held events in which he competed with the Empire's best sportsmen. In actuality, Abdul Hamid was a man of varied interests who often demonstrated seemingly inconsistent personality traits.

Possessing many talents, the Sultan was a skilled craftsman and carpenter who designed and constructed a number of pieces of furniture for his palace. "Pottering about his carpentry shop, and having the latest adventures of Sherlock Holmes read aloud to him at night," were among his "principal relaxations."[21]

In an earnest desire to emulate the West, the sultan was something of an innovator. He provided the empire with a basic structure of secondary education, with a network of railways and, late in his reign, with plans to improve the network of roads."[22] In addition, Abdul Hamid established an extensive telegraph system and developed a great interest in the "informational value" of photography.[23] Of course all of these "innovations" further increased the sultan's ability to gather information on his potential enemies and to further centralize his tight governmental control.

Both a poet and lover of western music, Abdul Hamid was a great patron of the arts and personally translated many classic operas into Turkish while actually composing a small number of original pieces himself. The Sultan, "who by nature had both wit and humor," took great "pleasure in French farces and light opera, detective novels and the society of Europeans,"[24] but his western leanings abruptly ended when it came to the matter of establishing a European-style constitutional monarchy.

It was not long after coming to the throne before Abdul Hamid betrayed personality flaws often bordering on the ridiculous. Ever fearful for his reign, the Sultan detected threats in the most amazing places. One particular example of the monarch's growing paranoia defies rational belief.

It was reported that, "An American mission college imported some elementary chemistry text-books from England. The consignment was held up in the customs-office, and the professor in charge was informed that the volumes were 'highly seditious.' When he expressed surprise, he was told a dangerous cipher against the sultan had been discovered, and he was shown the familiar formula for water, H2O. It was gravely explained to him that 'H' undoubtedly indicated [Abdul] Hamid, and '2' even more clearly connoted 'Second,' while 'O' was a palpable covering for 'nothing.' The cipher therefore obviously read, 'Abdul Hamid Second equals, or is good for nothing,' a deliberate incitement to treason!"[25]

Outwardly the Ottoman monarch betrayed no sense of his empire's terrible decline. Despite his obvious personal paranoia, the sultan still viewed his own international position with jealous pride and superiority. The autocratic monarch of an empire of more than thirty million people, Abdul Hamid II was both Sultan and Caliph; the physical ruler of the Ottomans and the spiritual leader of the world's Muslims.

As such, Abdul Hamid and his advisors "considered themselves the equal of their European fellows, and the Ottoman State the peer to the European Powers."[26]

THE "SUBLIME PORTE"

The government of Sultan Abdul Hamid II was accessible to foreign diplomats through a special gate dubbed the "Sublime Porte" (a French translation from the Turkish for "High Gate"). Beyond the imposing portal (that still stands today) one entered the courts of the Topkapi Palace, the home to the sultans for more than four hundred years until the residences were moved to the modern *Dolmabahçe* Palace in the mid nineteenth century.

In the ensuing years, the complex continued to house the principal offices of the foreign ministry and it was there that the Grand Vizier, the Sultan's most trusted and powerful minister held court. The "Sublime Porte" eventually became the name by which diplomats referred to the Turkish government.

The Turkish court at Constantinople was a strange mixture of East and West. At the close of the nineteenth century the Ottoman Empire was bent on westernization yet the sultan was still served by imperial eunuchs who looked after the royal harem of more than five hundred wives and concubines. Turkey under Abdul Hamid was an odd mixture of Mozart and the "Arabian nights."

The empire was comprised of dozens of administrative provinces or *Vilayets* that stretched from the Balkans to the Caucasus; from North Africa to Persia. Consisting of numerous ethnic and religious groups, the Ottoman Empire was a polyglot of languages, customs, and beliefs. With numerous minority Christian and Jewish subjects, the Ottoman Empire was the center of Islam, and home to thirty million Mohammedans.

As Caliph, the sultan in Constantinople was the overseer of the world's 300 million Muslims. The Mohammedan holy city of Mecca was situated in the Ottoman province of Arabia, and ever since the empire's inception at the close of the fourteenth century, the Turks "were determined to conquer the world for Islam."[27]

Ever since 1453, when Sultan Mehmed II conquered the city of Constantinople and effectively ended the Byzantine Empire, the Turks were both greatly feared and afforded a near mythical reputation. "From the moment when Constantinople fell, Europeans regarded the Turks with a mixture of horror and fascination. They were outside the bounds of society, and almost beyond the realm of humanity."[28]

The "Terrible Turks" were considered to be God's punishment for the sins and failings of Christendom, and it was anticipated that the Islamic juggernaut would soon overrun the continent of Europe. Finally checked at the gates of Vienna in 1683, the Turkish tide first began to slowly recede and then rapidly reverse by the end of the nineteenth century.

"THE SICK MAN OF EUROPE"

At its illustrious height the Ottoman Empire stretched from Vienna on the Danube to the shores of the Arabian Gulf; from Persia in the East, directly across the desert sands of Egypt and North Africa to Morocco in the West. In addition to present day Turkey, the Ottoman domains once included the modern states of Iraq, Syria, Jordan, Lebanon, Israel, Saudi Arabia, Yemen, Kuwait, the Persian Gulf Emirates, Egypt, Libya, and Algeria. The Empire's extensive holdings in the Balkans included Greece, Serbia, Bulgaria, Romania, Macedonia, Montenegro, Bosnia, Albania, Croatia, Hungary, and extended into Austria.

Now Sultan Abdul Hamid II was the absolute ruler of a once supremely powerful and enormous empire that had since fallen into abject decline. Under his watch, the formerly extensive Ottoman possessions in the Balkans, and North Africa had virtually disappeared. Following the earlier example of Greece; one-by-one, the Balkan states threw off Turkish rule with the often overt support of the Great Powers. The newly independent European states of Serbia, Romania, and Montenegro were created as the result of a disastrous Turkish war against Russia. In addition, by the terms of the 1878 Treaty of San Stefano, greater autonomy was granted to Bulgaria.

Later that same year, fearful that Russia had gained too much influence in the Balkans, the Congress of Berlin was convened at the insistence of the European Great Powers. Of paramount concern to Great Britain, Germany, France, Italy, and Austria-Hungary was the further encroachment of the Russians on the Dardanelles. Intent on keeping Constantinople in Turkish hands, the powers blunted the Russian gains in the war, and prevented their long dreamed-of access to the Straits.

Not all was beneficial to the Sultan, however, as the Great Powers continued to carve out additional portions of the Ottoman Empire. As recompense for their support, Great Britain assumed a "protectorate" over Egypt, Sudan, and Cyprus; shortly later, France occupied Tunisia; Austria-Hungary took administrative control of Bosnia and Herzegovina; the provinces of Macedonia and Albania were granted greater autonomy within the Turkish Empire; and Bulgaria was granted virtual independence. Although all these possessions were still technically part of the Ottoman Empire, their control was effectively lost forever.

German Chancellor Otto Von Bismarck, who hosted the conference, felt certain that he had achieved stability in the Balkans. As time went on, however, it became increasingly apparent that indeed, quite the opposite had occurred. As we shall further discuss below, the resentment felt by Russia, particularly towards Germany; the dissatisfaction over territorial boundaries between Serbia, Greece, Romania, and Bulgaria; along with the growing expansionist aims of Austria-Hungary; all escalated into the eventual eruption of the Balkan Wars of 1912-1913, and the subsequent start of the First World War.

Through it all, Turkey, dubbed disparagingly "The Sick Man of Europe," continued to steadily decline. The external pressures exerted by the Great Powers, along with the ever-increasing internal rumblings of those minorities still tied (or "chained") to the empire, hastened the rise of a strongly nationalistic and forward thinking movement within the empire. Determined to end the despotic and inept rule of the Sultan, forces within Turkey were mobilizing with the mutual aims of reversing Turkey's decline and propelling her into the modern world.

The westward winds of revolt were approaching at gale force.

A NECESSARY BEGINNING

The Constitution of 1876, the reinstatement of which had caused such exuberance, particularly amongst the Christian population, was the product of decades of increasing liberalism in the Sublime Porte. The movement to embrace western-style reforms, and hopefully to usher in the attendant economic and military advantages enjoyed by the Great European Powers, can be traced to the beginning of the *Tanzimat* period in 1839. With the formal declaration of the Imperial Edict (*Hatt-i sherif*) of Gulhane, the Sultan Mahmoud II ushered in the subsequent forty-year period of "reordering" (*Tanzimat*).[29]

The *Tanzimat* introduced to the Ottoman Empire "new European-originated concepts such as nation, freedom, homeland, and equality."[30] David Kushner states that, "the interests of the Ottoman Empire seemed indeed to demand the adoption of these concepts."[31] He notes that "beginning with the successful Greek uprising in the 1820's the Ottoman Empire was no longer facing only threats of encroachment from the outside, but also threats of disintegration from within."[32]

The large minority Christian populations, "affected by Western ideas, were becoming increasingly restless and demanding rights of freedom and equality which hitherto had been denied them."[33] Their cause was increasingly being championed by European public opinion and the danger was not lost on the Ottoman government. The ever-increasing threat of Great Power intervention on behalf of the Christian minorities, as well as the comparative weakness of the Turkish military, persuaded the Sublime Porte to "reorder" the empire.

Among the highest priorities were military reform, education, legal and administrative restructuring, and economic development.[34] Ever since the "invincibility" of Turkish arms was forever dispelled at the Battle of Lepanto (1571), "the military might of the Ottoman Empire had shown progressive deterioration as it had suffered important military setbacks in the seventeenth, eighteenth, and nineteenth centuries."[35]

Similarly, illiteracy was rampant within the empire and the goal was not only to teach, but also simplify the Turkish language.[36] The legal system was a shambles of corruption, and "the administration had reached such a state that the *rishvet* (bribe) had become a way of life."[37]

Finally, in order to compete economically the Tanzimat leaders understood the need to emulate the Great Powers. "Through borrowing advanced European technology and science the reformers hoped to bring the Ottoman Empire up to the level of a strong and civilized state."[38]

PAN-OTTOMANISM

In order to compete with the West, the empire had to embrace European strengths without abandoning the Islamic faith or reducing the overall control of the Muslim plurality. What evolved was the concept of "Ottomanism" (*Osmanlilik*) "which would counteract separatist nationalistic tendencies among the minorities and help to preserve the empire intact by winning stronger allegiance of all subjects to a beneficent imperial government."[39]

Prior to the *Tanzimat*, the Christian minorities "were referred to as *giavurs* (infidels) and *rayas* (cattle)."[40] They were distinctly subordinated to the Turkish majority, and often forced to "wear certain types of clothing as distinguishing marks of their inferior national or religious affiliations...[Similarly] they were obliged, in the presence of the ruling class, to observe certain elements of protocol on the street and elsewhere."[41]

To the minority populations "the traditional dividing lines among people were religious, not national. The *millet*, the religious community, to which an individual belonged, was the determining factor in his self-identification and in his identification of others."[42] The millet system proved a barrier to *Osmanlilik* in that their "continued existence as separate legal entities, whose rights the great powers frequently supported," ultimately tended to promote "separatist nationalisms."[43]

Rather than fostering Ottomanism, the millet system seemed to support a "dualism' of Islamic and non-Islamic communities subsisting "side by side."[44] Much like the Jewish ghettoes of Eastern Europe that tentatively co-existed alongside the hamlets of the Christian majority; the millets often helped breed suspicion and hostility between neighboring communities. Despite the difficulties, however, the Tanzimat did attempt to enact an atmosphere of "equality under the law of all Ottoman subjects regardless of sect."[45]

Ethnic and religious differences, notwithstanding, the Armenians were well represented in the Tanzimat reform movement. The Sultan relied heavily on a number of Armenian advisors, and Mahmoud II's "closest personal friend" was Haroutioun Bezjian Amira (known as Kazaz Artin among the Turks), the Director of the Imperial Mint.[46]

It was thought "that Mahmoud II never made a decision without first consulting Bezjian who had more access to the royal presence than did the grand vizier."[47] It is even suggested that "Bezjian's most far-reaching effect on reform was his role in dividing and conquering the Janissaries...[which] helped lay the ground-work for the reform era."[48]

THE "AUSPICIOUS INCIDENT"

By the start of the nineteenth century the "elite" cadre of the Turkish military organization known as the Janissaries epitomized all that was wrong and backward in the Ottoman Empire. Having long-ago developed into the most fabled fighting force of the Turkish army, the Janissaries were initially formed as a corps (*ocak*) of Christian slaves. Through strict discipline and military success the Janissaries later evolved into a separate Turkish aristocracy. Eventually they became a dominant force in Turkish society exerting great political influence and strict internal military control.

"In battle, the Janissaries fought for the honour of the sultan and their order."[49] Eventually, however, the *ocak* became the makers rather than merely the instruments of policy. Time and again the Janissaries placed and replaced sultans upon the Ottoman throne, becoming a true political power unto themselves.

Their presence was ubiquitous, and influenced government and political life throughout the Ottoman domains. "Every great city of the empire—Aleppo, Damascus, Salonika, Adrianople, Bursa— had its contingent of Janissaries...By the end of the eighteenth, the Janissaries in many cities had abandoned all pretense that they were a fighting force," rather preferring to establish networks of local political control rife with corruption, and bribery.[50]

By the reign of Mahmoud II, the once "Spartan" Janissaries had regressed in military effectiveness due to lives of ease and indulgence. Stubbornly refusing to adopt the use of modern European weapons and military tactics, which they viewed as cowardly and unworthy of the martial traditions of Islam, the Janissary corps had become virtually obsolete by the middle of the nineteenth century. "They saw no honour or bravery in the methods of the West. Despite defeat after defeat on the battlefield, they remained convinced that their way of war, hand to hand with the enemy, was right—the true Islamic path."[51]

Seeing them as a barrier to modernization, Mahmoud II finally concluded that the *ocak* had become a great impediment to the stability and future growth of the empire. As a result the sultan "prepared a plan not to reform the janissaries but to remove them entirely."[52] In 1826 the Turkish leadership tricked the antiquated Janissaries into launching a futile revolt against the well-armed troops of the sultan.

In what has since been dubbed the "Auspicious Incident," the leaders of the Janissaries were executed and the corps of more than 135,000 members was disbanded forever to be replaced by a more modern imperial army.

THE LOYAL MILLET

After Haroutioun Bezijan's death, in 1839, the Tanzimat was formally launched with the notable support of other influential Armenians. Reschid Pasha, whom Bernard Lewis called "the architect of Turkish reforms in the nineteenth century,"[53] was also closely aligned with an Armenian confidante, Hagop Gerjigian. A number of other high-ranking Turkish officials also worked closely with Armenian advisors,[54] and the Armenians soon came to be called the "loyal millet" by the Turks,[55] or the *millet-i-sadika* (the loyal people).[56]

Ironically, the more reforms the Turks granted, the less it seemed that the Christian minorities responded. The Turks blamed Russian agitation for fanning nationalist movements amongst the Christian minorities and the Crimean War forced the Turks to revisit the status of reform in the empire.[57]

The Porte viewed Russian claims of the "right to protect all Greek Orthodox subjects of the sultan...[as] the direct cause of the Crimean War."[58] In an effort to curtail Russian influence and to prevent Great Power interference, Sultan Abdul Mejid responded with the *Hatt-i Humayun* of 1856, "guaranteeing Christian privileges."[59]

In the Sultan's own words, "...each sect...shall be free from every species of restraint as regards the public exercise of its religion... As all forms of religion are and shall be freely professed in my dominions no subject of my Empire shall be hindered in the exercise of the Religion that he professes nor shall he in any way be annoyed on that account."[60]

Of particular importance was the added instruction that "no one shall be compelled to change their religion."[61] The imperial edict guaranteed to "every subject of the Ottoman Empire without distinction of creed or class: (a) personal liberty; (b) equality before the law; (c) complete religious freedom; (d) eligibility to hold public office, civil or military; (e) equality of taxation; (f) equal representation in the communal and provincial councils; (g) equal representation in the Supreme Council of Justice; and (h) complete security of property."[62]

The 1856 Treaty of Paris further "guaranteed the integrity of the Ottoman Empire... [and] the preservation of the essential freedoms of the Christians living in that empire."[63]

One of the benefits that the Christian communities "had reaped from the proclamation of 1856 was that they were able to secularize what political power was allowed them in the settlement of intra-community affairs [and they] took this power out of the hands of the patriarchs," where it had been previously vested.[64] The Armenians even drafted their own constitution and as Serif Mardin suggests, "the idea of constitutionalism and popular representation thus gained a limited toe-hold in the empire."[65]

THE "NEW OTTOMANS" AND
ALLEGIANCE TO THE *FATHERLAND*

At the death of the sultan, in 1861, his successor Abdul Aziz leant his support to reform and appointed Midhat Pasha to oversee the Tanzimat process. It was Midhat Pasha who best understood that adherence to reform was the best insurance for preventing Great Power intervention on behalf of the Christian minority populations. "Midhat wanted to show the powers that the empire was capable of reforming itself and dealing with its own problems."[66] Immediately upon taking office, Midhat embarked on a program aimed at ending corruption, even conducting "an investigation of the finances of the government and of the Sultan's court."[67] It was a similar such investigative action by Midhat, into the finances of his sultan that would later bring the unrelenting enmity of Abdul Hamid II down upon his Grand Vizier.

During this period a new "group of young intellectuals who called themselves for a time the "New Ottomans" (*Yeni Osmanlilar*) began to petition for "constitutional government."[68] Their concern, however, was that the Sultan's government was giving too much latitude to the Christian minorities, had not done enough to curtail great power interference, "and because it had pursued secular reforms in disregard of the traditional law and culture of Islam."[69]

Although they "harped constantly on the need for economic development, scientific knowledge, and modern education,"[70] their true passion was Ottomanism and the preservation of the *Vatan*, or Fatherland.

Formerly defined simply as "home,"[71] David Kushner suggests that it was "during the *Tanzimat* period the term *vatan* underwent a major transformation, assuming the meaning of the French word *patrie*."[72] Roderic Davison concurs and further notes that "a play by Namik Kemal, entitled *Vatan* and produced in 1873, aroused such enthusiastic street demonstrations that the fearful government closed it down."[73]

To the New Ottomans, the Vatan encompassed the entire Ottoman Empire, and all citizens, regardless of their millet were to give it their allegiance. Unfortunately, things were not going well for the Fatherland. By 1875-1876 "the empire was confronted by troubles of a very serious nature. Bulgarian and Serbian nationalist aspirations, compounded by crop failures and Turkish misrule, led to open insurrection."[74]

Finally, despite the best efforts of Midhat Pasha and other reformers, "...as a direct consequence of the Sultan's extravagances, the Ottoman Government was forced to declare itself bankrupt."[75] The New Ottoman intellectuals and the supporters of reform were all becoming increasingly impatient. They had become "disappointed and disillusioned in the face of entrenched vested interests that resisted change,"[76] and to add to the sense of futility, as Chalk and Jonassohn observed, "...the Tanzimat era, for all its fanfare, brought virtually no improvement in the daily life of the common person."[77]

THE "RIGHT CHOICE"

Not just beset with internal discontent, things were again becoming increasingly hostile for the Sublime Porte internationally. Russian supported "Pan-Slavism" was causing significant problems in the Balkans and the Sultan appeared to lack the vigor to curtail its threatened progress.

As Davison notes, "When government action against the Bosnian revolt of 1875 was so lethargic as to allow its spread, and when pan-Slavic pressure from Russia was exerted in favor of the Balkan rebels, the cup was full."[78]

As a result, on May 30, 1876, Midhat Pasha, and a group of military officers deposed Abdul Aziz and placed his "liberal-minded"[79] nephew, Murad V, on the throne. In addition to being liberal-minded, the newly crowned monarch was also soon found to be weak-minded as well. Within a few months, Murad V suffered a nervous breakdown, and was himself, in turn deposed and replaced by his brother, Abdul Hamid II. The new Sultan would reign for more than thirty years and during his tenure would paint a bloody swath across the empire; most particularly against the Armenians.

Initially, however, Sultan Abdul Hamid II appeared to be the right choice for the Ottomans.

Looked upon by many at home and abroad as a moderate, forward-looking young monarch, the new sultan was welcomed with eager anticipation. This was particularly true of the Turkish reformers.

The first positive impression created by Abdul Hamid apparently even fooled the Grand Vizier. "Midhat Pasha and his supporters seemed at last to have found a ruler who would cooperate with them in an effort to revive the failing empire."[80] It now seemed likely that Midhat and his associates, such as the influential Armenian Krikor Odian Effendi,[81] would at last be permitted to draft their long-awaited constitution.

As Davison explains, "during the summer of 1876 a constitution had been under discussion. Abdul Hamid having promised to promulgate one, the discussions were accelerated through the fall in an atmosphere of growing patriotic and fanatically Islamic reaction against pan-Slavism and European intervention."[82]

Finally, in December (after the Sultan had personally inserted a provision "giving him[self] power to exile any who endangered state security")[83] the first written constitution in Ottoman history was officially enacted. As Ernest Ramsaur observed, "A parliament was summoned, and the Ottoman Empire appeared to be on the path marked out for it by the reform party."[84]

Nothing could have been further from the truth.

PERFIDY, PARANOIA, AND PERSECUTION

Shortly thereafter, on February 5, 1877, the Sultan, exercising the "right" that he had so cleverly reserved for himself, "constitutionally" exiled Midhat Pasha. Betraying the paranoia for which he would later become famous, Abdul Hamid developed a fear of assassination,[85] and "was not disposed to have near him the man who had already deposed two sultans."[86] In addition, the new sultan never forgave Midhat's temerity in launching financial investigations into Abdul Hamid's treasury.

Eventually permitted to return to Constantinople, Midhat Pasha was later arrested and tried for regicide in the death of Abdul Aziz. Although it was at first reported that the former sultan had "committed suicide after his deposition;"[87] it was later discovered in Abdul Hamid's memoirs that the Red Sultan truly believed that his uncle had been assassinated on Midhat's own orders.

Indeed, upon his being imprisoned in the former sultan's own Feriye Palace; the circumstances that surrounded Abdul Aziz's "suicide" were quite suspicious.[88] Sean McMeekin acidly explained that Abdul Aziz dubiously killed himself, "By slashing his wrists--both of them, which may have been a difficult trick, the second wrist cut by a knife-wielding hand already incapacitated by the first thrust."[89]

Midhat Pasha was sentenced to life imprisonment, exiled to Arabia, and later strangled to death, presumably on the direct orders of the Porte. His head was reportedly sent to the capital in a box labeled "Japanese Ivories."[90] As one historian laconically observed, the affair, "did no credit to Sultan Abdul Hamid."[91]

The demise of Midhat Pasha was merely the start of Abdul Hamid's self-sustaining safeguards. His secret police operatives began a systematic regimen for cracking down on those suspected of disloyalty to the Porte. *Tanzimat* reforms were a thing of the past and the absolutist Sultan embarked on a repressive policy of strict centralization. It soon became evident that Turkey was now being governed "under a stark tyranny worthy rather of the ninth than of the nineteenth century."[92]

The obsessive fear of his own assassination dictated much of the sultan's decision-making. It took great effort to persuade Abdul Hamid to allow the introduction of modern means of illumination in

Constantinople. He mistook the term "dynamo" (a necessary electrical component) for the word "dynamite," fearing that he would be "blown up at night if he had electricity installed in his palace."[93]

On at least one occasion the Sultan's acute fears actually proved to be beneficially advantageous for his subjects. Having heard a prediction by a Muslim holy man that he would one-day die in a plague, Abdul Hamid took extreme precautions to ensure the cleansing and sanitation of the capital. He also instituted a strict quarantine that was actually credited with saving thousands of lives.[94]

In growing fear of his life, the Red Sultan became ever more reclusive. Rarely leaving the safety of his custom-designed fortress at *Yildiz*, Abdul Hamid felt secure behind the palace's high walls, and in the private knowledge that the myriad subterranean passageways and secret exits ensured a speedy escape if necessary.[95] Aside from the pleasures and security of the royal harem, all else was suspect.

The Christian minorities were particularly targeted for suspicion. The Sultan's intrusion into the daily lives of his Christian subjects often ranged from the violent to the banal. Aside from the very serious threat of government sponsored persecutions, confiscations of property, and even physical harm; the Sultan's agents sometimes lapsed into absurd measures for safeguarding his throne. The use of media censorship was a key method.

One contemporary observer remarked that "Liberty of press became such a farce that virtually no one would read a Turkish newspaper, because everything of the least interest, even on non-political subjects, was carefully excised by the vigilant censor."[96]

Christian missionaries from the United States, and Great Britain endured countless petty and often laughable intrusions from Abdul Hamid's censors. Books and religious texts were often confiscated or burned by customs agents upon their importation into the country. Those that were permitted entry were sometimes edited.

In one strange example, a passage in the Bible was "corrected." The government censor at Constantinople ordered that the text of the seventh and eighth verses of I Thessalonians be amended by striking the revolutionary name of "Macedonia" and replacing it with the "Vilayets of Salonica and Monastir."[97]

The Armenians were among the hardest hit by Abdul Hamid's paranoid machinations. *The Independent,* a New York publication reported that, "The Sultan, being convinced that the extirpation of the Armenian nation by force is next to impossibility, has fallen on an ingenious method of coercing its national spirit. He has put the Armenian school text-books and the Armenian press under strict censorship."

The article then explained how even seemingly harmless words were expunged from the texts, such as the noun "star" which in the Turkish language is translated *yeldiz,* the name of the Sultan's palace. Amazingly, even the word "astronomy" was purged from the school book's pages because of its relation to the word star![98]

Another petty example of the censorship that was commonplace in the Ottoman Empire concerns the American missionary founded "Armenian College," whose name the Porte forcibly changed into "Euphrates College."[99]

The Sultan's hatred for all things Christian and western was intense. "Christendom had torn from him some of his fairest provinces, and to the best of his ability he would make Christendom pay the price."[100]

He did not have long to wait.

BULGARIA AND THE *BASHI-BOZUKS*

During the first year of Abdul Hamid's reign, events came to a violent halt in Bulgaria. In April 1876, the Christian Bulgars began a nationalist uprising after suffering generations of persecution by the Turks. The Bulgarian leadership felt that "with the continuation of the revolts in Bosnia-Hercegovina and the obvious preparations for war being made in Serbia, Montenegro, and Greece, the opportunity for a successful revolt seemed highly favorable."[101]

Terribly overextended elsewhere in the Balkans, the Sultan had few remaining regular soldiers to commit to action in Bulgaria. As a result, the Turks recruited large numbers of irregular troops; mainly Albanian mercenaries to bolster their depleted ranks. Evidence suggests, however, that the so-called *Bashi-Bozuks* were enlisted with the prior intention of suppressing the restive Bulgarians without conscious regard of any imminent revolt. For more than a year, foreign visitors and missionaries had been warning of impending Turkish reprisals against the local population. The Turks, Circassians, and Muslim irregular cavalry had now escalated violent attacks against Christian civilians.[102]

Prof. Philip Shashko suggests that British and American diplomats anticipated the forthcoming Turkish massacres of Christians and that they were convinced that "some Ottoman officials concocted a scheme designed to persuade and incite Muslims to murder as many Bulgarians as possible or to make their condition so miserable that they would be forced to either emigrate or to submit totally to the will of the Turks."[103]

To execute the order, the Ottomans recruited cadres of the mercenary Bashi-Bozuks. The Turkish title *başıbozuk* (literally "corrupted head" or "leaderless") identified them as being undisciplined and disorderly mercenaries who were recruited as raiders.[104] Without any military oversight or restraint, the "undisciplined and disorderly" Muslim marauders were unleashed upon the Bulgarian Christians. Paid only by plunder, the Bashi-Bozuks were little more than government sanctioned bandits. Leaving in their wake a burning swath of looting, rape, and murder, the mercenary irregulars were something of an Ottoman version of Quantrill's Raiders in the American Civil War, only infinitely more brutal.

The fears and forecasts of the foreign observers had been accurate. Citing the subsequent widespread reprisals as evidence, "it can be concluded that the views of the American and British diplomats... possibly indicate the existence of some kind of premeditated scheme that entailed coordinated action by Ottoman officials, *bashi-bozuks,* Circassians, and the army against not just the rebels but unarmed Bulgarians as well."[105]

If Shashko's interpretation of British diplomatic reports is correct, Abdul Hamid's response would be the first "premeditated" government slaughter of a national group since the time of Tamerlane. It was also to be the start of a systematic pattern of genocidal atrocities that would continue unabated for the balance of his reign and later be adopted by the succeeding Turkish government in 1915.

"BY JINGO!"

In 1877, for the fourth time in the nineteenth century the Russians again declared war on Turkey. Under the pretext of defending the persecuted Christians in the Balkans, the Tsar also hoped to regain the territory and prestige that was lost in the Crimean War. Most importantly the Russians were determined to reestablish naval control over the Black Sea, and finally solve the question of the Straits.

Invading the Balkans through Romania (which had declared its independence from the Ottoman Empire) the Russians also advanced into the Caucasus opening a two front offensive against the Turks. It is noteworthy that the Russian Caucasus Corps was led jointly in the field by four Armenian generals. Through their concerted efforts the Turks were driven from the disputed Armenian homeland as far as Erzerum. Similarly, on the Balkan front after a spirited defense the Turks finally collapsed, and fell back to the outskirts of Constantinople. With Russian forced converging on the Straits the Turks were ultimately forced to accept the Treaty of San Stefano.

The Ottoman Empire suffered terribly from the war. As terms of the treaty, the Turks were forced to recognize the complete independence of Rumania, Serbia, Montenegro, and a large autonomous Bulgarian state. In addition, the Turks ceded Bessarabia, Kars, and Ardahan to the Tsar.[106] Flushed with victory, the Russians were prevented from taking the greatest prize, however. Concerned with a possible threat to India, the British Fleet was quickly dispatched to the Golden Horn, and the Russians were denied access to the Bosporus.

Back in England, ubiquitous Russophobes were musically venting their ire, and as Barbara Tuchman writes, the pubs and music halls resounded with the chorus:

> *"We don't want to fight but by Jingo if we do---*
> *We've got the ships, we've got the guns,*
> *We've got the money too---*
> *Russia shall not have Con-stan-ti-nople!"*[107]

For the moment the Straits remained in Turkish hands, but as Robert Massie observes, "for six months, British naval guns and Russian artillery lay within range of each other while the helpless capital of the Ottoman Empire stood between."[108] Finally, German Chancellor Otto von Bismarck offered to mediate, and the real threat of war with Great Britain and Austria-Hungary, persuaded the Tsar to agree to an international conference in Berlin.

Once again the Great Powers patronizingly decided to deliberate upon the fate of the Ottoman Empire.

REALPOLITIK

In June 1878, Germany's "Iron Chancellor," Prince Otto von Bismarck set events in motion that would have monumental repercussions for more than a century to come. In order to prevent a European war looming as a result of increased tensions in the Balkans, Bismarck called for a congress of the Great Powers to sort out the issues that stemmed from Russia's drubbing of the Ottoman Empire.

The pragmatic policy of *Realpolitik*, so masterfully practiced by Bismarck, had culminated in nothing less than the unification and subsequent declaration of the German Empire, and its quick emergence as the principle continental European power. Never one to shy away from military action if it served his national goals, Bismarck concluded that at present things were going quite well for Germany and a war would only stand to upset the favorable situation.

After soundly defeating the Turks in the War of 1877-78, Russia fully expected to receive ample rewards as was rightfully due the victor. Such was not to be. Great Power interests, particularly those of Great Britain and Austria-Hungary, were seriously threatened by the specter of unbridled Russian hegemony in the Balkans. The Pan-Slav crusade was seen as an overt Russian attempt to exert full imperial control over the Balkans, and ultimately gain naval access to the Mediterranean.

Forcefully denied the much desired occupation of the Dardanelles by the rapid deployment of the British Fleet; the Russians sought ancillary entrance to the Mediterranean by the creation of a super Slavic state in Bulgaria with access to the Aegean. In addition the Tsar's government demanded the award of Adriatic ports to the land-locked and newly independent Slavic Principality of Montenegro.

Considering the Eastern Mediterranean to be their own exclusive sphere of influence, the British were prepared to stop the Russian threat by any means necessary, including military action. Having fought the Russians little more than twenty years earlier in the Crimean War (1853-56); Great Britain, along with France and Sardinia, had blunted Russian designs on the Dardanelles. The British were ready and willing to do so again.

Furthermore, the French were similarly alarmed by what they saw as Russian advances into southern Europe, and the threat to their own potential colonial expansion in the Middle East. France and the newly unified Kingdom of Italy both looked for opportunities to increase their influence in North Africa and the Levant at Ottoman expense, and they viewed the Turkish playing field as already busy enough without Tsarist inclusion.

Finally, the Russian aspirations in the Balkans placed them in direct competition with another European power. Austria-Hungary had its own designs in southern Europe and also planned to make territorial gains at Turkish expense. In addition, the Hapsburg Monarchy feared the rapidly growing Slavic influence, particularly as it pertained to neighboring Serbia. In response Austria-Hungary planned the take-over of the buffer region of Bosnia-Herzegovina.

With these potentially explosive issues about to ignite into a major European war, Bismarck called for an emergency convention of the Great Powers to be held under his strictly neutral mediation. With his aim of preventing any war that upset the personally favorable status quo, the Iron Chancellor was able to convince the other powers of his German government's "impartiality."

DREI-KAISER-BUND

The Tsar was certain that the Reich's leading minister would be sympathetic to his imperial interests just as Russia had tacitly aided Bismarck's Prussians in their recent 1870 war with France. Fully anticipating Germany to support her claims, Russia agreed to the conference with high expectations.

Ever since 1815 and their joint participation in the defeat of Napoleon I; Russia, Austria-Hungary, and Germany (formerly the Kingdom of Prussia) had remained on friendly terms. Finally, in 1873, Bismarck formed the "League of the Three Emperors" (*Drei-Kaiser-Bund*), a formal alliance consisting of the Tsar of Russia; the Austro-Hungarian Emperor; and the German Kaiser.

With the aim of preserving the conservative, monarchist status quo against the rising tide of Western European liberal socialism, the three governments had mutually agreed to stand together. In 1870 Bismarck had precipitated the defeat of Imperial France, and with the abdication of Napoleon III, alarmingly witnessed the subsequent rise of the socialist French Republic. He further noted the rising "solidarity of the revolutionary and republican factions in Europe."

In a cautionary message to the Tsar, Bismarck opined, "In view of the elements, not only republican but distinctly socialist, that have seized power in France, the firm closing of the ranks of the monarchist and conservative elements of Europe is all the more desirable."[109]

As they had in the late eighteenth century, the three great imperial continental powers of Austria, Russia, and Germany would once again be forced to unify against the threat of republican, anti-monarchist themes emanating from Paris. Cooperation amongst the same three conservative monarchies that had defeated France in 1815 was deemed by Bismarck "as the most certain guarantee of order and civilization [and] the monarchial principle."

On paper this sounded good, but the reality of competing national interests was about to expose the shallowness of the alliance. The result was to have very dire long-term consequences, and ultimately help set the stage for two world wars.

CONGRESS OF BETRAYAL?

The Congress of Berlin convened on June 13, 1878, and for the next thirty days the "Great Powers" of France, Austria-Hungary, Italy, Great Britain and Germany arbitrated the aftermath of the Russo-Turkish War with individually subjective zeal.

After considerable wrangling, much of the Treaty of San Stefano was confirmed although to Russian chagrin, the size of the newly independent nations of Serbia, Montenegro, and the semi-autonomous Bulgarian State were greatly scaled back. The latter was denied access to the Aegean preventing Russian sponsored Slavic ability to flank the Dardanelles and gain an open sea lane to the Mediterranean.

To further exacerbate Russian feelings that the congress had been for them a dismal failure, the Austrians were awarded occupation of Bosnia and Herzegovina. Additionally, "by separate agreement forced on the sultan, Britain also gained the right to administer Cyprus...in return for a promise to defend Turkey against Russia."[110]

The occupation of Turkish Armenia, awarded to Russia in the original Treaty of San Stefano was fully rescinded. Once again, the Christian Armenian population found itself virtually imprisoned within the Ottoman Empire. In retrospect, as a result of the Congress of Berlin the Armenians would suffer even greater disappointment than the Russians.

The Tsar did receive some minor compensation by retaining the annexation of South Bessarabia, and the award of Batum on the Black Sea. Above all, the Russians were once again denied control of the straits and unrestricted access to the Mediterranean. Ultimately, they blamed Germany for failing to support them.

Bismarck later explained that the Tsar sought "to lay the guilt of the unsuccessful issue of the war on the German policy, [and] on the 'disloyalty' of the German friend." Casually dismissing their anger with characteristic Machiavellian nonchalance, Bismarck acidly added, "The desire of the Russian government to arrive at peace with Turkey by means of a congress proved that they did not feel themselves strong enough on the military side to let the matter come to a war with England and Austria, after they had once let slip the opportunity of occupying Constantinople."[111]

What is also telling about Bismarck's assessment is his lack of mentioning the additional threat of Turkish arms as a deterrent to further Russian demands. The Ottoman Empire was summarily ignored as a serious obstacle. In the collected opinion of the Great Powers it was only the combined might of Britain and Austria that had foiled the Russian Bear. Turkey, once the "terror of the world," had now truly been relegated to "the sick man of Europe."[112]

BERLIN LEGACY

As a result of Otto von Bismarck's attempts to preserve peace in Europe; political forces were unleashed that would ultimately lead to the death of tens of millions, and result in Germany's total defeat in two world wars.

Still unresolved and permitted to fester, was the growing competition between Austria and her Slavic neighbors. Serbian national aspirations, particularly in Slavic Bosnia-Herzegovina, would lead to increased tensions with the House of Hapsburg, finally culminating in the 1914 assassination of the heir to the Austrian throne. The spark that ignited the First World War was lit at Sarajevo, but the matches were first supplied by the Congress of Berlin.

Other crises were later precipitated by Great Power manipulation of the national borders of Bulgaria, Romania, Greece, Montenegro, and Serbia, and would lead to those countries entrance into further conflict with Turkey and amongst themselves in the two Balkan Wars of 1912-13. Meanwhile, desperately trying to hold onto the last vestiges of their once extensive European possessions, the Turks were being pushed further into a friendless vacuum with only the waiting arms of the Kaiser extended in their direction.

Among the newly created issues that dangerously emanated from the Congress of Berlin was nothing less than a dramatic shift in the European balance of power. As a result of their bitter feelings of betrayal, the Russians began a steady drift away from Berlin and inexorably moved towards an alliance with Paris and London. It was the resulting so-called *Triple Entente* of Great Britain, France and Russia that would later square off against Germany in the First World War.

For the "impartial" Germans the long-term legacy of the Congress of Berlin would have resounding repercussions over the next century. As a consequence of Russia's growing intransigence, the German Empire bonded more closely with Austria-Hungary. The ensuing "Triple Alliance" (that tepidly included Italy in a purely defensive pact) pledged Germany to back Austria-Hungary against any future Russian aggression.

The alliance with Hapsburg Austria would prove disastrous for the Germans. Ultimately the Kaiser's complete inability to curb the *carte blanche* agreement that had been bestowed upon the House of Hapsburg precipitated Germany's fatal entrance into the First World War.

Bismarck's coolly calculated handling of Russian interests, and subsequent siding with Austria-Hungary began the long chain of unforeseen events that would one day destroy the royal houses of all three empires.

LOST IN THE SHUFFLE

The provisions of the Congress of Berlin were also to have enormous repercussions for the fate of the Armenians. Initially awarded with a sizable portion of Turkish Armenia by the Treaty of San Stefano, the Russians were later denied possession of the entire tract, thereby leaving the Christian minorities once again in the hands of their Muslim overlords. Whether the liberated lands would have led to Armenian independence is problematic.

There is no reason to believe that the Russians would have relinquished sovereign control over even a few acres. Nonetheless, it is certain that the Christian minority would have enjoyed far greater success in the domain of an Eastern Orthodox ruler than it had in that of the Muslim sultan. One can only speculate how differently the Armenians would have fared with much of northeastern Anatolia under Tsarist control.

Having been denied the protection that would have likely been provided to them by direct Russian annexation, the Armenians now looked to the Great Power guarantees of the Berlin congress, for their ultimate security. Of paramount importance to the Armenian population of the Ottoman Empire were Articles XXIII and LXI of the Treaty of Berlin. By these provisions, the Great Power signatories were granted the right of intervention in favor of the Christians of Macedonia in the Balkans, and the Armenians living in the six eastern provinces of the Empire.[113]

Armenian survival again anxiously depended upon Turkish behavior, and that was to presumably be held in check by the direct threat of European chastisement. The question remained, however, whether

Great Power rhetoric would actually be backed by military force if and when the need arose. As subsequent developments would reveal, the intervention by the Great Powers, who had the vested responsibility of protecting Armenian rights, instead had inadvertently helped pave the way for their eventual destruction.

For their part, the Turks promised improvements, reforms, and pledged to protect the Armenians from the Kurds and Circassians.[114] It was thought that Abdul Hamid had finally been intimidated into refraining from his policy of Armenian repression. Stephen Astourian laconically notes, that "the ensuing internationalization of the Armenian Question at the Congress of Berlin failed, however, to provide any concrete improvement."[115] Later events would actually prove quite the contrary...that the worst was yet to come.

The Sultan would soon ignore his promises!

THRONE IN A GILDED CAGE

Having emerged from the Russo-Turkish War politically bruised but intact, Sultan Abdul Hamid II became convinced that Great Britain and the West would never permit Russia to gain access to the Straits. William Stearns Davis suggested that the wily sultan was actually emboldened following the military defeat. "As he watched events not unshrewdly two things became increasingly clear to him: first, that the great powers of Europe were intensely jealous of one another, that in scarcely any circumstances would the other nations allow Russia a second time to punish the sultans for their sins, and that although the 'concert of Europe' might present joint notes and threaten him, it could almost never act decisively. Secondly, that there was developing in central Europe a powerful friend to the Ottomans."[116]

Bismarck's erstwhile rescue of the Turks at the Berlin Congress was to presage a future long-term partnership between the Germans and the Ottomans that would ultimately end in the demise of both their empires.

Meanwhile, Abdul Hamid had the diplomatic clout of the "Iron Chancellor," and the guns of British battleships to thank for his safety from external threat. With the belief that Great Britain would selfishly keep his empire free from further Russian incursions, the Red Sultan quickly began to consolidate his internal domestic position as well.

In 1877 he boldly dismissed the parliament and suspended the constitution. "Nominally, the Ottoman Constitution was still in force, but even mention of the word *constitution* had become a ground for exile during the period 1878-1908."[117]

Ever the self-promoter, Abdul Hamid attempted to justify his actions by invoking precedent from the imperial regimes prior to his reign. In February 1878, he confessed to his ministers that, "I made a mistake when I wished to imitate my father, Abdul Mejid, who sought reforms by persuasion and by liberal institutions. I shall follow in the footsteps of my grandfather, Sultan Mahmud. Like him I understand that it is only by force that one can move the people with whose guardianship Allah has entrusted me."[118]

Ironically, even as he felt fairly secure in foreign policy, Abdul Hamid became progressively fearful at home. The paranoia of the Sultan now became increasingly apparent, and he began to assemble an intricate network of spies and secret police operatives. Davison notes that Abdul Hamid "became the prisoner of his own fears and suspicions. He tended more and more to seclude himself in his palace compound at Yildiz, outside the capital."[119]

On the rare occasions that Abdul Hamid ventured from his fortress-like compound, he always carried a pistol and even resorted to wearing a shirt of chain-link mail.[120] Contemporary British diplomat, Viscount James Bryce observed that "the sultan lives in complete seclusion. Fearful of his personal safety...intensely suspicious...he never quits the grounds of his palace...His favorite method of government is the employment of spies, which has reached such a point that no one ventures to speak freely to anyone else in Constantinople."[121]

William Langer wrote that Abdul Hamid was the victim of a "persecution complex," noting that "he was terrified, and for that reason surrounded himself not only with high walls, but with all sorts of dubious characters, especially spies and dilators who justified their existence by bringing ever more alarming reports."[122]

Ramsaur further notes that Abdul Hamid was "concerned only with the problem of maintaining himself on the throne. His whole reign was devoted to that end. The notorious espionage system... in short, the entire Hamidian system, had but one aim: the security of the Sultan, himself."[123] Apparently, self-preservation had become Abdul Hamid's chief objective.

Perhaps the anxious monarch had ample reason to fear for his safety, however. Robert Krikorian, in discussing Abdul Hamid II wryly observed that, "just because you are paranoid does not mean that someone is not out to get you."[124]

In Abdul Hamid's case there was justifiable cause for concern. Following his suspension of the Constitution of 1876, a group of Turkish intellectuals, and military officers were indeed "out to get" the Sultan.

Those ominously converging forces would be known to history as the "Young Turks."

3

PRELUDE TO HOLOCAUST

B Y THE END of the nineteenth century the truth was clear that the dream of Pan-Ottomanism was becoming more and more the exclusive purview of the Turkish majority, but increasingly less of a reality amongst the empire's seething ethnic and religious minorities. The legitimacy of this label was all the more questioned as the Ottoman Empire's Christian subjects continually demanded more autonomy, even as they looked to the Great Powers to intervene on their behalf.

At the same time, a competing, but not mutually excludable movement had also risen throughout the empire and beyond. Long before the emergence of Ottomanism this other "cause" had attracted legions of adherents. "Pan-Islam," the unification of the world's 300 million Muslims, had been a rallying force for a millennium.

At its height, the followers of the Prophet Mohammad had taken Islam from its birthplace in Arabia and spread it in all directions. Throughout central Asia, to the East Indies; across the desert sands of North Africa to the Atlantic shores of Morocco; penetrating the mountain passes of the Balkans; thrusting to the gates of Vienna; and ultimately crossing the Pyrenees border separating Spain and France in the West; the sword of Allah had once appeared to be unstoppable. It reached its apogee in the seventeenth century, however, and then just as abruptly as it had begun, the threat of all-out Muslim conquest steadily subsided.

By the nineteenth century the Islamic movement had suffered from centuries of decline, due to the realization of the obvious technological, military, and economic advantages that the Christian West had long since developed and now held over the Muslim East. Beginning in the sixteenth century, the high tide of Islamic conquest was already beginning to recede, and after the passage of another three hundred years were but a long-ago memory. In short, the glorious days of Saladin, Suleiman the Magnificent, and Tamerlane were shrouded in the far distant past and European armies now threatened to invade and colonize ever increasing portions of the Islamic world.

Many of the followers of Mohammad have long awaited the return of the *Mahdi*, a messianic Muslim conqueror who will one day destroy all infidels and usher in an everlasting era of worldwide Islamic justice. Then as now, many have dreamed of a leader who will unify Islam into another irresistible military force, and restore them to world dominance.

Meanwhile, another emerging movement looked toward gaining a rightful place in the sun.

"MARCHE SLAVE"

In 1876, the Russians justified their intrusion into the Balkans as a show of support for their Slavic brothers—a true pan-Slav crusade.[1] Using the Hamidian depredations as a pretext for invading Bulgaria, the Tsarist government had a convenient excuse for reversing the losses it had sustained twenty years earlier in the Crimean War. The Imperial Russian army was determined to liberate all ethnic Slavs from Turkish suzerainty and to ultimately unite them under the Tsar's protection. If in the process they could also gain the long-desired access to the Bosporus so much the better.

Pan-Slavism first formally emerged as the result of an 1848 Prague convention of Slavophile intellectuals, poets, and academics whose stated purpose was to force the Austrian Empire to improve its treatment and assimilation of her Slavonic minorities. Since the 1860's Slavophilism, the exaltation of all things culturally, traditionally, and historically Slavic, took immense hold within the Russian Empire. The interest in Pan-Slavism had grown in public popularity particularly when coupled with Orthodox Christianity, and Russia soon became the self-appointed champion of the ethnic South Slavs.

The great Russian novelist Fyodor Dostoevsky saw Pan-Slavism as a vehicle to rescue degraded Europe from the slide into liberalism and religious heresy. He believed that the Russo-Turkish War of 1877-1878 was the beginning of an apocalyptic European conflict that would ultimately result in a resurgent Orthodox, Slavic Empire under Tsarist rule.[2]

As the temporal head of the Russian Christian Church the Tsar undoubtedly felt a real sympathy for the fellow Slavonic peoples of southern Europe; particularly those in Eastern Orthodox Serbia, Bulgaria, Macedonia, and Montenegro. Even the Roman Catholics of Croatia and Slovenia; and the Muslim Slavs of Bosnia could find a friendly patron in St. Petersburg. The shared vision of a "Greater Serbia" embracing Slavonic peoples of all three faiths into one nation under the growing patronage of Russia electrified Balkan Slavs intent upon throwing off both Turkish and Austrian rule.

On November 17, 1876, in public support of the Balkan struggle against the Turks, Pyotr Ilyich Tchaikovsky premiered his "Serbo-Russian March" before a Moscow audience. Known afterward as the *Slavonic March* (French: *March Slave*) the orchestral tone poem stirred Russian pride as had the composer's similarly evocative *1812 Overture*. Within six months the Tsar declared war on the Ottoman Empire. Ethnic and religious kinship notwithstanding, the real Russian motivation was to make territorial gains at Turkish and Austro-Hungarian expense.

Taking a cue from his ancient Tsarist enemy, Abdul Hamid II found his own convenient cause to embrace.

PAN-ISLAM AND THE CALIPH

Ever since the glorious reign of Mehmed the Conqueror (1451-1481) the center of Islam had been the Ottoman Empire. By virtue of his exalted position the Sultan began to double as the *Caliph*, the living successor of the Prophet Mohammad for all "true believers" within the vast "Nation of Islam" (*ummat-al-Islamiyah*). After the Ottoman defeat of the Muslim Mamluks in 1517, the Turkish Sultan Selim I took the titles "Caliph of Islam" and "Servant of the Two Holy Shrines" of Medina and Mecca.

In reality the Turks recognized the caliphate more as a political entity than a religious office. Historically, "the Ottoman sultans had never made formal claim to the title of caliph, except in some general, honorific sense."[3] Their military and economic power had been so vast that there was no need to appeal to a movement such as Pan-Islamism in order to achieve further political success.

By the late-nineteenth century however, due to the enormous decline suffered by the Ottoman Empire; the Red Sultan began desperately searching for a means of reversing the imperial fortunes and more importantly of securing his throne. Witnessing the Tsarist use of "Pan-Slavism" as a unifying ethnic and religious force; Abdul Hamid likewise considered Pan- Islamism, and the caliphate as potential tools for unifying the Muslim world into a movement with which to help restore past Turkish glory.

As a result, in direct response to the growing expansionist threat of Pan-Slavism that emanated from Russia and had now saturated the Balkans; Abdul Hamid borrowed and eagerly cloaked himself in the mantle of Islamic zealotry to further his own ambitions. For the first time the Ottoman caliphate was seen as more than a mere ceremonial post and, "Abdul Hamid transformed the claim into a statement of temporal power."[4] Henceforth, as Caliph he could use the threat of religious "holy war" as a weapon against his enemies both foreign and domestic.

Never personally religious, the Red Sultan characteristically acted the part of a devout Muslim for the benefit of his observant subjects. In an effort to curry great favor with Islamic pilgrims, Abdul Hamid commissioned the construction of a rail line linking Constantinople with Damascus and on through the Arabian Desert (*Hejaz*) to the holy cities of Mecca and Medina.

Seen as a benevolent attempt by the Caliph to improve the travel difficulties of the *hajis* during the mass annual pilgrimage to the *Kaaba*, in truth, "the motives behind the Hedjaz Railway were strategical and political rather than religious."[5] The new railroad gave Abdul Hamid the added ability to transport troops and ordnance to the often restless Arabian Peninsula in a much shorter time.

The sultan's real reasons for its construction aside, the Hejaz Railway was nonetheless quite popularly appreciated. Joan Haslip wryly observed, "...as Pan-Islamic propaganda it was enormously successful."[6]

Outwardly the sultan enthusiastically embraced Pan-Islam and, "as caliph, Abdul Hamid claimed the loyalty and the service of all true Muslims, from the East Indies to the shores of the Atlantic."[7] In the late-nineteenth century the Pan-Islamic movement had now suddenly gained new momentum and some Muslim observers gave the full credit for its apparent resurgence to the Ottoman Sultan.

One contemporary Indian-born admirer glowingly described the Turkish Caliph, "as being the very cause of the revival of this very spirit of Pan-Islamism."[8] In addition, the Head of the *Pan-Islamic Society of London* strongly lamented and complained that the unflattering, and to him the unfair western characterization of Abdul Hamid II as a tyrant was indeed hypocritical.

Shaikh Mushir Hosain Kidwai suggested that despite their ingratitude and constant acts of rebellion, the Sultan had benevolently bestowed "unparalleled toleration" upon his Christian minorities. He then righteously declared that Abdul Hamid's Christian subjects were, "...given rights which England, notwithstanding her boast of impartiality and justice, has not given to Indians or any other non-Christians [within the British Empire]."[9]

No one could truly applaud Abdul Hamid when it came to "unparalleled toleration" but certainly the record of the European imperialists in the treatment of their colonial populations was in no way exemplary either. Aware of the Great Powers' underlying fear of the ever-present threat of native restiveness; Abdul Hamid wielded the Caliphate as a bargaining chip against future European harassment. He invoked the mere possibility of Muslim insurrections in the far-flung colonies of France, and Great Britain, as well as within Russia's Islamic domains in Central Asia, as insurance against further Great Power interference.

As one contemporary observer remarked, "Great Britain naturally felt the point of this weapon most as governing wide Moslem territories."[10]

THE SWORD OF ISLAM

The realization that the sultan held the potentially devastating power of declaring *Jihad* as a sacred call to arms for the world's 300 million Muslims also became a distinctly increasing tenet of Turkish military doctrine during the decades immediately leading up to the First World War. Even after the rise of the Young Turks, the military need to retain a figurehead sultan, and the preservation of the caliphate was clearly recognized. In the event of war the Ottoman High Command would order the puppet caliph to incite the faithful into revolt against their European masters.

Interestingly, the military potential was not lost on the new German Kaiser Wilhelm II, who also envisioned such a declaration of "holy war" as a useful threat to greatly disrupt the British Empire. In a future time of war with England, the Germans saw a Turkish alliance and Muslim *Jihad* as the possible pathway to the conquest of India. Having no Muslim colonial holdings of his own, the German monarch felt free to fan the flames of Muslim religious zealotry even if it meant the unfortunate persecution of Christian minorities.

In reality, the threatened hammer of Muslim Holy War never squarely hit the inviting anvil of European colonialism. After Abdul Hamid's later fall from power, his successor caliph who was fully controlled by the Young Turks had apparently neither the charisma nor the ruthlessness of his predecessor. More importantly, the aims of Pan-Islamism began to run head-long into the rising mutually excludable goals of Arab nationalism. This very tangible obstacle would later be clearly seen during the First World War when the dream of Arab independence forcefully competed with the Ottoman Sultan's call for *Jihad* in attempting to gain the hearts and swords of the empire's non-Turkish Muslim population.

Writing less than a year after the conclusion of "The Great War," G. Wyman Bury observed, "those Britons who have handled Oriental affairs for the past twenty years can appreciate the extent of that interest [Pan-Islam and Arab nationalism] while we remember that even while Yamen [Yemeni] Arabs were fighting the Turks, their neighbors on the Aden side of the frontier were praying in their mosques that the Sultan and his troops might be victorious."[11]

In the Levant, Lawrence of Arabia and the Arab revolt would also strike a blow against the myth of Turkish jihad. Ironically, Col. Lawrence's later success in fomenting an effective "fifth column" against the rear of the beleaguered Ottoman army would inadvertently exacerbate the already hostile Turkish suspicions of their Armenian and Greek subjects. The Young Turks would justify and excuse their harsh treatment of the Christian minorities as being necessary for the prevention of a full-scale military insurrection.

The overall aim of Pan-Islamism had always been the restoration of a unified and universal Islamic religious state as originally envisioned in the days of the Prophet Muhammad. To this day it is still the ardent desire of such contemporary Pan-Islamic organizations as the ubiquitous Muslim Brotherhood. Never as truly interested in the religious significance of the movement as he was in its value for protecting his own person, Abdul Hamid nevertheless outwardly embraced the cause of Pan-Islam.

For the present, however, the ever-paranoid sultan used the offices of Caliph to secure the fierce loyalty of "true Believers," not for the furtherance of the *Koran*, but rather to ensure his own survival on the throne. One important use of his caliphate was to suppress nationalistic sentiments of Arab tribes within the Arabian Peninsula, and the Levant. To resist the caliph was to resist the will of God!

To help assuage his ever increasing fear of insurrection and physical overthrow, Abdul Hamid continued to solidify his own personal protection. The sultan vastly heightened counter-espionage capabilities within his domains; increased the size and power of his secret police; and retreated more and more to the sanctuary of his *Yildiz* palace-fortress. What he also sought was the enlistment of a fanatical cadre of personal bodyguards whose allegiance to the caliph would be unquestioned as directly following the will of Allah.

In order to keep them motivated, and loyal, the mercenary recruits had to be materially satisfied and well-paid. In addition, Abdul Hamid needed to provide his new cohorts with a specific target. Ideally he would focus the energies of this newly created host upon a helpless group of victims to both plunder and physically exploit. By necessity, the targeted people would have to be non-Muslim infidels; ideally either Christians, or Jews.

In essence, what the sultan proposed to enact was the wanton persecution of a distinct minority group of his own subjects in order to unify his Muslim majority and thereby secure his throne.

THE BLOODY RIDE OF THE "HAMIDIYE"

Using his position as Caliph, and enveloping himself within the mantle of "Pan-Islam," Abdul Hamid II began inciting the Muslim Kurds.

For centuries the Turks and Kurds had experienced a tense and often violent relationship. With a Kurdish population of 1.5 million, the Sultan was faced with yet another sizeable ethnic minority that threatened the tranquility of the empire. One great difference prevailed, however. Unlike the Armenians, Bulgarians, and most Balkan minorities; the Kurds were Islamic. By the powerful call for *Jihad*, the Caliph could transcend past Kurdish differences with the mutual goal of destroying the infidels.

The Sultan's policy had two convenient outcomes. Abdul Hamid increased his personal control of the Kurds by offering their leaders gifts, positions, and titles to land, thereby allowing him to use them against the internal and external enemies of the Empire. As Siyamend Othman observed, "this policy bore fruit during the massacre of the Armenians."[12]

In addition, Abdul Hamid was able to recruit a fiercely loyal military formation to act as a large personal bodyguard. The sultan formed regiments of irregular Kurdish cavalry that he patterned after the Tsar's Cossacks. To guarantee his grip on the throne, the Sultan now had his own "Praetorian Guard."

Taking the name of their monarch, the new light cavalry regiments were called the *Hamidiye* (meaning "belonging to Hamid"). At their initial formation, Lord Kinross estimated their numbers as, "...in all, some fifteen thousand men, and which continued to increase year by year."[13] Perhaps to deflect western criticism it was claimed that the light cavalry was originally mustered to patrol the Russo-Turkish frontier. In reality, the sultan would eventually billet units of his Hamidiye corps in villages throughout Anatolia, and far from the potentially hostile border. He particularly targeted the Armenian *vilayets*.

Soon the paranoia of the Sultan began to focus on his Armenian subjects. In an effort to thwart a suspected revolutionary uprising, as had previously occurred in Albania, Bulgaria, Serbia, and Greece; the Muslim *Hamidiye* systematically plundered Armenian villages and terrorized the civilian Christian population.[14]

Whether or not a serious revolutionary threat existed has been debated. Armenian apologists generally dismiss the escalating revolutionary activity as merely the arming of "the inhabitants for defense against any future attacks by Turks, Kurds, and Circassians."[15] Certainly an armed insurrection was being avidly prosecuted by some with many Muslim civilians caught in the bloodshed, but the vast majority of Armenians remained peaceable. Even the pro-Turkish scholar Justin McCarthy granted that the creation of the predominately Kurdish Hamidiye "must have been seen by the Armenians as putting the fox in charge of the henhouse."[16]

The Hamidiye were often paid by plunder in similar fashion as the *Bashi-Bazouks*; the Ottoman Sultan's irregular cavalry that had terrorized Christian Bulgaria and Serbia during the nineteenth century. The difference was that the Hamidiye were officially uniformed military regiments supplied with the best arms and equipment that the government could furnish.

On the other hand, the infamous Bashi-Bazouks were little more than armed Albanian and Circassian bandits that were often used by the Ottoman military in reconnaissance, raiding supply lines, and for terrorizing and suppressing enemy populations. Their brutality and lawlessness during the Russo-Turkish War of 1877-'78 had been so excessive, and their actions so hard to control, that the Ottoman government finally became convinced to abandon their use.

In reality, however, the later result was much the same. The Hamidiye were simply better dressed and better equipped. The Sultan had merely repackaged a brutal device for controlling and terrorizing his Armenian subjects.

KURDISTAN

Like the Armenians, the Kurds are an ancient people with deep roots to the land. Unfortunately for their Christian neighbors, however, the Kurds claimed the very same territory. With a history possibly dating back three millennia, the Kurdish people draw descent from the Medes and possibly further back to the time of the Sumerians.[17]

G.S. Reynolds associated the Kurds with ancient *Qardu*, and reference is made in an ancient Sumerian cuneiform to "Kar-da," believed to be adjacent to Mt. Ararat.[18] The Kurdish strong attachment to Mt. Ararat mirrors that of the Armenians, and their geographic claims to a national "Kurdistan" likewise encompass much of eastern Turkey, northern Iraq, and western Iran.

It is likely that Xenophon also referred to the Kurds in the *Anabasis* as the "Carduchi." He reported that they were a people who, "lived in the mountains and were very warlike and not subject to the king. Indeed a royal army of a hundred and twenty thousand had once invaded their country, and not a man of them had got back, because of the terrible conditions of the ground they had to go through."[19]

In 401 BC, Xenophon, and his famous "Ten Thousand," would also be forced to fight their way through the Kurdish mountains on the way to entering the land of the Armenians. (It should be noted that both the Kurdish and the Armenian peoples were here listed as early as the 5th Century BC, laying claim to contiguous lands in Asia Minor).

In the ninth century, the Kurds had established a principality on the shores of Lake Van. They enjoyed relative autonomy under the over-all suzerainty of the Abbasid Caliphate until the invasion of the Mongols in the 13th century. The greatest ethnic Kurd was Saladin, who rose to become sultan of Egypt and the founder of the Ayyubid Dynasty. Famed for the conquest of Jerusalem in 1187, and his battles with Richard the Lionheart during the Third Crusade; Saladin was greatly respected in the Christian West for his chivalry, generosity, and military genius.

In 1898, Germany's Kaiser Wilhelm II visited Saladin's mausoleum in Damascus. He sought to honor the Great Saladin while seizing the opportunity to ingratiate himself with his Muslim hosts. Portraying himself as a friend of Islam, and the Turkish Sultan; the Kaiser offered a new, ornate marble sarcophagus for the tomb, and personally composed an inscription for the occasion. He described the Kurdish-born leader as, "A Knight without fear or blame who often had to teach his opponents the right way to practice chivalry."[20]

In 1514, the Kurds, and Armenians were both annexed into the Ottoman Empire by Sultan Selim I. Allowed a degree of semi-autonomy, the Kurds, were initially permitted to govern themselves. By the nineteenth century, however, the new centralist policies that were designed to vest greater authority with the Ottoman Sultan had disenfranchised the Kurds.

Nationalist sentiments began to emerge with some scattered outbreaks eventually escalating into open insurrection. Unable to physically wrest their independence from Turkey or Persia, the Kurdish revolt was defeated in 1880.

Ironically, Sultan Abdul Hamid II switched from derision to a policy of inclusion and actually invited Kurdish leaders into positions within the Ottoman government. The result was the emergence of a Kurdish movement loyal to the Turkish sultan, and the formation of Abdul Hamid's personal military squadron, the *Hamidiye*.

Despite their loyalty to the sultan, the Kurds eventually fell out of the protection of the government with the overthrow of Abdul Hamid and the rise of the Young Turks. In a strangely ironic twist, the Kurds suffered a somewhat similar fate as the Armenians whom they had so sorely oppressed. During the final years of the First World War, the Young Turks began a systematic deportation of the Kurds for much the same reasons as those visited upon the Armenians.

No longer able to rely on the commonality of Pan-Islam, the Turks were fearful of possible Kurdish cooperation with the Allies, as had been so terribly demonstrated in the Muslim Arab revolt led by T. E.

Lawrence. It has been estimated that by 1918, nearly 700,000 Kurds had been displaced with perhaps half that number killed.

Following the war, the Kurds echoed the demands of the Armenians with a similar call for international recognition. Sadly, they and their hated Armenian neighbors were each promised an independent homeland by the 1920 Treaty of Sèvres, but both peoples were later suppressed in a bloody conflict with Turkey's new postwar government of Mustafa Kemal Attaturk.

To the present day, the Kurds aspire to procure a fully independent national homeland. Their continual struggle has long crossed international borders. Beginning with Attaturk's bloody repression in the 1920's the Kurds have faced a number of other notable modern Middle Eastern "strong-men."

Having sizeable Kurdish minorities located in Iraq, Iran, and Syria as well as in Turkey; the peoples of "Kurdistan" have also battled against the repressive forces of Saddam Hussein, Mahmoud Ahmadinejad, and Bashar Assad. Savagely persecuted, and even the victims of Iraqi biological warfare in the 1990's, the Kurds were partially spared by the demise of Saddam Hussein. Now that they are similarly threatened by Syria's ruthless dictator, the Kurds must hope that Assad will soon suffer a similar fate.

"KURDISH JERUSALEM"

Since the overthrow of Saddam Hussein, a portion of northern Iraq has been designated as the semi-autonomous Kurdistan Regional Government (KRG). With its own president and parliament, Kurdistan remains a Federal Region within Iraq. Rich in oil reserves, if Kurdistan was an independent nation it would rank twelfth in the world.

Strangely, at the time of this writing the Kurds are struggling with a newly emerging enemy that has suddenly appeared seemingly from nowhere. The insurgent *Islamic State of Iraq and al-Sham* (ISIS) claims much of Iraq and the Levant for the formation of a Sunni Islamic State. In a scene reminiscent of the depredations of 1915: ISIS has butchered and beheaded thousands of Christians, Yazidis, and rival Muslims in a sudden wave of terror. Their atrocities have included crucifixion and the burning alive of innocent civilians. After taking and decimating the city of Mosul in northern Iraq, ISIS fighters threatened to sweep north against the Kurds. Wasting no time, the Kurds mobilized and in June 2014 took decisive action, and after centuries of longing, occupied their ancestral "capital" city of Kirkuk.

Reuters reported that, "The collapse of Baghdad's control of northern Iraq in the face of an onslaught by Sunni insurgents has allowed Kurds to take the historic capital they regard as their Jerusalem, and suddenly put them closer than ever to their immortal goal: an independent state of their own... [the Kurds] seized full control of Kirkuk -- and tracts of land besides. In all, they expanded the territory they control by as much as 40 percent, without having to fight a single battle. The new territory includes vast oil deposits the Kurdish people regard as their national birthright and foundation for the prosperity of a future independent homeland."[21]

The "map" of Kurdistan presently occupies a tenuous geographical position overlapping the borders of Turkey, Syria, Iran, and Iraq. The Kurds jealously witnessed the emergence of an independent Armenia in 1991, but have failed to follow suit with a fully free country of their own. In July 2014, KRG's President Massud Barzani announced that a referendum for independence is imminent noting that the insurgency of the Islamic State had already "effectively partitioned" Iraq.

Not surprisingly, just as it was a century ago, the Kurds greatest opposition comes from Turkey.[22]

MOTIVE FOR MAYHEM

A number of theories have been advanced for Abdul Hamid's motives in mobilizing the Kurds. It was certainly accepted practice that an autocrat would raise levies of troops for his own designs. Rarely, however, does one freely arm and empower a potential adversary within its own domain.

As an advocate of the Turkish position, Langer offered the explanation that the Kurds were actually organized "to satisfy the chiefs and keep them from joining forces with the Armenian revolutionaries."[23] There was in fact, at least one time that the two groups had acted in concert against their Turkish rulers. "Less than three decades earlier both Armenians and Kurds had fought as brothers in Van (1862) against Ottoman misgovernment."[24]

It is also certainly true that the Kurds have had a stormy and violent historical relationship with their Turkish overlords, even culminating in the deaths and deportations of tens of thousands during the early years of Mustafa Kemal Attaturk's republic. To this day, the Kurdish minority, that comprises more than one-fifth of Turkey's national population, harbors strong separatist feelings.

Indeed during the past forty years nearly continual armed resistance and guerrilla warfare has resulted in the government destruction of an estimated three thousand Kurdish villages within Turkey.[25] In addition the Turkish air force launched a number of punitive sorties into Iraqi Kurdistan in 2010.

At the time of this writing, the Kurdish fighters have been actively aiding the targeted victims of the Jihadist *Islamic State of Iraq and ash Sham* (ISIS) even as the Turkish government has adamantly refused to commit military to any intervention despite vehement United States and NATO requests. Suffice it to say, the Kurds have traditionally had less than amicable relations with the Turks.

Ethnic hostilities notwithstanding, there is no reason to suspect that the Kurds would have sided with the hated Armenians against the sultan. That scenario seems highly unlikely given the age-old animosities that existed between the two peoples, and the fact that the Kurds were Muslims who looked upon the Armenians as infidels. As such, Abdul Hamid was able to use his position as Caliph to enflame

Kurdish hostilities, and exploit "the differences between Moslem and Christian."[26]

The brief cooperation that had taken place between the two peoples at Van in 1862, was a rarity. "Alliances between Armenians and Kurds were the exception rather than the rule. Kurdish bands frequently attacked Armenians...Occasionally whole villages were terrorized unless they submitted to the arbitrary demands of Kurdish chieftains and bands."[27]

Rather than extend any degree of cooperation with the Armenians, the Kurds saw them as "fair game," and ripe for exploitation. One Ottoman government employee "observed that the Armenians were virtually 'the serfs of their ferocious neighbors.'"[28] Indeed, the Kurds had viewed the *Tanzimat* reforms that had been pushed upon them as being too favorable to the Armenians, and restricting their ability to plunder and victimize them.

Armenian scholar, Stephan Astourian suggested that, "Their response was simple: they sabotaged the reforms, condoned violence against the Armenians, and refused to bring the guilty parties to justice."[29]

It is very difficult to believe that Sultan Abdul Hamid II feared any possible Kurdish alliance with the Armenians, and needed "to satisfy the chiefs" in order to prevent them from joining forces. No matter how much the Kurds resented their Muslim Turkish overlords they far more despised the Christian Armenians

The sultan consciously took the step of pitting one hated minority against the other even though both groups were his royal subjects. With amazing ruthlessness Abdul Hamid clearly understood the Kurdish antagonism for the Armenians and coolly utilized it to further his own ends. "These consisted of consolidating centralization of the country, reasserting Islamic superiority, promoting Islamic unity within and without the empire, and getting rid of the *Tanzimat* reforms, in particular those reforms favorable to the Armenians."[30]

Finally, by his arming of the Hamidiye, the sultan "nipped in the bud the nascent Armenian revolutionary movement in the 1890's."[31]During the past two decades of the century, underground Armenian militants were planning open revolt in the vain hope that the Great Powers would then come to their aid. Louise Nalbandian noted that in fact, the Hamidiye regiments "were a formidable force in counteracting Armenian revolutionary activities."[32]

Whatever the reasons may have been, despite a long history of Turkish antagonism; at the end of the nineteenth century the Kurds were briefly used, and even rewarded by the "Red Sultan. "

VICTIMS APLENTY

When one reads of the Hamidian depredations against the Christian minorities, and the Armenians in particular; it must be clearly understood that in the decades prior to the First World War many thousands of innocent Muslim civilians were brutally persecuted and slaughtered by Christians as well.

The Russo-Turkish War of 1877-78 saw the death or displacement of some hundreds of thousands of Muslim refugees from their homes in Bulgaria. Justin McCarthy suggested that more than a quarter million died with at least twice that number displaced and forced to flee to sanctuary in Turkey.[33]

An immense refugee column numbering as many as 200,000 Muslim civilians was reportedly attacked by Russian soldiers on January 19, 1878. Known to posterity as the "Harmanli Massacre," the terrible atrocities visited upon the helpless caravan were no less horrifying than those perpetrated by the Bashi-Bazouks or the Hamidiye. Those who could not safely flee to the mountains were butchered and their possessions plundered. The sick, the elderly and the very young who survived the attack were left to die in the snow.[34] Some two thousand children drowned in a nearby river. Russian soldiers raped and carried off the young Muslim women even as local Bulgarian villagers massacred those refugees that could not escape.[35]

The virtually non-stop warfare that devastated the Balkans for decades was no respecter of persons. People of every race, religion, ethnicity, age, or gender were indiscriminately slaughtered. Terrible crimes were regularly committed by both the Turks and the Bulgars, and one can endlessly argue as to whether one side was the initial cause or the effect. The infamous Bashi-Bazouks despoiled, raped, and slaughtered thousands of Christians with little or no Turkish attempt to restrain them. The Turks on the other hand, claimed to be reacting to Bulgarian atrocities.

Although numerous civilians were killed on both sides, "the Ottoman reprisals, the so-called Bulgarian horrors, received great publicity in Europe where only the Bulgarian side of the story was known."[36] Contemporary Bulgarian estimates of the number of those killed in the revolt ranged from 30,000 to 100,000. Whether the similarly violent Bulgarian depredations against the Turks were acts of vengeance in response to the Muslim attacks, or vice versa, are problematic. Blood feuds eventually lost all track of their own origins.

The Harmanli Massacre was but one notable example of countless such atrocities that were perpetrated against both Christian and Muslim civilians by those on either side. They were not the sole victims, however. Another group was also terribly threatened.

Fearing persecution by the advancing Russians many from Bulgaria's Jewish population also fled alongside the retreating Turks, ultimately seeking refuge in Constantinople. The large combination of Muslim, and Jewish escapees swelled the population of the already crowded capital.

Arriving in the city for a personal visit barely a few days after the cessation of hostilities; Gen. Ulysses S. Grant commented on the sad state of "more than a hundred thousand refugees, men women and children who have fled to the capital before a conquering army." Describing the pitiful scene in a letter to the American Consul in Paris, the former U. S. President wrote, "They are fed entirely by charity and mostly by foreigners. What is to become of them is sad to think of."[37]

In light of today's circumstances in the Middle East, it is interesting to note that the persecuted Bulgarian Jewish population of 1878, that was desperately fleeing from their Christian pursuers, sought the benevolent protection of the Muslim Turks.

HUNCHAKS, DASHNAKS, AND GOOGONIANS (OH MY!)

During the last two decades of the nineteenth century, as the Sultan was recruiting the *Hamidye*, an Armenian revolutionary movement also began to emerge. Unlike the Kurdish experience, however, Abdul Hamid did not attempt to assimilate the Armenian leaders into his government. Rather than appease, attract, and disarm them, he decided to meet the new threat to his regime with brutal force.

Terribly disillusioned by the failure of the European Powers to grant them greater autonomy at the Congress of Berlin, the Armenian Patriarch of Constantinople Archbishop Mkrtich Khrimian exhorted the people to take action. Disgusted with the lack of enforcement of the civil reforms that were promised in Article LXI of the Treaty of Berlin, the Catholicos of the Armenian Church gave numerous sermons and speeches in an attempt to arouse his constituents.

In a veiled call to arms "he explained that the reason why Armenians had lost ground in the treaty was that the weapon they were using to bring about change was made of paper, and that to take a share of the 'soup' being offered in Berlin an iron 'ladle' was needed."[38]

Confronted with the realization of the Great Powers "lack of interest in pressing for reforms, the Armenians formed their first political parties between 1885 and 1890."[39] Louise Nalbandian notes that "among the Russian Armenians a rapid growth of revolutionary organizations, which concentrated their efforts on the political affairs of Turkish Armenia ...wanted a change in administration in that area and advocated rebellion as a means of achieving it."[40]

Earlier successful revolutions in Greece and Bulgaria began to convince them that the Armenians could also be liberated from the Ottoman Empire. Armenian militants drew inspiration from Balkan revolutionary organizations and even began building loose ties with some of them. The leaders of the Macedonian Revolutionary Organization, Gotse Delchev and Giorche Petrov developed a dialogue with, and enlisted the aid of Armenian revolutionaries to help foment terror.

As Philip Shashko observed, "Petrov and especially Delchev, wanted the Internal Organization and the armed detachments to bring about a degree of violence and destruction which the Ottoman system could not tolerate indefinitely. Delchev...wanted to use sabotage and partially calculated political terror to induce a state of anxiety within the Ottoman ruling group and thus force them to make concessions to the Macedonian revolutionaries."[41]

Cooperating clandestinely, the Armenian revolutionaries drew closer to their Balkan counterparts. Perry Duncan described the actual "swapping of services," and the Macedonian contracting of Armenian explosives experts to blow up Turkish banks.[42] Drawing inspiration from other anti-Turkish revolutionary organizations, the Armenian militants soon began to formally mobilize.

In 1887, *The Hunchakian Revolutionary Party*, a Marxist organization, was created in Geneva, Switzerland.[43] Their stated objective "was the political and national independence of Turkish Armenia."[44] The Hunchaks were formed on the heels of an earlier Revolutionary group, the *Armenakins* who had not been able "to develop the political scope and momentum" needed to become a nationwide movement.[45] Three years later, in 1890, *The Armenian Revolutionary Federation* (or *Dashnaktsuthian*) was officially organized.

A confederation comprised primarily of Russian-Armenian social-ists, nationalists and student groups; the *Dashnaks* circulated revolu-tionary newspapers, raised funds, and sought to agitate and enlist the support of the Great Powers at Turkey's expense.

At first, the two groups attempted to work together. It was not long however, before the Dashnaks, who were ideologically more national-ist than socialist, split with the Hunchaks. Preferring to act for change and greater autonomy within the Ottoman Empire, the Dashnaks were less open to the struggle for all-out Armenian independence as being advocated by the more militant Hunchaks.

Indeed the Hunchaks saw the revolution as also ultimately includ-ing both the Russian and Persian portions of "Greater Armenia" with the goal of the creation of one large independent state. Nonetheless, both groups continued to share the overriding general aim of achiev-ing greater Armenian freedom.[46] An obscure third group would inad-vertently complicate matters.

In September 1890, a small Armenian force, under the leadership of a former Russian university student named Sarkis Googoonian, attempted to cross the Trans-Caucasian border into Turkey. Foiled, ironically, by Russian Cossack border guards, the revolt collapsed be-fore ever reaching Ottoman territory. Despite its failure, however, the ill-fated and inept Googoonian Expedition was to have a serious effect on the Armenian revolutionary movement.

"As the first major revolutionary enterprise emanating from Russian Armenia and directed at Asiatic Turkey...this event helped create a stronger spirit of national unity among Armenians in Turkey, Russia, and Persia."[47] Unfortunately, it also served notice to the Turkish Sultan that hostile forces were forming amongst his Armenian sub-jects. As a result, the Hamidye were unleashed and allowed to act without restraint in the Armenian provinces.

Ironically, the affair also caused the Russian Tsar to distrust the Armenians.

"WITH FRIENDS LIKE THAT..."

Always suspicious of Dashnak ties to the Russian underground revolutionary movement, the Tsar was now convinced, however erroneously, that the Googoonian fiasco was evidence of Armenian designs on his own territory.

"He feared that an autonomous or independent Armenia might deprive him of Russian Armenia, a small part of his domain."[48] It was also apparent that "Russia did not relish the idea of an independent Armenia, filling in Asia Minor the role of the new Bulgaria in Europe."[49] In the latter case, the new Bulgarian State had emerged fully independent of Russian controls, and although Orthodox Christian, it had therefore actually become a potential threat. (The Tsarist fears would later be proven correct when Bulgaria sided with Germany in the First World War).

Russian misunderstanding of Armenian intentions had surfaced as early as 1828, when it nearly provided "the spark" for a war with Persia,[50] and this latest affair contributed to a lingering distrust of Armenian motives. It might also help to explain the virtual lack of any direct Russian military intervention during the genocide of 1915.

As a result of the perceived threat of revolt, "the Hamidiye regiments, sometimes supported by regular troops, began to raid the Armenian settlements, burning the houses, destroying crops and cutting down the inhabitants."[51] Whatever the provocation, Abdul Hamid's response was merciless and often indiscriminately targeted innocent women and children, as well as suspected "revolutionaries."

Wheatcroft compares the Turkish depredations with contemporary Russian pogroms against its Jewish citizens, in which the "authorities simply encouraged long-standing hatreds to spill over into massacre."[52] As a result, a number of Armenians began to take up arms and finally, under the direction of Hunchak and Dashnak revolutionaries, a full-blown confrontation took place against the Ottoman army garrison at Sassun.

Although the Armenians were defeated by numerically superior Turkish and Kurdish forces, the precedent of armed resistance had been breached. The consequences for the vast majority of Armenians who remained innocent non-combatants would be catastrophic.

Organizing a full-scale uprising in 1894, Ramsaur suggests that the Armenian revolutionaries "were fully conscious that the Turks would take drastic action in return, but they were prepared to sacrifice their own people in order to attract the attention of the European powers to their desires."[53]

One Hunchak leader was even quoted by an American missionary as having callously admitted to a willingness of causing the death of innocent Armenian civilians in order to achieve their goals. Dr. Hamlin, the founder of Robert College recalled his conversation with the Armenian revolutionary who icily explained how the Hunchaks would, "watch their opportunity to kill Turks and Kurds, set fire to their villages, and then make their escape into the mountains. The enraged Moslems will then rise, and fall upon the defenseless Armenians and slaughter them with such barbarity that Russia will intervene in the name of humanity and Christian civilization.[54]

Langer also excuses the Turkish reprisals and squarely blames the Armenian Hunchakian revolutionaries whom he believes acted without the approval of the vast majority of the Armenian populace. He suggests that most of the persecuted Armenians simply "wished the patriots would leave them alone."[55]

Still, the revolutionaries anxiously "relied on the sincerity of the European Powers, which had made commitments for reforms in Turkish Armenia in Article LXI of the Treaty of Berlin."[56] The Armenian revolutionaries understood that without international help they could never wrest independence from the sultan. They counted on and fully expected some form of Great Power intervention.

In Constantinople, on October 1, 1895 a group of some two thousand Armenians assembled and peacefully petitioned Abdul Hamid to honor the reforms that had been promised. Instead, the orderly demonstration was violently dispersed by Hamidian soldiers.[57]

Within a month of the ill-fated rally in the capital, an open revolt took place in the city of Zeitun. The reason is open to debate. Depending on one's own preference between the choice of conflicting claims; the bloodshed was either the direct result of Christian resistance against local Muslim persecution or it was a justifiable Turkish government response to Armenian insurrection.

In either case, the Turks fared badly. Armenian fighters inflicted huge casualties on the Ottoman forces and despite numerical superiority, the Sultan's troops failed to retake the city.

One contemporary Hunchak leader reported the terribly lopsided casualty figures of 20,000 Muslim dead to a mere 125 Armenians, "...60 of whom had died in battle, and 65 of whom were dastardly killed during the ceasefire." Certainly exaggerated, Johannes Lepsius the German missionary pastor suggested that 6,000 Armenians were slain at Zeitun[58]

Soon after a British diplomat stationed in the city of Van warned of a possible Turkish government assault against the local Armenian population. In early January 1896, Vice Consul W.H. Williams described widespread looting and persecutions writing that, "Armenians are everywhere in a state bordering on panic, afraid lest the spring will bring still further disasters."

The following June, forecasts of violence were confirmed when in answer to local depredations an armed group of Armenians revolted and held out against Turkish army units for more than a week.

For his part, Abdul Hamid relied upon the jealousies and mistrust of the European guarantors of the Berlin treaty to prevent them from reaching any concerted action against him. The 1894-1896 massacres of Armenians in Sassun and Van, actually "revived the European call for Armenian reforms, but failed to generate any actual Great Power military intervention."[59] As so often before, the actions of the Great Powers failed to match their rhetoric.

It had finally become apparent to the less militant Dashnak leadership that European support (or lack thereof) for the beleaguered Christian minorities of Ottoman Turkey ranged from the tepid verbal denunciations in the West to outright Tsarist antipathy in the East. What they needed was a catalyst to help persuade the Russians and also to shock those openly sympathetic Great Powers (such as France, Italy, and Great Britain) into exercising decisive military action.

As a result the Armenian Revolutionary Federation decided to take a dramatic step.

BREAKING THE BANK

In August 1896, an event occurred in Constantinople that would have enormous international repercussions, and send shock-waves throughout the Ottoman Empire.

A small group of Dashnaks boldly entered the Ottoman Bank and, declaring themselves "Armenian patriots," threatened to blow it up.[60] Hoping to attract "foreign attention," the Armenians were prepared to kill everyone in the bank.[61] The plotters had apparently chosen that particular financial institution for attack "because it contained people of so many nationalities that the representatives of the powers would have to act to save their nationals."[62]

The Turks quickly besieged the structure with every intention of destroying it rather than succumb to Armenian black-mail. The Ottoman authorities were eventually persuaded to prevent the destruction of the bank by its English Director, Sir Edgar Vincent, who had personally escaped out of a window when the attack initially occurred.

Just before Abdul Hamid's orders "to direct artillery fire to the bank were executed, the Armenians were persuaded to end the siege, and were provided safe passage from the country aboard an English yacht."[63]

The aftermath was horrific, however. During the course of the next two days nearly six thousand Armenians were massacred by mobs in the Turkish capital.[64]

The evidence suggests that Abdul Hamid was somehow fore-warned of the attack on the bank for immediately after the take-over, "...armed bands appeared in various quarters of the city and, at a given signal, set out to attack and pillage every house inhabited by Armenians."[65]

Although Ottoman authorities later claimed that the killings were the result of a spontaneous mob demonstration, "the massacres were on a highly selective basis, since no other minorities were molested, and the government looked the other way."[67]

It was also corroborated by Baron Wladimir Giesl, the Austrian military attaché in Constantinople that the Turks actually knew in advance of the Bank assault and orchestrated the massacres that fol-lowed. As evidence, he claimed to have witnessed the police distribu-tion of weapons on the night prior to the attack, and even reported that the Turkish mob was signaled to action by a "bugle-call."[68]

Whether the sultan had advanced warning or not his reaction was swift, brutal, and vengeful. Three weeks following the Bank attack two thousand Armenians were slaughtered in the Eastern Anatolia vil-lage of Egin (present-day *Kemaliye*); the hometown of one of the slain Dashnak leaders.[69]

That Abdul Hamid used the bank take-over as a convenient pre-text to launch a Pan-Islamic assault against the Christian Armenians is hard to deny. The Kurdish *Hamidiye* had been groomed for just such a purpose.

Nonetheless, the facts suggest that a small cadre of Armenian revo-lutionaries knowingly provided the convenient match that lit the fuse of Turkish reaction. Even Vahakn Dadrian, the "Dean" of Armenian Holocaust scholars, acknowledges that the bank attack was contrived to persuade the European Powers to seize Constantinople.[70]

The revolutionary provocation had been made in the hopes of gen-erating a strong Great Power response. The result would be disastrous.

———

4

STRONG WORDS, WEAK ACTIONS

TAKING A CALCULATED risk the Armenian Revolutionary Federation (*Dashnaks*) had placed the minority Christian population of the Ottoman Empire in great peril. In the belief that the Great Powers would forcefully come to their aid, the Armenian militants now braced themselves for the violent Hamidian response that was sure to come.

Unfortunately for the innocent Armenian population, "many of those who died were not aware of what was happening."[1]

THE BLOODY RED SULTAN

In the ensuing months, following the Ottoman Bank attack, Abdul Hamid II launched a massive retaliation against the Armenians. In her biography *Sultan*, Joan Haslip mournfully observed, "during the whole of these eleven months one massacre followed on another, till the rivers of Eastern Anatolia were polluted by rotting corpses and jackals and carrion birds were the only inhabitants of Armenian villages."[2]

By October 1896 the expressed number of Armenians that were wantonly massacred approached unprecedented epic proportions. The *New York Times* Best-selling author, and Armenian apologist Prof. Peter Balakian exclaimed, "When the main period of the Hamidian massacres ended in 1896, the death toll of innocent civilians exceeded anything the modern era had known."[3]

With no reason to inflate the numbers, the German, pro-Turkish propagandist of the First World War, Dr. Ernest Jackh estimated the total number of Armenian victims at, "200,000 killed, 50,000 expelled, and one million pillaged and plundered."[4]

The forever unknown sum of those who eventually died from wounds or later succumbed to starvation only increases the final fatality count. It was actually concluded at the time by other observers, that an estimated additional, "150,000 children, old men, and women were doomed to die during the winter from hunger and cold."[5]

That an atrocity of such magnitude could have been perpetrated without the full knowledge and support of the government simply defies credulity. American missionaries who witnessed the massacres left no doubt as to their belief that the Sultan was personally responsible.

In writing about the Armenian victims, Dr. Caleb Gates stationed at Harpoot stated that, "it is perfectly clear that this thing emanated from the Sultan. For two months the Dersim Koords [Kurds] and Moslem Koords have been declaring that they had orders from the Sultan to kill the Christians."[6]

The leaders of the Great Powers were virtually united in their collective condemnation of Abdul Hamid, all that is, except Kaiser Wilhelm II of Germany. Even though the German Ambassador co-signed the joint European note of protest to the Sublime Porte, the Kaiser privately nullified it.

With amazing callousness, the German Emperor took the opportunity to express his full support to the Sultan with the hope of ingratiating the Turks. It is reported that the Kaiser chose this moment to emphasize his personal friendship by actually sending Abdul Hamid a signed photograph of himself, the Kaiserin and their family.[7]

The German Kaiser notwithstanding, the overwhelming European and American consensus was that Abdul Hamid was to personally blame for the excessive Turkish reaction to the Armenian revolutionary activity. Newspapers on both sides of the Atlantic publicly denounced the Ottoman Sultan. Western political cartoons ubiquitously depicted the Sultan as being a lecherous, craven, sadistic butcher.

FROM "SABRE RATTLING" TO "WINDOW RATTLING"

Despite the universal outrage at the excesses of Abdul Hamid's tyrannical regime; the Great Powers, beset by mutual distrust, offered little more than angry rhetoric in response. A few western governments threatened military action but to no final avail.

England's Lord Salisbury had been diligent in insisting that Abdul Hamid II dutifully abide by the terms of the Treaty of Berlin, and that he finally institute the promised Armenian reforms throughout the Ottoman Empire. In light of the Sultan's defiance of that demand, the British Prime Minister eagerly sought Great Power consensus but to no avail.

Stanford Shaw noted that, "At this point Lord Salisbury attempted to get the support of the new Tsar Nicholas II...for the British fleet to come to Istanbul to persuade the sultan to give the Armenians what they wanted. Russia, however, feared this would increase British control in the empire and joined France in opposing unilateral intervention to pressure the sultan. Salisbury's initiative was frustrated, and nothing was done."[8]

Now faced with the apparent refusal of the Turkish Sultan to comply with the provisions of the Treaty, the British Prime Minister lamented the fact that the Red Sultan was effectively beyond the reach of Her Majesty's Royal Navy. As much as he may have personally wished to aid the Armenians, Salisbury realistically bemoaned that he "could not sail the Fleet across the Taurus Mountains."[9]

The King of Belgium, Ludwig II offered to muster colonial Congolese forces "for the purpose of invading and occupying Armenia and so putting a stop to the massacres."[10] What he did not promise, however, was also putting an end to his own murder of some ten million African natives in the Belgian Congo.

In the United States, the *New York Times* presciently posted the headline, "Armenian Holocaust," using a term that would one-day, become synonymous with genocide.[11] The American Press, well-informed of the Anatolian depredations due to the improved access to news provided by the telegraph, was terribly outraged. Reports flowed continuously from Christian missionaries regarding the first-hand witness of alleged Muslim atrocities against Armenian women and children.

Throughout the United States humanitarian relief efforts were organized to assist the Armenian sufferers. Philanthropists such as John D. Rockefeller gave hundreds of thousands of dollars even as the less fortunate donated blankets, clothing, or whatever else they could reasonably afford.

The composer of the widely popular *Battle Hymn* of the American Civil War, Julia Ward Howe used her personal popularity to create the "United Friends of Armenia." Her husband had formerly fought against the Turks as a volunteer in the 1825 Greek War of Independence. Another famous female humanitarian also answered the call.

Another heroine from the Civil War, Clara Barton, the "Angel of the Battlefield," raised considerable donations of cash and needed supplies. She received Turkish permission to enter the country on the condition that her organization's symbolic *Red Cross* not be visibly exhibited in any way, and that food and necessities be equally distributed to displaced Muslims as well.

Although she was closely scrutinized by Ottoman authorities and initially forced to remain primarily headquartered in Constantinople, the founder of the American Red Cross was eventually permitted to travel to Eastern Anatolia. The tenacious seventy-four year-old woman was able to guarantee the delivery of her entire inventory of food, medicines, and means of warmth to those in need.

Even the Turkish government was impressed and duly awarded her with a medal for her extraordinary humanitarian efforts.[12] The following year, the tireless Clara Barton continued her benevolent work in the military hospitals of Cuba during the Spanish-American War.

American women were particularly apt to become concerned about the plight of the Armenians with the continual stream of news dispatches describing the widespread reports of rape and female slavery. It took little to fuel the already huge aversion that nineteenth century predominately "white, Christian America" held for the Asiatic, Islamic Turks.

One clergyman angrily demanded that, "the warships of the western powers ride up as close as possible to the palaces of Constantinople and blow that accursed government to atoms."[13] The 1896 Hamidian Massacres even became a political issue.

In his bid for the White House, Republican presidential candidate William McKinley ranked "saving the Armenians" as one of his future administration's top three foreign policy objectives (along with the annexation of Hawaii, and Cuban freedom from Spanish rule). After his election, in response to calls from the American Ambassador in Turkey to send a fleet of gunboats that would "rattle the Sultan's windows."

McKinley did in fact dispatch the battleship *U.S.S. Kentucky* to the Turkish Port of Smyrna as a show of force. Duly impressed by the threat of the warship's combined armament of four large 13 inch guns, along with fifty more of smaller caliber; the Sultan agreed to give $83,000 in compensation to repair damage done to American Christian missionary schools.[14] That was the total extent of the "penalty" imposed upon the Sultan by the Great Powers. With all of the "saber rattling" on both sides of the Atlantic, the Red Sultan's windows barely shook. Meanwhile, the Armenian toll of death and suffering from the "Hamidian Massacres" was immense.

Kaiser Wilhelm was informed that by the end of 1895, some 80,000 Armenians had perished. At the same time the French reported 200,000 fatalities and the English claimed half that many were killed. The Armenian patriarchate argued that by the conclusion of the massacres, "the real number was in the area of three hundred thousand."[15]

The German missionary Pastor Johannes Lepsius, an eyewitness who personally travelled amongst the various sites of the massacres, "estimated 100,000 dead from the killing and another 100,000 from famine and disease."[16]

With the possible exception of Imperial Germany, the worldwide consensus was that Abdul Hamid II was personally responsible for the murder of as many as 300, 000 Armenians. Even the Turks could not deny the Ottoman government's culpability for that savage and unprecedented persecution.

Little more than two decades later the Turkish National Congress, in its 1919 official "explanation" (and denial!) of the holocaust of 1915, admitted at the very least to, "the responsibility for the innocent Armenian blood spilt in the course of the blind repression of 1895-96...and blamed Abdul Hamid II for their deaths."[17]

Before the watchful eyes of the world, the bloody Red Sultan had struck...and had thus far survived unscathed.

FROM POGROMS TO GENOCIDE?

It has been debated whether the violent persecution of 1894-1896 was the beginning of genocide or more resembled the anti-Jewish pogroms that were currently underway throughout the Russian Empire. Interestingly, the Armenian apologist Vahakn Dadrian differentiates between the violent actions of the Sultan's minions with those that followed two decades later. He contrasts the events of 1896 and 1915 by noting that "decimation is not coterminous with genocide."[18]

Dadrian does not minimize the severity of the Hamidian persecution, but neither does he consider it "genocide," for a number of reasons:

"The victims involved were: (a) mostly menfolk, to the exclusion, as a rule, of women and children of both sexes; (b) mostly from urban centers; (c) those who were massacred, lost their lives in periods of relatively short duration, ranging from two to four days; [and] (d) killed or burned outright in or around their places of residence or business."[19] As there were no "wholesale deportations and massacres," the Sultan had not yet determined to fully settle the Armenian Question.

The Sultan's biographer, Joan Haslip offered the suggestion that the atrocities of 1894-1896 were perpetrated as the result of perceived Armenian *Hunchak* revolutionary activity. She noted however, that the Turkish response was brutally excessive and took on the guise of a government sponsored *Jihad*. "In Constantinople, the Sultan heard with rage that Moslems were being killed by Christians furnished with foreign arms and, in a *firman* addressed to his provincial governors, Abdul Hamid invested them with full powers to repress the rebellion."[20]

In a scene reminiscent of the horrible religious pogroms of the Crusades or the Spanish Inquisition; "the terror had begun and once begun there was no going back. Age-old grievances and hatreds, jealousies and fears, cupidity and lust allied themselves under the green banner of the Prophet. Incited by their sheikhs and *imams*, men were free to pillage and to murder, to rape and disembowel, all in the name of Allah."[21]

Certainly misdirected religious zeal had taken on a violent form many times in the past, and the atrocities of 1894-96 were not without historical precedent. Eric Weitz goes even further in suggesting that the Hamidian massacres were merely typical for the period. He argues that, "while horrific and tragic, these were still traditional forms of violence, much like pogroms against Jews in the Russian Empire, though on a vastly greater scale."[22]

MODEL FOR MAYHEM

The thousands of anti-Jewish Pogroms that enflamed the Russian Empire from 1881-1917 were launched with the tacit approval of the Tsarist government, if not actually precipitated by it. In countless reports, the attacks took place while local Tsarist police or military personnel stood by and did nothing.

A correspondent for *The New York Times* reported witnessing a deadly attack perpetrated upon Russian Jews stating, "The scenes of horror attending this massacre are beyond description. Babies were literally torn to pieces by the frenzied and bloodthirsty mob." The astonished reporter then exclaimed, "The local police made no attempt to check the reign of terror."[23]

"They could not fire on Christians to protect Jews."[24]

Events in Russia sometimes took on the appearance of an actual prelude to planned government genocide. An advisor to Nicholas II suggested to the Tsar a hoped-for solution to the "Jewish question." He coldly forecast that, "A third will emigrate, a third will convert to Christianity, and a third will die out."[25] Those few in the government sympathetic to the Jews were unable or unwilling to prevent their persecution.

Even the Tsar's liberal thinking Prime Minister, Count Sergei Witte found himself powerless to prevent pogroms from being officially sponsored by his own government subordinates! "Witte was shocked to discover from a department official that while fighting against Jewish pogroms the Department of Police was simultaneously preparing proclamations inciting the population... to Jewish pogroms!"[26]

It is all the more remarkable that Witte could have been so unable to curb, or would even be unaware of the government instigated atrocities when one considers his usual organizational brilliance. Among his giant achievements, the minister was the man personally responsible for the Herculean construction, and efficient administration of the 5,500 mile Trans-Siberian Railway; an achievement rightfully called "one of the wonders of the world." His abilities and insights were so profound that Lenin later referred to Count Witte as a "conjurer."[27]

If even the brilliantly efficient Russian Prime Minister could be fooled by those within his own government, it can be also argued that the later heads of the Turkish triumvirate might have unknowingly acquiesced to subordinate sponsored minority persecutions as well. Such would later be their claims.

In Russia, as in the Ottoman Empire, both Jews and Armenians were hated and envied by the poor and peasant classes as generally being successful entrepreneurs and wealthy merchants.[28] "Pure-blood" ethnic Turks and Russians could not accept the fact that despised foreign minorities could enjoy better economic circumstances within their respective national homelands.

In Turkey, the imams incited the Muslim faithful against the infidel Armenians. Similarly, in Russia organized religion played an ugly role in the repression of the Jews. Often times the Russian Orthodox Church was directly implicated in the anti-Semitic persecutions. Many local priests actually participated in the pogroms under the pretext of punishing the Jewish "killers of Christ." Amazingly, a number of church organized pogroms took place on the annual celebration of Eastern Orthodox Easter.

The *New York Times* reported a 1903 pogrom in the Tsarist city of Kishinev. "The anti-Jewish riots...are worse than the censor will permit to be published. There was a well laid-out plan for the general massacre of Jews the day following the Orthodox Easter. The mob was led by priests, and the general cry, 'Kill the Jews,' was taken up all over the city. The Jews were taken wholly unaware and were slaughtered like sheep."[29]

It was certainly a bitter commemoration and remembrance of the resurrection of Him who taught us to "love" our enemies!

THE DOOR SWINGS BOTH WAYS...

The terrible anti-Semitic Tsarist pogroms of the late nineteenth century were not the only examples of Russian depredations aimed against their own minority subjects. In 1860, what can truly be described as a grisly prelude to the later Armenian deportations of 1915; the Tsarist government brutally persecuted the Circassians. In a virtual mirror-image scenario to that of the repeated Turkish actions; the Russian leadership similarly attempted to control and practically eradicate a sizable minority population. This time it was Christians persecuting Muslims instead of the other way around.

The Circassians had resisted Tsarist military pressure for more than half a century, refusing to be pacified and incorporated into the Russian Empire. They "inhabited a poor and difficult mountainous region with few riches, but the area was strategically important, as it controlled a part of the Black Sea coast and access to the Ottoman Empire."[30]

In a brutal four-year campaign nearly half of the Circassian population of two million died, with an additional 150,000 forcibly resettled within the Russian Empire. In an ironic twist of fate, nearly 700,000 fled across the border into Turkey seeking asylum in a totally reverse direction of the later attempted Armenian exodus to Russia. When the Russians finished the violent action only ten percent of the original Circassian population remained in their ancestral home.

Nonetheless, the Circassians were victims of the harsh government policy only after they refused to be pacified by the Tsarist government. Sociologists Daniel Chirot, and Clark McCauley noted that the Russians were often quite willing to incorporate non-Slavs into the empire but had only "resorted to what amounted to a costly military operation because all else had failed."[31]

Unlike the situation with the Armenians, who historically were generally passive and cooperative ("the peaceful millet"); the Circassian depredations more closely paralleled the nineteenth century United States government pacification campaigns aimed against native Americans. It is true that many of the Indian nations, particularly the so-called "Five Civilized Tribes" (Choctaw, Chickasaw, Creek, Seminole, and Cherokee) of the Southeastern United States were reasonably content as semi-autonomous entities within the Federal jurisdiction.

President George Washington had early recommended the assimilation of native peoples and their cultural integration and transformation into European culture was often successful. Ultimately, however, white western expansion (often triggered by greedy episodes of "gold fever") encroached continuously onto Indian lands.

The result was decades of conflict, treaty violations, and destruction of the Indian habitat, including the vast Buffalo herds upon which they depended for survival. The ravages of disease, starvation, and periods of open warfare decimated the indigenous population. Resistance to change was also partially to blame and what was progress for some became disaster for others. It was never the result of a planned, government genocide, however.

The forced relocation to reservations west of the Mississippi River were no less violent and deadly, as the 1830-1838 Cherokee "Trail of Tears" experience would confirm. To this day the memory of the sufferings of those who were deported is no less painful to their living descendants than they are to the Armenians. (My son's full-blooded Cherokee Mother-in Law still harbors great personal disdain for the memory of Andrew Jackson). The harsh government actions were not intended to destroy the American Indian population, however.

Today, according to the U. S. Bureau of the Census, the Cherokee Nation has rebounded and is currently the largest Native American Tribe in the country. "Genocide was never American policy, nor was it the result of policy."[32]

The Circassians similarly were victims of government territorial expansion. Refusing to assimilate, they chose to resist and were defeated. Rather than being the victims of planned genocide; the Circassians suffered terrible losses as the result of a punitive expedition that the Russians would have likely preferred to avoid.

In any event, it is the terrible but simple historical reality that minority populations were systematically persecuted and abused not only in the Middle East, but also throughout Europe and North America; by "Christian" governments as well as Muslim. Armenian-style depredations were all too widespread and commonplace during the late nineteenth century but as such, more resembled pogroms or punitive actions than systematic genocide.

Nonetheless, the Turkish atrocities of 1895-1896 "retrospectively may be characterized as a rehearsal for the subsequent 1915-1918 cataclysm."[33]

JOHN BULL CHANGES SIDES

In the wake of the Armenian massacres, the Great Powers initially expressed outrage, and public opinion, particularly in Great Britain, had become decidedly hostile to the Sultan. Having typically sided with Turkey, particularly when Russia was involved, this was a decided British departure from their former ally of the Crimean War.

The subject of many anti-Turkish political cartoons portrayed in the daily newspapers; the "Red Sultan" was widely vilified and denounced. British passions were audibly displayed once again by the "Jingoistic" tune now on many peoples' lips. This time quite differed, however, from the events of twenty years earlier.

No, longer did the British sing of *defending* the Turks:

> *"We fear not Frank nor Muscovite*
> *When liberty is calling,*
> *With British pluck for those we'll fight,*
> *'Neath Moslem vengeance falling;*
> *Cease your preaching! Load your guns!*
> *Their roar our mission tells,*
> *The day is come for Britain's sons*
> *To seize the Dardanelles!"*[34]

British opinion had changed dramatically. Akaby Nassibian writes that "the widespread Armenian massacres of 1894-96 had made the British public deeply aware of the misgovernment of the Turkish Empire and had aroused a genuine interest in the identity and the history of these oppressed peoples."[35]

Oddly enough, British public opinion, so enflamed by the plight of the Armenians, was greatly muted regarding the Russian Jews. London newspapers were replete with stories of the bloody pogroms and persecutions of <u>both</u> peoples. Atrocities from the East filled the pages of the *Times* on an almost regular daily basis.

Although the depredations were similar to those visited upon the Armenians, British sympathy for Russia's Jews was far less evident. The reason was less one of religious identification than as a matter of simple economics.

The cities of Great Britain were experiencing a great influx of Jewish immigrants fleeing Tsarist oppression. As a result of the exodus caused by the pogroms, the already overcrowded working class communities were becoming further stressed by increased competition for jobs, adequate housing, and an upwardly spiraling crime rate.

It was actually feared by London authorities that the "Jack the Ripper" scare of 1888 would possibly incite severe anti-Semitic reprisals, due to the widespread belief that the grisly murderer was a Jewish immigrant.

The end result was that the usually sympathetic British "man on the street" became far less supportive of the plight of oppressed foreigners, in the wake of real threats to his personal domestic order.

Driven by the thousands from their homes in the East, the Jews were still persecuted in the West. The Armenians, however, remained for the most part in eastern Anatolia.

DARWIN'S "RACIAL HIERARCHY"

Without the threat of large-scale immigration from the oppressed minorities of the Ottoman Empire, British public support for them remained selfishly high. Sympathy for the Armenians also translated into scorn for the Turks. It was often, however, a matter of condescending racial views.

European images of the Turks as "barbarians," dated back to as early as 1453, and the fall of Constantinople.[36] By the late nineteenth century, Turkey had disdainfully been epitomized as the "sick man of Europe," and had long lost its terror for the West. Now rather than fear of the Turks, Europeans loathed and looked down on them.

Thomas Carlyle, without intended "pun," spoke of "the 'unspeakable Turk' [who] savaged women and children, and raped, murdered, and pillaged, sparing neither young nor old."[37] In a widely popular pamphlet published in 1876, former British Prime Minister William E. Gladstone reviled the Turk as "the one great anti-human specimen of humanity."[38] Some years later another British diplomat wrote of his personal disdain for the Turks after serving for a time at the Sublime Porte. Sir Harold Nicolson confided, "For the Turks I had, and have, no sympathy whatsoever. Long residence at Constantinople had convinced me that behind his mask of indolence, the Turk conceals impulses of the most brutal savagery...The Turks have contributed nothing whatsoever to the progress of humanity: they are a race of Anatolian marauders."[39]

In 1853, the French aristocrat Count Arthur de Gobineau wrote a racially incendiary treatise title provocatively *An Essay on the Inequality of the Human Races*. Circulated throughout Western Europe, it is considered today to have been the catalyst for the rise of "Racialism" in later nineteenth and early twentieth century political thought. The book greatly influenced the Aryan supremacist teachings of Friedrich Nietzsche, Richard Wagner, Houston Chamberlain, and was later studied and widely disseminated by Adolf Hitler and the Nazis. Equating all Turanian peoples with a common Mongolian ancestry, Gobineau wrote that, "...the Turkish people belonged to the yellow race." He then acidly described all ethnic Turanian people with the hostile observation that no "creatures were so incontrovertibly ugly and repulsive as the ordinary specimens of the Mongolian race."[40]

Even Charles Darwin placed the Turk at the bottom of his "racial hierarchy," expressing himself as having a low opinion of "the Turkish race."[41] The original subtitle for his opus *Origin of the Species* was "The Preservation of Favoured Races in the Struggle for Life." Darwin had only the harshest regard and racist condescension for the non-white peoples. He wrote of the Turks with particular disdain.

"Remember what risk the nations of Europe ran, not so many centuries ago of being overwhelmed by the Turks, and how ridiculous such an idea now is! The more civilized so-called Caucasian races have beaten the Turkish hollow in the struggle for existence. Looking to the world at no very distant date, what an endless number of the lower races will have been eliminated by the higher civilized races throughout the world."[42]

Such flagrantly racist words were worthy of the Third Reich and would have made a Hitler or a Himmler proud. No wonder the Turks were militantly offended by European attitudes of the late nineteenth century!

Darwin's racist views towards the Turks were widely shared in England. They were often visually lampooned in art and political cartoons as the "Terrible Turk;" "Indolent Ottoman;" "Lustful and Craven Turk;" and other odious epithets. Abdul Hamid himself was portrayed as a drunkard, a lecher, and as "the Red Sultan," covered in his victim's blood.[43]

Quite often the Turks were depicted as savage rapists. One popular British cartoon portrayed a determined John Bull, backed by French and Russian sailors, confronting the Sultan with the caption:

"Deeds not words! Look here---we've had enough of your palaver! Are you going to let the girl go or have we got to make you?"

The "girl" in question was a weeping Christian beauty, chained to a tree.[44]

Ironically, for all of their threatening "words," no "deeds" were forthcoming. The Great Powers were deeply divided on how to respond. Russia was looking towards expansion in the Far East and agreed with Austria to" keep the Balkans quiet."[45]

While being energetically exhorted to action by Georges Clemenceau, Anatole France and other notables,[46] the French Republic was similarly distracted elsewhere, particularly in Saharan Africa.[47]

Finally, the vituperative British were stymied, and the government rejected the course of going alone. It was apparently easier to sing about chastising the Turks than in actually proceeding to do it.

When Queen Victoria pressed him to take action on behalf of the Armenians, Lord Salisbury, British Prime Minister, responded that, "England's strength lies in her ships and ships can only operate on the seashore or the sea. England alone can do nothing to remedy an inland tyranny."[48]

OPPORTUNITY KNOCKS

Perhaps not surprisingly one European power, seeing an opportunity for influence and ever-eager to gain strategic advantage, came to the aid of the Sultan. Germany, and its new, young Kaiser Wilhelm II, discarded the Eurocentric policy of Bismarck, and sought adventure in the Middle East.

In November, 1889, the German emperor paid a lavish state visit to the Sublime Porte. Aboard his Imperial yacht *Hohenzollern*, the Kaiser sailed through the Dardanelles to the ubiquitous sights and sounds of great official welcome. On the sultan's orders, "all the forts hoisted the German flag, the military bands played the German anthem, and as the Imperial yacht passed between the castles where the straits are narrowest the forts on either side thundered forth their welcome in a salute of 101 guns."[49]

Thoroughly intoxicated by the warm welcome, the Kaiser began a new friendship with Abdul Hamid that despite the Turkish monarch's later "bloody" reputation would last for the remainder of the

Red Sultan's reign. The euphoria did not last long, however. Upon his return to Berlin, Wilhelm failed to follow-up on his overtures with the sultan for a number of years, and as historian Sean McMeekin observed, "...his attention, characteristically wandered elsewhere soon after returning home from Constantinople."[50]

As is so often the case great historical events are sometimes decided by the most seemingly trivial circumstances. In 1895, the Great Powers were trying to gather a consensus as how best to respond to Abdul Hamid's persecution of the Christians within his empire. The British government, under the constant goading of Queen Victoria, was particularly interested in some sort of mutual intervention. Germany was at first, equally concerned about news of events in the Sublime Porte.

The German monarch was personally enamored with his British cousins and as the grandson of the Queen was predisposed to the island empire. Originally receptive to British policy, the Kaiser abruptly changed course after a perceived personal snub by Prime Minister Salisbury, during an August meeting regarding Turkey. Stood-up for an audience not just once, but also a second time in as many days; the Kaiser was greatly upset at the apparent affront from someone with whom he had previously enjoyed a relatively warm relationship.

Despite Salisbury's apologies and the explanation of certain extenuating circumstances, Wilhelm was indignant, and incredibly, the affair jaded his opinion of Great Britain ever after.[51]

One immediate change in course was the Kaiser's renewed interest in the Ottoman Empire. Perhaps due in part to Wilhelm's emotional sensitivity, and "in order to improve Germany's world position vis-à-vis Britain, France, and Russia," strong overtures were soon made to the sultan.[52]

In the race for overseas colonies, Germany had come too late into the game. Little remained but, "a secondary share of colonial spoils. In the scramble for Africa, England and France had secured the lion's share. Russian ambitions blocked the way to the Far East and the only road for the *Drang nach Osten* lay through the Sultan's empire."[53]

It was not just the Kaiser's dream of the German "drive toward the East" that fueled his courtship of Abdul Hamid. In addition to being a market for German manufactured goods, the Ottoman Empire was rich in natural resources that the Fatherland lacked. As Haslip observed, "Economic necessity had brought the Kaiser to Constantinople."

In the days to come, even while in the midst of the Hamidian massacre of Armenian Christians, the opportunistic Germans began "to ingratiate themselves with the Turks, and to win a steady stream of economic concessions."[54]

BERLIN TO BAGHDAD

The idea of creating a rail line from Berlin to Baghdad was born from the Kaiser's desire to build Germany into a global colonial power. Rejecting the decades-old continental foreign policy of Bismarck; under Wilhelm II the Reich would henceforth aspire to become a true world empire.

The German foreign ministry became committed to fostering a strong alliance with Turkey. In essence, the Kaiser was intent on supporting the regime of his fellow monarch and that meant helping to personally bolster Abdul Hamid himself. Sean McMeekin observed, "In building the Baghdad railway, then, the Germans were betting on the Sultan's political future."[55]

In 1888, "Sultan Abdul Hamid decided to reward Wilhelm II by granting the Germans the first railway concession, which was followed by subsequent concessions subsumed under the Baghdad Railway Project."[56] The Kaiser began pouring financial investment as well as military advisors into Turkey and the results were dramatic. In the period "...between 1886 and 1910, Germany jumped from 15th to 2nd place in Ottoman trade, surpassed only by England."[57]

Never willing to miss an opportunity to upstage the British, the Kaiser had memorably visited the Sublime Porte in 1889, and once again in 1898. "On the second occasion Wilhelm, speaking at Saladin's tomb in Damascus, proclaimed himself the friend of the world's 300,000,000 Muslims."[58]

The effect on the Turks was electrifying. Here was a leader of one of the European Great Powers who not only refrained from coveting Ottoman territory, but who even praised the Turks rather than treating them with condescension.

One witness to the Kaiser's visit exclaimed, "In Damascus...I was struck by the powerful impression the visit of His Majesty the Kaiser had made on the Mohammedans of Syria, and it was not difficult to observe what a particularly fine reputation the German name is endowed with, now more than ever."[59]

Despite the Kaiser's posturing, Vahakn Dadrian acidly noted that, "the episode that is believed to have exerted a great influence in cementing Turco-German ties of friendship was the German response, or rather the lack of it, to the 1894-1896 empire wide massacres against the Armenians."[60]

Germany had indeed exhibited a generally tolerant posture to the excesses of the Hamidian regime. At times, the Reich even aided the Red Sultan in his draconian enterprises. One of the requirements for obtaining Turkish concessions regarding the building of the railway was the Sultan's demand that Germany provide sensitive information to the Sublime Porte. "As early as June, 1898, Abdul Hamid, through his ambassador to Berlin, had demanded that the Germans share intelligence on revolutionary opponents of his regime, and be ready to deport, on request, specifically named 'agitators' from Germany."[61]

The Germans were only too eager to comply and thus began a pattern of unconditional support that would eventually culminate in their officially ignoring the barbaric atrocities being committed against the Armenians.

"MUSLIM" KAISER

Interestingly, Kaiser Wilhelm's apparent lack of concern for the fate of Christians in Eastern Anatolia may have a curious explanation. In 1898, immediately after his second visit to the Ottoman Empire, the German Emperor took in the confidence of Tsar Nicholas of Russia and in paraphrasing his sentiments explained that he had virtually "fallen in love with Islam."

Writing of his own preference for the simplicity of the Islamic shrines in Jerusalem when compared to the ostentation of the many Christian Churches he had visited; Wilhelm went on to declare, "My personal feeling in leaving the holy city was that I felt profoundly ashamed before the Moslems and that if I had come there without any Religion at all I certainly would have turned Mahommetan!"[62]

Thus was born, in Sean McMeekin's words, *"Haji Wilhelm, the Mythical Muslim Emperor of Germany."* It was even being rumored by some that he had been ordained by Allah to defend Islam from European infidel rule.[63] The fact that Germany also had nearly three million Muslim subjects in her African colonies was apparently forgotten, however.

Ever a man of contradictions, Kaiser Wilhelm's effusive praise of the Islamic Turks apparently masked an underlying racist viewpoint that would have pleased his later successors in the Third Reich. Robert Massie observed that Wilhelm, "hated Orientals, and often raved about the 'Yellow Peril.'"[64]

During the Chinese "Boxer Rebellion" of 1900, the Kaiser was intent on having Germany take a leading part in the relief expedition to free the European legations then being besieged in Peking. Addressing a detachment of German Marines embarking for China, the Kaiser betrayed a deep-seeded racism in his loud exhortation. He militantly exclaimed, "You must know, my men, that you are about to meet a crafty, well-armed, cruel foe! Meet him and beat him. Give no quarter. Take no prisoners. Kill him when he falls into your hands. Even as a thousand years ago, the Huns under King Attila made such a name for themselves as still resounds in terror through legend and fable, so may the name of Germany resound through Chinese history a thousand years from now."[65]

Later, in a personal letter to Tsar Nicholas II, the German emperor vehemently announced his support for Russia's impending 1905 war with Japan. Declaring the upcoming campaign to be nothing less than a "Holy Mission," the Kaiser wrote, "Clearly, it is the great task for the future of Russia to cultivate the Asian continent and to defend Europe from the inroads of the Great Yellow Race. In this you will always find me on your side, ready to help you as best I can. You have well understood the call of Providence...in the Defense of the Cross and the old Christian European culture against the inroads of the Mongols and Buddhism."[66]

One can only wonder if Nicholas was perplexed as to the true religious sentiments of his Prussian counterpart. Was he *Haji Wilhelm*, or a sincere defender of the Cross? It seems that the Red Sultan also harbored suspicions about the Kaiser's true colors having been informed of the German monarch's racist ravings against the Chinese "heathens."[67]

"THE PANTHER'S POUNCE"

During Wilhelm's second visit to the Sublime Porte in 1898, he dramatically exclaimed, "May the Sultan and his 300,000,000 subjects scattered across the earth, who venerate him as their Caliph, be assured that the German Kaiser will be their friend for all time."[68]

By so patronizingly claiming to uphold the rights of the worldwide Islamic population, the overzealous monarch had stepped on the toes of those colonial powers that ruled over Muslim lands. Great Britain, France, Russia, Spain, and Italy all had reason for alarm, as did Persia who did not pay allegiance to an Ottoman caliph. The mere threat of Islamic unrest, instituted from Constantinople with the Kaiser's prodding, brought understandable concern to the capitals of the Great Powers.

As if to confirm their suspicions, Wilhelm actually confided to the Russian monarch Nicholas II that, "British India...could be brought low by an Islamic jihad, launched by either Sultan or Tsar [or Kaiser!] who was himself the 'master of millions of Mahometans.'" As Sean McMeekin aptly points out, however, "The idea that Russia was just as vulnerable to Muslim unrest as Britain does not seem to have occurred to Wilhelm."[69]

Germany's not so veiled threat had undoubtedly occurred to the leaders of the other powers, however, as later events would seem to illustrate.

Ever the opportunist, Kaiser Wilhelm II was the friend of Islam only when it served his purposes. At the same time that he was courting first Sultan Abdul Hamid, and then the Young Turks, the German monarch was recklessly instigating a major controversy in another part of the Muslim world.

Morocco had never been a formal part of the Ottoman Empire which had reached its furthest North African extant with the capture of Algiers in 1516. Preferring to avoid conflict with another Islamic power, the Turks maintained a relatively amicable relationship depending upon who sat on the Moroccan throne. Ottoman military expeditions met varied success during a long period of struggles between rival Moroccan ruling factions. Finally, by the end of the sixteenth century, the two remained independently separate with Morocco's Sunni population paying respectful religious obeisance to the Ottoman Caliph in Constantinople.

In 1905, amidst French efforts to gain greater control over Morocco; Kaiser Wilhelm II visited Tangier professing to lend his personal support to Sultan Abdel Aziz, and his nation's efforts to remain independent. Although wishing to appear as the benevolent friend of an Islamic potentate, the German Emperor's true motive was purely political. He wished to test the strength of the Anglo-French Entente and hopefully help split it asunder.

As a result of the Kaiser's visit, the Moroccan leader rejected French proposals and called for an international conference to mediate the situation.

France was outraged, and in the succeeding months the issue almost escalated into war with Germany. Finally, in January 1906, the parties agreed to an international conference to be held in Algeciras, Spain. For the next five months, delegates from twelve nations in addition to Morocco arbitrated that kingdom's independence. Hoping initially to drive a diplomatic wedge between Great Britain and France, the Kaiser soon discovered his great lack of support within the international community. Only Austria-Hungary joined with Germany in supporting the Kaiser's proposed settlement, the other ten powers, including Great Britain, Russia, Italy, Spain, and even the United States, solidly backed France. Morocco remained technically independent but in reality was well entrenched within the French sphere of influence.

Five years later, a second Moroccan crisis again threatened to escalate into a European war. Under the pretext of protecting French citizens during domestic rioting against the Sultan, the Paris government dispatched troops to the Moroccan capital. Sensing that this was merely a French ploy to gain complete control of the sultanate, the German government objected and quickly ordered the gunboat *Panther* to the port of Agadir. Ostensibly sent to safe-guard German business interests, the *Panthersprung*, or "Panther's Spring" as the crisis was dubbed, soon spiraled into another international war-scare.

Again raising the ire of Great Britain, who objected to the operation of any German warship so close to Gibraltar; the Kaiser looked for some way to extricate himself, and still save face. It was only after Germany received a small territorial concession in the French Congo that they agreed to France having a free hand in the North African kingdom. That effectively ended Moroccan independence.

So much for the Kaiser's lasting Muslim friendship!

HAMIDIAN REASSURANCE

In any event, the fickle "Muslim Kaiser" had earlier been afforded the opportunity to once again show his predilection for siding against the Christians in another dispute with Islamic Turkey.

In April 1897, the Kingdom of Greece and the Ottoman Empire went to war after a protracted dispute over the Greek annexation of Crete and additional pressures in Macedonia, turned into open hostilities.

As had now become so previously typical, the Great Powers, ever distrustful of one another, failed to act in a cohesive manner. Germany characteristically supported the Turks in order to gain greater favor with the Sultan while also frustrating England. Meanwhile, the British demurred once again and failed to intervene.

The Ottoman military, newly armed by the Kaiser and trained under the direction of German General von der Goltz, was now becoming increasingly confident. William Langer wrote, "Of the victory of the Turks there could be no serious question."[70]

Before a short time elapsed, Greek forces led by Crown Prince Constantine were soundly defeated by the Turkish commander Edhem Pasha in parallel campaigns in Thessaly and Epirus. The eminent military historians R. Ernest Dupuy and Trevor Dupuy observed, however, that "the ineptness of both sides was remarkable."[71]

Within a month of the commencement of armed hostilities, an armistice was arranged through the mediation of the recently crowned Russian Tsar Nicholas II, and a peace treaty signed the following September.

It was the only military victory of Abdul Hamid's thirty-year reign. Under the terms of the agreement, Turkey would receive some small territorial concessions and a sizeable financial indemnity from the Greeks. The situation on Crete was less beneficial to the Turks, however.

Despite his victory, the sultan was pressured by the Great Powers to accept a joint peace-keeping administration of the island which would still technically remain under the suzerainty of the Ottoman Empire. A joint naval demonstration that included warships from all six Great Powers had arrived off of Crete to ensure order.

As a result, France, Italy, Russia, and Great Britain each respectively took effective jurisdiction of a fourth of the island under the terms of the treaty. Only Germany, and Austria-Hungary withdrew from the venture; a gesture that was not lost on the appreciative sultan. With the fruits of victory all but nullified, Abdul Hamid was further insulted when the four occupying Great Powers appointed Prince George of Greece as the island's Governor.[72] Its nose proverbially under the tent, the Greek government in Athens patiently waited out the occupation which finally ended in 1908.

Taking advantage of the Young Turk revolt against Abdul Hamid that was simultaneously occurring in Constantinople; the Greeks declared union with Crete in October, 1908. The full annexation was later recognized by the Great Powers after the resolution of the Balkan Wars of 1912-1913. Once again, the Ottoman Sultan had lost territory from his continuously eroding empire.

Nonetheless, Abdul Hamid came away from the episode with two firm conclusions.

Even though the Great Powers had finally intervened with a naval show of force, the sultan was never truly endangered. Things could have gone much worse as a result of European anger over the plight of the Christian minorities. This rebuff was small recompense, and after all, Crete still technically remained under Ottoman rule.

While vexing, the situation in Crete was not crucial to the sultan's own domestic survival, and indicated that as far as further European meddling was concerned, the worst was over. It also convinced him that for the most part the Great Powers were truly to be counted on for bluff, more than action.

Secondly, Abdul Hamid became further convinced of the legitimacy and value of his close relationship with the German Kaiser. Once again, Wilhelm found a way to ingratiate himself with the Sublime

Porte at the expense of his rivals. Sadly, his actions inadvertently harmed the Christian minorities that the Treaty of Berlin had pledged to protect.

Secure in the knowledge that the Great Powers were unlikely to intervene, and basking in his newfound friendship with Germany, Abdul Hamid increased the pressure on his domestic enemies, and the Christian minorities.

As Dadrian observes, "the pervasive fears of punitive measures that had gripped the Sultan and his perpetrators prior to the massacres not only evaporated quickly but gave way to a new level of Turkish perception in which the Armenians were defined as an utterly vulnerable nationality."[73]

In addition, the Sultan's own mistaken delusions about the West prevented him from recognizing the deep hostility by which he was commonly viewed. It was only Great Britain that vocally objected to the sultan's excesses, and the other Great Powers appeared to be blindly disinterested.

In fact, Viscount Bryce noted that the Sultan had long lost his concern over British demands because "they came from one power only."[74] Abdul Hamid did not even take the lone British objections seriously.

As early as 1876, the Sultan had actually convinced himself that the British truly viewed his actions against the minorities with passive indifference. Salisbury wrote to the Earl of Derby that Abdul Hamid appeared "to be fully convinced, in spite of my assurances to the contrary, that the alienation of a large portion of the English people was due rather to the repudiation of the Turkish debt than to the atrocities."[75]

With Britain's response to the Armenian depredations confined exclusively to scathing newspaper editorials, disparaging cartoon caricatures of the "Red Sultan," and patriotic songs regaled in the pubs; it was becoming apparent that the Turks had little to actually concern them.

The current reluctance of the British Government to intervene once again had confirmed to Abdul Hamid that his greatest personal threat was not external, but rather came from within.

5

THE RISE OF THE YOUNG TURKS

THE CELEBRATED HISTORIAN Carlton Hayes remarked that "The Sick Man of Europe," as Turkey had so often been called, was apparently tottering to his end. Despite the sultan's tight grip on his throne, the empire was coming apart. There was, however, a group of politicians within the Ottoman Empire who dared dream of rejuvenating Turkey. As Hayes eloquently observed, "Some of their number were actually advanced in years, but all were 'Young Turks' in their exuberance of patriotism."[1]

THE "COMMITTEE OF UNION AND PROGRESS"

The Young Turk movement of the last quarter of the nineteenth century primarily traced its origins to the literary Turkish intelligentsia that had resided in Paris and London in the 1860's. "Under the influence of western European institutions and customs, its leaders began to demand freedom from the despotism of the Turkish sultans and the adoption of constitutional government in the Ottoman Empire."[2]

Initially formed in 1889, from a student "patriotic society," the group eventually became known as the *Ittihad ve Terakki Cemiyeti* or "Committee of Union and Progress" (CUP). By 1895, the Young Turks, led by Ahmet Riza, and headquartered in Paris, had developed a manifesto in which they demanded "reforms, not especially for this or that province, but for the entire Empire, not in favor of a single nationality, but in favor of all Ottomans, be they Jews, Christians, or Moslems."[3]

Influenced by their French surroundings, the Young Turks were impressed by all things western. They soon came to believe that the future of Turkey depended on the "borrowing" of western methods and institutions. Ironically, this would in turn allow them to "repulse the encroachments of the West."[4] Subsequently, the study of European practices, "most of which dealt with military science,"[5] was viewed as paramount for future Turkish success. In essence, "the purpose of westernization became the attainment of superiority over the West through the adoption of western technology."[6]

Even though the impetus for the Ittihad movement was the necessary attainment of the military and technical prowess of the Great Powers, many in the CUP leadership also sincerely embraced the egalitarian spirit that they had observed during exile in Paris, Geneva, and London. Greatly influenced by the humanist teaching of the French philosopher August Comte, a number of Young Turks eagerly embraced the notion of altruism, and sought to replace the strong Islamic influence in the Ottoman Empire with a secular "Religion of Humanity" or *Positivism*. It is even thought that the very name Committee of Union and Progress was derived from Comte's famous motto, "Order and Progress."[7]

It is important to note that in its original formation the Committee of Union and Progress was intent on guaranteeing the equal rights of all citizens of the Ottoman Empire. Aside from the egalitarian "rights of man," another long-standing western philosophical institution greatly impressed the leadership of the Ittihad.

To the Young Turks, the vehicle to achieving westernization was obvious. "Like many of their former subjects in the Balkans, these Young Turks cast about them and came to the conclusion that the most significant thing about the states of modern Europe was parliamentary government."[8]

Greatly impressed with the British form of governance, the Young Turks sought to achieve a similar balance of democratic principles with royalist tradition. To them, "the logical solution to their own problems was limited constitutional monarchy," and they concluded that by merely erecting the framework, the mechanics would take care of everything else.[9]

To achieve their goals the Young Turks believed that they needed to concentrate their attention on removing the single greatest barrier to constitutional government. For them, the remedy for all of their problems was simplicity itself: "remove the sultan (but not the dynasty) and restore the short-lived Constitution of Midhat Pasha."[10]

Therefore, the focus of their loathing, and the unifying force within their diverse movement, was Abdul Hamid II.

"LOOSE LIPS SINK [REVOLUTIONS]"

After years of internal debate and power struggles, the Young Turks in the capital planned to stage a coup d'etat and depose the sultan.

The Istanbul branch of the CUP had evolved from an organization comprised of medical doctors, academicians, and college students into a group led by military officers, Islamic legal scholars, and high-ranking government officials. Tired of the seeming inactivity of the Paris branch, and rejecting Ahmet Riza's call for peaceful reforms, the new leadership was prepared for violent action. "In a short time this branch obtained support from many officers, and the War Office became a CUP center."[11] In fact, the military commander of Istanbul, Marshal Kazim Pasha would lead the revolt.

One of the conspirators, Doctor Mekkeli Sabri wrote about the lengths to which the CUP leadership were willing to go. In his diary he described the unanimous decision to assassinate Abdul Hamid if the Sultan attempted to resist and ordered the members of his personal guard to open fire. He also explained that the heir to the throne, Abdul Hamid's brother Reshad Effendi had been notified and even offered a room at the War office.

Sultan Abdul Hamid II, in Dr. Sabri's own words "was going to be dethroned and the constitution was going to be reproclaimed."[12]

In August 1896, under the leadership of Haji Ahmet Efendi, the Young Turk society finally felt strong enough to achieve its goal. With the support of many high-ranking government and military leaders the coup seemed sure to succeed. Ironically, on the very eve of the planned revolt, one of the conspirators, in a fit of drunken bravado, accidentally revealed the whole plot to an agent of Abdul Hamid.

One of Turkey's leading mathematicians, Mehmet Nadir Bey, had in Ramseur's words, "apparently exceeded his capacity for alcohol," and divulged the full details of the coup to Ismail Pasha, who immediately informed the Sultan. That same night, many of the participants in the ill-fated enterprise were rounded up and subsequently exiled.[13] The conspiracy had been wide-ranging as is clearly evident by the more than 350 people who were arrested, including the military commander of Constantinople, the Police Commissioner, and the head of the Gendarmes.[14]

Even at the moment of victory, Abdul Hamid still restrained from having the main perpetrators executed. It was not out of any inability to do so, nor from any merciful feelings of leniency. Rather the Sultan reckoned that the public execution of so many high-ranking officials, particularly within the military, would only invite more trouble from their supporters. Instead, many were exiled to far-flung posts in the hopes that they would just disappear. The Highest ranking offender was the former military commander in the capital Marshal Kazim Pasha who was sent off in disgrace to become governor of Scutari in Albania. As one observer wryly mused, "it was a lenient punishment for a soldier known to have been seeking the overthrow of his sovereign."[15]

The Istanbul branch had collapsed and would never regain the power that it had attained prior to the failed coup. Elsewhere, the Committee of Union and Progress attempted to re-gather and re-group. As a result the society was shaken, but was far from broken. The leadership, most of who escaped the Sultan's exile, mustered in Paris and continued to plot. For the time being, however, the paranoid monarch had escaped with his throne still intact.

Meanwhile the CUP leadership patiently licked its wounds and waited to fight another day. The following year, however, matters again came to serious a head.

THREE CONVERGING FORCES

Those Young Turks that had remained in Turkey weathered continuous government crackdowns until their movement was inexplicably betrayed by the largest European exile faction: that headed by Murat Bey. After constant pressure and coercion from the Sultan, Murat agreed to return to Constantinople and forge a rapprochement with Abdul Hamid.

As a result of the truce, he was promised amnesty and safe passage home for the revolutionaries. In return Murat believed that the Sultan would be amenable to positive changes within the government. With Murat Bey's unexpected defection, the movement effectively collapsed and only the minute hard-line faction led by Murat's exiled rival, Ahmet Riza, remained committed to the cause.

Not surprisingly, Abdul Hamid reneged on his promises, but the damage to the movement was too late to reverse, or to remedy. As Ramsaur observes, "the main result of the truce of 1897 was to destroy almost entirely the organization of the society within the Empire and to set back the Young Turk cause for a number of years. Not until 1906 did the society commence to rebuild, or rather to build anew, inside Turkey."[16]

Despite the seeming demise of the Young Turk Society, however, a newly emerging political, cultural, and social movement would eventually breathe unexpected life into the revolution.

Throughout the nineteenth century, two schools of thought had dominated the thinking of both the intelligentsia, and the rulers of the Empire. Foremost was the notion of Pan-Ottomanism, whereby all subjects, regardless of religious affiliation, millet, or ethnic identity, were first to be identified as "Ottomans."

The legitimacy of this label was becoming more questioned, as the Christian minorities continually demanded more autonomy, and as they looked to the Great Powers to interfere on their behalf. Similarly, the Turkish plurality began to resent the way in which they were being portrayed by Europeans, and longed for affirmation of their own racial value. CUP leader, Ahmet Riza, and others were even complaining that "every nationality in the sprawling Ottoman domains had its protector save for the Turks."[17]

Similarly, Pan-Islamism had long been a rallying point within the Ottoman Empire. Strangely enough, both Abdul Hamid and his opponents both recognized the potential unifying power of *Jihad,* or religious "Holy War," in reviving the Empire to past glories. Even the Young Turks, a secular movement often comprised of atheists, and relatively open to Christians, and Jews, understood that retaining the monarchy, and consequently protecting the caliphate, were essential to preserving the Empire.[18]

Nonetheless, the reality of the Turkish need for westernization was having a militating effect on Islamization. Centuries of technological stagnation had hurled the Islamic East far behind the Christian West both militarily and economically. Used more as a vehicle to suppress nationalist risings within the Arab communities, and in continual opposition from the competing Muslim Shiites of the Persian Empire, the forces of Pan-Islam as a Turkish movement, were realistically on the wane. A third movement, however, was about to offer a dynamic alternative to both Ottomanism and Islamization.

ATTILA THE TURK?!

Thanks in large part to the writings of a young generation of patriotic ethnic zealots; a new and potentially explosive concept was gaining influence. Since Namik Kemal, electrified the Turks with his play *Vatan*, the idea of "Fatherland" was becoming more appealing.[19] The notion of Turkish nationalism as a response to increasingly difficult minority aspirations, and as a symbol of ethnic pride, was catching the imagination of Turanians both within the Empire, and those of similar racial stock living elsewhere.

At the same time that "racialism," espoused in the white Aryan supremacist writings of Count Arthur de Gobineau and others, was greatly influencing the rise of nationalism and imperialism in Western Europe;[20] the Turks were finding their own expression of ethnic pride and solidarity.

"Pan-Turkism," or "Pan-Turanism," was being embraced throughout Central Asia, and the efficacy of expansion north to the gates of Kazan, and east to the Indus, was now being discussed in the coffeehouses of Constantinople. The press was "vociferous in its calls for support for the Central Asian Turks and even some sort of union with them."[21] Two Ottoman intellectuals, Shemseddin Sami, and Necib Asim Yaziksiz, "the leading Turkists of the Hamidian period,"[22] were vocal in their belief in the kinship of all Turanian peoples.

Often used interchangeably, the terms Pan-Turkism and Pan-Turanism actually represent two different audiences which nonetheless, often overlap. The first embraces the unification of all Turkic speaking peoples and is limited exclusively to ethnic Turks. Pan-Turanism, on the other hand was racial, and embraced a much wider potential field including not only the Ottoman Turks, but also the "Turcomans of Central Asia and Persia, the Tatars of South Russia and Transcaucasia, the Magyars of Hungary, the Finns of Finland and the Baltic provinces, the aboriginal tribes of Siberia and even the distant Mongols, Manchus and Japanese people."[23]

In a surprising twist, writing in 1917, T. Lothrop Stoddard also added Bulgarians into the Pan-Turanian camp by dismissing them as ethnic
Slavs and suggesting that originally the migrating Bulgars more racially
aligned with the Turks. He felt that this helped to explain Bulgaria's
entry into the First World War fighting against the Slavic Russians and
Serbs; preferring instead to come in on the Turkish side.[24]

At the time of the 1897 Turkish-Greek War, an upsurge in patriotism prompted the publication of the works of Turanist, Leon Cahun,[25]
which glorified the Turkish past. It also inspired Mehmec Emin's celebrated *Poems in Turkish*.

One of which, "Going to the Battle" began with the words:

> *"I am a Turk; my faith and my race are mighty,*
> *My chest, my essence, is filled with fire.*
> *A man is the slave of his fatherland,*
> *A Turkish son will not stay at home, I shall go."*[26]

Another influential writer was Yusuf Akçura, a Russian-born,
Turkish-bred Tatar who was a strong voice for Turkish nationalism. His
chief work, *Three Types of Policy*, published in the Egyptian-based Turkish
revolutionary magazine *Türk*, called for an end to the Ottoman Empire
with its diverse multitude of ethnic and religious peoples, and permanently replacing it with a purely Turkish nation. He also dismissed Pan-
Islam in favor of a secular state fearing that the Muslim religion would
likely inhibit the national limitation to Turks only. Originally dismissed
as radical, Akçura's ideas later caught on with the Young Turks and ultimately helped to set the stage for Ataturk's secular Turkish Republic.[27]

The most influential philosopher and spiritual guru of the Pan-
Turk movement, and later a mentor to the Young Turks, was Ziya
Gokalp. Reviled by Peter Balakian as the author of Turkish "racial
nationalism," and branded as the Turkish "Himmler,"[28] Gokalp published numerous works through which he exerted an enormous influence on Pan-Turkish thought.

First as a student and later as a secondary school philosophy teacher, Gokalp joined the Ittihad in Salonika, then a hotbed of CUP activism. Writing in numerous nationalist and revolutionary periodicals, he soon became a major intellectual leader in the organization. In 1912, Gokalp went to the capital where he was named chair of the Sociology Department at the University of Istanbul. It was from there that he wrote extensively, and became the leading voice for Turkish nationalism.[29]

The late Turkish apologist Stanford Shaw positively eulogized Ziya Gokalp as the one whose "ideas created an intellectual movement that provided the inspiration needed for a change in popular mentality from empire to nation, from religious to secular, [and] from East to West."[30]

Gokalp firmly believed in a historical "Turkish past, not in the Ottoman past, a Golden Age that predated the coming of Islam. He gloried in the military exploits of such 'Turkish' conquerors as Attila, Ghengis Khan, and Tamerlane [and] contrasted their times with the weakness and decadence of the present."[31]

In his final opus, *The Principles of Turkism*, published years later at the birth of the modern Turkish State, Gokalp posited that "the regions of Khwarizm, Iran, Azerbaijan and Turkey are, in an ethnographic sense, the homelands of the same people." He went on to call "the totality of these four regions *Oghuzistan*," (after the descendents of Oghuz Khan) and that their common origins were a "scientifically established fact."[32]

With his ethnocentric worldview, Gokalp professed that "the long-range ideal of the Turkists is to unite in language, literature and culture the Oghuz, Tatars, Kirghizes, Uzbecks and Yakuts once they have joined together under the name Turan." He further stated that "the prospect of uniting one hundred million Turks in a single nation is a source of great rapture for Turks."[33]

Dreamily standing in the Pan-Turanian "utopia" (*Kizil Elma*, literally translated "Red Apple") "...the Turkish peasant imagines the ancient Turkish kingdoms pass before his eyes." Gokalp recounted those "Turkish kingdoms" as successively comprising the Huns, Avars, Sky-Turks, Oghuz, Kirghiz-Kazaks, and the empires of "Genghiz Khan and, finally Tamerlane."[34]

TURKEY FOR THE TURKS!

Not surprisingly, Gokalp's images of past Turkish military greatness, and his call for a future resurgence, were becoming popular in officer's barracks throughout the Empire. One particular army officer, Djemal Pasha, a man who would later rise to prominence (along with Enver Pasha and Talaat Pasha) as a member of the ruling government "Triumvirate," wrote in his published memoirs, "I am a Turk, and nothing can shake my belief that the Turkish Race is the foundation-stone of the Ottoman Empire."[35]

Djemal saw Pan-Turkism as the last defense against minority nationalism.[36] Many of his brother officers were beginning to arrive at the same position. Yusuf Akçura even concluded "that the Turks were the only *loyal* element...and constituted the chief bulwark and support of the State."[37] With the increasing military support for Pan-Turanianism, the position of the Armenians and other non-Turks became ever more tenuous. After all, the last recorded historic genocide was perpetrated by none other than Gokalp's Pan-Turanian standard-bearer: Tamerlane.

As Yusuf Akçura had described in his work *Three Types of Policy*, the choice for the Young Turks was threefold: Ottomanism and its identification with territory; Pan-Islam and its reliance on religion; or Pan-Turkism and the glorification of ethnicity and nationalism.[38] For Akçura, Gokalp, and their CUP adherents the decision was clear. Ottomanism and Pan-Islam were each "a grave error,"[39] and Pan-Turkism was the only patriotic option. As Gokalp succinctly wrote, "Turkism means to exalt the Turkish nation."[40]

Henry Morgenthau, the United States Ambassador to the Sublime Porte from 1913-1916, summed up the motive and the result of Gokalp's nationalism, "The time had come to make Turkey exclusively the country of the Turks."[41]

Ambassador Morgenthau would later personally witness what a disaster that policy was to be for the Armenians.

"STRANGE BEDFELLOWS"

Gokalp's influence notwithstanding, the Young Turks' attitude towards the Christian minorities and the Armenians in particular, was initially one of tolerance, both during the formative years before the revolution, and in the immediate days that followed. Although predominantly Muslim, with an additional number of atheists; the leadership accepted the constitutional religious guarantees, and generally welcomed Christians into the organization. That is not to say, however that the Young Turks were "pro-Armenian."

It appears that the early benevolent attitude exhibited by the Young Turks towards the Armenians emanated less from any altruistic philosophical concern, and more due to pragmatic political expediency. Perhaps operating under the adage that "the enemy of my enemy is my friend," the Young Turks openly embraced the Christian minorities that had been so savagely persecuted under the Hamidian system.

In particular, the Armenian population had been the recipient of excessive violence and depredations. As such, in their desire to mobilize all who opposed the Red Sultan, even the Armenians were initially welcomed. It was a Turkish practice of *Realpolitik* that would have even impressed Bismarck!

Ramsaur views the attitude of the Young Turks towards the Armenians and other subject minorities as "imperialistic."[42] As Ottomans, they felt that all subjects owed equal allegiance to the Empire, and had a place therein, but the rapid emergence of minority nationalism was becoming a disruptive force. As Islamic Turks, the ancient forces of Pan-Islam and the new Turkish nationalism both held strong appeal, and Ottomanism was acceptable only under those circumstances that were compatible with the other two.

Predominately secular and humanist, the CUP leadership had little personal allegiance to the caliphate. They understood, however, that the Turkish mainstream was devoutly Muslim. Rather than upset the populace and incite the mullahs, the best policy remained one of Pan-Islamic devotion, and outward respect to the Caliph. To the Young Turks, Islam was to remain "the cornerstone of the state."[43]

At the same time, as already stated, the notion of a nationalist "Turkish" identity was rapidly evolving from the fraying remnants of traditional Ottomanism. Both Islam and Turanism held little prospect for the future inclusion of the empire's Christian minorities.

For their part, the Armenians were also growing less concerned with Ottomanism, as they were more hopeful of the threat Great Power intervention as the true guarantor of their rights. Often seen as being little supportive of the Ottoman State, the Armenians were viewed with suspicion by many in the Ittihad party.

The rising tensions between the Young Turks and their Christian partners began to reveal themselves at the various CUP conferences that had been held in Paris during the years of exile, and finally became fully apparent during the 1902, "Congress of Ottoman Liberals."

ROYAL REVOLUTIONARIES

In the years following Murat's abandonment, and the near collapse of the Young Turk society, Ahmed Riza vigorously attempted to maintain a viable anti-Hamidian movement. His efforts were greatly enhanced "...by a completely unexpected event. In December 1899 Damat Mahmut Pasha, the Sultan's brother-in-law, fled the country with his two sons, the Princes Sabahaddin and Luftullah."[44] Upset over the Sultan's continued refusal to reinstate the Constitution of

1876, Damat Mahmut now intended to expose Abdul Hamid's perfidy to the world. Ahmet Riza, and the remaining members of CUP were delighted to have such highly placed members of the royal family join them in Paris, and the wave of publicity caused by their defections, was enormous.

Enraged at his brother-in-law's "treason," Abdul Hamid launched a publicity campaign of his own. At first, he demanded Damat Mahmut's immediate arrest and extradition by the French government, on the basis of trumped up criminal charges. When that was rebuffed, he changed tactics, and tried to lure the émigrés' return through promises of concessions and bribes, again to no avail. With the renewed foreign public attention that Damat Mahmut's arrival had provided, it now appeared that CUP was rebounding from the disaster of 1897.

Moving quickly into a leadership role, Damat Mahmut's charismatic son, Prince Sabahaddin, brought an idealistic focus to the movement. His aim was to forge an "Ottoman Confederation," consisting of the various nationalities within the Empire, and by granting each separate group greater individual autonomy help revive the notion of Ottomanism. Ahmet Riza, less personally inspiring, but demonstrably more zealous, was determined to promote "Turkish nationalism" and to him the plight of Christian minorities was of lesser importance.[45]

The opposing "visions" came to a head at the 1902 "Congress of Ottoman Liberals." Fearful of a dilution of Turkish authority within the movement, Ahmed Riza and his supporters were suspicious of the motives of the large number of non-Turkish minority delegates. Their concerns appeared justified when the Christian minorities inserted a provision in the CUP manifesto "calling upon the European powers to intervene on behalf of the oppressed peoples of the Ottoman Empire."[46]

Even more alarming was an Armenian demand that the Great Powers enforce Article LXI, of the Treaty of Berlin, with the aim of eventually granting them an independent national homeland.[47] To

Ahmet Riza, and the Turkish nationalists, this was heresy. As tempers became heightened, Ismail Kemal, a Turkish nationalist, heatedly responded to the Armenian delegates, "If you wish the creation of an [organic] law exclusively unto yourselves, I say, no! No! Always no will be your answer, and we will oppose you on every occasion from this point onward."[48]

At the end of the day, all that the diverse groups within CUP could agree to was their joint determination to depose Abdul Hamid II. Their internal disputes, however, actually ensured that the Sultan would not be overthrown at any time soon.

Following the congress, and with his father's natural death in January 1903, Prince Sabahaddin became the ranking "royal" exile, and for the next two years, he and Ahmet Riza continued to develop their two divergent "schools of thought."[49] The lack of an effective and coordinated policy relegated the European branch of CUP into a virtual non-player in the events that were to follow.

It would now be the responsibility of the Young Turks who had remained within the borders of the Empire, to take decisive action.

OFFICERS' CALL

After the failed coup of 1896, the effective resistance in Turkey seemingly disappeared. What began in its stead was an ancillary movement of disenfranchised military officers that eventually evolved into a revolutionary organization. "The causes of this disaffection in the Turkish officer corps are not to be found in nationalism alone."[50] Promotion, in the army "was rarely accorded on the basis of ability [and] pay was constantly in arrears,"[51] Indeed, for the enlisted men, regular pay did not exist at all, proper food was scarce, clothing inadequate, and living conditions were generally poor.

One of the obvious advantages, and inducements to persecuting minorities, such as the Armenian villagers, was the opportunity for spoils. In fact, the Kurds later reacted negatively to the reforms of the

Young Turk revolution when it was feared that they would lose "their right to despoil and oppress the Armenians at will."[52]

Armenians, Greeks, and Jews had for centuries taken on the traditional role of merchants and businessmen, with the Turks employed primarily in military occupations. The economic disparity that often resulted, bred further Turkish animosity towards the more affluent minorities, and further marked them for plunder. Ambassador Morgenthau commented that the "Turks present the most complete illustration in history of the brigand idea in politics...the mechanism of business and industry has always rested in the hands of the subject peoples."[53]

If the Turk was destined to fill a military role in society, the declining fortunes of the empire had now made that an impoverished profession. Officers were becoming more personally exposed to their European counterparts, especially the Germans sent to train their army. Invariably, the young Turkish junior officers became aware of their relatively low standard of living. "They could not help but feel shame when they contrasted their shabby uniforms and their menial status under Abdul Hamid with the resplendent dress and relatively pleasant life of the European officers."[54]

In this climate of jealousy and indignation, the future leaders of the revolution, including Enver Pasha, and Mustafa Kemal, were influenced, and recruited. Ramsaur makes the extraordinary point that "within a relatively short time it was difficult to find a Turkish officer in all European Turkey who was not pledged to overthrow the government he served."[55]

A Model To Emulate

Another totally unrelated event was to have a major impact on the evolving world view of the Young Turks, and further convince them of the need for westernization. It would also help to reinforce and affirm their Asiatic identity.

In 1905, the Empire of Japan soundly defeated Tsarist Russia in a short but brutal war. Victorious on both land and sea, the rapidly emerging Asian power had in a very short time successfully forged a modern European-style army, navy, and supporting industrial base. In less than fifty years, Japan had miraculously risen from an internally divided medieval backwater, into an industrial, commercial and military giant ready to take its rightful place at the table of Great Powers.

Little Japan had defeated the Russian Goliath, emerging from obscurity and isolation only decades earlier. As Denis and Peggy Warner wryly observed, "...half a century before the Japanese destroyers sprang from the night to attack the Russian fleet in Port Arthur, Japan lived in a feudal isolation, its shutters drawn, its face unseen. Russia, yet to be humbled by the Crimean War, was still the world's preeminent military power; Japan was not even a pygmy among giants."[56]

The Japanese demonstrated their new-found naval proficiency with the decisive destruction of the Russian Imperial Fleet at the Tsushima Straits. That crushing victory shocked the western world, and no naval force had exhibited such efficient tactics and surgically destructive proficiency in exactly a century. The Battle of Tsushima was simply "the greatest naval battle of annihilation," since Nelson's triumph at Trafalgar.[57]

No Asian nation had successfully crossed swords with the West since the days of the Mongol and Turkish invasions. Until the smashing Japanese victories at Tsushima, Mukden, and Port Arthur; European military dominance had not been seriously challenged since the seventeenth century. One may argue that the defeat of the Turks at the gates of Vienna in 1683, was the high water mark of the Ottoman Empire, and began its steadily rapid decline along with that of all non-European arms for more than the next two centuries.

That is not to say that western-style white armies had not recently been defeated by peoples of color. Barely three decades earlier indigenous native forces had smashed a large British formation at Isandlwana,

South Africa (1879), and three years earlier, Native American warriors destroyed the 7th U. S. Cavalry at the Little Bighorn in Montana.

In each event, however, the commands of both Lord Chelmsford, and George Armstrong Custer were annihilated due to a combination of their own rash decisions; vastly large enemy numerical superiority; and while in the process of dangerously splitting their own smaller forces as they penetrated deep into hostile territory. In the case of both debacles, the careless white invaders were brutally counterpunched by determined Zulus or Sioux bravely defending their family domiciles. On this occasion things were different, however.

In the Russo-Japanese War, the opposing forces were fairly matched; both sides fighting far from their homes; and each drawing from the same well, the most modern weaponry, and military tactics.

This time the playing field was leveled, and the white chess pieces were being evenly challenged by the dark. Finally, at Tsushima the Japanese declared "check-mate," and this small island empire had rightfully claimed a place of equality alongside the Great Powers.

Non-European observers took both proud satisfaction and hopeful inspiration from the Japanese victory. The lesson that a westernized Asian nation could defeat the white Europeans was not lost on the Young Turks. It also appealed to their sense of pride, previously degraded by decades of European condescension.

The racial superiority felt almost universally by whites, and stuffed down the throats of people of color the world over, was now being vividly challenged for the first time. The Ottoman intellectual and Young Turk ideologist, Dr. Abdullah Cevdet took particular satisfaction in confronting a famous French anthropologist. "When Abdullah Cevdet met Gustave Le Bon in 1905; he questioned him about where the European thinkers had erred when they placed the Japanese at the bottom of the racial Schema."[58]

Another Turkish observer gleefully wrote, "Some Europeans and some Ottomans, who imitate whatever they see without understanding, regard us a race in the lower part of the racial hierarchy. Let's say it in plain Turkish: They view Turks as second-class human beings. Japanese people, being from the same stock of the yellow race, are obliterating this slander against nature with the progress in their country, and with their cannons and rifles in Manchuria."[59]

Perhaps no one summed up the importance of the game-changing Japanese victory more eloquently than the incomparable father and son military historians, R. Ernest and Trevor N. Dupuy. "Psychologically and politically, Japan's victory in the war marked a turning point in world history. Asia woke to the fact that the European was not always invincible; 'white supremacy,' as such became a shibboleth."[60]

Perhaps a strong dose of the Japanese elixir could help revitalize the "Sick Man of Europe."

FRATERNAL FOUNDATIONS

Encouraged by events transpiring outside the empire, and impatient with the steady decline within; widespread forces were coalescing to seriously challenge the sultan. By 1906, new cells of opposition to the Hamidian regime were springing up in military installations throughout the Empire.[61]

The center of the movement was in Salonika, the headquarters of the Turkish Third Army. "Abdul Hamid's control was weaker there than in the capital, his censorship less effective; in addition contact with European ideas was easy, a Freemasonic lodge existed, and Jewish citizens of Salonika could help with finance and communications."[62]

The affinity that revolutionary groups and secret societies often had with Freemasonry is evidenced by their frequent adoption of Masonic rituals[63] and their oft-stated embrace of "ideals such as brotherhood, equality, tolerance, and reason."[64] Such was the case in Turkey as well.

Masonic historians point to the beginning of Ottoman Freemasonry in Istanbul, circa 1721. The Turkish Grand Lodge was first established in Macedonia in 1856, but was later outlawed by the Sultan in 1876.

Freemasonry proliferated throughout the Ottoman Empire during the Crimean War due in large part to the presence of so many British, French, and Piedmontese military personnel. It was probably through their auspices that the Turkish officer class first became acquainted with the Lodge. The Young Turks were also greatly influenced during their Paris exile by other para-Masonic revolutionary societies such as the Italian "Carbonari" of Mazzini and Garibaldi.

By the early twentieth century, the Turkish officer class was heavily involved with the lodge, despite the fact that freemasonry had been outlawed by the Sultan. In Salonika, the hotbed of Masonic membership, Turkish officers often met in the lodges of Spanish, Italian, and French chapters where they were legally beyond the reach of the Sultan's police.

One of the leaders of CUP in Salonika was Talaat Bey, himself a freemason.[65] He would later become the revolutionary government's principal administrator, and an eventual member of the ruling triumvirate.

Along with various army officers in the outlying military districts, the members of the secret societies were poised and ready for action, with only the smallest spark necessary to ignite the dry tinder of full-scale revolt.

Through it all, Turkey, dubbed disparagingly "The Sick Man of Europe," continued to steadily decline. The external pressures exerted by the Great Powers, along with the ever-increasing internal rumblings of those minorities still tied (or "chained") to the empire; hastened the rise of a strongly nationalistic and forward thinking movement. Determined to end the despotic and inept rule of the Sultan, forces within Turkey were mobilizing with the mutual aims of reversing Turkey's decline and propelling her into the modern world.

The "Young Turks" were mustering at the Red Sultan's door.

6

UTOPIAN "SUNRISE?"

THE LONG AWAITED demise of the Red Sultan actually came as a virtual accident and was a complete surprise to foreign observers and diplomats. Despite the fact that military discontent was widespread, and that in 1906 and 1907 some army units had even mutinied to secure over-due pay,[1] the actual Revolution of 1908 happened almost randomly. "It is impossible to ascertain if a definite date had been set for the projected revolution, but it is possible to say that the uprising was not scheduled to commence when it did."[2]

"LIKE A THIEF IN THE..."

In late June 1908, a series of government investigations into alleged military plotting in Salonika "caused a wave of spontaneous and perhaps unrelated revolts" among various Third Army units.[3] At that moment, Enver Bey, "a member of the Committee of Union and Progress but not at the time any more important than the average young officer who had become affiliated with the society," decided to flee into the Macedonian hills rather than face certain Hamidian recriminations. His disappearance produced some excitement in the Turkish press, and a German news dispatch ironically claimed that he was a "victim of the Young Turks." [4]

Events then developed rapidly, with other officers leaving their posts, and the random formation of scattered mutinous bands. Seemingly oblivious to the impending threat, the Porte publicly expressed the opinion that they were dealing with, "...single cases of insubordination, [that] have probably since been remedied."[5]

In addition, the Great Powers were virtually impervious to the potential gravity of the situation. Oddly enough, despite the listless response of the Sultan, and freedom from foreign interference, an all-out order to revolt still was not forthcoming as the various Young Turk cadres in Macedonia were not organized under a single central authority. Neither the Sultan's court at Yildiz; the European governments; the foreign press; or quite possibly the Young Turks themselves, had the slightest idea of what was about to come.

The "Final Act" began on July 7, with the public assassination of Shemsi Pasha, the General sent by Abdul Hamid to investigate and suppress the mutinies.[6] Virtually overnight, "one unit of the Third Army Corps after another came out into the open and declared for the constitution."[7] Other troops, dispatched to Macedonia to stop the revolt, also mutinied.[8] The assassination of a second Hamidian general barely a week later, and in the same location, had in the words of *The New York Times*, "created a great sensation."[9]

Suddenly beset and anxiously fearing for his life, the "justifiably" paranoid Abdul Hamid, was now forced to back down. Battered but not yet completely beaten, the crafty Sultan declared the Constitution of 1876, to be in effect, and claimed that he had "zealously been preserving" it until such time as seemed appropriate.[10] He had betrayed his true sentiments however, by issuing his first public proclamation of the reinstatement of the Constitution as an apparent afterthought.

On July 24, the first page of the morning *Sabah* contained a lengthy list of the Sultan's Army promotions (clearly a feeble last effort aimed at bribing his discontented officers). As *The London Times* acidly noted, "near the end of the fourth column appears the announcement of the grant of a Constitution—eleven lines to the most important decision of the Sultan's reign."[11]

THE SULTAN'S SURPRISE

Not at all convinced of his sincerity, the Young Turks desired to depose Abdul Hamid once and for all. Amazingly the Sultan's public embrace of the Constitution had "been fairly successful in making it appear that the idea was his own."[12] In Constantinople, the local populace was far less influenced by the provincial cadres of the Young Turks and mistakenly believed that Abdul Hamid was acting on his own volition.

One member of the foreign press observed that "the Constantinople populace seems to have been totally unprepared for the revolution which the provinces had prepared, and certain notable differences stand out in the manner of its reception. It would appear that in the capital the Constitution was seriously treated by the crowd as a sudden and purely spontaneous act of grace by the Sultan and that much enthusiasm was displayed for the person of the monarch."[13] In another dispatch it was reported that a deliriously enthusiastic crowd of fifty thousand marched on the Yildiz palace "to thank the Sultan in person."[14]

Responding to the huge show of support, Abdul Hamid, who for three decades had routinely hid himself from his subjects, now publicly exhorted his grateful listeners with a speech that is astonishing for its unabashed hypocrisy. The Sultan's words as reported by *The London Times* included the following: "Since my accession I have worked for the security and prosperity of the country. My desire will ever be the happiness and security of my people, whom I regard as my children. God is my witness."[15] Remarkably, Abdul Hamid had once again saved his throne.

One can readily imagine the chagrin of the Young Turk leadership at the misplaced appreciation being lavished on the "Bloody Sultan." Even in the provinces the citizens began to equate the Sultan with the benevolent policies of the Young Turk movement. A report from Athens indicated that "the Greek, Armenian, and Jewish newspapers are unanimous in their expressions of gratification at the re-establishment of the Constitution and their sentiments of loyalty to the Sultan."[16]

More importantly, despite their miserable state under his command, the ranks of common soldiers also retained a blind allegiance to their Sultan and Caliph. Mostly illiterate and accustomed to subservience from birth, the common soldiers were still fanatically loyal as ardent Muslims, and they now obediently rallied to the Sultan's defense. Although the Turkish officer corps was decidedly with the Young Turks, for the present the army could not be fully relied upon to overthrow Abdul Hamid without risking the mutiny of many within the common ranks.

As Ramsaur indicates, "The reason for the retention of Abdul Hamid on the throne is to be found in the simple fact that the Committee of Union and Progress did not feel strong enough to force the issue in 1908."[17] Nonetheless, the Young Turks had achieved the reinstatement of the constitution, and had effectively wrested full control of the government.

ROYAL REALITY CHECK

Despite his outward pretensions of confidence, the Sultan was finally convinced of the danger of his situation, and fully aware of who was actually in control. As a result, he was described as appearing "aged and depressed."[18] He was also said by another to look like a "living corpse."[19] One observer wryly commented that "the Committee holds the Palace in its grasp, for it has garrisoned the barracks which surround Yildiz, and the searchlights of the men-of-war moored at convenient points in the Bosporus, haunts even the Sultan's sleep."[20]

It was also made very clear that any attempt by the Sultan to interfere with the Young Turks administration or to renege on the Constitution would be immediately dealt with. In an open letter to the Viennese press, Enver Bey flatly stated that "the Sultan has accepted all our demands, and already begun to fulfill them. For the moment we cannot doubt that his intentions are serious, and have already given the signal to suspend operations... [but] we shall be in a position to renew the struggle at any moment and [are] even more determined to strike as hard as we have ever done."[21]

Incredibly, despite their overwhelming military power, the Young Turks had taken effective government control almost by accident, and virtually without any bloodshed. Caught by complete surprise, foreign observers were simply astonished at the outcome. One admiring commentator was moved to confess that "authorities on the Eastern Question admit that they are now sitting as schoolboys, open-mouthed for the next wonder... There is a feeling that the Young Turks have at any rate established a title to the benevolent respect of Europe."[22]

Although they were initially caught totally unawares, once the revolution had commenced, the foreign press became rapidly aware of the totality of the change in power. Abdul Hamid's retention of his throne was clearly understood as a facade, and there were no delusions as to the end of his regime.

Within weeks, one British observer already wrote, "there is no need to recapitulate the intolerable conditions of life which existed until a few days ago for every class of the Sultan's subjects. The whole Hamidian system was rotten, and it needed but a touch from within to crumble into unhallowed dust."[23]

Without any shots being fired the long-awaited regime change in Constantinople had finally commenced. As Shaw observed, "The Age of Abdul Hamid II was over, though the Sultan was to remain on the throne for another year, and the era of the Young Turks was about to begin."[24]

"WE WILL ALWAYS HAVE PARIS..."

The CUP leadership in Paris had performed almost no function in the final revolt, and as such had ceased to be of major influence. Ahmet Riza, who had carried the CUP banner for so long, was invited to chair the newly reopened parliament, but his position was mostly ceremonial and henceforth, his impact was minimal.[25] The Paris faction had simply been absent when fortune suddenly appeared.

For his part, "Abdul Hamid played what for him was a very strange and most unwelcome role---that of constitutional monarch."[26] With the opening of Parliament, Abdul Hamid was inundated with congratulatory messages from various foreign legislative bodies. Telegrams of good wishes were received from the French Senate, the Russian Duma, the German Reichstag, and from King Edward, on behalf of the British Parliament.[27]

Despite his personal revulsion, Abdul Hamid continued his public charade of endorsing the Constitution. At the ceremonial first session of parliament the figurehead sultan gave a flowery and typically disingenuous address. With a straight face, Abdul Hamid paternally claimed that the "temporary" dissolution of the first assembly was due to his belief that his subjects were not yet prepared for such grave responsibility. He sanctimoniously suggested that "...popular education had not been brought to a sufficiently high level. The intellectual standard of the people having [now] reached the required height, His Majesty acquired the conviction that a parliament should once more assemble."[28]

Some accepted the sultan's self-serving explanation, but not all were fooled. Politely received by the parliamentary audience, *The Times* scornfully reported that "the deputies listened without even an augur's smile to the first part of the speech, surely the strangest defense an autocrat has ever offered for his suppression of the liberties of a nation."

The Sultan's absurd suggestion that he had only acted in the nation's best interest by temporarily suspending the national assembly until it was better prepared for a successful implementation, was not the most insincere of his patronizing pronouncements. Abdul Hamid's hypocritical performance at the parliamentary session concluded with a visual tour de force.

Hamidian biographer Joan Haslip poignantly writes, "When the deputy from Mecca intoned a prayer and the words of the Koran drifted across the silent room...[Abdul Hamid] suddenly came to life, rising from his throne and extending his hands in a simple, child-like gesture, with the palms turned upwards as if to gather the blessings falling from heaven. There was something so moving, so apparently spontaneous about this gesture, that even the most cynical were touched and Jews and Freemasons, Atheists and Christians, prayed with the Caliph of Islam."[29]

Even Abdul Hamid II could not continue his weak deception indefinitely, however.

BLACK LEGACY

In a final desperate move to preserve his throne, Abdul Hamid instigated a populist revolt against the Young Turks.

On April 13, 1909 conservative reactionaries within the army attempted a counter-coup known to history as the "31 March Incident" (both being the same date as calculated on the Islamic *Rumi* Calendar then in use within the Ottoman Empire). At issue was the apparent government slide toward liberal, European-style constitutional reform and secularization. Muslim fundamentalists abhorred what they viewed as the Young Turk's departure from traditional Pan-Islamism as evidenced by the overthrow of their Caliph.

Abdul Hamid had diligently courted the Islamic faithful even though privately, he was never considered to be a devout Muslim.[30] To some observers that had relatively close contact with him, it appeared that the caliph merely paid lip-service to his religious duties in order to curry favor with the devout. One can never truly know the heart-felt spiritual beliefs of another but suffice it to say, at the very least Abdul Hamid earnestly nurtured his public image as Islam's protector.

Sensing his opportunity, the Sultan fostered the plan to restore the caliphate, and even promised to impose *Sharia* law within the empire. Islamic clerics, students, and conservative elements within the army rallied to the Caliph's defense. At the head of Abdul Hamid's Islamic fundamentalist supporters was a newspaper editor from Cyprus.

Dervish Vahdeti was the publisher and editorial writer of the Constantinople news organ *Volkan*. A devout Muslim, he had fully memorized the *Koran* thereby qualifying as a *Hafiz*; "one who can accurately recall all passages from the sacred text."[31] Inciting Turkish soldiers who were already unhappy with their living conditions, Dervish Vahdeti encouraged them into an open rebellion. Some military officers and members of parliament were slain as infidels, and the countercoup briefly appeared to be successful.

In response to the upheaval, the Young Turk military commander of the Turkish Third Army marched rapidly from its headquarters in Salonica to retake the capital. Led by General Mahmud Shevket Pasha, the relief force was dubbed *Hareket Ordusu* ("The Army of Action"). Among its officer corps were both Enver Bey, the future member of the ruling Triumvirate, and the young Mustafa Kemal, eventual founder of the Turkish Republic known to the world as Ataturk.

In a lightning march from Salonica to Constantinople that took only six days to complete, the Young Turk forces rapidly converged on the Sultan's palace. With characteristic cunning, Abdul Hamid now claimed to have personally sent for the Macedonian Third Army Corps in an attempt to "restore order in the capital."[32]

With the arrival of Shevket Pasha and the Army of Action, the countercoup collapsed. For his part Dervish Vahdeti was hanged, and civil order was again restored in the capital, with or without the Sultan's prior approval.

Sultan Abdul Hamid II was finally deposed a few weeks later following the unsuccessful countercoup attempt, and his brother Murad V, was subsequently installed as a "puppet" sultan. The question that remained was what to do with Abdul Hamid II?

Some called for imprisonment and even the Sultan's execution, but eventually, to avoid an Islamic upheaval in defense of the Caliph, it was decided to send him into a forced but very comfortable exile.

One observer noted that, "No reigning monarch could have been treated with greater consideration than Abdul Hamid."[33] He was never prosecuted for any crimes. Rather the former caliph was sent into respectful house-arrest in Salonica. When that city later fell to the Greeks in the Balkan War of 1912, the ex-sultan was brought back to Constantinople where he resided in the luxury of the fabulous Beylerbeyi Palace overlooking the Bosporus.

In an action that would in many ways presage the future benevolent American, and Allied treatment of Japan's Emperor Hirohito at the conclusion of the Second World War; the Young Turks opted to preserve the Sultan's dignity and therefore avoid any possible further conservative religious back-lash.

The Japanese Emperor was worshiped and revered as god-like by his subjects and any forced removal would have certainly precipitated a violent and widespread civil uproar. Similarly, as the Islamic Caliph, Abdul Hamid also commanded the fanatic devotion of legions of the faithful.

Hirohito, who unlike Abdul Hamid had been permitted to remain on the throne, would enjoy his final years in the avid study of marine biology. Similarly, if somewhat less scholarly, the former caliph spent the remainder of his days pursuing his carpentry hobby, and reading Sherlock Holmes tales amidst the company of his thirteen wives.

Later watching the escalating war clouds with increasing concern, and perhaps feeling a trace of cynical pride at the growing failure of those who had deposed him; Abdul Hamid II died in his palace on February 10, 1918.

He had somehow beaten the odds. Having feared assassination for most of his adult life, and after himself being the personal cause of so much violence and suffering; the "Red Sultan" had passed peaceably in his sleep.

It was less than nine months before the final collapse of the Ottoman Empire.

COMPETING EPITAPHS

The once promising young man who three decades earlier had ascended the Ottoman throne to such universal approbation, had finally reached the end of his blood red reign.

What is perplexing is the current Pro-Turkish view of Sultan Abdul Hamid II.

Nearly a century after his death his alleged crimes are often times either ignored or completely glossed over.

In a recent book describing the ethnic cleansing of Muslims at the hands of Christians in the Balkans, Anatolia, and the Levant (during the century 1821-1922); one prominent Turkish apologist only mentions the name of Abdul Hamid II three times in a 340 page manuscript. Not once is he named in reference to the plight of the Armenians (except as their being a security threat to the empire) but rather they are brief allusions to the formation of the *Hamidiye* as a defense against revolutionaries, and in condemning the Sultan's alleged inadequate military preparedness prior the First Balkan War.[34]

While it is certain that during the same period many thousands of Muslim non-combatants, including innocent women and children were also murdered by Christians (as this particularly well-documented book effectively illustrates); the lack of even the slightest mention of Abdul Hamid's complicity is concerning.

After all, the Hamidian government depredations were virtually committed entirely against the Armenians who were the actual subjects of the Ottoman Sultanate.

At least one modern Islamic, American scholar actually reveres the Sultan's memory. Nearly a century after Abdul Hamid's death, a web-site is dedicated to the "Last Great Caliph." With no mention of the brutality of his reign, the commentator applauds Abdul Hamid's resistance to secularism, and his defense of Pan-Islam.

It is also noteworthy, that the observer also heartily approved of the sultan's rejection of Zionist Theodore Herzl's request to purchase land and settle in Palestine. In 1896, backed by a coalition of wealthy financiers, Herzl reportedly approached the Turkish ruler who declined a Zionist offer to defray the Ottoman Empire's national debt.

While these sentiments are understandable from a contemporary Muslim perspective, it hardly justifies Abdul Hamid's well-documented depredations against hundreds of thousands of his own Ottoman citizens. In a telling statement, the historian wrote, "With about 3/4th of his empire Muslim, Abdülhamid decided to emphasize Islam as the dominant uniting factor among his subjects."[35]

Clearly Islam was <u>not</u> the "uniting factor" for the remaining quarter of the Red Sultan's "subjects."

A British editorial in the December 16, 1908 edition of *The Times*, titled <u>The Passing of Hamidianism</u>, provided a more fitting epitaph to Abdul Hamid's despotic reign. It read, "The story is worth telling...for it is a dramatic page of history and marks the close of a sinister regime which weighed like a nightmare for more than thirty years, not only on the unfortunate people of Turkey, but on the prestige and conscience of civilized Europe."[36]

LOVE FEAST"

Sultan Abdul Hamid II's minority subjects, the Armenians in particular, were elated with the change of governmental power. "There were scenes of public reconciliation; Young Turk leaders such as Mehmed Talaat, Ismail Enver, and Ahmed Djemal visited churches, and prayers were said for the future of the new order of national harmony."[37] The Young Turks believed that they could satisfy the aspirations of the minorities and proclaimed that all would enjoy "equal rights within law."[38]

One British diarist in Constantinople approvingly recorded, "The Young Turks rely on the support of the Christians; they preach fraternity, and denounce massacre; their ideal is to bring about unity of all races and religions in a well-governed Ottoman Empire. Whether this noble ideal can be realised is not here the question; that the object of the Young Turks to try to realise it, is admitted by everyone.[39]"

With the restoration of constitutional rights, ethnic Turks and minority Ottomans alike celebrated with "a wave of mass demonstrations, without equal in the empire's long history."[40] Shaw notes that in Istanbul, and other major cities, "happy mobs of Turks, Arabs, Jews, Greeks, Serbs, Bulgars, Armenians, and Europeans embraced in the streets and made eternal vows of brotherhood for the common good."[41]

American Ambassador Morgenthau approvingly noted that, "a general love feast now followed the establishment of the new regime, and scenes of almost frenzied reconciliation, in which Turks and Armenians embraced each other publicly, apparently signalized the absolute union of the long antagonistic peoples."[42] Other observers were equally impressed.

The correspondent to *The London Times* enthusiastically enumerated, "...certain scenes lately witnessed here of close fraternity between Turks and Armenians. The presence of numerous Turkish officers at Armenian churches on Sunday last, Young Turks going in numbers to a cemetery where victims of the massacres lay buried and kissing their graves, the cadets of the military school requesting an Armenian priest to say prayers before them at another such cemetery, are as many instances in point. The new bond of common Ottoman nationality for which a generation ago Midhat had striven embraces Turk and Armenian, Greek and Bulgar, Albanian and Vlach, Moslem, Christian, and Jew—All the races and creeds of the Empire."[43]

As amazing as it seems from hindsight, Guenter Lewy suggested that, "The Armenians now became the most ardent defenders of the new regime."[44]

THE WINDS OF EGALITARIANISM

That the Young Turks originally intended to construct an administration that was open and inclusive is evident from many early indications. Numerous newspaper reports of the early days of the revolution suggest that the new government made great efforts to reconcile Moslems, Christians and Jews, and unite them into one unified Ottoman confederation. One such contemporary account noted that "the Young Turks are inviting Christian co-operation, reassuring the Christians as to the outcome of the movement."[45]

This change in attitude and application of justice was becoming apparent throughout the Empire. On a similar occasion it was reported that "an Albanian at Djakova who, unmindful of the changed routine of life, insulted his Serb shoemaker and shot another Albanian who reproved him in the name of 'equality and fraternity,' was himself shot by order of the people in the first flush of liberty...Since then the fraternization between Albanians and Serbs has been general." The observer went on to remind his readers that "to Europeans who know the country, and understand the Albanian contempt for the Serbs and the murderous feud which has existed in the past, this fraternization is almost incredible, but is none the less true."[46]

In another surprising development, it was reported that Turkish troops had been dispatched to protect Armenian villages from Kurdish raiders.[47] Amazingly, the same newspaper had reported only one month earlier that a similar unit of Turkish soldiers had been ordered to burn four Armenian villages and "to outrage women and children."[48]

In an action once thought unimaginable, a court-martial was convened to try and punish perpetrators of the massacres at Adana. "Eventually fifty Turks were condemned to death for murder and incitement to riot; twenty of these were actually executed--the first time that Muslims had been hanged for murdering Christians."[49]

In another entry it was asserted that the new leadership was "doing their best to win the good will...and maintain even justice between Moslems and Christians." The same article went on to recount how a Moslem who had killed a Christian was subsequently hanged "to the great astonishment of his fellow countrymen."[50]

The euphoria that was sweeping the Ottoman Empire at the overthrow of the Red Sultan was most surprisingly being felt in the leadership of the Armenian Revolutionary Federation. At their fifth congress (held in the fall of 1909) the Dashnaks affirmed their policy of cooperation with the Young Turks, and they decided to discontinue their underground activities."[51]

It seemed that conditions in Turkey were so dramatically changing from the decades of Hamidian oppression that it had now become vividly apparent to foreign observers. An editorial in *The London Times* suggested that "bewildered skepticism has now given way to general satisfaction at the present idyllic condition of affairs and to a solid, though not an assured, hope for the future."[52]

In a letter to the Editor of the same paper, one English diplomat then stationed in Constantinople went even further in praise of the new leadership, and in his exoneration of past Turkish depredations. He wrote, "The almost bloodless character of the recent revolution in Turkey has not failed to excite deserved admiration...But apart there from, the recent occurrences should go far to dispel the mischievous impressions which particularly in England has so long passed current regarding the bloodthirsty fanaticism of the Turk. The recollection of 12-year-old massacres still causes any expression of contrary opinion to seem a dangerous paradox."[53]

Even the Hamidian massacres at Adana, that immediately followed the Sultan's short-lived countercoup failed to curb the optimism felt by the Ottoman minorities. Nearly everyone blamed Abdul Hamid for the depredations and excused the Young Turks, even with an estimated death toll of close to twenty thousand, most of them Armenians.[54]

Quoted in a letter to the *Times*, Sir William Whittall, considered by many to be, "the leading figure of the British Colony of Constantinople," was convinced that the depredations against the Armenians were not the actions of the new Ottoman government.[55] Shortly before his death in 1910, the long-time president of the British Chamber of Commerce in Turkey insisted that, "the Armenian massacres were rather the work of Kurds and Lazes than of Turks." To which the letter-writer to the *Times* wistfully concluded, "suffice it to say that the regime which was guilty of such atrocities is over."[56]

SHORN LIKE SHEEP

As fashionable as it may have become to dismiss the Turks and blame the Kurds for the previous atrocities against the Armenians; the reality was that in fact, they were indeed the one group that remained vehemently opposed to the new reforms. The Kurds had been granted a free hand under Abdul Hamid II and had considered the Armenians to be open targets for exploitation. William Langer observed that the Kurds, who were Muslims, "looked down upon the Christians and felt perfectly justified in exploiting them."[57]

In 1900, traveler Sir Charles Eliot (writing under the pseudonym "Odysseus") wryly explained that the Kurds regarded the Armenians "as harmless, serviceable, comfortable infidels, whom one could not expect to meet in Heaven, but who were very useful here below."[58] Armenian apologists Tessa Hofman and Gerayer Kotcharian further suggest that "the Kurds were not happy about the Constitution. During Abdul Hamid's reign their most influential class, the landlords, tribal leaders, and sheiks, had enjoyed considerable economic and political advantages at the expense of the Armenians; these advantages could be lost by reforms that advocated equality."[59]

The Kurdish "Hamidiye," the Cossack-style cavalry that had been created and employed by the "Red Sultan", was reliant on plunder for their sustenance. Like the *Bashi-Bazouks*, the cadres of Muslim irregulars so savagely utilized for centuries by the Turks against Christians in the Balkans; the Hamidiye were unpaid troops who were permitted and encouraged to systematically raid Armenian villages for spoils.

Another European traveler to the scene of the atrocities at Adana painted a haunting picture that could easily be culled from today's contemporary news reports of the grisly horrors being daily inflicted by terrorists of ISIS.

In his diary, the Biblical archaeologist Sir William M. Ramsay recorded, "...the massacres began simultaneously in the villages, where the Armenians were unarmed, and made no resistance, and where certainly there was no quarrel to provoke the riot. The massacres there were largely the work of Kurds. In many cases they did not waste [gun] powder on the wretched villagers...but ordered them to lie down in rows on their faces, and went along the rows decapitating the miserable and unresisting people. It is said that not a single Christian house is left standing in or near Adana...The helpless acquiescence of the peaceful Armenian[s] ...in their fate seems to northern people almost incredible...In the streets many of the victims quietly held out their heads in a convenient position for the assailant to inflict the death-stroke. An old friend described the whole hideous business in a few words, 'they had their throats cut like sheep.'"[60]

To put it delicately, the Kurds were not easily persuaded by the altruistic notions of "equality, fraternity, and liberty," preferring the local ascendancy they had historically enjoyed.

BE CAREFUL WHAT YOU WISH FOR...

Despite the animosity of the Kurds, the general feeling of the different ethnic, national, and religious groups that comprised the Ottoman Empire was one of hope and euphoria.

The ubiquitous feeling of enthusiasm, and gladness for the Young Turk revolution was eloquently and astonishingly encapsulated by an anecdote published in *The London Times* of August 15, 1908. It read, "...only the other day a Turkish officer addressed a crowd of Greeks, when one of them cried out, 'Down with the Bulgarians.' The officer went on to say 'We must each of us dig a grave; dig it wide and deep, and in it bury all our resentments and all our hatreds, private and public, and place over it a marble slab bearing this inscription, *There shall be no resurrection.*'"[61]

Ironically even the Turkish government would later point to the "delirious joy which Turks and Armenians experienced in common at being at last delivered from the cruel omnipotence of Yildiz,"[62] as being evidence of the "injustice" of post-First World War claims of genocide. One Young Turk, writing in 1909, even described the Armenians as "the most useful, after the true Turks, [and] the most patriotic community of the Ottoman Empire."[63]

The enthusiasm of the Armenians, and other minorities, would soon turn to sour disillusionment, however. T. E. Lawrence (later known to the world as the celebrated "Lawrence of Arabia") observed that "the gullible subject races---far more numerous than the Turks themselves---believed that they were called upon to cooperate in building a new East."[64]

To many, the good intentions initially expressed by the Young Turks now appeared to be hollow words when finally converted into action. "Asked what the difference was between the old and the new regimes, a German arms salesman confided that nothing had changed, except the bribes required were larger."[65]

The blatantly Pan-Turanist policies continued by the CUP that had been disguised as "Ottomanisation," were having a dilatory effect on the Christian minorities. Such things as the government requiring "the teaching of Ottoman Turkish and the promotion of Ottoman culture in the schools and colleges," were mainly responsible for the decline of minority support.[66]

Of far greater concern, the renewed massacres at Adana perpetrated during Abdul Hamid's futile 1909 counter-coup, painfully demonstrated to the Armenians the inability of proclamations alone to dispel centuries of racial and religious hatreds.

As one contemporary British journalist had presciently suggested, during the euphoric early days of the revolution, "the feuds of centuries will not easily be reconciled, and the traditions of Moslem supremacy are too firmly rooted to be removed by a stroke of a pen."[67]

Sultan Abdul Hamid II

"DEEDS—NOT WORDS!"

John Bull: *"Look here,—we've had enough of your palaver! Are you going to let the girl go, or have we got to make you?"*

Great Britain, France, and Russia protest the Turkish treatment of the Armenians.

French Political Cartoon portraying Sultan Abdul Hamid
as a butcher for his treatment of the Armenians

Kurdish *Hamidiye* Cavalry

An Armenian woman and her children who had sought help from
missionaries, after fleeing the *Hamidiye* that had killed her husband

The paranoid Sultan Abdul Hamid II on a rare public
excursion beyond the safety of the *Yildiz Palace*

"The Three Pashas" The Young Turk Ruling Triumvirate
Enver Pasha
Talaat Pasha
Djemal Pasha

Kaiser Wilhelm II

THE NEW HAROUN AL RASCHID.
A DREAM OF BAGHDAD, MADE IN GERMANY.

British Political Cartoon of the "Muslim Kaiser" Wilhelm II, dressed as the 9th century Islamic Caliph, riding the Berlin-to-Baghdad Railway

The "Red Sultan," near the end of his life in forced but luxurious retirement

The Battlecruiser *SMS Goeben*

Sir Winston Churchill, 1912
His actions as Lord of the Admiralty helped to push the hesitant
Turkish Government into the welcoming arms of the German Kaiser

"His Master's Voice"
The Ottoman Empire rashly follows Germany into the First World War

The Turkish Trenches at Gallipoli
Lt. Col. Mustafa Kemal (Atatürk) leads a brilliant defense as
Commander of the Ottoman 19th Division...The Turkish victory
would later have terrible consequences for the Armenians

Kaiser Wilhelm II, Sultan Mehmet V, and Enver Pasha during
the German monarch's visit to the Sublime Porte in 1917

Death March, Kharpert, Western Armenia, Ottoman Empire, April, 1915

The Armenians were packed into the concentration camp bound
cattle-cars, *"after having been compelled to pay their railway fare."*
--- Eyewitness Dr. William Dodd

The *Yildiz* Palace in 1905

Ambassador Henry Morgenthau, Sr.

"[We] began to see bodies by the roadside...There were between five
and ten thousand all entirely naked, nearly all women and children."
---Eyewitness Dr. Tacy Atkinson

The Lucky Ones?!?
"A group of Armenian girls who escaped from the Turks and sought refuge
in Russia. Some of them are the only remaining members of their family."
Chicago Examiner (December 19, 1915)
One can only guess their ultimate fate---living later
under the severe repression of Lenin and Stalin!

Mustafa Kemal Atatürk, Founder of the Turkish Republic

Soghomon Tehlirian
Depending upon one's viewpoint, either the cold-blooded
assassin, or the justly avenging executioner of Talaat Pasha

The "Loyal Millet"

A prosperous Armenian family... The young girl and mother holding
her were both slain in the genocide. The boy nearly starved but survived
and eventually lived in Beirut. The father had earlier emigrated from
Turkey to America in the hopes of later sending for the rest of the family.
The Grandmother, (seated) knit her own burial cloth as she
marched through the desert with her daughter-in-law. She
was later wrapped in her shroud and left at the side of the
road as the survivors did not have time to bury anyone.
All were peaceful citizens of the Ottoman Empire
victimized by their own government.

"Der Voorghmia, Der Voorghmia" ("Lord have mercy, Lord have mercy")
An Armenian woman mourning over her dead child

7

THE TRIUMVIRATE OF TERROR

T HE YOUNG TURKS came to power with the apparent best of intentions. Welcomed by Muslims and Christians alike, the new regime initially promised greater acceptance of minorities and a commitment to western-style values. Echoing the notions of "liberty, equality and fraternity," the Young Turks (many of whom had been exiled in Paris) patterned much of their early philosophy after the French revolutionary example of the late eighteenth century. Unfortunately, for the ethnic minorities within the Ottoman borders, the euphoric dreams of autonomy, and equality once promised by the rise of the Young Turks, were soon to give way to bitter nightmares. Something had indeed changed that would eventually have the gravest of consequences for the Armenians.

"WOLVES AT THE DOOR"

It can be argued that whatever their actual commitment to reform might have been, the Young Turks had little chance of success almost from the beginning.[1] The European Powers, along with antagonistic nationalist groups in the Balkans, began almost immediately to take large bites out of the Ottoman Empire.

Seeing themselves as the "Japan of the Near East,"[2] the Turks were greatly disappointed in their inability to copy the Japanese success in forming European alliances, and receiving Great Power respect. Only the German Kaiser, determined to threaten both Britain and Russia with his "Berlin-to-Baghdad Railroad," offered any material or moral assistance to the Empire.

It was not just a general lack of Great Power respect that alarmed the Ottoman Government but a deepening mortal danger as well. In the years immediately preceding the First World War, a series of international crises intensified the deepening political division in Europe represented by the two opposing grand alliances. The Triple Entente of Great Britain, France, and Russia, was increasingly growing at odds with the Triple Alliance formed by Germany, Austria-Hungary, and their erstwhile lukewarm partner, the Kingdom of Italy. The Ottoman Empire was caught in the midst of the global competition between the Great Powers, and was quite often the victim of their separate imperialist designs for colonial expansion.

Like wolves sensing a wounded prey, the European powers began to quickly exploit the temporary power vacuum that had been caused by the regime change in Constantinople.[3] As a result the Young Turks became the victims of a continual European power grab and events deteriorated rapidly. In October 1908, Austria-Hungary formally annexed Bosnia-Herzegovina; Greece annexed Crete; and Bulgaria, with Russian backing, declared its full independence from Turkey. During the winter of 1909-1910, Albania also began a successful two-year revolt for independence. This was followed in 1911, by the Italian conquest of Tripolitania, and then subsequently the rest of Libya.

The following year, the nations of Bulgaria, Greece, Serbia, and Montenegro jointly declared war on Turkey, and in a series of short but devastating campaigns, drove the Turks out of virtually the entire European portion of their Empire. Only the small territory extending from Constantinople to Edirne, and immediately adjacent to the Straits, remained in Turkish hands. A second Balkan War in 1913, in which Greece and Serbia defeated the Bulgarians in a quarrel over spoils, resulted in the Turks ability to regain a small portion of their European territory, but it was small consolation.

Despite any initial plans to preserve it, during the five years immediately following the accession of the Young Turks the Ottoman Empire had eroded enormously. For them, the sum total of the years 1908-1913 had been a disaster. As Feroz Ahmad forcefully illustrates, "the significance of these losses is difficult to exaggerate. In terms of territory and population alone, the Turks lost about 424,000 square miles out of a total area of about 1,153,000 square miles, and approximately 5,000,000 souls from a population of about 24 million."[4]

Controlling the Balkans for centuries, the Turks were virtually expelled from the continent of Europe. "Put differently, by 1913 the Ottomans had forfeited 83 percent of their European territories."[5]

With the rapid attrition of both a third of its territory and a fifth of its population, the Ottoman Empire was no longer just a "sick man," but was actually lapsing into mortal danger.

FICKLE FRIENDSHIP

Only Germany remained steadfast in its support of Turkey. Unfortunately, with the fall of the government of Abdul Hamid II the Germans found themselves in a quandary. Having strongly supported the Red Sultan; the Kaiser had backed the wrong horse and the Reich was now forced to come to terms with the new revolutionary government. On principle alone, it was difficult for an absolutist emperor to embrace the republican overthrow of another authoritarian royal monarch.

Nonetheless, always unpredictable the Machiavellian Kaiser easily shifted gears and reached out to the new regime. In so doing, the "fickle" Reich was able to quickly turn the Sultan's picture to the wall and begin to build relations with the CUP leadership.

For their part, the new Turkish government had good reason to accept the Kaiser's overtures. Germany had the distinction of being the solitary European power that had not stripped any portion of sovereign territory from the Ottoman Empire, and this realization was not lost on the Young Turks. The desperate need for military alliances, economic investment, and international trade partners remained the paramount aims of the Turkish government regardless of who actually ruled in the Sublime Porte.

For Germany's part, they were initially skeptical about the rise of the Young Turks, and suspicious of their seeming predilection to French egalitarianism. The Kaiser was naturally more at ease with the autocratic sultan than with a western style parliamentary alternative. As events unfolded, this became a moot concern. Circumstances would soon sway the Young Turks toward the adoption of ever-expanding government centralization.

As pressures steadily mounted both without and within, the ruling Committee for Union and Progress, became increasingly nationalistic and dictatorial. To the delight of the Germans, "the limitations on democracy instituted by the CUP echoed the semi-authoritarian structures of imperial Germany."[6]

Turning away from the democratization of the west, the Young Turks, like their bloody Hamidian predecessor, began to believe that a firm iron-hand was required for the very survival of the empire. To the delight of the Kaiser, "...German forms of governance had a recognizable counterpart in the late Ottoman Empire."[7]

In 1909, the Kaiser demonstrated his callous determination to place politics above principle. After hearing of the Adana massacre, "in the mistaken belief that the lives of Germans were in danger, he had approved the dispatch of two cruisers. Upon learning, however, that there was no such danger for the Germans, he became irritated at the false report and exclaimed, '...why send then two cruisers. The Armenians [being killed] are of no concern for us.'"[8]

In turning his back on the Armenians, and the apparent German abandonment of Turkey's Christian minorities, Kaiser Wilhelm had exhibited a remarkable indifference from one who was the reigning monarch of a large Christian nation. Moreover, his publicly declared protection of Islam, however insincere, was now playing very well with the Young Turks.

After putting down the conservative counter-coup instigated by Abdul Hamid, the secular and often atheistic members of the CUP leadership were beginning to succumb to the idea of keeping the useful internal threat of Pan-Islamic *Jihad* alive. For that reason the caliphate was kept intact under the figurehead Sultan Mehmed V. As was so often effectively the case with his predecessor, the unifying call for religious repression was again being echoed in Eastern Anatolia.

By his tacit acquiescence of both the persecutions, and the Young Turk's swing to the right in support of Pan-Islam; the German monarch had actually "come around to support them only after they had jettisoned their ideals."[9] It seemed that the more autocratic and centralized the Turkish government became the better for German liking.

Once the self-professed "friend for all time" to the world's 300,000,000 Muslims, and the close personal crony of Abdul Hamid; the Kaiser had pivoted and the Turkish leaders that had deposed the Red Sultan, and repressed the capital's conservative Islamic elements were now suitably assured of future German support.

DIRECTION CHANGE

As a result of the Turkish defeats during the period 1908-1913, the Young Turk movement finally completed the philosophical shift from Ottomanism to Turkish nationalism. Some liberal Turkish visionaries had previously exhibited a preference for an "American-style" model, in which there would be one nation composed of many equal elements, but this now suddenly changed to the adoption of "British-style" nationalism, in which the subject minorities were to be subordinated and administered under imperial rule.[10]

In October 1911, the Ittihad party passed a resolution that dramatically evinced the change in direction. It read in part, "...in the Ottoman Empire the dominant race is the Turk, and it is our necessary duty and policy to organize an Islamic state of the Turkish race. The non-Moslem races are negligible, and shall be deprived their languages."[11]

Nevertheless, for the moment the Young Turks continued to take a pragmatic approach, and freely borrowed from each of the doctrines of Pan-Turanism, Pan-Ottomanism, and Pan-Islam, as the situation dictated. Akcam Taner suggests that, "the CUP never felt bound to a single ideology. The Unionists determined their approach according to practical needs, and easily jumped from one ideology to another when necessary."[12]

Even the ideological mentor of Turkism, Zia Gokalp instructed, "let the Turkism movement cease being the opposite of Ottomanism, in truth it is its most powerful support...There has never been a contradiction between Turkism and Islam because one possesses the character of nationalism, the other of international unity. Turkism is simultaneously Islamism."[13]

No matter how it was packaged, however, the Young Turk leadership was becoming increasingly pro-Turk, and less inclined to concern itself with the rights of the empire's ethnic and religious minorities. International events were to soon push the Young Turks even deeper into the Turanist camp.

Meanwhile, partly due to the Ittihad's authoritarian swing to the right, and its embrace of Pan-Turkism; things were coming to a crisis in Istanbul.

"The CUP failed to sustain its support within and outside Parliament due to the waning of its revolutionary appeal and its failure to take charge of the government despite its strength in Parliament. Following the failed counterrevolution of April 1909, the CUP took a more active role in government and sponsored centralizing policies, which revoked some of the liberties of the immediate post-1908 period and subjected the CUP to charges of attempting to 'Turkify' the empire's various groups."[14]

It was not only the Christian minorities who were becoming opposed to the new course the CUP was taking, but many Turkish liberals were alarmed as well. There was a call for a new voice in Turkish politics.

As a result, the Young Turks split apart.

THE FREEDOM AND ACCORD PARTY

In November, 1911, dismayed over the direction it was heading, a new political organization rose in the capital in direct opposition to the Committee of Union and Progress. Within a month of its formation the fledgling party stunned the leaders of the Ittihad.

"The Liberal opposition reorganized itself as the *Hürriyet ve Itilaf* ("Liberty and Entente" or the "Liberal Entente") and jolted the CUP by winning the contested seat in the November 1911 by-election in Istanbul 196 to 195."[15]

Also known as the "Freedom and Accord Party," the new political organization had portrayed the CUP as being opponents of both Ottomanism and Islamism, and being solely intent on the promotion of Pan-Turkic objectives.

As Hasan Kayali observes, "The CUP was particularly vulnerable to charges of Turkification. Its main cadres consisted of Turkish speakers, and that contributed to the perception of its centralizing policies as Turkification."

Ironically, the leaders of the Freedom and Accord Party were not much different in appearance than their adversaries. "The prominent leaders of the Entente were Turkish-speaking and no different from the Unionists as far as their basic attitudes toward Islam were concerned. Nevertheless, they sought to frustrate the CUP by encouraging non-Turkish groups to attack it for pursuing a policy of Turkification and by pointing out to the [religious] conservatives its alleged disregard for Islamic principles and values." Kayali further suggests that, "The overall effect of this propaganda was to instill ethnic and sectarian-religious discord."[16]

The CUP lost no time in attempting to curtail the efforts of its new opposition party. In the subsequent 1912 general elections, the Ittihad used such strong-armed tactics that the April polling had been dubbed the "Election of Clubs," in an infamous reference to the numerous reported beatings perpetrated by CUP upon opposition candidates. Amid the additional widespread charges of CUP initiated voter fraud, members in the military took matters in hand.

Angered at the terribly lopsided and obviously fraudulent final election returns, a group of military leaders calling themselves the "Savior Officers," pressured the allegedly corrupt Grand Vizier to resign, and forced the formation of a new government.

The new leadership was dubbed the "Great Cabinet," in recognition of its being comprised of three former Grand Viziers. Led by Ahmed Muhtar Pasha, the new administration, void of any CUP representation, lasted barely three months when the disastrous events in the First Balkan War brought down the government. The next succeeding cabinet head was the former military commander who had once led the unsuccessful coup against Sultan Abdul Hamid II; the anti-CUP former three-time Grand Vizier Kamil Pasha.

Almost immediately upon taking office, Kamil Pasha entered into peace negotiations with the Bulgarians resulting in the devastating loss of most of the remaining Ottoman territory in Europe. Altogether, the humiliating conquest of Libya by the Italians, coupled with "Turkish territorial losses in the Balkan wars and the declaration of independence by Albania ended the power of the remaining moderates and liberals in the government."[17]

Finally fearful that the Grand Vizier would also agree to the Bulgarian occupation of Edirne (Adrianople), which had once been the European capital of the empire from 1365-1453; a pro-CUP military faction decided that it was high time to intervene.

Turkey was in crisis and strong hands were required to keep what remained of the tottering empire from totally toppling into the abyss.

COUP D'ETAT OF THE TRIUMVIRATE

Desperate to end the further erosion of the empire, the Young Turks finally took direct and decisive action. On January 23, 1913, a coup led by the ultranationalists gave full dictatorial powers to a small group, "led by the triumvirate of Enver Pasha, as minister of War, Talaat Pasha, as minister of Interior, and Djemal Pasha, as the Military-Governor of Constantinople."[18]

Marching on the Sublime Porte, a group of armed conspirators, dramatically led by Enver mounted upon a white horse, stormed the offices of the Grand Vizier. Despite their expressed intention of taking control of the government without bloodshed, random gunshots resulted in a few deaths including the head of the government's Ministry of War, Nazim Pasha.

Enver was not blamed for the death even though there was some speculation that in the ensuing exchange of fire, either he or Talaat may have actually been the one to accidentally shoot the War Minister. *The New York Times* called Enver "one of the suspected assassins" even though it reported that he and Talaat were probably only trying to defend themselves when Nazim Pasha was killed.[19]Although it is believed that Enver had not planned to harm Nazim, it is ironic that he would soon succeed to the dead man's position as War Minister.

With no further attempt made to halt them, the conspirators proceeded to the cabinet chambers of the Grand Vizier. Upon entering Enver and Talaat confronted Kamil Pasha and forced him at gunpoint to write a letter of resignation. Wasting no further time, Enver immediately went to the palace of the figurehead Sultan and presented the signed document to Mehmet V. Meanwhile, Talaat took over the administration of the all-powerful Ministry of the Interior.

During the commotion in the Sublime Porte, another prominent CUP leader was immediately designated the Military Governor of Constantinople. Djemal Pasha described in his memoirs that, "the corpse of Nazim Pasha was still lying in the room," as he was officially being appointed by the new Grand Vizier.[20]

Deciding to forgo any recriminations against the former Grand Vizier Kamil Pasha, and his administration; the Young Turks preferred instead to keep them under heavy surveillance for the moment. It would not take long, however, for things to change once again.

The CUP's newly appointed Grand Vizier was Mahmud Shevket Pasha, an Ottoman general credited with being the father of the Turkish Air Force.[21] His administration was also to be short-lived when he was assassinated less than five months later in a revenge killing by a relative of the slain Nazim Pasha. The Young Turks now feared that an imminent coup attempt would be led by the long-time liberal opposition leader Prince Sabahaddin.

The CUP leadership would now use the murder of their Grand Vizier as a final pretext for cracking-down on any further opposition, and most of the remaining members of the Freedom and Accord Party fled out of the country. Prince Sabahaddin returned to Geneva where, just as had been his occupation in the days of the Red Sultan, he again took up the role of opposition leader in exile.

In an act of apparent magnanimity, Djemal was personally involved with affording safe passage for Kamil Pasha and his family to Egypt. The benevolent gesture may have also had something to do with the very close personal friendship that the former Grand Vizier still maintained with England's Lord Kitchener. It would not be wise to antagonize the British unnecessarily.

With the death of the Grand Vizier, three men emerged to jointly head the Young Turk government.

Thus began the Triumvirate that would lead Turkey until the end of the First World War

THE THREE PASHAS

The assassination of the Grand Vizier Mahmud Shevket Pasha placed into public prominence a trio of Young Turks who had been actually orchestrating the Ittihad Party's moves for some time, and were the true power in the capital. Enver, Talaat, and Djemal each had been given large roles to play on the day of the overthrow of the government of Kalim Pasha and the Freedom and Accord Party. As a result they individually became Minister of War, Minister of the Interior, and the Military Governor of Constantinople, respectively. It was now time for them to take full control of the Ottoman Empire.

To history, these three individuals who now formed the ruling Triumvirate would be called the "Three Pashas."

In the Ottoman Empire, one rose to prominence by first earning the designation of *Effendi*, then *Bey*, and finally that of *Pasha*. The first, *Effendi* was affixed at the end of an individual's given name and was similar in respect to the English "Sir." It was awarded in recognition of a gentleman of higher education, breeding, or rank. The title of *Bey* was reserved for lower-level military officers and administrative officials of the Ottoman Empire. They were higher in ranking than the first group, and likewise could aspire to attaining the third designation, *Pasha* which was roughly the equivalent of the British title of "Lord." The latter term was afforded only to the highest government dignitaries, generals, and admirals.

Enver had earned his right to the "Pasha" suffix after his successful re-conquest of the city of Edirne from the Bulgarians in the second Balkan War of 1913. Talaat never served in the military, and prior to the coup of 1913 was employed primarily in fairly low-level administrative roles in the Ottoman Postal Service. His strength was as a politician and he had a mercurial career in the Committee of Union and Progress where he ultimately rose to prominence. Finally, Djemal was recognized as the Governor of Baghdad in 1911 and later service in the Balkan Wars.

All three were heavily involved in the Ittihad party of Salonica, which became the catalyst for the overthrow of Sultan Abdul Hamid II, and later of coup against the administration of Kamil Pasha.

T. E. Lawrence later described the three as "the most ruthless, the most logical, and the most ambitious of the Young Turks."[22]

Very different in appearance and demeanor, Talaat was "large, tough, and earthy, whereas Enver was small, handsome, and reserved." Using a "silent movie" analogy of the time, Alan Moorehhead described Talaat as a "Wallace Beery," to Enver's "Rudolph Valentino."[23]

Djemal Pasha, the final "triumvir" and oldest of the three, was described by Lord Kinross as "black-bearded and short in stature but dynamic in energy...with dark, piercing eyes."[24] (In deference to the early film star analogy...perhaps a "John Barrymore"?)

Despite their physical differences, all three of the Young Turk leaders, Enver, Djemal and Talaat, appear to have exhibited certain personality quirks that might help to offer reasons for their later decisions regarding the Armenians.

SMALL MAN/HUGE AMBITION

The first of the three leaders, Enver Pasha, was the public face of the Triumvirate. That "face" helped betray his strong Pro-German sentiments. He conspicuously sported a waxed moustache in the exact style of the German Kaiser which unbeknownst to him had reportedly aroused no little amusement among the European diplomatic corps.[25]

Enver reportedly had an obsession with personal appearance. His concern with his physical image was extreme and may have actually affected his actions. Small in physical stature the Young Turk made up for it in vanity. As such he chose as his personal role-models two of history's greatest military leaders with whom he shared a distinct physical characteristic.

Barbara Tuchman, the Pulitzer Prize winning historian, personally traveled to Constantinople in 1915, to visit her grandfather the American Ambassador.[26] Later recalling the diminutive leader, she described Enver as the Young Turks' "little Napoleon."[27]

It was no secret that Enver "saw himself as a man of destiny in the Napoleonic tradition."[28] Franz Werfel observed that Enver Pasha had prominently hung behind his office desk, the portraits of two eminent military geniuses that he personally emulated. In addition to the aforementioned Napoleon I, the other monarch greatly esteemed by Enver, was also conspicuous by his short physical stature. The second portrait reverently exhibited behind Enver's chair was that of Prussia's Frederick the Great.[29]

Might Enver's choice of heroes possibly suggest an inner desire for validation as a commander, as well as wishful self-identification with those equally diminutive but truly great military geniuses? Ironically, it also may have led him to suffering similar delusions as those exhibited by his equally short Hamidian predecessor. Both Enver, and the Sultan Abdul Hamid stood considerably less than average height.

Interestingly, Enver's own possible fixation with physical stature had actually been preceded by that of the father of Frederick the Great. King Frederick William took great pride in his special military unit that was comprised of exceedingly tall men who had been recruited (or kidnapped) for his army, from all over Europe. The formation was dubbed the "Regiment of Giants."[30] So obsessed was the king with adding towering personnel for his regiment that he once reportedly remarked, "the most beautiful girl or woman in the world is a matter of indifference to me, but tall soldiers, they are my weakness."[31]

To instill much needed martial fervor in his uninterested son, the King gave over the command of his "Potsdam Giants" to the young prince at the age of fourteen. Nonetheless, by the time of his own reign, Frederick the Great disbanded the regiment as an unnecessary expense and placed the individual tall soldiers into other units.

For whatever reasons, whether height or personal hero worship, Enver Pasha exhibited great jealous pride and became noted for his "flamboyant vanity." He was good-looking, and as Lord Kinross described, "...cool and imperturbable."[32] Morgenthau described Enver as dashing and compared him in looks to an American "matinee idol."[33]

Having humble working-class origins he eventually married a royal princess (once again following in the Napoleonic tradition) "thus acquiring the noble title Damad."[34] In Constantinople, it was said that because of his royal pretensions, "Enver Pasha has killed Enver Bey."[35] It would also later become apparent that Enver would permit no challenge to his authority and that he would zealously maintain a strong need for autocratic control.

Of course the lack of physical stature has absolutely nothing to do with one's aptitude for personal bravery. For proof one need only recall the heroic exploits of Congressional Medal of Honor recipient Audie Murphy, America's most decorated combat veteran.

Similarly, just like his illustrious autocratic "heroes" Frederick and Napoleon; Enver had also shown conspicuous personal bravery in battle. One amazing story from Enver's service in the Balkan Wars testifies to his fearlessness and iron nerves in the wake of great danger. It was recounted that "during the war in Albania, an artillery regiment had mutinied, [and how] he, cigarette in mouth, had stood before the muzzle of a howitzer and challenged the mutineers to pull the firing-cord."[36]

That story of heroic crisis management is eerily familiar. Perhaps Enver had consciously emulated the actions of Napoleon I, who recently returned from Elba and marching on Paris, personally faced down a regiment of French soldiers sent to stop him. "Advancing alone he bared his breast to the leveled muskets. 'Soldiers of the 5th, [he challenged] you can shoot your Emperor if you dare!'"[37]Needless to say, despite the loudly repeated orders to "fire," not a single marksman fired upon the solitary monarch. Instead, Napoleon was wildly cheered by the hardened veterans who once again joined the service of their emperor and marched with him in triumph to Paris.

The two historic anecdotes have seemingly great similarity, and as a result of such courageous conduct Enver "inspired loyal admiration" among his fellow officers. As was also the case with the French emperor, however, Enver was equally noted at times for being reckless in his decisions, and "impulsive in action."[38]

Morgenthau similarly identified War Minister as audacious. He wrote that Enver was quick in making decisions, always ready to stake his future and his very life upon the success of a single adventure."[39] He was also described by the American Ambassador as being cold-blooded, remorseless, and lacking in pity. Those particular attributes would one-day have grave consequences for the Armenians.

Nonetheless, Enver's personal valor was never in question, and during his military career he was often in harm's way. One later episode was truly ironic when considering the subsequent events of 1915. It was reported that during the early days of the First World War, Enver was literally saved from imminent Russian capture by an Armenian army officer under his Ottoman command.[40]

BLAME AND PARANOIA?

Djemal Pasha was nine years the senior of Enver Pasha, and was also a career army officer. In actuality, his role in the triumvirate was somewhat lesser than that of the other two. He was to Enver and Talaat, as Crassus was to Caesar and Pompey, or as Lepidus to Octavian and Antony. Nonetheless, his memoirs written after the First World War betray a similar vanity and attitude of moral superiority.

Kinross described how as the army commander in Syria, Djemal "ruled as a dynastic prince."[41] His greatest passion was the cause of

Pan-Turkism and he was zealous in defense of the ideas formulated by Gokalp and the other Turanists.

He was often "ruthless to the point of cruelty in the discharge of his responsibilities and the pursuit of his interests...As military governor of Istanbul...he showed skill in the organization of the police force and in its relentless use for his party's ends."[42] Morgenthau recalled that Djemal was imperious and stubborn, often being a thorn in the sides of his other two partners in the ruling Triumvirate. He remembered that, "there was little about Djemal that was pleasing."[43]

A medical doctor who saw him stated that, "he had never seen a face that so combined ferocity with great power and penetration....His eyes were black and piercing... [and] signalized cunning, remorselessness, and selfishness to an extreme degree."[44]

Stanford Shaw, normally a sympathetic and ardent admirer of the Young Turks, described Djemal Pasha as, "ruthless and without pity when dealing with enemies."[45]

Djemal's memoirs are replete with severe denunciations of his "enemies" and are often defensive in tone. A typical example is illustrated by his casting of blame upon others for his failure to take the Suez Canal in the early years of World War I.

One target of his wrath was the Hashemite Emir of Mecca who had declared an Arab revolt against the Turks. In Djemal's words, "It was the treachery of Sherif Hussein which made that desirable object [the Suez Canal] unattainable for us."

In his further explanation of the failure of the campaign, Djemal also complains that he was given insufficient means for achieving military victory. In a self-serving defense against his Turkish critics he wrote, "...the resources at our disposal [were] inadequate to make the execution of this project possible."

Prior to his embarking on the Suez expedition, the now chastened commander had dramatically declared, "If our enterprise failed, and my corpse and those of the brave men going with me were left at the Canal, the friends of our country who would then have to take up our work must sweep over us and rescue Egypt, the rightful property of Islam, from the hands of the English usurpers." It was a speech worthy of Barrymore but now returned to haunt the beaten general.

In a truly unusual passage, Djemal next defended the fact that he returned alive from the failed Suez campaign rather than remain with the Turkish dead, fallen on the battlefield as many of his enemies now questioned. He writes that his critics were complaining, "How could Djemal Pasha have the audacity to come back from Egypt? Wasn't it his business to drive out the English or die?"

Making a defensive (and similarly dramatic) response he then asks rhetorically, "But what do all these critics really want?...It is no fault of mine that I am still alive...Who knows whether I have not been called on to remain alive to suffer still more sorrow and slander in the conflicts into which I am still prepared to enter for the good of my country!"[46]

Djemal Pasha also made good use of an excuse that would later serve Nazi war criminals in the aftermath of yet another world war. In all that happened, as a good soldier "he was just following orders." The equal partner of the ruling Triumvirate took pains to create the impression that his disastrous Suez campaign was actually the plan of Enver Pasha who Djemal then claimed had appointed him as commander of the Fourth Turkish Army.[47]

Due to his almost constant service in the field, and virtual absence from Constantinople during the First World War, Djemal's personal impact on the events of 1915 is less apparent than that of his colleagues. It is a fact that he takes pains to present in his post-war defense of his own involvement in the genocide.[48]

THE "DANTON OF THE TURKISH REVOLUTION"

The final member of the ruling triumvirate, while outwardly the most affable and gregarious, was quite possibly "the ablest of the three."[49] He was also the most ruthless and calculating.

Talaat Bey had been forced to abandon a planned military career when, upon the death of his father, he left "his early army education in order to make a career in the postal bureaucracy."[50] Upon joining the Committee of Union and Progress, Talaat used his official government position as "Director of Posts and Telegraphs"[51] to help secretly circulate Ittihadist propaganda in Salonica and throughout Macedonia.[52] His initial role in the 1908 military revolt was probably limited due to his civilian status, but he rapidly rose to prominence after the Young Turks seized power. Eventually he would become Minister of the Interior and later rise to Grand Vizier.

Kinross noted that Talaat "was a patriot to the point of chauvinism, wedded to his country's interests."[53] A member of the Freemason lodge *Macedonia Risorta*,[54] Talaat would have been influenced by the liberal tenets of fraternity and equality that were also the early expressed ideals of the Committee of Union and Progress. Rising to the position of Minister of the Interior, he "had come, through his apparent moderation, to be known as 'the Danton of the Turkish Revolution'."[55]

Henry Morgenthau, the United States Ambassador in Constantinople, was originally quite taken with the Young Turk leader. Of all the leading Turkish politicians he had met, Morgenthau considered Talaat Pasha to be, "the only one who really had extraordinary native ability. He had great force and dominance, the ability to think quickly and accurately, and an almost superhuman insight into men's motives. His great geniality and his lively sense of humor also made him a splendid manager of men."[56]

Talaat's outward appearance convinced his observers that he possessed a jovial and welcoming personality. Franz Werfel in his semi-historical work, The Forty Days of Musa Dagh, (based in part on the personal reminiscences of Dr. Johannes Lepsius) descriptively stated that "Talaat's mighty head was grey at the temples. Above the pursy lips of the Oriental there hovered a small, pitch-black moustache. Fat double chins thrust out of a stick-up double collar... [while] a white picque waistcoat, like the symbol of candid open-heartedness, curved over a jutting expanse of belly."[57]

Best-selling historian Barbara Tuchman observed Talaat on a visit to her grandfather, Ambassador Morgenthau. She later described him as "a stout Levantine adventurer who could devour a pound of caviar at a sitting, washed down by two glasses of brandy and two bottles of champagne."[58]

His physical demeanor identified Talaat as, "a man of virility and gusto, powerful in frame, humorous in talk, warm and genial in manner, with a rough, frank simplicity which masked a swift supple mind and a ruthless outlook."[59] His later discussions with Dr. Lepsius, Ambassador Morgenthau, and others would betray a dark side of avarice and Machiavellian cunning. His policies and actions would also reveal a sinister contempt for human life.

It was in Talaat's hands, along with those of Enver and Djemal that the fate of nearly two million Armenians would eventually lay.

An Unacceptable Barrier

Through it all, the Armenians continued to be the single Christian minority-group within the empire that remained reasonably peaceful. Although the Armenian Revolutionary Federation was still fomenting unrest, in its hope of attaining an independent national homeland,[60] the lack of direct support from the geographically distant Great Powers, and the "relatively thriving state"[61] of the scattered population, maintained a tentative status quo. The Armenians immediately fell under the suspicion of the new Turkish leadership, however.

The formerly tolerant policy of the Young Turks towards the Christian minorities was about to change. Regarding the Armenians in particular, it would evolve to one of pathological genocide. It is truly ironic, and on the surface seemingly inexplicable, that those sworn antagonists of Sultan Abdul Hamid II eventually came to emulate his paranoia, autocracy, and rabid persecution of the Armenians.

Actually, it was a combination of motives that ultimately drove the new Turkish government to the holocaust of 1915, and without excusing their actions one might at least find an explanation as to why they so violently departed from their original course.

8

DESCENT INTO DEPRAVITY

Located as they were, at the crossroads between three opposing empires; the Armenians now found themselves living directly in the path of Pan-Turkish ambitions to the east. The geographic disbursement of the Armenian people between Russia, Persia, and the Ottoman Empire, ensured that despite any peaceful intentions they would be embroiled in the coming conflict.

WRONG PLACE, WRONG TIME!

The approach of war intensified the Pan-Turanist ambitions of the Young Turks. "The retreat of the Empire from Europe to Anatolia was nothing less than a military and political disaster for the Turks, but it was a disaster that had even more serious consequences for the Armenians...[now becoming viewed as] a deadly threat to which a deadly response seemed appropriate."[1]

Recently driven from their European and North African possessions, the Pan-Turkism of the new leadership convinced them to look eastward and forge a natural unification with the Turanian peoples of Central Asia.

Alois von Paikert, considered by some as the originator of Pan-Turanism, claimed "that no fewer than 600 million people across vast areas of Asia and Europe were Turkic in origin."[2] G. S. Graber further asserts that, "by the time Turkey was involved in the First World War, its leaders were intent on cementing the Turkish hold on what they considered the irreducible minimum of Turkish territory. This was Anatolia... [and it] was needed to justify Turkey's continued hegemony there."[3]

From the security of that base, Enver wished to pursue his dream that all "people of Turkic origin might be united.[4] He ultimately looked to move against Persia in the East, and Russia to the north. Once again, the Armenians, with populations living along the borderlands of all three empires, were in dire straits. By virtue of their physical barrier to the lands of the East, they were perceived by the Turks as an unallowable obstacle and targeted for removal.

Sadly, those Armenians that lived on the other side of the Persian border fared no better than their kinfolk in Turkey. Traditionally exploited by their Muslim rulers, the Christian situation in Persia was often worse than even that in Eastern Anatolia.

In 1876, during extensive travels in the Persian Empire, Britain's Viscount Bryce complained that, "modern Persia, from all that one can hear, is more execrably misgoverned than even Turkey itself. The duty of the governor of a province or town is simply to squeeze as much as he can out of the [Christian] inhabitants; his methods are the bastinado, impalement, crucifixion, burying up to the neck in the ground, and similar tortures."[5]

It is little wonder that most Armenians, whether residing in Turkey or Persia, welcomed the thought of liberation by the Russians.

CHESS MOVES AND POWER POLITICS

Just prior to the commencement of the First World War in August 1914, the Turkish government found itself bereft of allies, and still recovering from the devastating territorial losses of the previous half-decade. The new leaders of the Turkish government now scrambled to strengthen ties with the European Powers.

Enver Pasha was decidedly pro-German. The Reich was the only European Power that had never enriched itself territorially at Ottoman expense. Early in his career Enver had been posted as a military attaché in Berlin, and soon learned to speak fluent German. While there he developed a strong admiration for the Kaiser's imperial army, and navy. He even emulated the distinctive mustache of the Kaiser, and grew to greatly admire the autocratic ruler, whom he grew to know personally. In describing Enver, the United States Ambassador to Turkey, Henry Morgenthau recalled that, "The man who returned to Constantinople was almost more German than Turkish."[6] Not surprisingly, Enver was quite favorably disposed to the German efforts to rebuild and modernize the Turkish military, and urged forging an alliance between the two empires.

His two partners in the Triumvirate that ruled Turkey were not so enthusiastic, about increasing reliance on the German Kaiser, however.

Both Djemal Pasha and Talaat Pasha looked backwards at Turkey's long historical friendship with England and France, and although recently strained, it was still the hoped-for basis of future cooperation. Nonetheless, the two Entente Powers declined the serious overtures made by Djemal and Talaat to forge stronger ties. The two leaders were greatly dismayed by the obvious rebuff to their offer of mutual military assistance, and after Djemal returned from a visit to Paris, became convinced that the third Entente member had influenced the result.[7]

Turkey's age-old enemy Tsarist Russia still harbored strong aspirations to occupy the Straits, and it was now believed that England and France were acquiescent to their partner's aims. Great Britain strongly urged the Ottoman Empire to declare strict neutrality, thereby permitting Russian naval access to the Mediterranean without the need to force the Dardanelles.

A belligerent Turkey would undoubtedly attempt to close the Straits, and the Allies understood that such action might "dry up the westward flow of Russia's grain and [equally] obstruct the eastward flow of arms to her."

It was also feared by the British high command that a Turkish threat to the Suez Canal might inhibit "the fast passage of Indian troops to France." Lord Kitchener, the British Secretary of State for War, "insisted that Turkey must be kept neutral, or, if this was impossible, her entry into the war should be delayed at all costs."[8] The War Office reasoned that Turkey must be at least held in check until the full European deployment of the Indian Army was achieved. For the Allies, it was essential that the Ottoman Empire remain neutral for as long as possible.

The Germans had other notions, however.

"GOLDEN [HORN] OPPORTUNITY!"

Ever seeking an opportunity to undermine their likely future enemies, the German government was early to appreciate the value of a strengthened Turkish ally in a potential contest with Russia and/or Great Britain.

During the years leading up to the First World War the Germans began to give strong consideration to the potential benefits of an alliance with the Ottoman Empire. In the event of a conflict with Russia, the Turks might be expected to open a southern front against their age-old hereditary enemies.

The Ottomans dreamed of expanding their Pan-Turkish crusade into the Caucasus and forever unite with the Turkic peoples of Central Asia. Long subjugated by their hated Russian masters, it was believed that given the chance, those descendants of Tamerlane would again rise up and ride against the West.

This valuable Turkish help, along with the expected thrust of the Austro-Hungarian army into the Carpathians, might just tie-up enough of the Tsar's initial manpower to provide the Kaiser's limited forces allocated on the Eastern Front the precious time needed for Germany to defeat France in the West.

An alliance with Turkey held other possible benefits for Germany in a future war against Tsarist Russia. The continued Ottoman control of the Bosporus and the Dardanelles also ensured the virtual isolation of the Russian Black Sea ports and guaranteed the inability for the Tsar's forces to receive material supplies from the their allies in the west. The unfulfilled age-old Russian dream to acquire the Straits and occupy the Golden Horn, so long obstructed by British foreign policy, would soon rise to haunt them both. Indeed, the extreme difficulty with which the Allies were later able to support Russia during the First World War, eventually helped hasten the Tsarist collapse.

The Ottoman Empire was also viewed as a valuable potential ally in a prospective war with Great Britain. Sitting astride the Suez Canal, and positioned at the crossroads between Europe, Asia, and Africa; the Turks could pose a serious strategic threat to the British colonial empire.

Even the gem of India would be a potential target, with the real possibility of Germany and Turkey attempting to incite a native Islamic revolt against the British crown. After all, the Turkish Sultan was the Caliph to the sub-continent's many millions of Muslims. At the very least, with Turkish assistance India could be hampered from sending men and resources to fight elsewhere for England.

From very early on, the Germans appreciated the potential strategic value of a strong Turkish friendship.

TIMING! TIMING! TIMING!

German military doctrine, as it began to evolve in the last decades of the nineteenth century, was focused on a quick and decisive war against France, with the possible addition of Great Britain. With the defeat of France in the 1870 Franco-Prussian War; the German occupation of Alsace-Lorraine left great bitterness in Paris. It was only a matter of time before war would return to the two European neighbors. Striving to isolate France both diplomatically, and militarily,

Bismarck had sought Great Power alliances with Russia, England and others. The only result was the 1882 "Triple Alliance" defensive pact that Germany signed with Italy and Austria-Hungary.

Ever fearful of a dreaded "two-front war," the Germans watched with alarm as Russia and France formed a military alliance in 1894. This was further complicated ten years later by a formal British and French agreement, the *Entente Cordiale*. The English had shifted from a position of relative neutrality as the result of the threat of Germany's growing naval power. Finally, the Russians, already allied with France, came to an understanding with the British, and entered into the "Triple Entente" in 1907.

As a counter to the war on two-front scenario, the German Imperial General Staff, under the leadership of Field Marshall Alfred Von Schlieffen, designed a strategic plan intended to decisively defeat the Entente powers in detail. Believing that the Russians would need considerable time to fully mobilize their enormous, but relatively cumbersome military forces, the German High Command needed a swift victory in the west. This was to be achieved by a willful violation of the neutrality of Belgium, Luxemburg, and in the original plan, Holland as well.[9] Invading France by way of the less defended Low Countries, the massive German right-wing would be able to flank the French and British Armies and smash them in a colossal envelopment.

Consequently, the overwhelming percentage of German manpower and materiel was committed to the invasion of France. With most of that immense force assigned to the hammer on the right, the much smaller German left wing was intended to hold back the expected French thrust into Alsace-Lorraine until they were hopelessly encircled and destroyed. Meanwhile, a relatively miniscule force would attempt to hold the Tsar's slow-moving invasion of East Prussia in check until the bulk of the victorious German army could be transferred to the east.

Absolute perfect timing was required to ensure German victory. To make the complete success of this plan possible, and to allow the swift passage of armies from one front to the other, the Kaiser constructed an extensive railway system. Having the benefit of interior lines, the Germans believed that because of their highly efficient mobility, they could effectively wage a two-front war. German engineering and Europe's most sophisticated rail system would allow the German High Command to successively defeat the French first, and then the Russians.

THE BEST LAID PLANS...

Turkish war aims in 1914 were fairly simple. They simply didn't exist.

Unlike the elaborate and complex mobilization and operational plans of the European Powers, the Ottoman Empire was bereft of an offensive military policy due to the disastrous losses incurred in both of the Balkan Wars of the previous two years. The Turkish Army was exhausted and many formations had been decimated. As a result, the Ottoman Empire was little concerned about fighting the next war as it merely tried to recover from the last one.

Military historian, Lt. Col. Edward J. Erickson observed that, "Turkey had no elaborate mobilization plans designed to deliver large forces to a decisive point, nor did it have territorial or irredentist ambitions. In fact, beyond the simple act of the preservation of the state and the preservation of territorial integrity, the Turks seemed to have had no clearly defined war aims."[10]

That is not to suggest that obvious military goals shouldn't have existed. Certainly, in a perfect world the Turkish High Command longed to regain as much of their recently lost territory as possible. Since the majority of Ottoman losses had been at the hands of the members of the Entente, it was clear where their natural enemies lie. The Allies had collectively despoiled the Ottoman Empire and the potential wish-list of re-captured territories was large indeed.

Looking ideally (if unrealistically) to regain Egypt, and Cyprus from British control; Libya from the Italians; and Batumi, and the Crimea from Russia; the most optimistic Turkish planners could even dream of eventual western expansion into French Tunisia, Algeria, and Morocco, and ever-eastward into the vast reaches of Central Asia. The myriad of old Turkish enemies in the Balkans were less directly accessible to Ottoman arms without the unlikely cooperation of Bulgaria, a kingdom being heavily wooed by both sides.

Although Bulgaria did later join the Central Powers, joint military action with Turkey never did effectively materialize. It was also clear that in the event of victory, the aspirations of Austria-Hungary would bar any future Turkish concessions in Serbia, and Albania. As an inducement to forge an alliance, Germany did guarantee the return of Aegean Islands held by Greece in the event that nation entered the war and was defeated.[11]

At least one Turkish leader still dared to dream of Turkish military victory. Enver Pasha, the Minister of War and part of the three-man ruling junta, had become entranced with visions of martial glory. His near-fanatic support for Pan-Turkism, and a personal belief in the potential power of Muslim *Jihad*, had convinced him of the importance to urgently get Turkey into the war. His worldview was faced toward the eastward, however.

As a Pan-Turanist, Enver was less concerned about regaining the non-Turkish territory that had been previously lost in the Balkans. He loathed the return of Christian minorities into the empire, and planned instead to link-up with the Turkic peoples of Central Asia.

Unable to militarily regain their lost territories or expand into new ones on their own, Enver planned to align with the one nation that had not made gains at Turkey's expense. Believing that Germany would win the coming war and ultimately defeat Turkey's mortal Russian enemy; the only thing necessary was for the Ottoman Empire to procure a place at the victory table.

The ultimate goal for Enver Pasha was the Turkic crusade into Persia, Azerbaijan and throughout Central Asia to the gates of India. The dream of creating a Pan-Turkish super-state would obsess him for the rest of his life...and ultimately be the cause of his death.

The Turkish Minister of War, without the consensus of the other members of the Ottoman government, possessed an optimistic set of war aims. The reality was for any of that to possibly happen however, the Germans would have to prevail.

Ardently pro-German, Enver Pasha had developed a close relationship with the German Ambassador, Baron Hans von Wangenheim, but was less favorably influenced by his highly competent military advisor, General Liman von Sanders.[12] Despite the belief that von Sanders and his staff had a "firm grip on the Turkish Army,"[13] for reasons of his own Enver often kept him in the dark or disregarded his sound advice on important matters. As events would later prove, that was to be a costly mistake.

Just prior to the start of the war Limon von Sanders was reassigned to take command of the Turkish Fifth Army where he would later brilliantly lead the spirited defense of the Dardanelles at Gallipoli. Although the post was of great importance, it effectively took the German General out of the high-level decision-making then being done in the capital.[14]

The actual head of the German military mission to the figure-head Turkish Sultan Mehmed V, was the aged Baron Colmar von der Goltz who had earlier helped to modernize the Ottoman Army from 1877-1895. Back again in Constantinople after so many years, the Baron was thoroughly disliked by both Sanders, and Enver who nonetheless would eventually grant him field command of Ottoman forces in Mesopotamia.

Now, with war in Europe looming, the ubiquitous presence of German military advisors, foreign office diplomats, and business entrepreneurs was felt everywhere in the Sublime Porte. Above it all the Turkish War Minister awaited events with the hope of exploiting the coming conflict in his own favor and that of the Porte.

Enver Pasha had set his entire hopes, and that of the future of the Ottoman Empire, on a complete German victory. All he needed to do now was convince the rest of the Turkish leadership, including a skeptical Talaat Pasha to get on board.

The Entente Allies meanwhile sought earnestly to ensure Turkish neutrality in order to keep open access to the Straits. In a remarkably shortsighted move however, the British Admiralty completely nullified any Allied chance of securing Turkish cooperation and inadvertently provided the final impetus for Turkey's entrance into the war.

Due to a catastrophic British miscalculation, the sudden arrival of yet another German would provide Enver Pasha with just the argument that he needed.

FRIENDS IN NEED

In a remarkable case of diplomatic blunder, John Bull inadvertently solved Enver's problem. Professing to guarantee Ottoman sovereignty, the British foolishly persuaded the Turks of their own duplicity, and actually drove them into the welcoming arms of the Kaiser.

Upon the direct orders of the Lord of the Admiralty, the Royal Navy "requisitioned," (in Sir Winston Churchill's own words) two newly completed warships that had just been built in England for the Ottoman government who was anxiously awaiting their delivery.

Claiming the necessity of war, the British Admiralty felt justified in reneging on their Turkish contract as a result of the opening hostilities in Europe.[15] Fearful to entrust a pair of modern Dreadnoughts to the uncertain future use of the Imperial Turkish Navy; the ships were quickly added to the British Fleet.

In Constantinople the government reaction was predictably hostile. Turkish public opinion was outraged and support for the Entente eroded precipitously. One pro-German newspaper reportedly invoked "a thousand curses" on perfidious Albion.[16]

In a strange twist of fate, the Turkish Navy found seemingly "miraculous" redress when on August 10, two modern German warships, trapped by the British in the Mediterranean and bottled-up by Gibraltar, sailed down the Bosporus and sought safe harbor at the

Sublime Porte. Acting under the orders of Grand Admiral Alfred von Tirpitz, head of the German Navy; the commander of the small naval squadron had successfully eluded the British Fleet since the formal start of hostilities a week earlier.

Declared to be gifts from Kaiser Wilhelm (who actually had not approved of their transfer) the two German ships, the powerful battle cruiser *SMS Goeben* and the light cruiser *SMS Breslau*, duly hoisted the Turkish Ensign and now mysteriously arrived to replace the two vessels that had previously been purloined by the English. Ecstatic Turkish crowds cheered the newly re-named *Yavuz Sultan Selim*, and *Midilli*, and wildly welcomed German Admiral Souchon whose sailors were now gloriously arrayed in fezzes and Turkish naval uniforms.

As Barbara Tuchman observed, "the sudden appearance of the two German warships, as if sent by a genie to take the place of the two of which they had been robbed, put the populace in transports of delight and invested the Germans with a halo of popularity."[17]

The *Yavuz* would later be personally inspected by the Kaiser on his 1917 visit to the Golden Horn to the approbation of the Turkish people, even though the two warships' original change of ownership had actually been done without his prior knowledge or approval. The former German Battle Cruiser remained the flagship of the Turkish Navy until it was finally decommissioned in 1950.

The Young Turk Triumvirate was especially pleased with the amazing turn of events. Djemal later recounted that upon the arrival of the *Goeben*, a joyful Enver Pasha cryptically quoted Judeo-Christian scriptures with the Messianic words of salvation, "Unto us a son is born" (Isaiah 9:6 & Luke 2:11).[18]

The apparent "treachery" of the British, followed by the perceived "charity" of the Kaiser, played directly into the hands of the Pro-German Enver. Long an advocate of siding with Berlin, the War Minister persuaded the Sultan to "rubber-stamp" his appointment of German Admiral Souchon to command the entire Turkish Fleet.

Talaat and Djemal, cognizant of the shift in public sentiment, and frightfully aware that the two powerful warships were still manned by *German* sailors, came around to Enver's position. The presence of the "former" *Goeben* in the Golden Horn was a stark, visual reminder of the changed circumstances. "As Talaat Bey pointed out, the government, the palace, the capital, they themselves, their homes, their sovereign and Caliph, were under her guns."[19]

Queried on his support for a Turkish-German alliance, Djemal was more pragmatic. Reminded of their present paucity of foreign friends, he told Talaat, "I should not hesitate to accept any alliance which rescued Turkey from her present position of isolation."[20]

In the ensuing weeks, Turkey drew closer to Germany and promised to come in on the side of the Central Powers. Needing time to fully mobilize their army, the Turks publicly declared neutrality while rapidly preparing for war

OTTOMAN "PEARL HARBOR"

In late September, Enver closed the Straits to foreign shipping and mined the Dardanelles.[21] The Turkish navy, greatly bolstered by the addition of the *Goeben* and the *Breslau* was being rapidly refitted for war. Admiral Souchon repeatedly took the vessels into the Black Sea for maneuvers and on one occasion he brazenly brought his ship to an abrupt halt directly opposite the Russian Embassy.

It was reported that in a rare example of Teutonic humor, "The sailors appeared on deck in their German uniforms and treated the enemy ambassador to a concert of German national songs. Then, putting on their fezzes, they sailed away again."[22]

Finally, on October 28, Admiral Souchon, now in command of the entire Ottoman Navy, led the two former German warships and a flotilla of Turkish gunboats in a sneak attack on the Russian Black Sea ports of Odessa, Sevastopol, and Theodosia. Kinross suggests that the Turkish squadron was acting under secret orders from Enver which "he had concealed from his ministerial colleagues."[23] That is quite possibly the case.

At the time of the sneak attack, Djemal Pasha, the Turkish Minister for Marine, was actually playing cards at his club in the capital and upon being told the news, "declared that he had not ordered the raid and that he knew nothing about it."[24] If Djemal was being truthful, it illustrates the great personal lengths that Enver took to enter the war on the German side.

As a further indication of Enver's secretive planning for the attack and further distancing from his top German military advisor; Liman von Sanders was completely surprised when first informed by his aide of the news of the naval sneak attack against Russia. It clearly illustrated von Sanders' limited access to the Turkish War Minister and "how far from the nexus of power he really was."[25]

The surprise Turkish bombardment without a formal Declaration of War, probably emulated the 1905 Japanese naval assault on Port Arthur. That "undeclared" naval action presaged yet another more "infamous" sneak attack that would later be launched by Imperial Japan in December, 1941. In any event, the presence of the two German cruisers ensured virtual Turkish naval supremacy in the Black Sea for the balance of the war.

Lord Grey denounced the Turkish action stating that, "Never was there a more wanton, gratuitous and unprovoked attack by one country on another."[26] Within days Great Britain, France and Russia declared war on the Ottoman Empire.

As Mr. Churchill so somberly concluded, because of the voyage of the *Goeben* there would result "more slaughter, more misery and more ruin than has ever before been borne within the compass of a ship."[27] One million dead Armenians would later provide quiet "testimony" to the correctness of that claim.

Oddly enough, Sir Winston Churchill's miscalculated appropriation of the legally contracted Turkish vessels had precipitated the *Goeben* affair, and arguably provoked the Ottoman Empire to enter the war. It at least gave Enver the justification needed for having Turkey side with his German friends.

Strangely, that episode, and the subsequent Turkish entrance into the conflict would nearly precipitate Churchill's own professional ruin, as well. In the wake of the disastrous Gallipoli campaign that followed, for which he was publicly blamed; the Lord of the Admiralty would be forced to resign and summarily went into a self-imposed "exile" from which it was believed he would never again publicly emerge.

STRANGE BEDFELLOWS

Turkey now found itself at war with the Triple Entente.

Interestingly, aside from once-again fighting against their age-old Russian nemesis, the Turks were also opposed to their three previous allies from a conflict they jointly fought against the Tsar sixty years earlier. Great Britain, France, and the Italian State of Sardinia, had sided with the Ottoman Empire in the Crimean War of 1856.

Just as ironically, the Turks decided to join forces with two of their harshest traditional enemies. Austria-Hungary and the Kingdom of Bulgaria had both fought vicious engagements with the Turkish Empire.

Dating back to Suleiman's failed siege of Vienna in 1529, the Turks and Austrians clashed numerous times. The Hapsburgs and the Ottomans incessantly fought against each other throughout the sixteenth and seventeenth centuries. In 1683, the Turks returned to besiege Vienna only to be repulsed once again. The Great Turkish War of 1683-1699 was a disaster for the Ottoman Empire which lost substantial European territory to the Austrians. That conflict also was the start of centuries of future Turkish warfare with the Hapsburg's momentary ally, Tsarist Russia.

Defeated again in the Austro-Turkish War of 1787-1791, the Ottoman Empire was now suffering a precipitous decline which continued unabated throughout the nineteenth century. Oddly enough,

Austria-Hungary also diminished in prestige relative to the other European Powers sustaining separate military defeats at the hands of the French (1859), Prussians (1866), and in the Third War of Italian Unification (1866).

Similarly, during both the nineteenth and early twentieth century the Turks had also fought savage conflicts with the Bulgarians. A Turkish possession since the Ottoman conquest of 1372, Bulgaria first gained full independence in 1908 after thirty years of intermittent bloody revolt. In the subsequent Balkan Wars of 1912-1913, the Bulgarians squared off twice against the Turks. Now, only two years later, the two ancient enemies were both fighting on the same side.

Courted heavily by both alliances, the Kingdom of Bulgaria eventually opted to join the Central Powers in the desire to settle old accounts with Serbia, Romania, and Greece. The Germans assured Bulgaria that pending victory they would see the return of all territory that had been lost to her hostile neighbors in the Second Balkan War.

The alliance with the Sublime Porte ensured Bulgaria of the freedom to attack Serbia and Romania without fear of being stabbed in the back. Nonetheless, Bulgarian hatred of the Turks was undoubtedly a bitter pill to swallow. One contemporary observer noted that, "To multitudes of the Bulgarians, and especially to the Macedonians, the alliance with Turkey was almost intolerable."[28]

"FOUR-FRONT" WAR

Almost immediately from the opening salvo, Turkey found itself with the daunting prospect of fighting on four separate fronts. In addition to the early standoff against the British in Egypt and Suez; the Turkish High Command was also gravely concerned about a looming Anglo-Indian Army expedition into Mesopotamia; massive Russian troop concentrations along the mountainous northern border; and the imminently much anticipated Allied strike against the Straits. Attacked from all corners of the Empire, the Turks would have been wise to utilize their interior lines in meeting the multiple threats.

Enver Pasha would not counsel a defensive posture, however.

As a result of the War Minister's irresponsible directives, in a very short time the Turks mounted a series of disastrous offensives that would almost serve to knock themselves out of the conflict.

Within a week of the start of hostilities the Germans began to aggressively urge Enver to invade Egypt and wrest the Suez Canal from the British. It was believed in Berlin that the loss of the Canal would be a "mortal blow" to Great Britain while having the additional benefit of fomenting "a rebellion in Egypt against British rule."[29]

The Turkish Minister of War immediately asked Djemal Pasha to lead an expedition across the Sinai, while simultaneously pacifying the Syrian Arab population and preventing any potential revolt against their own government. (Even if the Germans did not, the Turks were already realizing that the call for *Jihad*, or Muslim Holy War, was being purposely ignored by the Empire's restive Arab minorities.)

Djemal Pasha's army secretly penetrated the Sinai Peninsula with a force of 22,000, and subsequently attempted an amphibious assault on British defenses at the canal. Losing ten percent of his command, by the end of the following January, Djemal's expedition had been repulsed by the British forces, and he withdrew the Turkish Fourth Army back across the Negev Desert to defensive positions in Syria and Palestine.

No further large-scale Turkish attacks were ever again launched against Suez. With characteristic rationalization, however, Djemal noted that although unable to take the Canal, he was at least partially effective by stalemating the British forces stuck in Egypt.[30] Military historians, Ernest and Trevor Dupuy suggest that Djemal was probably correct to the extent that his continued threat to the Canal later "held much-needed British reinforcements back from Gallipoli."[31]

Meanwhile, more disappointing news was received from Mesopotamia where the British Indian Army advanced against Basra, taking the city on November 23. In addition, one week later British warships commenced a bombardment of the Turkish Dardanelles forts in anticipation of an imminently expected amphibious assault. Before the end of the year, however, the real showdown would take place on the snow-covered slopes of the Caucasus.

"TURKISH NAPOLEON"

With Turkey's entrance into the First World War, Enver Pasha likely envisioned that fate had given him the opportunity to personally restore the Ottoman Empire to its former glory.

Ever since the previous year with his retaking of the city of Edirne (Adrianople) in the Second Balkan War, Enver was considered a "national hero."[32] Having previously served with distinction against Greek and Bulgarian partisans in Macedonia (1903); and again in Libya during the Italo-Turkish War (1912); Enver had risen to effectively take supreme command of the entire Turkish Army.

In December 1914, against the sound advice of General Otto Liman von Sanders, his German military advisor (who eighteen months earlier had ably assisted him at Adrianople); Enver Pasha decided to order an invasion into the Russian Caucasus. Coinciding with the strike against the Suez Canal, the Turkish High Command had also planned to launch a simultaneous pre-emptive advance against the British in Mesopotamia.

The main theater of operations would be against the Russians, however. Once again the army would be personally led by a member of the ruling Triumvirate. Enver Pasha, the self-styled "Turkish Napoleon," would lead the invasion himself.

The goal of the campaign was to surround and destroy the Tsar's army and in the process to regain Kars and Batumi, both cities lost in the 1877 Russo-Turkish War.

Hurriedly rushed into action, the Caucasus campaign was doomed from the beginning. Poorly planned and inadequately equipped for a mountainous winter campaign, the Turkish army of nearly 100,000 troops lost at least 15,000 through frostbite and desertion before the battle even commenced. Advancing on Kars, the Turks were decisively routed at the Battle of Sarikamish by a Russian counterattack on New Year's Day.

Enver's rash invasion plan was shattered, and the Turks lost 30,000 combat fatalities with many thousands more later freezing to death in the ensuing retreat.[33] *The New York Times* tersely reported that, "The Best Army Corps in the Turkish Army, the Ninth...has been destroyed."[34] Out of the 100,000-man host that had initially set out on the campaign, only 18,000 effectives returned to the Turkish base at Erzerum. Amazingly, Enver himself was personally in danger of being cut-off from the retreating army and was ironically saved by an Armenian soldier in the Turkish army.[35]

The debacle at Sarikamish was the greatest Ottoman military loss of the war. It was solely the lack of any immediate Russian pursuit that prevented a final collapse of the entire front. Shaken by the disastrous defeat, Enver relinquished field command and returned to Constantinople.[36] By virtually losing his entire army in an ill-fated invasion of Russia, Enver had once again emulated his hero Napoleon Bonaparte in a way that he had not foreseen.

The Young Turks regime, reeling from the setbacks in Russia, Mesopotamia, and the Sinai, while also fearing an imminent Allied attack on the Dardanelles, looked to avoid responsibility and shift criticism away from the capital. The War Minister, himself being previously accustomed to the "hero-worship" of the Turkish Army, was now coming under increasingly harsh criticism for his handling of the war, and support of the Kaiser.[37]

On January 7, *The New York Times* printed an interview reportedly made with a Turkish Colonel who was captured by the Russians. With obvious bitterness he complained that "Enver Pasha has been our ruin. This wretched, brainless puppet of Wilhelm and [Liman] Sanders Pasha has brought Turkey to a pass which imperils the

Ottoman Empire...There is no Turkey now. It is only a German province."[38]

It is my belief that Enver Pasha may have become greatly fearful after the terrible military setbacks of January-February 1915. Although personally fearless in battle, I believe that he exhibited paranoia regarding his potential loss of control over the government and the army. The "Turkish Napoleon" was now seen more as the Ottoman embodiment of the inept Napoleon III rather than of the former French monarch's grandly illustrious uncle.

SACRIFICIAL SCAPEGOATS

After so recklessly destroying the army that had been entrusted under his direct command, the Turkish Minister of War was now intent upon becoming distanced from the disaster. To shift the recriminations from himself, Enver Pasha now looked for someone to whom he could personally pin the blame.

One telling incident that made front-page headlines in the American Press, reported that Enver had seventeen of his officers executed for a suspected mutiny in the days immediately following the Russian fiasco. Rather than being comprised of a group of craven traitors, the same news dispatch also mentioned that the slain men were "...officers who had distinguished themselves in the Balkan Wars."[39]

It is apparent that the Minister of War was desperately seeking to implicate and brand someone else with the responsibility for his own military disaster in the Caucasus. It would certainly be desirable if he could identify a convenient internal threat as a physical reason for the catastrophe.

In a strangely familar reaction, Enver's colleague Djemal Pasha also sought to procure a self-serving explanation for his military defeat in the ill-fated Sinai campaign. Although the loss of 2,000 men was miniscule when compared with Enver's massive casualties, Djemal still sought to deflect his responsibility and exonerate himself for the Ottoman repulse.

Writing after the war, Djemal was quick to point out that the failed Suez attack had been actually ordered by Enver, and that his command had been given "inadequate" resources to successfully complete their mission.

In his post-war memoirs he also described the "secret betrayal" of the Muslim Arabs as a further partial reason for the Turkish defeat. The Sultan's call for a Muslim *Jihad* against the infidel enemy Christians was for the most part ignored by the Arab tribes of Arabia, and the Hejaz. The lure of complete Arab autonomy from the Ottoman Empire trumped waging a Holy War on behalf of the Turkish Caliph.

The following year, the Grand Sherif of Mecca proclaimed Arab independence and the Turkish forces facing the British in the Sinai, "found themselves hampered by Arab dissidence threatening their entire line of land communications north through Syria to the Taurus Mountains."[40]

Djemal placed severe blame for his ultimate defeat on the threat to his rear that was orchestrated by Sherif Hussein in what would later become a full-blown Arab revolt. Djemal Pasha called the Sherif's actions a "secret betrayal...and an unforgivable sin against the Mussulman world."

It is important to note the justifiable Turkish concern over what would later be identified during the Spanish Civil War as "fifth column" activities. The same suspicious fears that they expressed over rear-guard Arab threats would also be focused on the Armenians the following spring. There is little doubt that many Armenians looked upon the Russians as Christian liberators and willfully took up arms against the Turks. The vast majority of Armenian fighters were Russian citizens from the other side of the border, but those living in Ottoman Armenia were also recruited in large numbers. It must also be noted that the Turkish army also included a large number of Armenians loyal to the Ottoman Empire.

My personal belief is that the fear of an Armenian uprising was genuine, and was fair cause for Turkish concern. It was only after his military debacle in the snows of Sarikamish, however, that Enver Pasha took actual steps against the Armenian "threat."

The Armenians had a sad record of being conveniently blamed and terrorized during times of Turkish internal discord. During the countercoup of April 1909, between the conservative loyalists of Sultan Abdul Hamid II, and the Young Turks; the Christian minority was brutally persecuted.

As R. P. Adalian observed, "The Adana massacre demonstrated that even in a power struggle within Turkish society, the Armenians could be scapegoated by the disaffected and made the object of violence. In this context, Enver's embarrassment at his defeat in early 1915 and the government's casting of blame on the Armenians had a precedent."[41]

However real or imagined the military danger of an Armenian fifth-column may have actually been, the Minister of War would use it to own his personal advantage. He was handed a convenient source of blame for his own dismal failure. In the Armenians, Enver Pasha ultimately found his perfect scapegoat.

What followed was the beginning of the Armenian genocide.

"PLAN D"

In a brilliant study of the causes of genocide, Michael Mann described four separate levels of government escalation that takes place dubbing them "Plan A," through "Plan D" in succession. He suggests that rarely does one start out with the intent of committing all-out ethnic genocide. Mann writes, "It is rare to find evil geniuses plotting mass murder from the very beginning. Not even Hitler did so."[42] Rather it is by the continual failure at each successive step of an escalating process that one is led to an ultimate Nazi-style final solution.

In essence, the initial stage, Plan A typically envisages a carefully planned solution in terms of compromise and even alliance. Plan B is a radically repressive adaptation to the failure of Plan A, more hastily conceived amid rising violence and some political destabilization. When these both fail some of the planners radicalize further. Plan C becomes more violent and widely applied, and finally the Plan D decision is made for the out-right extermination of the target group.

Mann concluded that the Armenian and Jewish holocausts were different in that Hitler and his minions saw the Final Solution of the Jewish question as "the logical escalation of an ideology ruthlessly overcoming all obstacles in its path. For the Young Turks, however, the final solution to the Armenian problem seems much more contingent, flowing out of what they saw as their suddenly desperate situation in 1915."[43]

In the case of Eastern Anatolia, the Young Turks were originally hailed as the liberators of Turkey's ethnic and religious minorities from the tyranny of Abdul Hamid. Very early on they embraced the Armenians in the spirit of Pan-Ottomanism. Plan A was the proposed assimilation and alliance of all peoples within the multi-ethnic empire.

Plan A was somewhat successful at first. It should be remembered that the Young Turks and the Armenian Nationalists had been allied in 1908. For their part, I believe that many of the Young Turks were sincerely idealistic in the beginning but the terrible military disasters they suffered during the first years of the CUP administration changed their direction towards the embrace of Hamidian-style centralized control. The commensurate rise of Pan-Turkism coupled with a government perception of growing nationalism among the Armenian population, led to the adoption of Plan B.

Prior to taking the next step Mann believes that in August 1914, the Young Turks tried one last time to persuade the Armenians to join in an Ottoman alliance against their "common opponents."[44] It should be noted, however, that from very early in the war, the Armenian intelligentsia was forcibly detained and all available Armenian manpower had either been hastily drafted into the Turkish Army for unarmed work details; or those who escaped had already chosen to join sides with the approaching Russians. There actually were no "common opponents" as even those Armenians who were conscripted by the Turkish army were little better than slave-labor.

The Armenian position is that the Turkish government had effectively neutralized their ability to later defend themselves with the forced conscription and virtual detention of the able-bodied male population. The Turks on the other hand claim the necessity of preventing the military age Armenian men from revolt and providing fifth column support for the Tsar's advancing army.

There never was a real attempt at forming an alliance at that late date. It is true, however, that "sometime between August 1914, and February 1915, Plan A was replaced."[45]

What is at issue is merely the timing of Plan B which was the targeted deportation of the Armenian male population. It is likely that once the Turks found themselves at war with the very nations that had upheld the Armenian cause for decades, the government found itself in the position to finally do whatever they liked without restraint. Here the competing pressures of war, combined with the passions of Pan-Turkism, Pan-Islam, and long pent-up ethnic jealousies towards the generally more affluent Christian minorities finally spilled-over.

In essence Plan B was quickly leapfrogged during the months in question and following the military debacles of January 1915, Plan C, the general forced deportation of the entire Armenian population was ordered. As will be later discussed, the Young Turk leaders never denied the deportation decision.

What has been challenged is whether Plan D, the planned systematic extermination of the Armenians was ever intentionally called for. In fact the Turks still deny that the subsequent depredations were actually genocide at all.

The Young Turks were following a path that had risen meteorically out of control. The question of pre-meditation, however, still remains to be answered. Mann frankly admits that to argue the degree of intentionality and pre-meditation is for him "morally uncomfortable" when one looks from the perspective of the victims.

Simply stated, the Jews and Armenians both suffered genocide regardless of the steps that it took to get there.

Just What the Doctors Ordered?

For the past century the fact that the Armenian population of Turkish Anatolia was forcibly deported, and as a later result virtually ceased to exist, has not been seriously debated by apologists from either side. What is in question is whether their ultimate destruction was an act of pre-meditated government sponsored genocide or merely the unfortunately tragic consequences of the fog of war.

Scholars have searched for evidence that would settle the matter either way. What was needed to find is a "smoking gun." According to Turkish born genocide scholar Uğur Ümit Üngör, the issue of how to deal with Armenian and other minority groups was discussed by the CUP government months before the First World War actually began. He suggests that in the spring of 1914, "Enver Pasha organized a series of secret meetings at the War Ministry at which 'the elimination of the non-Turkish masses' was discussed."[46] If true, that would clearly establish a government plan of premeditated genocide and dismiss the Turkish claims that the deportations of 1915 were orchestrated to counteract fears of possible Armenian fifth column activity in support of the advancing Russian army.

Great efforts have been taken by others in further trying to establish the existence of definitive proof similar to that which clearly authenticated another genocidal crime.

Without question the Jewish Holocaust of Hitler's Third Reich was perpetrated under the direct orders of the Nazis hierarchy. The evidence for Hitler's planned destruction of the Jews is ubiquitous and beginning with his anti-Semitic ravings in *Mein Kampf*, is confirmed in mountains of captured Nazi documents, photographs, and eyewitness testimonies.

No one that believes the earth is round seriously doubts the planned, pre-meditated Nazi genocide of Europe's Jewry; and the actual date for its formal adoption as a government policy has been firmly established. On January 20, 1942, a formal conference was held in the quiet Berlin suburb of Wannsee. Its purpose was to officially inform and involve the representatives of the various Nazi ministries of the "Final Solution of the Jewish Problem."[47] The chairman of the meeting was one of the darkest, and most sinister, characters of the Third Reich.

The head of Nazi Germany's carefully planned answer to the "Jewish Question" was Reinhard Heydrich, a sadistic butcher who was personally appointed by the Fuhrer himself. Described by Adolf Hitler as "the Man with the Iron Heart,"[48] Heydrich had been one of the organizers of the infamous *Kristallnacht* of November 9-10, 1938.

Considered by many as the actual start of the Holocaust, that nationwide pogrom was described by William Shirer as the night that, "the Third Reich had deliberately turned down a dark and savage road for which there was to be no return."[49]

For his part, Heydrich was given ever greater roles of responsibility including the personal orchestration of the phony Polish "attack" that was staged by the Nazis to justify Hitler's invasion of that country on September 1, 1939.[50] Rising rapidly through the ranks from private to General, Heydrich became a personal favorite of Hitler's and a member of the most inner circle of Nazi elites.

At the Wannsee Conference, Heydrich formally announced the German government's stamp of approval given to the planned systematic genocide of the Jewish people that had already been underway for some time. Henceforth the holocaust was the "official" policy of the Third Reich. The infamous proceedings at the secret meeting were later used as evidence against the Nazis at the Nuremburg Trials. Interestingly, just such a conference is said to have taken place that if authentic would clearly implicate the Turkish government in the Armenian Holocaust.

In February, 1915 a meeting of the CUP leadership was allegedly convened under the direction of Talaat Pasha. The secret minutes were reportedly recorded by Mevlanzade Rifat and later published in 1929. According to the book, *The Inner Aspects of the Turkish Revolution*, the author related witnessing a damning report given by a high-ranking member of the Young Turk leadership.

During the meeting Dr. Nazim Bey, a member of CUP's Central Committee allegedly called for the complete annihilation of the Armenian people. He has been quoted as suggesting, "If we are going to be satisfied with the kind of local massacres that occurred in Adana and other places in 1909...if this purge is not going to be universal and final, instead of good, it will inevitably result in harm. It is imperative that the Armenian people be completely exterminated; that not even one single Armenian be left on our soil; that the name Armenian be obliterated."[51]

He then goes on to explain that due to the existing state of war, "the usual protests of the newspapers" was no longer a consideration, and that the matter would finally be completely settled anyway even if that had been a concern. Dr. Nazim allegedly closed his remarks with the words, "The procedure this time will be one of total annihilation--it is necessary that not one single Armenian survive this annihilation."[52]

Rifat then reported that after a period of deliberation the members of the CUP central committee voted unanimously to adopt Dr. Nazim's proposal and officially authorized the extermination of the Armenian people. In Dr. Nazim Bey, Talaat Pasha had apparently found his Heydrich.

It is also important to note that according to Rifat's account the *Ittihad* leadership was also directly responsible for the violent persecution of the Armenians long before 1915. "Rifat asserts that the guilt for the Adana massacres of 1909 rests in truth on the government of the Young Turks."[53]

On the surface, the evidence of a premeditated Turkish "Wannsee Conference" appears to be damning. As early as 1929, the Rifat "minutes"were used by Armenian apologists in their post-war indictment of the CUP leadership. Unfortunately, upon deeper investigation, the story has very serious flaws. It seems that the credibility of Mevlanzade Rifat is in serious question.

In 1973, Gwynne Dyer reported that Rifat had never been a member of the *Ittihad* Central Committee and in fact was a Kurd with a long history of opposition to the Young Turk regime. He was even court-martialed by the CUP government for attempting a coup.[54] As Guenter Lewy indicates, Rifat was probably never in a position to have access to secret plans for the annihilation of the Armenians. He rather suggests that Rifat's book, "represented an attempt to absolve the Kurds of responsibility for the wartime massacres by putting all the guilt for the killings on the CUP leaders."[55]

Another Turkish physician has also been accused of complicity in the deportation and alleged extermination of the Armenians. Dr. Behaeddin Shakir was reportedly the head of a CUP counter-insurgency group called the *Te kilât-ı Mahsusa* ("Special Organization"). It was the duty of the paramilitary unit to suppress anti-government activities which included Arab separatism.

Turkish born Historian Taner Akçam suggests that the Special Organization was activated in 1914 and, "had two goals: externally, to incite a Muslim revolt against Russia and Great Britain, and internally, to take measures against the Armenians."[56]

The Special Organization was identified by the 1919 Turkish courts-martial as being responsible for carrying out the CUP execution orders of the Armenians. David Rausch suggests that Hitler may have philosophically patterned his infamous *Einsatzgruppen*, SS Death Squads after the Turkish Special Organization.[57]

Journalist Robert Kaplan observed that, "There is nothing new about physicians taking part in acts of barbarism." In a scathing analysis of the CUP leaders, he makes the comparison with other heinous examples of medical men gone bad.

Kaplan charges that, "Systematic participation of doctors in state terrorism began with the Armenian genocide in Turkey in 1915. Medical personnel were directly involved in the killings, often participating in torture. Behaeddin Shakir and Nazim Bey established extermination squads staffed by criminals. Nazim, in one of the most misguided appointments in the history of medicine, was professor of legal (ethical) medicine at Istanbul Medical School." Dr. Mehmid Reshid, the governor of Diyarbakir province, "was involved in the 'deportation' of 120,000 Armenians. Reshid's brutality included nailing red-hot horseshoes on the victims' chests, and then crucifying them on makeshift crosses."[58] Dubbed the "Butcher of Diyarbakir," he reportedly incarcerated some 800 Armenian children in a barn and then personally set it afire, burning them alive. When confronted with the query of how a doctor could commit such violent acts, Reshid responded, "Either they us, or we them...There are two alternatives: Either the Armenians will liquidate the Turks or, or the Turks will liquidate them...therefore, I proceeded eyes closed and without consideration, convinced that I was acting for the welfare of the nation... The Armenian bandits were a load of harmful microbes that had afflicted the body of the fatherland. Was it not the duty of the doctor to kill the microbes?"[59]

Mehmid Reshid's admission is perhaps one of the gravest violations of the medical professions' Hippocratic Oath on record. Unfortunately, it would be echoed, copied and further disgraced a short number of years later. Kaplan concluded, "The Armenian genocide provided the template for the Nazi holocaust, leading to the most notorious example of medical complicity in state abuse: Nazi doctors who participated in euthanasia and genocide, of whom the most well known is Joseph Mengele."[60]

FIFTH COLUMN? OR THIRD DEGREE?!

Ever since the end of World War I, the Turkish government has pointed to a threatened "fifth-column" uprising by Armenian nationalists as having been the cause that justifiably precipitated the Turkish deportations.

With their entry into the First World War (also identified by Joachim Remak as the "Third Balkan War")[61] the Turks feared an Armenian uprising in Eastern Anatolia, which they thought would be coordinated with Russian army advances from the Caucasus. The recent disasters that the Turks had experienced fighting the Christian nationalist revolts in Bulgaria, Macedonia and Albania, along with the territorial losses suffered in the "previous" two Balkan Wars understandably aroused Turkish concerns. Enver even blatantly confided to United States Ambassador Henry Morgenthau that "we are not going to let the Armenians attack us in the rear."[62]

It is perhaps justifiable, on purely military grounds, that the Turks sought to protect themselves from what a later generation would call a "fifth-column" assault. It was just such a concern that later prompted the United States government to physically intern Japanese-American citizens for similar reasons in 1941. What remains totally unacceptable, however, was the magnitude, and the severity of the Turkish "precautions." The resulting deportations and massacres culminated in the virtual annihilation of Turkey's Armenian population.

The Armenian people were Ottoman subjects in 1915 and it is a unique characteristic of the massacres that all of the Turkish government's eventual victims were citizens of the very same empire. There was, however, a strong and long-lasting tradition of Armenian sovereignty dating to before the time of Christ. That national identification and ethnic separation quite naturally contributed to the suspicions of the Young Turk regime.

Before further discussing the actual events of 1915, it is important to first ascertain whether Armenian nationalism actually posed a serious threat to the Ottoman Empire. In the next chapter we will attempt to answer that question by briefly examining the historical evidence and background for any Armenian claim to an autonomous national homeland.

9

TURKEY, ARMENIA AND THE CASE
FOR NATIONAL SOVEREIGNITY

MUCH OF THE modern world is today populated by peoples that long ago conquered their presently occupied piece of real estate from some other previous holder. History is replete with examples of invasions by migratory invaders who forcibly confiscated lands that were once held by someone else. Every inch of Planet Earth has been disputed and changed hands at least once. Even the uninhabited continent of Antarctica has no less than eight separate national claimants to a portion of its frozen territory.

If one accepts the traditional Biblical view, all peoples originally emanated from one solitary source and eventually coalesced into separate tribes, clans, and ultimately into entire civilizations. Secular anthropologists also agree that over many millennia world-wide migrations populated the far-flung world after originally embarking from a single place of origin.

The Native American domains that had been usurped by Europeans between the fifteenth through the nineteenth centuries were earlier fought over repeatedly by indigenous peoples that had once migrated from Asia over the Siberian-Alaskan land bridge that once connected the two continents. Wars of conquest were not newly introduced to the Indians as evidenced by the bloody Pre-Columbian subjugation of neighboring tribes by both the Aztecs and the Mayans.

The Magyars and the Huns were driven westward out of Central Asia by the Mongols, and forced to start over by forcibly occupying someone else's lands. The result more-or-less, is modern day Hungary.

From before Biblical times the "Fertile Crescent" of the Middle East was the theater for numerous migrations and incursions. The "Cradle of Civilization" ultimately had many occupants. Sumerians, Akkadians, Assyrians, Babylonians, Medes, Persians, Egyptians, Phoenicians, Greeks, Romans, Byzantines, Mamelukes, Seljuks, Mongols, and Muslim Arabs each stamped their footprints into the desert sand.

The Holy Land of ancient Canaan was once the domain of the Hittites, Hivites, Jebusites, Elamites, Amorites, Philistines and ultimately of the victorious Israelites who from Abraham to David had been promised the land by the Hebrew God.

Amazingly more blood has been shed at the world's most sacred city than virtually anywhere else. Jerusalem (the "City of Peace") has been fought over more times than any other piece of real estate on earth!

CLAIMS AND COUNTER-CLAIMS

As is also the case most everywhere else, the land that is modern Turkey has been contested, and fought over by many different claimants. What then is the historical evidence supporting the Turkish claims to eastern Anatolia, and those lands counter-claimed by the Armenians?

For centuries Turkey has laid claim to Anatolia by the ancient right of conquest. Physical possession has historically been seen as sufficient proof of actual ownership. Therefore it was a remote possibility that Turkey would ever have willfully relinquished the land claimed by the Armenians, as is the equally absurd notion that the Jews would abandon modern Jerusalem, or the United States Government would finally return Manhattan to the Indians.

The Ottoman Empire of the early twentieth century was comprised of a polyglot of peoples, and religious beliefs. It had been decaying, declining and diminishing for hundreds of years but was not yet ready to dissolve altogether. The Young Turk leadership was intent on preserving what remained and reversing the disastrous course. They truly believed that the converging forces of Pan Turkism, Pan-Ottomanism, and Pan-Islam would restore the empire to former glory. All subjects of the Ottoman Empire would be required, by force if necessary, to aid in that effort and support the national good.

Of course, for the empire's minorities that meant deferring to the well-being of the Muslim Turkic majority. The Christian Armenians were no exception, but were long viewed with particular condescension and contempt.

In perhaps an unintentional but seemingly dismissive denunciation of the Armenian struggle for an autonomous national homeland, written by a fairly sympathetic British career diplomat of the early twentieth century; a reason was given for their heretofore lack of success. Sir Charles Eliot argued that the Armenians were "doomed to failure," as they suffered from an inability to "succeed in forming national political organizations strong enough to hold their own against the adverse circumstances by which they are surrounded."[1]

He compared the Armenians to the Poles, who by the time of the writer's observations (1902) had also failed for centuries to regain an independent state. Eliot, who traveled extensively in Turkey, and often reported his observations under the pseudonym of "Odysseus," pointed out that both the traditional homelands of Poland and Armenia had been divided by the partition of neighboring powers for centuries.

At the start of the twentieth century, Prussia, Austria, and Tsarist Russia each owned a portion of Poland. Similarly, Armenia was divided between Russia, Persia and Ottoman Turkey. As a result Eliot quipped, "It is hard to say what are the limits of Armenia, for it is not a recognized division of the globe."

In fact, "Odysseus" noted that, "The name Armenia clashes to a certain extent with another local designation--Kurdistan."[2]

Rather than making a comparison with Poland, who along with Armenia would both achieve their own free national status by the end of the twentieth century (in defiance of Eliot's assurances to the contrary); the situation of another ancient people may have provided a more suitable resemblance.

Like the Armenians, the Jews had longed for an independent, "promised land" for many centuries. Often traditionally compared as peoples adept at commerce, finance and banking; the two also shared the distinction of each possessing a distinctly personal religion.

Most notably, however, the Jews and the Armenians each staked an ancient birthright. The Jewish claim to Palestine was perpetually as sacred to them as the age-old interest in Anatolia was to the Armenians. To this day, both peoples view the respective lands with passionate desire, and from a great historic vantage point.

DIASPORA PEOPLE

The rugged land of Armenia traditionally encompassed approximately 100,000 square miles, extending from Asia Minor to Persia, and was shielded by the Taurus Mountains in the south, and the Pontic range to the north.[3] In the center lie the twin summits of the fabled Mount Ararat, the Biblical site of the debarkation of Noah's Ark.[4]

At present less than ten percent of the ancient land belongs to the Armenians. In 1915, the territory was divided between the Ottoman Empire, Russia, and Persia, with no independent Armenian homeland. In an analogous sense, one might compare the Armenians to the Poles whose national homeland was also carved into thirds by the likes of Austria, Germany and Russia.

Like the Jewish people, to whom they have often been compared,[5] the Armenians survived as a group for centuries without a national state. This is rare in history with most defeated or displaced national groups either moving on to usurp new lands (eg: the Huns, Magyars, Vandals) or assimilating into the empire that conquered it (Hittites, Chaldeans, Etruscans, Saxons). Just as in the case of the Jews, the Armenians were also the beneficiaries of a strong ethnic culture tied inextricably to religious faith and traditions.

The Bible states that Noah's Ark rested "upon the mountains of Ararat" (Genesis 8:4) and Flavius Josephus, the Jewish historian of the first century, added the detail that the location was "in Armenia."[6] The Armenians traditionally trace their heritage to the descendents of Haik, a grandson of the Biblical Japheth, whom they claim were the original occupants of the land.[7]

Modern scholarship favors their descent from Phrygian tribes that arrived at Ararat by the sixth century B.C.[8] The Greek historian Strabo wrote of the revolt of Artaxias against Antiochus the Great (190 B.C.), and his subsequent founding of Artaxata (Ardaschad) as the capital of a newly created Armenian kingdom.[9] The city flourished due to its location on the commercial routes between east and west, and trade was established with Rome.[10]

The apogee of ancient Armenian power is reckoned from the forty-year rule of Dikran, or Tigranes II (90-36 B.C.) who expanded and solidified the kingdom only to eventually be forced to bow before Roman hegemony.[11]

TIGRANES MAGNUS

The illustrious reign of Tigranes the Great was the "high water mark" of the Armenian national experience.

Very little is known about the early life of the future Armenian king beyond what was first recorded by the Greek historian /geographer Strabo. It is believed that Tigranes II was born in c. 120 B.C., and that at the age of twenty the prince was taken royal hostage by the Parthian King Mithridates II following his defeat of the Armenian King Artavasdes I.

It is uncertain whether Tigranes was the son of Artavasdes, or his brother Tigranes I, who later came to the throne in 115 B.C. In any event, Strabo records that after twenty years of captivity, young Tigranes was able to purchase his release from the Parthians upon the news of the death of Tigranes I, and his succession to the Armenian throne. The price for his ransom was "seventy valleys" in Armenia which were duly ceded for his release.[12]

Rapidly consolidating his power, the new Armenian king turned against Parthia, and regained not only the aforementioned seventy valleys but a great part of the Parthian lands of Mesopotamia, and Media. Checked by the Roman dictator Sulla from an attack on Cappadocia, Tigranes marched against Syria and conquered the last vestiges of the Seleucid Empire.

After Sulla's death in 78 B.C., the Armenian king returned to Cappadocia and annexed it to his expanding empire. Conquering Phoenicia and Cilicia, Tigranes had dominion over the commercial crossroads of the Middle East. "In the following years, he consolidated his control over his conquests and was generally acknowledged the most powerful ruler of southwest Asia."[13]

Tigranes the Great now reigned from the center of his vast domains at his capital city of Tigranocerta. Resplendent in style, and a center of both art, and commerce, the metropolis was adorned with parks, hunting grounds and decorative lakes in the suburbs.[14]

His empire stretched from the Syrian shores of the Mediterranean in the west to that of the Caspian Sea in the East. From Damascus, and Antioch, to the Caucasus Mountains, the kingdom of "Greater Armenia" reached its zenith in 70 B.C.

Plutarch referred to him as "King of Kings," and Cicero later remarked that Tigranes had "made the Republic of Rome tremble before the prowess of his arms."[15] The Armenian monarch truly had taken claim to the title of "the Great."

Then disaster struck the Armenians.

ASIATIC VESPERS

Perhaps Tigranes' greatest misfortune was in whom he chose for a father-in-law.

In 89 B.C., Tigranes II forged an alliance with Mithridates IV of Pontus, and subsequently married the king's daughter. Both monarchs looked to further extend their influence with Tigranes looking to the east, and Mithridates seeking expansion in the west. The designs of the king of Pontus soon ran up against the aspirations of Rome.

By a cruel and barbarous action, Mithridates IV brought the full force of the Roman Republic against both his own Kingdom of Pontus, and eventually that of his son-in-law as well. He had wantonly embarked upon a campaign of carnage and death that was truly genocidal in nature. In 88 B.C., Mithridates ordered the slaughter of 80,000 Roman citizens, many of which were women and children, in a series of attacks coordinated to take place on the same day in towns throughout Asia Minor. The pre-arranged day of the atrocity was later infamously dubbed the "Asiatic Vespers," and Cicero reported that it was the cause of the first of the three "Mithridatic Wars."[16]

Despite initial success, King Mithridates' army was later defeated by the Roman Consul Lucius Cornelius Sulla first at the battle of Chaeronea, and again at Orchomenus, despite a numerical advantage of more than three to one, and peace was temporarily declared.

The two nations went to war again in 83-81 B.C., and Tigranes managed to continue his support of his father-in-law without provoking Rome into open hostilities. Finally, in 75 B.C., the two nations went to war for the third time. Mithridates invaded the Roman province of Bithynia with a host of 150,000 men, and was totally crushed at the Battle of Cabira by a Roman army barely one-fifth its size.

After his devastating defeat by the Roman General Lucius Licinius Lucullus; the king of Pontus fled to safety at the capital of his son-in-law who had thus far remained at peace with Rome. Demanding that Mithridates be handed over to Roman authority, Lucullus threatened war unless he the fugitive king was peacefully surrendered. Tigranes adamantly refused to give up his father-in-law, and the Romans duly invaded Armenia in 70 B.C.

With remarkable bravado, the Roman commander led a small force that the Dupuys' estimated to be as few as 10,000 legionnaires against an Armenian army that was possibly ten to twenty times that number.[17]   Appian of Alexandria estimated the Armenian host at roughly 250,000.[18]

In a legendary anecdote, Plutarch reported that upon observing the size of the enemy advance, the surprised Tigranes was prompted to scoff, "If they come as ambassadors, they are too many; if they are soldiers, too few."[19]

Nonetheless, the Romans won a brilliant victory and forced Tigranes to retreat. In the aftermath the capital city of Tigranocerta was totally plundered and destroyed. Suffering yet another setback the following year at Artaxata, the Armenian-Pontic forces were temporarily reprieved when the exhausted Roman army threatened mutiny rather than continue the campaign.

In 67 B.C., Lucullus was replaced by Pompey the Great who decisively defeated individual armies led by Mithridates, and Tigranes in successive battles. The former Pontic ruler committed suicide, but Tigranes was graciously treated by Pompey, who allowed him to remain on the throne after relinquishing a large amount of treasure and territory. He remained king, in an alliance with Rome, until his death in 55 B.C.

Fabled in legend as Armenia's greatest monarch, Tigranes the Great was the later subject of no less than twenty modern operas. It is also believed that from the evidence found on Armenian coins, Tigranes likely witnessed Halley's Comet as it became visible in the summer of 87 B.C. Such an unusual celestial event might have been deemed as particularly auspicious for the reign of the erstwhile "King of Kings."[20]

Armenia would never again attain such power but would remain relatively autonomous for four more centuries despite intermittent periods of Roman or Parthian occupation. The Jewish historian, Flavius Josephus noted Marc Antony's later subjugation of Armenia, and the later dynastic struggles that took place during the time of Nero.[21]

Tacitus also described the Armenian kingdom and reported on the fall of Artaxata to Nero's general Corbulo in A.D. 58.[22] For the next three centuries Armenia was caught in between the incessant warfare between Rome and Persia. The Romans placed Tiridates III on the Armenian throne after driving out the Persians in 288.

His reign lasted twenty-six years and was most notable for proclaiming Christianity as the state religion in 314,[23] the first country in history to do so. As such, Armenia lays claim to being the oldest Christian nation on earth.

In A.D. 370, the city Artaxata was once again taken and finally destroyed by the Persians. As a consequence, the Armenians remained the subjects of foreign kings for the next fifteen centuries.

It can hardly be contested that Armenia is an ancient land with strong historical attestation. What is remarkable is that the Armenians retained their strong individual identity for so long without a self-governing national homeland. It is my belief that just as in the case of the Jewish People, the key to Armenian national and cultural survival was their religious tradition.

Anthony Smith compares the Armenians to the Jews and Greeks whom he corporately identifies as "archetypal diaspora peoples." He links the three separate groups as all epitomizing "ethno-religious communities cultivating the particular virtues and attitudes of their traditions."[24] It can be argued that amongst the Jews, Greeks and

Armenians, the strongest traditions were truly religious in nature and centered around the church or synagogue.

As Sirarpie Der Nersessian observed, "the role played by the church throughout Armenia's turbulent history cannot be sufficiently stressed. Bulwark of Armenian language and culture, a rallying point for the scattered elements of the population, the Church was also one of the centers of resistance against all attempts at fusion or absorption."[25]

ARMENIA'S NATIONAL EPIC

One of the most intriguing chapters in the history of Armenia may help explain the strong traditional ties. It is a tale that is steeped in myth and legend yet might contain a basis in historical fact. A fourth century Christian historian tells a remarkable story about an Armenian king who lived in the time of Christ.

In his work, *The History of the Church*, Eusebius described a letter that was purportedly sent to Jesus by Abgar Uchama, the Toparch of Edessa (modern Urfa) asking him to visit his kingdom and heal him of an illness. The chronicler contends that Christ subsequently wrote back instructions to Abgar promising that he would "send you one of my disciples to cure your disorder and bring life to you and those with you."[26]

Eusebius claimed to have actually seen the written correspondence that had yet been preserved in the imperial archives. The story continues that in the year A.D. 30, immediately after Christ's ascension the apostle Thaddeus, "one of the seventy" traveled to Armenia and both healed and converted Abgar along with many of the local population[27].

Later documents, including the 6th century *Acts of Thaddeus*,[28] and ancient Syraic manuscripts recovered from the Nitrian Monastery in Lower Egypt, added the curious information that the Christian apostle had presented Abgar with a burial cloth upon which was imprinted the physical likeness of the savior.[29]

Egeria (Etheria), the 4[th]century Galician pilgrim, wrote of her visit to the palace of Abgar, and the Church of St. Thomas in the city of Edessa. She claimed to see the actual correspondence between Jesus and Abgar that remained in the physical possession of the local Bishop.[30] Once again, without passing on the actual reliability of the documentary evidence, it is clear that the Armenian Christian tradition was already quite strong by the middle of the 4[th]century.

Regardless of the questionable authenticity of this documentary "evidence," many believe that it helps to support the ancient tradition that Abgar actually received the burial cloth of Jesus, known today as the Shroud of Turin. Ian Wilson has brilliantly constructed a detailed, if circumstantial "chronology" of the Shroud dating from the time of Christ up to the present time.[31]

In his research he links the Roman Catholic traditions of the "Veronica Veil,"[32] the Eastern Orthodox "Mandylion,"[33] and the Shroud to weave a fairly persuasive, if un-provable account. It is not the purpose of this paper to debate the authenticity of the Shroud, or the Abgar legends, but what is important is that the Armenians have claimed the story as their own for many centuries.

The ancient Abgar Legend is to the Armenians as the *Niebelungen* is to the Germans, the *Kebra Negast* to the Ethiopians, or King Arthur's *Camelot* to the Britons. It is an enduring national epic that despite any actual authenticity proves nonetheless the antiquity and national integrity of the people.

ANCIENT PEDIGREE

The Armenians profess to be the first Christian nation in history.[34] That Abgar was an actual monarch living in Edessa, as reported by Tacitus, Pliny, and Eusebius, is a fairly well established fact. Esat Uras' exhaustive work *The Armenians in History and the Armenian Question* is one of many recent publications that acknowledge Abgar's authenticity.[35]

If as claimed, Abgar's people converted to Christianity between A.D. 30 and 50 (the usually accepted year of his death) the Armenians would have preceded the Apostolic Roman church by decades.

This was a notion adopted by the great medieval Armenian historian, Moses of Khoren. His "popular *History of Armenia* helped publicize the Abgar legend and constitutes an early version of the story in oriental Christianity." To him the legend "served the dual purpose of proving the apostolic origin of their national church and of heightening the pride of Armenian Christians."[36]

Nina Garsoian suggests that the prevailing modern belief is that "the account of St. Thaddeus's missionary activity in Armenia...and the legendary Christianization of Edessa has long been demonstrated to be apocryphal."[37] She readily admits however, "the early appearance of Christianity coming to Armenia from Palestine by way of Syria and Mesopotamia is equally beyond doubt.

The second century African church father Tertullian already listed the Armenians among the people who had received Christianity, and the mid-third-century letter of Bishop Dionysios of Alexandria to an Armenian bishop named Meruzanes indicates a sizable community."[38] (The existence of such an early Christian congregation might also lend some credence to Wilson's provocative Shroud chronology).

Despite the circumstantial case for a first century Armenian Church, virtually all agree that the Armenians were either converted, or restored to Christianity by St. Gregory the Illuminator, considered to be the "Apostle of Armenia," in the early fourth century A.D.[39]

The conversion of the pagan Armenian King Trdat (Tiridates) was told by a mysterious contemporary writer known only as Agathangelos. R. W. Thomson suggests that the author's name is fictitious since it "only too appropriately means 'bearer of good news'."[40]

The work is filled with myths and obvious falsehoods (the impenitent King suffers from lycanthropy and languishes in the form of a wild boar "for sixty-six days of instruction," prior to his acceptance of the faith).[41]

It is important nonetheless in that it suggests that the Armenians as a nation adopted Christianity in the years immediately prior to Constantine's conversion of the entire Roman Empire[42]

This would once again permit the Armenians to lay claim to being the oldest Christian nation, even without needing recourse to King Abgar.[43]

DEFENDERS OF THE TRUE FAITH

Just as important to the Armenians as was the claim of their priority of national conversion, was also their claim to doctrinal purity. Sebeos was another "shadowy" Armenian historian[44] who wrote in the mid-seventh century, and about who little is also known. His *Armenian History* has as its featured component, a lengthy letter that was ascribed to Nerses, the Armenian Catholicos. In it Nerses strongly reaffirms the Nicene Creed to the Emperor "in order to inform in writing your pious majesty, the definition of the orthodox faith which our fathers received from the very first."[45]

As R. W. Thomson suggests, "the basic argument of this letter is that the Armenians have preserved the true faith, of which the Nicene Creed is the touchstone. [In addition,] according to this letter, the Armenians had learned the true faith from St.Gregory 'almost thirty years' before it was confirmed at the council of Nicaea and reconfirmed on the occasion of King Trdat and St. Gregory meeting the Emperor Constantine in Rome... [as] is enshrined in the History of Agathangelos."[46]

A constant visual reminder to the Armenians of their religious faith and national identity could be found in the ubiquitous array of Christian churches that had been erected throughout the land. "Armenian tradition states that the first Christian church in the world was built in Armenia."[47] In his 17th century *Chronicle*, Deacon Zak'aria of K'anak'er stated that "the first church was built by Thaddeus" after the conversion of King Abgar.

He further recounted that during the fourth century, "many churches were constructed by the efforts of St. Gregory the Illuminator and the brave Trdat...First among them was the great cathedral in the city of Vagharshapat, holy Ejmiatsin...as is recorded by the knowledgeable secretary Agathangelos"[48] (John Douglas suggests that for Armenians today Ejmiatsin is "the planet's most venerable and sacred spot").[49]

Basilicas dating to the fourth century have been excavated at numerous sites including recent finds at Ejmiatsin, confirming the historian's account. In addition, many of the distinctive "cruciform" and "quatrefoil" churches from the time of Nerses still stand since their original construction in the seventh century.[50]

Possibly the most elaborate church was constructed by Catholicos Nerses at Zvart'nots, around the year 650. Sebeos contended that it was erected on the site where King Trdat went to meet Saint Gregory and was dedicated by Nerses "to the angels of Heaven."[51]

Today the Turkish landscape that was once Ancient Armenia is replete with abandoned church buildings that testify to Christianity's hold long before the coming of Islam. Their present emptiness is also a solemn reminder of the 20th century Diaspora of the Armenian people.

The Armenians held together as a society despite being overrun and occupied by a succession of conquerors that progressed from the Romans, to the Byzantines, Persians, Mongols, Seljuks, and finally culminated with the Ottoman Turks. Their physical geographic position placed them in the perilous path of powerful invaders, marauding back and forth between Asia and Europe.

Through it all the Armenians persevered and stubbornly held on to their strong Christian identification, even when their land was later physically "divided among Persians, Arabs, Turks, and Russians."[52]

It was their fervent religious faith that I believe, enabled the Armenians to survive more than fifteen centuries of persecution and oppression.

To this observer it is difficult to deny the long-standing Armenian presence in eastern Anatolia, and their legitimate claim to continued residency. After all as Suny suggests, the Armenians had lived there, "for nearly a thousand years before the Turks had arrived."[53]

LIONS OR LAMBS?

The reason most often given for the forced removal of the Armenians was the Turkish fear of a general uprising and a subsequent declaration for an independent nation. The evidence does not seem to support the Turkish contention, however. Although there was certainly the existence of an Armenian revolutionary movement in 1915, it was a relatively minor threat due to the fact that most of the population was apathetic to its cause.

In addition, a large majority of the able-bodied Armenian manpower had already been conscripted into the Turkish army and was simply unavailable to provoke any rear-guard hostilities. The simple truth is that by the twentieth century, after generations of oppression, the Armenians were a fairly docile and patiently long-suffering group.

As a people, the Armenians were historically regarded as peaceful, and cooperative. They do not have a strong warrior tradition, and for the most part the Armenians remained relatively passive and subservient. William Langer somewhat caustically suggested that no matter what the provocation "for the most part the Armenians did not try to fight back." He further reported that "one traveler after another was impressed with their cowardice and servility."[54]

One such observer, Henry C. Barkley recounted an 1891 conversation in which an Armenian remarked: "We are not like Bulgars and other Christians. When the Turk robs us, we see nothing; when he thrashes us, we say nothing; and so we have peace."[55] Such an image of docile passivity strongly conflicts with later Turkish assertions of an impending Armenian militant uprising.

Alexander the Great once said, "I do not fear an army of lions if they are led by a lamb, but I fear an army of lambs if led by a lion!" In Armenia, the long tradition under Turkish rule was one of passive obedience. During the First World War there was no charismatic leader that ever emerged to lead the army of lambs to revolt. The ancient Macedonian conqueror would have found no threat from the Ottoman Armenian population of 1915. Neither did the Turks.

As will be discussed more thoroughly in the next chapter, the available evidence does not lend itself well to the notion of Armenian militancy being a serious threat to the internal security of the Ottoman Empire.

Even more importantly, it defies any rational defense of the subsequent mass Turkish reprisals against the civilian population.

GENOCIDE REVISITED

Ironically, the holocaust of 1915 was not the Armenians first bitter taste of genocide. The Mongols had ruthlessly introduced them to the heinous concept six centuries earlier. As George Bournoutian asserts, "Tamerlane's invasion at the end of the fourteenth century...had a devastating effect on the population of historic Armenia."[56]

Unprecedented for its wanton cruelty, Tamerlane's irresistible foray engulfed an expanse from India to Anatolia and prompted the Dupuy's to later lament that "no more senseless, bloody, or devastating campaign has ever been fought."[57]

It was to be the world's last true genocide until reappearing in the fifteenth year of the twentieth century, when the Apocalyptic "Pale Horseman"[58] would once again ride into Armenia.

10

MANDATE FOR MAYHEM: THE
ARMENIAN GENOCIDE OF 1915

A s STATED AT the outset, the purpose of this manuscript is to attempt a determination of the motives for the Armenian Holocaust of 1915, and to search for answers within the political, moral, religious, cultural, and military climate of the times. It is my contention that at least ten separate but interrelated motives corporately precipitated the holocaust.

We will now briefly examine a sampling of the contemporary evidence and eyewitness reports in order to test those assertions, and to better ascertain what actually occurred on the plains of Eastern Anatolia exactly a century ago.

"ALL THE NEWS THAT'S FIT TO PRINT"

Peter Balakian reports that in 1915 alone, *The New York Times* published 145 articles on the Armenian Genocide.[1] An examination of contemporary daily editions of *The London Times* reveals no less an abundance of coverage. What is immediately clear, to even the most casual observer, is the vehement and ubiquitous condemnation that virtually saturates the pages of the western newspapers.

In fairness to the Turks, it is understandable that British editorial and public opinion would have been severely biased in 1915. Great Britain and Ottoman Turkey were mortal enemies desperately embroiled in an already horrifying world war. As we have previously discussed, the British public had been decidedly anti-Turk for many decades dating back to the regime of the "Red Sultan" Abdul Hamid II.

The United States was still a neutral nation, however, and possibly less apt to be prejudiced in its news reporting. If anything, the United States and Turkey enjoyed relatively good relations prior to America's entry into the war. After all, the Americans had never sought to acquire Turkish territory, nor did they openly support those European powers that did.

Indeed the United States had not crossed swords with the sultan's subjects since winning the brief naval action against the Barbary Pirates in 1803. If anything, the American public of 1915 was relatively well-disposed to the Ottoman Empire and saw it as a humanitarian and Christian "mission field."

It should also be noted that the plethora of eyewitness accounts being wired by American diplomats and missionaries stationed in Turkey were sent by those who actually possessed a strong desire to maintain friendly Turkish relations.

In order to gauge the depth of the catastrophe that beset the Armenian population and to help determine the motives for the events of 1915, an examination of such primary sources would be beneficial. Although the published literature is replete with the sordid and grisly details of the genocide, my purpose is to demonstrate examples that will corroborate the underlying causes.

RECIPROCAL CRIES OF "SELF-DEFENSE"

As previously indicated, the reason most given by the Turkish government for the precipitation of the actions taken was an expressed fear that the Armenian communities would rise in rebellion and aid the Russian advance. Yet, as Alan Moorehead contends, "there were grounds for the Turkish belief that the Armenians were a fifth column inside the country, and that, no less than the Greeks, they had gloated over every Turkish loss in the Balkan Wars."[2]

Turkish historian Esat Uras contends that the Tsarist government was arming the Armenians "with guns and explosives and supplying them with revolutionary programs and declarations... [and that] the militants were also given the task of inciting the Armenians to massacre the Turks and the Kurds."[3]

It is true that upwards of 200,000 Armenians volunteered to fight in the Tsar's Army, but that group consisted overwhelmingly of men who were Russian citizens prior to the war.[4] The Armenians also admit that 20,000 "volunteers" fought on the Caucasian front.[5] That is a very small percentage, however, of the available Armenian military-age population in the Ottoman Empire. (With a pre-war census in excess of 1.5 million, easily one fourth would have been of the required age).

The Turkish suspicion that their Armenian subjects would revolt was seemingly confirmed by an incident that commenced on April 20, 1915. After Enver's disastrous winter campaign in the Caucasus, and the other Turkish military setbacks of early 1915; the Ottoman high command expressed grave concern about reports of an Armenian uprising in the area of Lake Van. A hostile Armenian force placed directly behind the beleaguered Turkish army that was already facing the oncoming Russians, might prove to be disastrous and could not be ignored.

To Aram Terzian this government concern was merely a pretext to finally solve the Armenian question. Pointing to the disastrous Ottoman military campaign as the catalyst, he suggests that "the disappointment and violent passions caused by these failures inevitably led the Turkish leaders who had been responsible for the wild gamble to seek scapegoats. It is here that the unfortunate Armenians were shrewdly brought into the picture."[6]

THE DEFENSE/REVOLT AT VAN

Perhaps the most controversial action that preceded the wholesale deportation of the Armenian population in the spring of 1915 was the armed struggle at the city of Van.

Calling it a *revolt*, Turkish sources consider the uprising of Armenian revolutionaries in the *Van Vilayet* to be evidence of an impending fifth column, and use it as justification for the harsh but necessary government response that followed.

Armenian apologists counter that the *defense* of Van was in desperate response to the already existing Turkish order to persecute the Christian minorities and was therefore a matter of survival. The truth is likely found somewhere in between.

With the advance of the Russian army in the spring of 1915, a large number of Armenians welcomed them as liberators from decades of harsh Muslim, Turkish oppression. Some took up arms in revolt and others fled to enlist in the Tsar's forces. Many Armenians remained either passive, or in the case of some 50,000 were recruited into the Turkish army as unarmed labor-battalions.

It was recorded that Russian Tsar Nicholas II exhorted the Armenians to join him in the struggle against the Ottoman Empire. During a visit to the Caucasus Front late in 1914, he reportedly declared before God and the head of the Armenian Church, "Armenians from all countries are hurrying to enter the ranks of the glorious Russian Army, and with their blood, to serve the victory of Russian arms... Let the Russian flag wave freely over the Dardanelles and the Bosporus. Let...the peoples remaining under the Turkish yoke receive freedom. Let the Armenian people of Turkey, who have suffered for the faith of Christ received [sic] resurrection for a new and free life under the protection of Russia."[7]

Stanford Shaw contended that as a result the Armenians "flooded" into the Russian army forcing Enver Pasha to conclude that it would be, "impossible to determine which of the Armenians would remain loyal."[8]

In February, 1915, concerned with what they suspected as "increased dissident Armenian activity," the Turkish General Staff issued "Directive 8682," titled *Increased Security Precautions*. It was sent to the headquarters of the Ottoman Third Army with orders to increase security measures, and to remove any ethnic Armenian soldiers from critical command centers.[9] It is clear that the Turks believed that a danger existed, and that they planned to act accordingly.

The deportation order came very soon after.

Van had previously experienced violent depredations during the Hamidian Massacres of 1896, in which some 20,000 Armenians perished. In subsequent years, it had become a hub of revolutionary activity with both Hunchak and Dashnak contingents operating within the city. For years the local populace had remained peaceful but alert, all the while amassing a small store of weapons and ammunition for home defense.

Now less than twenty years following the persecutions that were formerly perpetrated on the orders of the Red Sultan, a brutal new Turkish overlord was about to descend on the Armenians of Van.

In spring, 1915, the Ottoman governor of the Van Vilayet, Cedvet Pasha began a crack-down on suspected dissidents in accordance with the instructions from Constantinople. He was the brother-in law of Enver Pasha, who undoubtedly knew and approved of his subsequent actions. Notoriously antagonistic to the Armenians, Cedvet was described as, "a man of dangerously unpredictable moods, friendly one moment, ferociously hostile the next, capable of treacherous brutality."[10] He would affirm his reputation.

It appears from eyewitnesses that Cedvet planned to launch a violent persecution of the local Christian populace. American missionaries living in Van later observed that the governor was already preparing for a major assault against the Armenian population of the Van Vilayet, prior to the rising in the city.

Grace Knapp confided that Cedvet, "planned a massacre of his Armenian subjects," whereas Elizabeth Ussher concurred writing in her diary on the day that the fighting began, "Although the Vali

[Cedvet] calls it a rebellion, it is really an effort to protect the lives and homes of the Armenians."[11]

On April 20, Rebel forces, claiming the need for self-defense, and a necessary response to the ongoing Turkish depredations already launched against the civilian inhabitants, did indeed take the City of Van and tenaciously held it against huge odds. In their massive *Encyclopedia of Military History*, Ernest and Trevor Dupuy succinctly indicated that, "Turkish massacres of Armenians, on suspicion they were aiding the Russians, precipitated an Armenian revolt."[12]

The New York Times reported on May 6, that the Armenian Bishop of Tabriz had "described the situation at Van as desperate. The Armenians have been standing off the Turks and Kurds for a week. Four Turkish regiments with artillery are advancing against these Armenians. They are also threatened by gendarmes from the Persian border."[13]

The small Armenian militia, estimated at no more than 1,300 men, fought for a month against Ottoman forces many times their number.[14] Despite the overwhelming Turkish pressure that was thrown against them, the Armenians held the fortress of Van until the arrival of a Russian relief force on May 19.[15]

At least one Armenian observer who served with the Russian forces suggested during the war, that the defense of Van may have been instrumental in thwarting the Turkish offensive into Persia as it tied down needed troops that if available might have provided an Ottoman margin of victory.[16]

The question remains, however, as to the real threat posed by the Armenians, and whether the Turks were justified in taking the subsequent steps to deport the population.

ACTS OF DESPERATION

The comparison might be made between the Armenian revolt at Van and the Jewish uprising in the Warsaw Ghetto during the Second World War.

Beginning in early 1940, the Nazis forced conquered Poland's population of some 3,000,000 Jews into terribly crowded sections of various Polish cities. The largest ghetto was in Warsaw and nearly 400,000 were crammed into a squalid sector barely three miles square. It soon became the staging area for mass deportations, presumably to slave labor camps.

By the beginning of 1943, however, those who remained in the Warsaw Ghetto finally learned that the nearly 300,000, who had previously departed, were actually sent to be exterminated in the death camp at Treblinka.

In the spring of 1943, the Jewish population that remained in the Ghetto, approximately 70,000 men, women, and children, decided to fight. On the Eve of Passover, German SS units entered the section and began a month-long operation to pacify the occupants. By the end of the rising, 13,000 Jews had been killed and another 50,000 were rounded up and transported to the death camp. Less than two dozen Nazis were reportedly killed in the futile but valiant effort. Although they failed to inflict even the slightest damage to their oppressors, the Polish Jews preferred to resist rather than submit meekly to equally certain death.

There are similarities between the Armenian and Jewish uprisings. In both cases, the desperate civilian population was threatened with imminent deportation, and even suspected extermination. Similarly, both risings were conducted against well-equipped, regular military units by poorly-supplied militia using an array of captured and makeshift weapons.

Finally, in each case, it was to be virtually the sole armed insurrection offered by either the Jews or Armenians during the entire length of the respective world wars.

Eyewitnesses tend to suggest that the Turks were already taking measures to suppress the Armenians long before the actual outbreak at Van. No less un-sympathetic an observer than Baron von Wangenheim, the German Ambassador to Turkey already warned the previous January that, "in the event of the Allied fleet's forcing the Straits, the Turks will vent their wrath by a massacre of the Christian population."[17]

In February, *The New York Times* article posted under the heading <u>Predict a Massacre</u> reported, "American missionaries...said that the fall of the Dardanelles would probably mean a massacre of Jews and Gentiles in the Holy Land."[18] In September 1914, Mary L. Graffam, an American evangelist in Turkey, was visited by a German army colonel who likewise warned her about a probable persecution, "...which might take place next summer... [as] a certain fate was in store for all Armenians." She later cited this as evidence that "the deportations were planned" long in advance.[19]

The Turkish "contention that the Armenians took up arms and joined the Russians, as soon as the latter crossed the Ottoman frontier," was quickly disputed by Arnold Toynbee. He noted that "the standard case sited is the 'Revolt at Van,'" which the eminent historian later dismissed altogether. He suggested rather that "the Armenians merely defended the quarter of the city in which they lived, after it had been besieged and attacked by Turkish troops."[20]

As proof of Turkish precipitation he pointed to the fact that "the deportations had already begun in Cilicia before the fighting at Van broke out." Invariably, Toynbee suggested that similar Armenian resistance at Zeitoun, Bitlis, and Sassun were also in self-defense against Turkish or Kurdish reprisals.[21]

Even Vice-Marshal Pomiankowski of Austria, who throughout the war was attached to the Turkish General Headquarters, asserted that the uprising at Van was an act of Armenian "desperation" (*Verzweiflung*) to avert a general slaughter.[22]

The claims and counter-claims as to what actually precipitated the defense of Van may never be fully proven, but it certain that there was shared responsibility on both sides. As both Dyer, and Lewy assert, it is "probable that Cedvet Pasha must bear most of the blame [but it is] by no means entirely certain that some Armenians in Van did not have plans for a rising."[23]

The truth is that with the long violent history of ethnic cleansing in the region, and the threatening actions of the Turkish governor; the Armenians were facing likely destruction long before any shots were ever fired at Van.

Of perhaps greater salience, however, was the simple fact that much of the Armenian population had been virtually stripped of its available able-bodied manpower prior to the reputed revolt.

ARMY OF THE DAMNED

In the months prior to the rising at Van, the Turks ordered the drafting of a huge segment of the Armenian male population into the Ottoman Army. Historically Christians were exempt from service in the Turkish military but that had changed. "Soon after the Young Turk revolution, the Armenians, now treated as equal citizens, became subject to conscription like other Turks."[24] Now, the draftees were permitted into the army but in comparison with ethnic Turks, they were treated anything but "equal."

Armenian resident Khacher Matosian described a government order that his village received in the summer of 1914 commanding them that "Turks from 20 to 25 years of age, and Christians from 20 to 45 years of age will become soldiers." He then described the villagers' understandable dismay and recalled hearing them ask about the Turks' maximum recruitment age being twenty years less than that for the Armenians. They rightfully exclaimed "Why this discrimination!"[25]

The reason for the disparity in the conscription age soon became answered by the total segregation of the Armenians into "labor battalions."[26]

German General Bronsart, the Turkish Chief of Staff, ordered that Armenians be placed "in the Labor battalions" for security reasons.[27]

Numerous eyewitnesses reported that the Armenians were forced into veritable slave labor. They were totally disarmed and according to a February, 1915 directive from the Ottoman High Command, were not to be employed in any military unit, including the gendarmerie."[28]

Even more disconcerting, there were numerous reports of the Armenian soldier-laborers being summarily executed in large numbers. In one example, western missionaries in Urfa reported the massacre of 600 men carried out by members of the Ottoman gendarmes.[29]

One Venezuelan officer, who had volunteered to serve in the Turkish Army, reported that he personally observed "thirteen or fifteen hundred unarmed Armenian soldiers, breaking stone and mending road" who had all subsequently become the victims of "a massacre."[30]

It appears in retrospect, that the Turks deliberately drafted a large portion of the military age population, in order to effectively neutralize the Armenians, as well as to provide forced labor. French historians, Chaliand and Ternon contend that "these soldiers were discretely eliminated, [and] shot in batches of 50 to 100."[31]

Dr. Tacy Atkinson, an American missionary at Harpoot, witnessed the herding of a number of defenseless Armenian soldiers who were "shut in a large building" and killed.[32] That a nation's own "soldiers" were rendered unarmed, segregated, forced into slave labor and subsequently massacred is without precedent in any modern army.

The effective elimination of the flower of Armenian manhood would place the remainder of the Armenian population at enormous risk and vulnerability. It also disputes Turkish claims of a massive revolutionary threat since virtually "every potential rebel force was wiped out before it could even be organized."[33]

Even at Van, the available Armenian manpower was extremely limited. Dadrian stated that the total number of Armenians who joined in the defense of the city amounted to no more than 600 fighters.[34] Walker estimated the Armenian militia to be a little more than twice that number.[35] In either event, this small but determined force repulsed no fewer than "twelve veteran battalions that comprised the Van Gendarmes Division."[36]

Nonetheless, even that Armenian victory would have been impossible without the arrival of Russian troops to finally drive the Turks into full retreat. The simple truth is that the Turks had ensured that there was not enough available Armenian manpower to mount a full-scale revolt, even if the population had been so disposed.

Successful in depleting the manpower pool, the Turks next sought to neutralize another important segment of the Armenian citizenry.

POETIC PURGE

The Armenian uprising at Van was immediately followed by systematic government reprisals against the Armenian intelligentsia. On April 24, within just four days of the Van uprising, "two hundred Armenian writers, poets, newspaper editors, teachers, lawyers, members of parliament, and other community leaders in Constantinople were taken out from their homes at night and later killed...By the end of the year, some 600 Armenian intellectuals, and a few thousand workers had also been arrested and deported into the interior."[37]

As Ternon and Chaliand suggest, the pretext was rebellion, but they are convinced that the arrests were "conceived like a strategic operation, aimed at disarming, then splitting, and scattering the enemy."[38]

Once again, the apparently systematic and efficient campaign to suppress the Armenians strongly indicates a planned and premeditated program by the Young Turk leadership. As *The New York Times* so alarmingly noted, "it is declared in Armenia that the Young Turks have adopted the policy of Abdul Hamid in 1905, namely the annihilation of the Armenians."[39]

The notion that the Turks were concerned with preventing Armenian revolutionaries from creating a "fifth Column" in eastern Anatolia is understandable on the surface. A similar argument would later prompt the United States Government's internment of Japanese-Americans living on the West Coast, in the days following Pearl Harbor.

Upon closer scrutiny, however, the evidence strongly indicates that whatever resistance the Armenians could offer was minimal due to the prior depletion of their manpower through the already ordered Turkish military conscription. It also appears that the rising at Van was conducted subsequent to the earlier initiation of depredations against the Armenians, and then used as an excuse for further Turkish actions.

That this was the early conclusion of the American press is illustrated by *The New York Times* editorial of September 17, 1915. It read in part, "Apparently the uprising of Armenian revolutionists at Van, which paved the way for Russian occupation of that city without resistance, has been seized by the Turks as a pretext for a general attack upon Armenians everywhere."[40]

The fact remains that the Russians did indeed threaten Eastern Anatolia to the general approval, if not the full armed support of the Armenians. It has been the Turkish argument for justifying their actions ever since. What immediately followed was the Ottoman government's order to deport the entire Armenian population.

It has been suggested that another serious situation also directly contributed to the final decisions made by the Turkish leadership.

THE GALLIPOLI FACTOR

After threatening for weeks to force the Dardanelles and attack Constantinople, a combined British, French and ANZAC amphibious assault landed at the Gallipoli peninsula exactly five days after the start of the Van uprising, and only one day following the purge of Armenian intelligentsia in Constantinople. One must wonder at the timing.

It has been suggested that the Turks were preparing for the expected allied onslaught by using the time to secure their rear. The combined British and French fleets initially began bombardment of the defenses at the entrance to the Dardanelles in mid-February.

Finally, on March 18, in a desperate attempt to run the Straits, the allied naval attack had been completely thwarted by the Turkish fortifications, with severe damage being inflicted upon two British Dreadnoughts and a number of smaller ships. To the Turks who were in dire need of a boost in morale, the repulse was deemed a great victory.

Now the long-awaited infantry landing had finally begun on April 25. During the interim it has been argued that the Ottoman government deliberately attempted to neutralize its Armenian population.[41]

Alan Moorehead proposed the intriguing notion that the Turkish military was virtually transformed on the night of March 18. After repeatedly suffering terrible defeats, the Ottoman Army had long been at a very low-point. But now all that changed.

"The British battle-fleet was the strongest armament in existence, its very name had been enough to strike terror among its enemies in every ocean, and no one had given the Turks the ghost of a chance against it. Yet by some miracle they had driven it away. Constantinople had been saved at the last moment. The Turk could hold up his head again."[42]

Flushed with success, the Turks went from months of being previously humiliated to finding a new exhilarating sense of pride. "Now at last the Turkish soldier was something in the world again."[43] According to Moorehead, what happened next was disastrous for the Armenians.

Enver and Talaat took credit for the apparent victory after coming close to completely losing their public confidence. Now they were again riding a crest of popularity, xenophobia and patriotic pride. In addition they had a pent-up hunger for revenge against the foreigners who had patronized and dominated them for so long.

In their elation, Moorehead suggested that Enver Pasha, and Talaat Pasha, "did a thing which was nothing new in the east...they set about hunting down their racial and political opponents. They were now strong enough to express their hatred and they wanted victims."[44]

The Turkish leadership, in fulfillment of their Pan-Turanist, and Pan-Islamic aspirations now focused ever more closely on the one people that presented the most likely target. All the generations of conflicting social and religious forces were coming to a head.

It was the age-old struggle of Muslim against Christian; poor against affluent; and the Turkic race against Armenian. Not only were they Christian infidels who had long treated their Turkish overlords with quiet condescension; the Armenians were now supporting the advance of the Russian enemy in the east.

The terrible fighting at Gallipoli had just begun, but for the Armenians, the die was already cast. Rolf Hosfeld contends that once the allied amphibious assault began, the Turks felt compelled to move against the Christian minorities. "The systematic persecution began on April 24, as the Allies began their landing action on the Gallipoli peninsula. The decision that they must evacuate the imperiled capital and reorganize the fight from Anatolia made the ruling Young Turk cadres view the Armenians living there as dangerous enemies who had to be brought under control."[45]

For the next nine months the Turkish and allied forces on Gallipoli would fight and die in huge numbers without much discernable change in position. In a spirited defense led by German General Liman Sanders, which included the brilliant tactical leadership of a front-line Division commander by the name of Mustafa Kemal; the allies were kept to a bloody standstill.

Finally, after the loss of a quarter million men dead on each side, the allies withdrew in early January, 1916. Although, the Turks had also suffered grievously, they were buoyed-up by the victory. The continued Turkish occupation of the Straits would have serious consequences for the isolated Russians who would be knocked out of the war two years later. The allied defeat also ensured the doom of the Armenians. Reprieved from the danger to their capital, the vengeful

Turks were further emboldened in their feelings of harsh retribution over their Christian subjects, who for the past year were being deported in the east.

During the same nine months that the Anzacs and Turks had brutally faced each other in the Dardanelles, the Armenian people of Eastern Anatolia had begun to disappear.

TURKISH "REVELATION"

In one of the more revealing passages, that has yet been written in the decades since the Armenian Holocaust; the Assembly of Turkish American Associations, in a 1987 publication gave their reason for the deportations of 1915. The report was written with the apparent approval of the current Turkish Government, as the *Preface* was penned by the Turkish Ambassador to the United States.

It contended that "the Armenian betrayal of the Ottoman State in time of war led the then-ruling government to relocate the Armenian population from the path of the invading Russian armies they were actively supporting." The Ambassador then continued with the startling revelation that "this relocation also stemmed from the necessity to forestall further bloodshed resulting from the rapidly escalating fighting between Armenian and Moslem civilian populations."[46]

Despite the lack of any Turkish admission of impropriety and subsequent blame of the Armenians, the important fact is that there is no denial that a government order was given for the "relocation." Talaat, Enver and Djemal repeatedly denied that government directives had precipitated the massacres yet it is now agreed by even the Turks themselves that the deportations were ordered by Constantinople.

As early as 1919, the new post-war Turkish Government published a report with the admission that "the forcible transplantation of an entire people at short notice is a cruel measure."[47] Even Djemal confessed in his memoirs that his "friends" (apparently Talaat and Enver) "held it more expedient to transfer the whole Armenian nation to another region where they could do no harm."[48]

Edward Alexander cites an official government order, signed on April 24, 1915, by three members of the committee: Talaat, Enver, and [executive secretary] Nazim," that ordered the deportations.[49] What must be clear, however, is that the Turkish Government, by virtue of their order of deportation,[50] pronounced a death sentence on the Armenians. Djemal admits that "600,000 of them died." How ludicrous then to insist that "this relocation...stemmed from the necessity to forestall further bloodshed."

Could the Armenians have fared any worse?

ARMENIAN DUPLICITY?

The deportations were preceded by government orders transmitted to officials in the vilayets, such as the one distributed in the village of Chomaklou in July 1915. At the beginning of the decree was the terse instruction that "All Armenians inhabiting the district of Caesaria will be deported to the state of Aleppo."[51]

Quite often the official Turkish pronouncements were accompanied by complaints of Armenian duplicity. Khacher Matosian recalled how the deportation in his village was blamed on Armenian revolutionary activity in nearby Evereg where a man was killed when a bomb he was making accidentally exploded. To Matosian, "the Turk Government was looking for just such an occurrence as an excuse for carrying out its program."[52]

In Caesaria, a missionary estimated 1,000 men were imprisoned "and subjected to torture in order to force them to confess that they had arms concealed."[53] Mrs. Harriet Atkinson, another American missionary stationed at Harpoot, was informed by a Turkish policeman that the "trouble" had all been precipitated by Armenian revolutionary activity in Van and elsewhere. She stated that "he told me of outrages which had been committed by the Armenians on the Turkish people. Whether true or not he evidently believed them."[54]

That the Turks truly believed in an Armenian threat to the security of the empire is clearly indicated from the record. It is also fair to suggest that such a danger was not entirely unfounded, as the existence of 20,000 revolutionaries would testify. The issue that defies any logical acceptance, however, is the Turkish response to the perceived Armenian "threat." The literature of the Armenian genocide is replete with grisly stories of heinous atrocities, and it is not within the scope of this paper to furnish an exhaustive recapitulation. It is imperative, however, to examine a cross-section of eyewitness reports in order to persuade the reader of the justice of the claims of "genocide," and also determine the underlying motives.

TAMERLANE'S REPRISE

The Western press was cognizant that something was happening in Anatolia for which modern society had not yet been prepared. For the first time since the murderous days of Tamerlane, wholesale civilian populations were reportedly being exterminated. Sir Mark Sykes, a contemporary British observer, clearly saw a Turkish reversion to the times of the Golden Horde, arguing that "the Turk, who in the last ten years had thrown back to the primitive Turanian Conqueror, was not content with dominating, but was now engaged in exterminating the Armenian."[55]

Although atrocities against Christians were hinted at as early as January,[56] it was not until July 1915, that British and American newspapers began reporting on wholesale deportations. Even to a reader in the 21st century, hardened by more than nine decades of unparalleled inhumanity, the atrocities of 1915 are not easy to digest. One can only imagine the shock to a post-Victorian society first confronted with such unprecedented horrors.

In a special cable to *The New York Times* from *The London Morning Post* dated July 11, the terrible story began to unfold. The report read in part, "that the Christians in the Ottoman Empire have never been in such stress and peril since the Turk first invaded the Byzantine Empire. Both Armenians and Greeks, the two native Christian races in Turkey, are being systematically uprooted from their homes en masse and driven forth summarily to distant provinces, where they are scattered in small groups among Turkish villages and given the choice between immediate acceptance of Islam or death by the sword or starvation."[57]

During the following summer weeks numerous articles were written on both sides of the Atlantic denouncing Turkish atrocities and lamenting the fate of the Armenians. In one front page story it was reported that the Turks, "after massacring all the males of the population in the Region of Bitlis, Turkish Armenia, assembled 9000 women and children and drove them to the banks of the Tigris, where they shot them and then threw the bodies into the river." The paper further estimated that "more than 40,000 people already are dead."[58] As subsequent events progressed, the images became ever more sickening.

HINTS OF HOLOCAUST

A *Reuters* dispatch eerily presaged the 1942 Nazi atrocities at Lidice. "In one village 1,000 men, women, and children are reported to have been locked in a wooden building and burned to death." Witnesses further reported that in another instance "several scores of men and women were tied together by chains and thrown into Lake Van."[59] One cablegram noted that "at Vardis, 2000 of all ages and both sexes were shut in a convent and burned to death."[60]

In perhaps the most remarkable prelude to the Jewish Holocaust, *The New York Times* presciently reported that "Armenians are being shipped to *concentration camps* at various points, being driven afoot or forwarded in *box cars*."[61] (Italics are the author's).

The Hejaz Railroad, constructed with the help of German engineering, was now being put to a similar use as that their countrymen would later employ in the transportation of Jews to the death camps.

With images so sadly reprised in the 1940's, eyewitness Dr. William Dodd described the plight of the Armenian railroad "passengers." He hauntingly recalled that "the refugees were packed into cars—baggage-cars, cattle-cars—packed...as thick as it was possible to crowd them on the floor...As they passed the station I saw them crying out for water piteously stretching out their hands through the bars asking for mercy."[62]

Other American witnesses (to somberly paraphrase Charles Dickens) described similarly *ghastly* visions of "Ottoman Present," and "Nazism Yet-to-Come." One eye-witness mourned his glimpse of the deportation trains reporting that, "we could see old men and old women, young mothers with small babies, men, women, and children, all herded like cattle."[63]

In a cold-blooded manner that even Hitler's minions would later fail to copy; Dr. Dodd incredulously explained that the Armenians were packed into the concentration camp bound cattle-cars, "*after having been compelled to pay their railway fare.*"[64]

In a strangely fitting irony, it was the German constructed "Berlin to Baghdad" railway that would be the Armenians' conveyance to hell.

OUT-DOING THE RED SULTAN

It was now becoming alarmingly apparent that the Ottoman Government was either in the process of willfully exterminating its Armenian population, or at least permitting them to be massacred by rogue elements within the empire.

To the editorial board of *The London Times* there was little doubt, however, as to who was ultimately responsible. Under the heading, "The Armenian Massacres: Exterminating a Race," the article decried "to one who remembers the rejoicings which welcomed the

Bloodless Turkish Revolution of 1908, the fraternization of Moslem and Christian, the confidence in a better future for the Armenians which survived even the Adana massacre of 1909, the story of the systematic persecution of the Armenians of Turkey is a bitter tale to tell. Talaat Bey and his extremist allies have out-Hamided Abdul Hamid... attaining an eminence in 'frightfulness' to which the 'Red Sultan' never soared."[65]

For the Young Turk leadership to be less than favorably compared to Abdul Hamid was certainly grim testimony to how far their revolution had veered from the promise expressed in those heady early days of "liberty; fraternity; and equality." Once embraced by the Armenians, the Young Turks were now intent on destroying them. The final descent into depravity had begun.

The great outcry of Western public opinion notwithstanding, it was not until Christian missionaries began to return from eastern Anatolia that the true enormity of the catastrophe became fully revealed. The wealth of eyewitness accounts that have been documented since the commencement of the genocide attest to the ubiquitous scope of the atrocities as well as the monumental scale.

Before addressing the magnitude of the genocide, the next focus of study will be on the barbaric ferocity that was exhibited by the individual perpetrators. In his book, *Becoming Evil*, James Waller suggests that ordinary people are apt to commit extraordinary evil.[66] As true as that statement certainly is; it stuns one's sensibilities when considering the depths of depravity to which man can descend.

What could possibly lead one to commit the types of unthinkable atrocities that were so commonplace in 1915?

CLIMATE OF HATE

In examining the detailed reports of individual acts of persecution, different sets of underlying motives begin to emerge. In many instances the depredations were carried out without actual government knowledge or consent. Simply put, local hatreds often spilled over into outrageous acts of violence. That such a hostile climate for the excesses to be perpetrated was nurtured by decisions in Constantinople should not be discounted, however.

The competing yet interwoven catalysts that promulgated the localized atrocities were the racial, economic and religious competitions that had festered for centuries into anathema and hatred. The Turks and particularly the Kurds harbored deep-felt resentment against the Armenians who often emoted reciprocally. Eyewitnesses attest that such animosity contributed greatly to the merciless depredations. The various tensions emanated from causal relationships that set Moslem against Christian; Asian against European; poor against affluent; man against woman; and master against servant. In each hostile pairing the Turks were represented as the former with the Armenians as the latter.

The call for Moslem Holy War (*Jihad*) provided the foundation for justifying actions against the Christian infidels. It was coupled with Turanian antipathy for European Caucasians upon whom the Turks unleashed the pent-up fury derived from years of Western condescension.

Class warfare also played a role in the persecutions. Viewed often as wealthy elites, the Armenians were systematically robbed of their homes and possessions. The plundering of the villages and caravans were equally within the purview of Kurdish brigands, and unpaid Turkish troops. G. S. Graber further suggests that the Armenians "were generally better educated, more industrious, and more literate than the Turks. It is from such rifts in status and cultural background that great antipathies grow."[67]

Undoubtedly the most heinous of the many crimes committed were perpetrated by men against women. Encompassing the gamut from forced marriage, and white slavery, to brutal gang rape, and murder; Armenian women and young girls were subjected to atrocities of unimaginable depravity and on a monstrous scale. Starvation, disease, and the cumulative miseries of the forced deportation were the least of their tragic sufferings.

In total it cannot be overstated that intolerance, material greed, lust, revenge, and jealous hatred were great determinants in creating the savage rage that was exacted upon the Armenians.

FIRST *JIHAD!*

In my opinion, the most unforgiving form of conflict is religious warfare. Whether wrought by Christian Crusader, Shintoist Samurai, Mahdist "Fuzzy-Wuzzy," or Turkish Jihadist; the concept of Holy War is as old as man's belief in Divine intervention. To fight and perhaps die as a martyr for one's God has implications for the receipt of immeasurable rewards both in this life and the next. The Islamists found *Jihad* to be a logical rallying point for preserving the Ottoman Empire's diverse Muslim constituencies, and to unite the religious faithful against their common "infidel" enemies.

Although the Turks actually failed miserably at convincing their Arab minorities to remain loyal, holy war had a devastating effect on the Armenians. In assessing what he called "the preconditions for genocide," Kevork Suakian cogently suggested that "the religious biases of the superordinate branch had considerably more impact on the aggravation of discontent than the religious orientation of the subordinate. The Muslim Koran provided ready avenues of legitimization of the superordinates' outlooks. Definite categorization of Muslims and non-Muslims was posited in The Book. The non-Muslim was often referred to as *goaour* (infidel). This characterization helped keep the two cultures at odds and at a distance from each other."[68]

At least one historian has traced the actual responsibility for the Muslim Holy War to a Christian monarch. Edward Paice suggests that Germany's Machiavellian Kaiser Wilhelm II was indeed the true instigator of *Jihad*. He had long courted the Ottoman Empire with the intention of one-day using the power of the caliphate to incite Muslim uprisings throughout Africa, Central Asia, and India.

As evidence of the Kaiser's attempts at instigation of a Muslim Holy War, a 1914-15 German-produced Arabic Jihad pamphlet proclaimed, "The killing of the infidels who rule over the Islamic lands has become a sacred duty, whether it be secretly or openly, as the great Koran declares in its word: 'Take them and kill them whenever you come across them.'"[69]

The German goal was to threaten Russia, France and Great Britain from within their own territory and colonial possessions, and to tie down enemy forces that would be needed elsewhere. "Turkey's support was central to Germany's strategy of *Drang nach Osten* ('the Drive to the East'), and as soon as the Ottoman Empire declared its allegiance German agents were sent eastwards to spread the word that the Kaiser had secretly become a Muslim, and to instigate a vigorous propaganda campaign publicising German victories on the Western Front."[70]

One unforeseen yet terrible by-product of the Kaiser's machinations was the destruction of the Armenians. The effect upon the Turks and their Kurdish vassals was electrifying, and prompted the violent release of centuries of pent-up animosity against the Armenian infidels. "Although this horrifying spectacle was not an intended consequence of German policy, it demonstrated emphatically just how powerful a tool the Kaiser's Holy War, aimed at eclipsing British and Russian power in the Middle East, might become."[71] From Dehli to Khartoum, the Germans hoped to fan the flames of religious hatred.

Nowhere was the religious divide more deeply riven than between the Armenians and the Kurds. Dating back as early as 1515, the Sultan Selim appointed a Kurdish governor to oversee the Armenians. "The governor soon brought about the transfer of large groups of nomad Kurds from their strongholds in the south...to the Armenian provinces and offered them free land...[and] exception from taxes on condition that they would act as an organized militia in the area."[72]

Centuries later, Abdul Hamid would also call upon the Kurds in forming his "Hamidye" to persecute the Armenians, and in 1915, the Young Turks did the same.

UNLEASH THE KURDS!

In a diabolically conceived recruiting program, Kurds were released from prisons and assigned to "police" the Armenians. Rev. Frederick MacCallum reported that "I saw hundreds of men in Constantinople dressed in a particular uniform, being drilled, as I supposed for military service. Afterwards they were sent off. On inquiry, I was informed that they were criminals condemned to penal servitude for life, but had been released from the prison...and then sent to take charge of the Armenians who were being deported from various centers in Asia Minor."[73] Mrs. Atkinson likewise reported that, "crowds of armed Kurds were seen moving about, who had a short time before been released from prison."[74] Another American missionary pastor dourly provided the additional detail that "the Koords did not assist the government in the deportation, but only in killing, the taking of captives, and booty."[75]

In some cases Turks and Kurds inhabited the abandoned homes of the deported Armenians. The President of Anatolia College, Dr. George White, wrote that "all the properties of the Armenians were confiscated...[The] Turks moved out of their more squalid habitations into the better Armenian houses whose owners had been 'deported'."[76]

Other Turks and Kurds were themselves displaced refugees from far-off battlefields who as Talaat had earlier predicted "found resting places in the villages which the Armenians had vacated."[77]

In Constantinople, Rev. Arthur Ryan noted that "laws were passed to make legal the confiscation of all the property of the deported people." He also witnessed how "the inmates of an old ladies home, under the auspices of some foreign ladies, were turned out one day and the building confiscated."[78]

EXTREME AND UNSPEAKABLE HORRORS

The Armenians were also systematically despoiled of their valuable possessions. At times the Turks and Kurds went to extreme ends to loot their victims. Kerop Bedoukian recalled how as a young boy he witnessed Turks searching through human excrement in order to find gold that had been secretly swallowed by Armenians.[79]

Even more appalling was the report of American diplomat, Leslie Davis. He testified that, "some of the bodies that we saw had been burned. I thought at first this had been done as a sanitary measure, although the Kurds seldom think of such things, but was told that they had burned these bodies in order to find any gold which the people may have swallowed. I subsequently saw many others that have been burned for the same object and learned that deported Armenians frequently swallowed their gold in their attempt to save it when they were attacked."[80]

Perhaps the most horrifying experience befell a woman who was deported from Ordoo. She explained to an American "the ways in which women tried to hide their money---in the bottom of water jugs, by swallowing pieces of gold, [and] by inserting into the vaginal orifice." She then depicted how the guards would pour out the water jugs, searched the victim's clothing and "in some case went so far as to examine the women internally."

The woman then went on to confide "that she had hid some money in her monthly napkin and when the men examined her clothes, she succeeded in convincing them that she was in an unclean condition, as according to Mohammedan Law, and they went no further in the examination." The woman also laconically explained that her condition kept her from being forcibly raped.[81]

The pent-up racial and cultural hatreds were clearly evident in the report of American missionary Isabelle Hartley. She recalled that in Harpoot, Armenian men were imprisoned on May 1, 1915.

Miss Hartley later wrote that "the Armenians in prison were tortured by having the hairs of their heads, mustaches, and beards pulled out, by having finger nails and toe nails pulled off, by being hung by arms for a day and night, by being beaten upon the head, body and hands until they dropped, by being starved, by being thrown and made to stay for a whole night in a filthy water closet, [and] by breaking fingers."

She also conveyed the insidious story that the mayor of the city savagely tortured an Armenian college professor until the Turk finally tired of the brutal exertion. He then "called upon anyone who loves his country and his nation to continue the beating."[82]

In yet another diabolical episode the *bastinado* was administered to "a prominent Armenian, 50-60 years old,[who] had received 700 strokes on the feet."[83]

In June, the deportations began in earnest. A witness in Erzeroum reported that, "the first group of people consisted of some forty families, some 250-300 souls...In fear and trembling they left the village and proceeded scarcely a mile when whistles sounded and a motley crew of Kurds, Turks [and] soldier police began to attack the caravan with guns, swords, scythes, clubs, fists, and everything that could be carried off was taken."

She added that "all the men were killed outright."[84]

WITH NO ONE TO DEFEND THEM

The vast number of reports regarding the harsh treatment of defenseless women and children instills the greatest revulsion against the events of 1915. A number of singularly pathetic images were witnessed by a female Christian missionary in Bitlis. "One day I saw an old woman left lying in the street near the school compound. She had just the strength enough to lift her hand faintly in an effort to ward off a dog sniffing at her face. Some of the Turks passing by stopped out of idle curiosity, others went on taking no notice. We later succeeded in having her brought to our premises where she died."[85]

The same witness, Miss Myrtle Shane, also described seeing "a gendarme beating an old white-haired woman who was stumbling along beneath the blows of his gun...Suddenly the gendarme sprang in front...and pointed his bayonet at the old woman as if to run it through her body. She fell in a heap at his feet, whereupon he seized her first by the girdle and then by the hair, dragging her through the rough street...She died soon after." Miss Shane concluded her narrative by laconically observing that the old woman's face "was very sweet and gentle."[86]

Not all of the unfortunate women who were brutalized under the horrified eyes of the young missionary were old, however. She further recounted, "Once I was startled from sleep by a woman's shriek of terror, followed by cries and pleadings which were answered only with the jeering laugh of men." The horrified missionary listened to the brutal gang rape of a young Armenian woman. She commiserated that "for about two hours I could hear the woman's low moans like those of a tortured animal."[87]

Such hellish depravity was also reported by Ambassador Morgenthau who asserted that "Turkish roughs would fall upon the women, leaving them sometimes dead from their experiences or sometimes ravingly insane."[88]

Women and young girls were particularly targeted during the deportation. Their young and middle-aged men had been conscripted into the Turkish army, imprisoned, executed or a combination of all three, and were no longer able to afford protection. One observer exclaimed, "...these poor unprotected women and children suffered in ways too horrible to describe. Those who suffered no actual harm were under a severe mental strain. Fear was a great monster stalking around and about them."[89]

In a cruel and ironic twist, it was rampant starvation and disease that often "saved" Armenian women from further sexual exploitation. An American doctor at Konia observed that the malarial and starving women were no longer being brutally visited at night as had so often previously been the case. Wilfred M. Post explained simply that "a vast assemblage of sickly and half-starved people is naturally comparatively safe from molestation."[90]

At the very least, the disrespectful treatment of women stunned the post-Victorian sensitivities of many Western witnesses. One wrote that, "...we saw the refined, educated women recoil from the beastly talk and rough handling of the gendarmes, as they were thrust out of their homes."[91] Unfortunately, "beastly talk" would be the least egregious offense to be showered upon the helpless Armenian women.

LIVING DEATH

Age offered no respite and even very young children were brutalized. Missionary, Dr. Ruth Parmelee stated that "in our school we had a little girl of 11 years of age who had suffered rape at the hands of a Turk... [Another] had been raped on the way to Harpoot. This child was nine years old."[92] A German nurse reported that "the girls were abducted almost without exception by the soldiers and their Arab hangers-on. Young female pupils at a Christian school in Harpoot, were actually "compelled to marry Turks." They had willingly sacrificed themselves "in order to save their own families."[93]

One father, on the verge of despair, "besought me to take... his fifteen-year-old daughter, as he could no longer protect her from the persecutions inflicted upon her."[94] An American minister commiserated how Kurdish gunmen "turned to work their will upon the defenseless women...All were stripped of their clothing. Then the brigands seized the most beautiful of the young women, threw them on their horses, and galloped away."[95] For many girls who were scarcely into their teens, rape and sexual exploitation had become a daily form of living death.

White slavery was another deplorable fate for many Armenian females who eventually ended up on the markets in Constantinople,

Damascus and elsewhere in the Moslem domains. One American missionary "took in a young girl who escaped after being sold to a Turk for $2.00."[96] Another described how "young brides and girls had been carried off as slaves in Kurdish and Turkish harems...In fact it was part of the day's program for the gendarmes to go through the camps at night selecting the pretty girls."[97]

Rev. Henry Riggs described a young girl who was forced in "marriage" to a six-year-old boy whose father then "tried to take her for himself."[98] Incredibly, one woman actually welcomed being bought by an old Turk so "that she might escape the further outrages of the Koords to which she was being subjected in the mountains."[99]

A Jewish eyewitness wrote that, "...nothing can convey to an Occidental mind the horror and shame of these slave markets. The writer has seen himself a grey bearded Mohamedan [sic] mustering with the eyes and fingers of an expert a row of such slaves, putting on his glasses in order to better see, feeling his victims one after the other and picking out a young maybe thirteen years old child." He concluded that, "untold thousands of Armenian women were sold in this way to Mohamedan harems."[100]

To protect themselves from being kidnapped or raped, Armenian women resorted to disfiguring themselves in order to appear unattractive. Mary Riggs, a missionary in Harpoot told that, "...the women and girls were dressed in very strange ways as they started out, so much so that I did not recognize some of my own pupils until they spoke to me and told me their names. They had disfigured their faces, marking them with charcoal and coloring them so as to make themselves look hideous. I could understand without asking them what the purpose was because of the reports that had come back to us of the treatment of pretty girls on the road."[101]

One survivor recounted that the women cut their hair and smeared mud on their faces "in order to appear ugly and detestable and thus evade the lustful eye of the Turk."[102] In some drastic cases, women actually permanently scarred themselves rather than fall prey to the abductors. Despite these extreme precautions, however, large numbers of Armenian women were being brutalized, and sent to Turkish slave markets in order to feed the harems of the Muslims.

By some perverse logic, one might have actually reckoned the harem slaves to be among the lucky ones. Rev. Alpheus Andrus described seeing the "corpse of a young woman almost entirely nude. She was on her back, her mouth open and distorted, and her expression was one of excruciating pain and agony and almost demonic ferocity."[103] One loathes to even imagine what transpired in her final moments of life.

Hideous stories were told of Armenian maidens, stripped nude, forced to dance in front of leering soldiers, then savagely doused with kerosene, and set ablaze.[104] One English witness "had seen women and girls brought up along a precipice and then had seen soldiers shoot at their feet so that they fell head-long down below."[105] If all that was not horrible enough, numerous witnesses "recalled seeing pregnant womens' stomachs being cut open by gendarmes, *in sport*, to determine whether the fetus was male or female."[106] (Italics are the author's). Finally, in a ghastly reversion to the sadistic methods of Tamerlane, a missionary stated "that at the door of one of the mosques they had seen a heap of womens' breasts several feet high."[107]

To be an Armenian woman in eastern Anatolia was to be a citizen of Hell.

ASSYRIAN GENOCIDE

Just as public knowledge and awareness of the Armenian Genocide is somewhat lost in the "shadow" of the Jewish Holocaust, the same may even more be said of the systematic ethnic cleansing of yet another persecuted people. During the same period as the Armenian holocaust, the Assyrian Christian population of the Ottoman Empire was also nearly destroyed.

By the start of the First World War there were an estimated 600,000 to 700,000 Assyrians living in southeastern Anatolia, inside the closest

Arab provinces, and along a narrow strip along the Persian side of the Turkish border.[108] Referred to as *shato d'sayfo* ("Year of the Sword") the Assyrian genocide that commenced in 1915 had witnessed the murder of at least 275,000 people. That number of deaths was officially reported at the 1923 Treaty of Lausanne, but according to one historian was possibly understated by some ten percent due to the fact that several Assyrian enclaves were located within larger Armenian communities and those killed were probably counted along with the other victims.[109]

All told, the death-toll reached between 250,000 to 300,000. Nearly half of the pre-First World War ethnic Assyrian population of the Ottoman Empire simply ceased to exist.[110]

Also known as Chaldean, or Nestorian Christians; the Assyrians are descended from an ancient people that has inhabited the land since Old Testament times. First appearing in the Middle Bronze Age (c. 2500 B.C.) the Assyrian Empire lasted for nearly two millennia until the fall of Nineveh to the Babylonians in 612 B.C.

Since that time the resilient Assyrian people have endured and survived the repeated depredations of one savage conqueror after another. Overrun in unbelievably bloody succession by Babylonians, Medes, Persians, Greeks, Parthians, Romans, Sassanids, Muslim Arabs, Saracens, Seljuks, Mongols, Kurds, Mamluks, and the Ottoman Turks; the Assyrians remain to this day only to again be persecuted at the time of this writing by the fanatical terrorists of ISIS.

Despite the tenure of four thousand years, the plight of the Assyrians, and especially the holocaust of 1915-1918, is little remembered today. Although it was widely reported in western newspapers at the time, very little research has been done about this sad episode, and genocide historians David Gaunt, and Hannibal Travis have both helped to re-introduce the Assyrian tragedy to the American public.

Once again, the questions of motive and intent weigh heavily on the debate regarding alleged Turkish responsibility. Gaunt clearly equates the Assyrian and Armenian tragedies as genocidal. He suggests that both Christian minorities were targeted immediately following Turkey's entry into the war.[111] Similarly, Travis suggests that the Assyrian persecution was clearly genocidal likewise perpetrated by Turks, Kurds, and Persians.[112]

It becomes apparent that the Turks were no longer concerned about the chastisement of world opinion. Already at war with Great Britain, France, and Russia; the Ottoman government need no longer fear Great Power intervention and the Turks were finally free of any restraints in dealing with their Christian subjects. This is borne out by the fact that in addition to the Armenians and the Assyrians; the Greek minority was also being devastated. It is estimated that nearly a half million Greeks were deported from Thrace with at least 250,000 perishing.

The United States Ambassador to the Ottoman Empire, Henry Morgenthau reported that the Turks "have massacred fully 2,000,000 men, women, and children—Greeks, Assyrians, [and] Armenians."[113]

DIPLOMATIC IMPOTENCE

The gruesome evidence that Turkey was destroying its Christian population became increasingly difficult to ignore.

The American consul in Aleppo, Syria, reported to the U.S. Secretary of State that, "...the [Ottoman] Government deported great numbers of Syrians, Catholics, Caldeans [sic], and Protestants, and it is feared all Christians may later be included in the order and possibly even the Jews. They cry 'Turkey for the Moslems.'"[114]

In London and Washington, vehement protests were lodged against the Ottoman Government. In a stern address to Parliament, Viscount Bryce described alleged Turkish atrocities in minute detail.[115] That noble hall had rarely heard such reports of civilian outrages since the Indian wars on the North American frontier, the Sepoy depredations in Calcutta, or Gordon's fall at Khartoum. Sordid tales of women and children robbed and stripped naked after their men had been bayoneted or shot elicited great public horror and condemnation, but unfortunately little else.

With Great Britain at war with the Turkish Empire, no diplomatic pressure could be directly expended beyond that of verbal threats. For the first time, the Turkish government was completely beyond the reach of Great Power reproach. "Now at last, after two hundred years of interference at Constantinople, the Russians, the British and the French were out of the way."[116]

As a result, Lloyd George and others promised full judicial accountability after the cessation of hostilities.[117] Of course for accounts to be justly settled; Britain had to first win the war.

Those neutral governments who attempted to bring humane or diplomatic pressure on the Turkish leadership found that their efforts were equally futile. In a Rome dispatch, *Reuters* reported that "the Pope has written an autograph letter to the Sultan interceding on behalf of the unfortunate Armenian population."[118]

Similarly, President Woodrow Wilson, kept abreast of events by his Ambassador in Constantinople, also lobbied directly to the Young Turk leadership. Ambassador Morgenthau even offered to "transport to America, the Armenians who have escaped the general massacres." He personally interceded with Enver Pasha, and Talaat Bey, but to no avail.[119]

The only nation that might have actually exerted enough influence to end the genocide was Turkey's ally and benefactor, Imperial Germany.

THE GERMAN POINT OF VIEW

The record is replete with sympathetic German eyewitness accounts of the Armenian plight. Missionaries, railway workers, military personnel, diplomats and others lobbied with their own government to intervene.

One example was published in the German missionary paper *Sonnenaufgang* (Sunrise) for July 14, 1915. A German female missionary wrote, "I visited another camp of exiles from Zeitoun, and heard stories of unspeakable sufferings. [They asked] 'Why don't they kill us at once? By day we have no water; our children cry with thirst. At night the Arabs come, steal our beds and clothing, carry off our young girls, and outrage our women. If we cannot walk, the soldiers beat us. Some women have drowned themselves, with their children, to escape outrage."[120] There is no question, with reports such as, that the Kaiser's government knew of the genocide that was taking place.

Strangely, the official response ranged from denial, to one of Turkish support, and finally to that of total indifference. Three different newspaper dispatches (amazingly all published within just two weeks of each other) graphically illustrate the various German viewpoints.

Denying any genocidal activity, the German Ambassador to the United States, Count J. Von Bernstorff, wrote on September 28 that, "the alleged atrocities committed in the Ottoman Empire appear to be pure inventions."[121]

Amazingly, only one day later, the Ambassador posted another letter *defending* the atrocities that he previously claimed did not exist. He stated that the depredations were in fact, provoked by the Armenians.[122]

Finally, Count Reventlow summed up German apathy towards the Armenian question in an article published October 12, in *Deutsche Tageszeitung.* His language perhaps betrays the true government position, however. "The Turkish Empire has had to put up long enough with interference in its affairs by all Great Powers who wanted to rob or destroy the Turks...It is a matter concerning Turkey alone what Turkey does with her revolutionary and *bloodsucking Armenians.*"[123] (Italics are the author's).

"HOW CAN I BEAR SO MUCH GRIEF!"

Regardless of the weight of world opinion, the genocide continued unabated. The British failure to seize the Straits and their subsequent evacuation from Gallipoli sealed the fate of the Armenians. Dr.Wilfred Post, a Turkish born American missionary, mournfully observed the unfolding events. "Suddenly towards the end of 1915 the British mysteriously disappeared from the peninsula on a misty night in December, and we realized the sad truth that the Dardanelles campaign had come to an end and that there was no deliverance for the Armenians."[124]

With the renewed vigor that stemmed from their success at Gallipoli, it is possible that the Turks became confident that there program in eastern Anatolia would go unchallenged. The deportations had become death marches and the desert was strewn with the grisly evidence of the genocide.

One witness contended "that wholesale slaughter was going on [and] was evident everywhere. One did not have to go more than an hour's journey from home to find signs of it in fresh dead bodies, skeletons, and dismembered bones and skulls."[125] Another wrote of a similarly gruesome scene.

"On the mountain, just off the road in the little gullies, we frequently saw bodies in various stages of disintegration and many skulls and other bones...In the gorge below us were countless naked bodies in positions showing how they had been hurled from above...As we went on our way we came to a field which seemed like a battlefield. It was strewn with skeletons and bodies."[126]

The New York Times reported "the roads and the Euphrates are strewn with corpses of exiles, and those who survive are doomed to certain death, since they will find neither house, work, nor food in the desert. It is a plan to exterminate the whole Armenian people."[127]

Dr. Tacy Atkinson from the mission at Harpoot also reported that she and her husband "began to see bodies by the roadside...There were between five and ten thousand all entirely naked, nearly all women and children." She added poignantly that, "all of the women showed signs of mutilation, let us hope after death."[128]

In evacuating the country one American traveled along a highway of horror. "Mr. Riggs, in coming home via Malatia and Sivas in June reports that he saw thousands and thousands of skulls and skeletons lying along the road west of Malatia for a distance of some fifteen or twenty miles."[129]

Starvation and disease were rampant. Sanitary conditions were deplorable. One witness was horrified to see Armenians forced to drink "sewage water," even though the guards had an abundance of fresh water.[130] Numerous Christian missionaries attempted to aid the victims but were often overcome by infectious diseases themselves. Dr. Clarence Ussher's wife died at Van during an outbreak of typhus fever[131] as did Dr. Atkinson, on Christmas Day.[132]

In addition to disease and starvation, the medical staffs of the various missions reported treating a vast assortment of wounds and injuries. Elvesta Leslie described wounds "from bullets, stones sticks, and various projectiles. There were broken arms, cut heads, (one child's head was cut to the brain), and injured faces. One woman...had her nose nearly cut off."[133]

Isabelle Harley wrote of "tired, sick, hungry, beaten, dirty, vermin infested, frightened, hunted, broken-hearted creatures pushed on... not knowing where they were going nor when the end would come." She further indignantly stated that, "it was the plan of the government to keep this up until the last had dropped. This was what they called deportation!"[134]

At Diarbekir, Dr. Floyd Smith treated "two children about seven and nine years old," that had been "attempted decapitations...[with] deep incised wounds on the nape of the neck." He also attended a woman whose nose had been cut off; a boy with a bullet in his face; a woman whose hand had been severed at the wrist; and a "boy about nine years old with a portion of his skull cleaved by a sword or axe."[135]

Perhaps the most shocking were the pitiful victims that visited the infirmary at Harpoot. A doctor remembered that, "one boy came back to us with about a dozen hacks and cuts from a hatchet on his back and head, and a bullet in his lung. We had many sick patients; one woman with a bullet in her jaw, one little girl with her neck cut.

She said they had been laid one on top of another and their heads cut off two at a time. She was underneath, so her neck was not cut through. One woman fell and feigned death then after found some of her children cut to pieces, others she did not find."[136]

The horrors in eastern Anatolia were unprecedented in modern society. For many of the Western missionaries and clergy, who witnessed the events of 1915, the unspeakable atrocities were beyond the boundaries of their post-Victorian sensitivities.

One Christian minister summed it all up with wrenching pathos. "Seared into my memory is the picture of an Armenian man---one of the few who had survived to see that day---who passed by as we stood waiting there. His two hands stretched out toward Heaven and his face turned upward as he walked along solemnly pouring out a stream of denunciation and curse against God. Curses on a God who, if he existed, would permit the awful injustice of such a horrible fate as was then falling on that innocent race."[137]

The unmitigated cruelty and the attendant suffering were also poignantly memorialized by Armenian Poet Avedik Issahakian who tragically lamented:

> "Bitter, vexed, day and night
> Cureless hurt in my heart.
> Paternal hearth ravaged, ruined,
> Bathed in Blood, sorrows untold.
> Blessed tots, mothers, sisters,
> Hurled unto fire, rapier, rivers.
> Grief, grief...so much grief:
> How can I bear so much grief?"[138]

11

THE GRIM LEGACY OF THOSE
"NOT RESPONSIBLE"

REGARDLESS OF THE violent events that were currently taking place within the Ottoman Empire, the external military situation continued to deteriorate outside the ever-shrinking Turkish borders. Not all seemed lost, however.

After their initial military setbacks in 1915, the Turks mounted a tough resistance against the British Indian Army in Mesopotamia, and also scored a brilliant success in defense of the Dardanelles. Despite the great valor of the ANZACS (Australian and New Zealand Army Corps) the repulse of the British assault at Gallipoli was a huge Turkish victory.

That success merely prolonged the inevitable, however, with perhaps the only lasting benefit being the recognition of the heroic actions, and subsequent rise of Mustafa Kemal. The dashing young Turkish division commander would one-day found and lead the modern Republic of Turkey under the sobriquet, Ataturk ("Father of the Turks").

Despite the able assistance of German General Limon von Sanders, and an influx of material support from Berlin; the Turkish military situation steadily worsened under the overall command of Enver Pasha.

THE END OF EMPIRES

In March of 1917, things at first appeared to be more promising with the complete collapse of the Tsar's government and the end of effective enemy opposition on the Russian front. The Turkish high command now had the opportunity to free up a large number of troops that were badly needed elsewhere. Rather than effectively transfer valuable resources to other hard-pressed fronts, the Turks quickly squandered their new-found advantage by shifting direction and committing to the "Pan-Turanian option."[1]

Long the leading desire of Enver Pasha and others within the Young Turk leadership, the Ottoman high command sent an expedition into Central Asia with the overall objective of uniting the Turkic peoples that had long been held under Tsarist control. The British High Command became seriously alarmed envisioning a joint Turkish-German invasion of Afghanistan, and a possible threat to the imperial prize jewel of India. As a consequence badly needed men and army supplies were diverted from British service in Mesopotamia in order to bolster defenses on the Indian frontier.

Ironically, the dilution of limited resources then being experienced by the British was an even greater problem for the opposing Turks. The unfortunate result of their thrust into the Trans-Caucasus was that during the subsequent British advances into both Palestine and Mesopotamia, the "combination of military overstretch and expansionary aims," severely impaired the Ottoman ability to resist.[2] The very same month as the Tsar's abdication, Anglo-Indian forces advancing up the Tigris and Euphrates captured the city of Baghdad.

Meanwhile, with orders from Prime Minister Lloyd George "to take Jerusalem before Christmas;"[3] the British Army under Sir Edmund Allenby relentlessly drove the Turks from Palestine. Taking in rapid succession the towns of Gaza, Beersheba, Jaffa, and finally entering the Holy City on December 9; Jerusalem was now in Christian hands for the first time in nearly seven centuries.

In a direct rebuff to Kaiser Wilhelm's grandiose mounted procession in 1898, General Allenby deferentially entered Jerusalem on foot and proclaimed that the sacred city would remain equally accessible to Jews, Christians and Muslims alike.

Ironically, Jerusalem is the single most fought over piece of real estate on earth. One historian calculated that Jerusalem, in Hebrew "The City of Peace," has been the site of 118 separate conflicts in the past four millennia. Eric H. Cline painstakingly laid out a bloody history that included "conflicts that ranged from local religious struggles to strategic military campaigns and that embraced everything in between."[4]

Supported on his right by the celebrated Lawrence of Arabia and the Arab guerilla revolt, Allenby launched the final decisive blow against the Turks. In what has been described as "one of the most brilliant operations in the history of the British Army," the Turkish Fourth, Seventh, and Eighth Armies were virtually destroyed in a 38 day campaign ending in October 1918.[5] That same month British efforts in the Caucasus were being met with stiff Turkish resistance, but the oil fields near Mosul were finally secured.

On October 30, 1918, the Ottoman Empire withdrew from the war signing an armistice three days before Austria-Hungary, and eleven days prior to Germany's final collapse. With the end of the First World War, all three empires ultimately ceased to exist.

The Central Powers had come close to winning the war on more than one occasion, but in the end the entry of the United States tipped the ever-precarious balance in the Allies favor.

With "uncanny" hind-sight, Adolf Hitler bitterly denounced the German Kaiser's poor choice of allies made prior to the start of the First World War. In *Mein Kampf*, written and published in 1925, the future Fuhrer described both Austria-Hungary and the Ottoman Empire as, "the putrid state corpses with which Germany allied herself in the last war."[6]

Hitler would eventually discover that his own choice of siding with Italy's Mussolini, and the Reich's inability to curb and coordinate the strategic actions of Japan, would later saddle Germany with another pair of ineffectual allies.

TRIUMVIRATE OF DENIAL

The end of the war witnessed the hurried escape of the Turkish leadership from their homes in Constantinople to places of safety well outside the Ottoman borders. It is provocative that the members of the Turkish ruling Triumvirate each felt the urgent necessity to flee into voluntary exile. One must conclude that their actions were done to avoid any personal recriminations or even the threat of possible physical danger resulting from the consequences of their decisions.

It certainly appears that at a minimum, the "Three Pashas" were concerned about possible criminal prosecution. If that was the case it proves that there was at least a strong suspicion from the very beginning that a huge crime had indeed taken place. There was really no modern precedent for the victors in a conflict placing the vanquished national leaders on trial. Nuremburg was still a generation away.

The architects of the genocide remained certain that all was done for the final good of the Turkish Nation. Enver Pasha, Talaat Pasha, and Djemal Pasha, the individual members of the Triumvirate that ruled Turkey, were jointly convinced that their actions were justifiable in light of the prevailing dangerous circumstances that had threatened the very survival of the Ottoman Empire. Their flight from Turkey indicates that they feared serious reprisals for their actions, however, and that they recognized that criminal charges were forthcoming.

Remarkably, despite their uniform protestations to the contrary; following the war each one was subsequently tried and found "guilty" (*in abstentia*) by a <u>Turkish</u> court of law.

Although the three leaders each individually professed personal innocence of any criminal responsibility, they were less than generous in blaming each other, and various additional members of the Turkish government.

One from another the three "Young Turks" were quite different in appearance, style and demeanor. Yet each individually exhibited marked character traits that may help to explain their infamous decisions. In addition, the testimony of witnesses as well as their own written accounts of the events of 1915, in which they unanimously decline any negative responsibility, actually may help to corroborate the charges leveled against them.

They also provide factual proof of their premeditated program of genocide.

"WITNESS FOR THE PROSECUTION"

The man that is probably the most often quoted by those who charge the Young Turks with pre-meditated criminal actions was Henry Morgenthau, the United States Ambassador to the Sublime Porte from November 1913 until his resignation in February 1916. Appointed by President Wilson in part due to his active role in Reformed Jewish affairs, the German-born naturalized citizen was viewed by the administration as a possible "natural bridge" connecting American Christians, with Muslims and Jews inside the Ottoman Empire.[7]

His son, Henry Morgenthau, Jr. would later be named the U.S. Treasury Secretary under Franklin Delano Roosevelt, and much as his father had earlier been in the case of the Armenians; was himself a tireless advocate for increasing American efforts to rescue Jews that were being persecuted by Nazi Germany.

Critics contend that Ambassador Morgenthau's version of the Armenian deportations is biased and therefore untrustworthy. With America's entrance into the First World War in 1917, both against Germany and the Kaiser's Ottoman ally; any assessment of events in Turkey prior to that time might rightly be riddled with subjectivity and even propaganda. Indeed, in the very opening paragraph of his personal memoirs, published after the end of the war in 1918, Henry

Morgenthau charged Germany with "the greatest crime in human history."[8]

Heath Lowry, and Guenter Lewy, both find fault with Morgenthau's recollection of events as published in his memoirs when compared to his original diary entries. They also agree that Morgenthau had harbored definite propaganda intentions after the American entry into the war. Finally, there is strong reason to suspect that the Ambassador's account was skewed by the literary license of ghost-writers that assisted in its publication. Perhaps Lewy is correct when he suggests that, "It has been given an importance that it does not deserve."[9]

While agreeing that the book contains possible errors and embellishments, Dadrian counters that Morgenthau's central message regarding the Armenian genocide was totally consistent between that written in his memoir and the Ambassador's wartime reports to the President.[10] Both Lowry and Dadrian agree "that Morgenthau's wartime dispatches and reports sent to Washington are the more important material on which to base any pertinent study of the events in question."[11]

Nonetheless, it is difficult to believe that Morgenthau initially harbored any pre-conceived aversion towards the Central Powers having spent the first ten years of his life in his native Germany. One should also note that Ambassador Morgenthau, as a close observer to the inner workings of the Young Turk leadership, is still considered by many to be an unimpeachable witness. Peter Balakian calls him, "a man of high moral conscience."[12]

His excellent reputation for integrity notwithstanding, it should be also mentioned that at the outset he not only failed to harbor any reason for personal bias, but for a time actually had a close personal relationship with many of the Turkish leaders. Until the Armenian deportations became a contested issue, the Ambassador actually enjoyed excellent relations with Enver, and Talaat. They were so cordial in fact, that in January 1915, Mrs. Morgenthau and her three daughters were decorated by the Sultan with the Turkish *Grand Order of*

Nichan-i-Chefkat, in recognition for her philanthropic work within the empire.[13]

The debate over accepting the testimony of Morgenthau and other third party western observers rages unabated and generally defaults toward which side one wishes to believe. The head of the *Turkish Historical Society* (TTK), Dr.Yusuf Halacoglu vehemently objects to the validity of the third-party testimony that was given by many of those witnesses held in equally high regard by Armenian apologists. He wrote, "Beside the U.S. Ambassador, the spread of the contentions that Armenians were massacred can be mainly attributed to Lord Bryce and the German Protestant priest Johannes Lepsius. Furthermore, Arnold Toynbee, a member of the Wellington House, was another avid user of information supplied by Morgenthau. The writings of these people have become a chief source for the subsequent books written on the so-called Armenian 'genocide.'"[14]

In summary, the reader needs with caution, to be aware of the subjectivity issue when considering the testimony of the American Ambassador and others. My own conclusion is that in the case of Henry Morgenthau there was absolutely no intention to deceive or lie about the events and conversations that he witnessed, and therefore his account should be treated as valid testimony.

It is also fair to say, however, that Morgenthau used his memoir wherever possible to paint the Young Turks in the worst possible light.

Having given due consideration to the subject of the degree of impartiality, it is appropriate to view a few disturbing anecdotes from Ambassador Morgenthau's account of his dealings with the Young Turk leadership.

The most stoic of the three was Enver Pasha. Ambassador Morgenthau noted a very revealing quirk, however, in Enver's nature, and one that may speak volumes about his alleged orchestration of the holocaust.

Describing an interview he had with Enver, Morgenthau writes, "I began by suggesting that the Central Government was probably not to blame for the massacres. I thought that this would not be displeasing to him.

'Of course I know that the Cabinet would never order such terrible things as have taken place,' I said. 'You and Talaat and the rest of the Committee can hardly be held responsible. Undoubtedly your subordinates have gone much further than you have ever intended'...

Enver straightened up at once. I saw that my remarks, far from smoothing the way to a quiet and friendly discussion, had greatly offended him. I had intimated that things could happen in Turkey for which he and his associates were not responsible."[15]

Perhaps caught off-guard, Enver, his supremacy challenged, immediately claimed responsibility "for everything that has taken place."[16]

Even more revealing, and terribly incriminating, was a personal conversation that Morgenthau reportedly had with Talaat. Again in the Ambassador's words, "One day Talaat made what was perhaps the most astonishing request I had ever heard. The New York Life Insurance Company and the Equitable Life of New York had for years done considerable business among the Armenians... 'I wish,' Talaat now said, 'that you would get the American life insurance companies to send us a complete list of their Armenian policyholders. They are practically all dead now and have left no heirs to collect the money. It of course all escheats to the State. The Government is the Beneficiary now."[17]

Morgenthau was understandably alarmed and categorically refused. Such an outrageous demand only underscored Talaat's later boast: "I have accomplished more toward solving the Armenian problem in three months than Abdul Hamid accomplished in thirty years!"[18]

The daily dispatches that were sent back to the United States, both under the direction of the Ambassador, and through the reports of missionaries in Eastern Anatolia were inciting the American public. In one revealing episode, the press reported that as early as January 1915, Talaat was already publicly betraying his designs for the Ottoman Christians. *The New York Times* recorded that when the Grand Vizier met with "the Greek Patriarchate, who was sent to Talaat Pasha to remonstrate against the excesses committed by the organs of his ministry, he unequivocally replied that there was no room for Christians in Turkey, and that the best the Patriarch could do for his people would be to advise them to clear out of the country and make room for Moslem refugees."[19]

Months later, Talaat was again quoted in the American press. He was reported saying that, "the Armenians are a damned race; their disappearance would be no loss. I intend to prevent any talk of Armenian autonomy for fifty years."[20] For those words, the editorial board of *The New York Times* dubbed Talaat Pasha the "chief author of these crimes."

The testimony of individuals who originated from nations that were at war with Turkey should understandably be viewed with suspicion. Regardless of a person's unimpeachable character, a natural degree of subjectivity might still affect both memory and judgment. That cannot generally be said, however, when the evidence emanates from someone whose bias would likely be in favor of the accused. The Germans were the allies of the Ottoman Empire, and yet a number still had some damning recollections about the actions of Talaat and the Young Turks.

German historian Rolf Hosfeld damningly writes, "At the time of its campaign against the Armenians, the Turkish government had far fewer compunctions about stating its intent frankly, at least to its German wartime allies. Talaat literally conceded to German Consul General Johann Heinrich Hermann Mordtmann that the deportations and massacres were intended to do nothing less than 'to destroy the Armenians,' reported German Ambassador Baron Hans von Wangenheim to Chancellor Theobald von Bethmann-Hollweg on July 7, 1915. The ambassador further quoted Talaat as stating that the Turkish government wanted to use the world war 'to get rid of its domestic enemies–native Christians–through and through, without being disturbed by foreign diplomatic intervention.' At the end of that year German Ambassador Count Paul Wolff-Metternich concluded in a telegram to the chancellor that Talaat himself was undoubtedly the cold-blooded 'soul of the Armenian persecutions.'"[21]

UNINTENDED SELF-INCRIMINATION

Djemal Pasha virtually washed his hands of any personal responsibility for planning, sanctioning, or executing the Armenian genocide. In his memoirs, published in 1922, he flatly states, "...a few days after the declaration of war, I was appointed to the Command of the 4th Army and left Constantinople to proceed to Syria. From that time I have learnt nothing further of the conditions in the vilayets of east Anatolia, nor on what grounds the Government saw itself called upon to deport all Armenians. I neither took part in the negotiations at Constantinople nor was I consulted. It was through the Government Proclamation to the vilayets that I first learned that all Armenians were provisionally to be deported."[22]

In other words, Djemal Pasha knew nothing!

The record is somewhat less incriminating when examining the general's actions as compared to his two partners in the Triumvirate. In fairness to him, Djemal was reported to have "ordered the chiefs of two Turkish Bands be hanged for ill treatment of Armenians."[23] Despite his public denial of any personal knowledge or responsibility for the genocide however, Djemal's own words, published elsewhere in his manuscript, appear to provide contradictory clues to his true feelings.

In the aftermath of the Balkan Wars, Djemal smugly stated that "the racial problem had been finally settled so far as the Bulgarians were concerned, and not a single Bulgarian was to be found within the frontiers of the Turkish Empire."[24] Apparently the Young Turks had grown to believe that the solution to their "racial problems" was deportation or extinction.

This would portend sinister implications when Djemal further explained that he and the Turkish leadership had now "decided to tackle our thorniest domestic problem, the Armenian question."[25]

Djemal Pasha's published protestation of innocence, regarding any personal complicity in his government's plan to "deport all Armenians," is revealing for a couple of reasons. First, it clearly admits that such an action was in fact premeditated and orchestrated by the Young Turk leadership. Secondly, the magnitude of the deportations is confirmed by stating that *all* of the Armenians were targeted.

Finally, his very <u>need</u> for a defense at all insinuates that he believed that crimes were indeed committed from which he wished to publicly distance himself.

Self-serving, and delusional to the end, Djemal justified his own actions at the conclusion of his post-war memoirs. Writing as if nothing at all had happened, the former leader advised that if the surviving, "Armenian minority desires to remain Ottoman, it has only to prove that... it is inspired with feelings of loyalty and true Ottoman ideals. This, in my opinion, is the only method I can suggest for finally burying the blood-stained past and preparing the way for a rich and happy future."[26]

Those words must have been greatly consoling to the Armenian survivors.

What is also interesting about Djemal's personal account of the events of 1915 is that he readily admits that, "the Ottoman Government deported a million and a half Armenians from the East Anatolian Provinces, and that 600,000 of them died, some murdered, some collapsing on the way from hunger and distress."[27]

He then justifies that horrible tragedy by insisting that an equal number of Turks and Kurds were similarly slain at the hands of the Russians and the Armenians. His notion that two wrongs make a right is revealed by his rhetorical questions, "If the Turks are to be made responsible for the Armenian massacres, why not the Armenians for the massacres of Turks? Or are the Turks and Kurds of no more value in the eyes of humanity than flies?"[28]

The tortured logic of such a specious argument need not be further addressed. Suffice it to say that whatever the total of Turkish fatalities inflicted during the war, and many thousands of innocent civilians certainly perished, the overwhelming majority were military combatants.

By contrast, in the case of the Armenians nearly all of the deceased were civilians, many of whom were women and children who were killed with the full knowledge and likely instigation of their own government.

What is clear, however, is that Djemal actually tacitly acknowledges the government-sponsored genocide in his memoirs.

Whatever were his personal excuses for it, the end result is not denied.

A GRIM MATTER OF SCALE

In the aftermath of the war, Talaat Pasha preserved his private records of the deportations that he apparently intended to use in some fashion. Whether he ever planned to publish the documents remains a mystery for he died less than three years after the war ended. His widow retained and preserved his notes until her death in 1982. Finally, in 2005 portions of Talaat's personal records were published by Turkish journalist Murat Bardakçı first in a series of articles posted in Turkey, and later in book form. In 2011, his material was published by Ara Sarafian in a disputed edition published in London.

Although Bardakçı disagrees, Ara Sarafian cites the documents as being evidence for planned genocide by illustrating that the information that is contained therein carefully documents the great disparity in numbers between the 1914 and 1917 population statistics in twenty-nine different Ottoman vilayets.

Sarafian contends that, "Talaat's report clearly shows that the deportation of Ottoman Armenians in 1915 was part of an effort that aimed at the destruction of Armenians. The object of the authorities was not a population transfer...but the destruction of entire communities. This fact is quite apparent in the organization, implementation and outcome of Talaat's policies, as can be seen in the discrepancy between the number of Armenians who were deported, and the number of deportees who were found in the resettlement zone in 1917." The observer finally concludes that, "Talaat was well aware of this discrepancy since he closely supervised deportations throughout 1915-16."[29]

The existence of such documentation found in the private papers of the man who was both Grand Vizier, and Interior Minister gives some credibility to the claims of Grigoris Balakian, an Armenia villager that was arrested in 1915, and whose experiences as a holocaust survivor was published in 1922. He contended that Talaat Pasha was party to the issuance of a secret government plan to exterminate the Armenians and that he was to receive daily reports of local police "blacklists" which recorded the numbers of those already massacred, compared with those still alive.[30]

Published along with the deportation records is a so-called *Black Book* (due to the color of its untitled cover) that was also obtained by Murat Bardakçı, and reports on the deportation of nearly one million Armenians and the confiscation of their properties often for the use of relocated Muslims. These are the only surviving records that indicate the scale of the deportations as understood by the Turkish Grand Vizier.

Scholars and observers are in great disagreement over the final number of Armenian victims of the holocaust. Robert Melson correctly observed that, "An extensive massacre or genocide always leads to a controversy over the number of victims. Those who deny it minimize the number; those who would affirm it maximize the number."[31]

That is typically true but how much more compelling if one from the "deniers" side of the argument actually *maximizes* the claim?

Djemal Pasha's own words attest to the colossal scale of the deportations and the subsequent massacres. His statement that "one and a half million Armenians" were displaced, offers a demographic figure that is equal to or greater than the estimates of some modern historians.

Justin McCarthy agrees that there were "one and a half million Armenians who had lived in Anatolia before World War I."[32] He cited official Turkish census figures of 1914-1915 where the population was categorized by *millet* or religion. In 1915, the combined Armenian Christian community was identified as including 1,329,007 individuals.

Stanford Shaw flatly suggests that the total number of Armenians living in the empire before the war "came to at most 1,300,000."[33] That number is actually a third less than the two million person census figures that were provided by the Armenian Patriarchate in 1912.[34]

Although one would presume that Armenian apologists would consider the Patriarchate's figures to be indisputable, even that number is often contested as being too low. As early as 1913, Krikor Zohrab, who ironically was a respected member of the Ottoman Parliament, "...contested the Patriarchate's 2.1 million figure as probably a terrible under- calculation."[35]

Others concurred. Jacques de Morgan estimated in 1919 that "there were 2,380,000 Armenians in the Ottoman Empire on the eve of World War I."[36] Haigazn Kazarian, who served in 1918 as a civilian employee with British occupation forces in Constantinople, examined Turkish archival information germane to the deportation and massacres of Armenians. In his later book *Tzeghazban Turkeh* he reported that according to his findings, "more than 2.6 million Armenians" had resided in Turkey before the holocaust.[37]

This number would have actually been a plausible progression supported by the Ottoman Government's own official calculations from its *first* census conducted in 1844. Administered for taxation purposes, that census stated that "the number of Armenians was 2.4 millions—two million in Asia Minor...and 400,000 in European Turkey."[38]

My own contention is that we should accept Djemal's estimate as the *lowest* likely Armenian population figures for 1915. As a prominent member of the Turkish government he would certainly have had no reason to inflate the number, especially given his understandable proclivity to wish to minimize the obvious attrition of the Armenian population. On balance, Djemal would also have needed to present a believable figure in order to persuade and not strain the credulity of his contemporary observers.

Conversely, Djemal Pasha's fairly conservative estimate of 600,000 genocidal deaths is contrasted with Armenian estimates often put at twice that number and more. It should be remembered, however, that at the time of Djemal's writing he had already been exiled from Turkey for nearly four years and no longer would have been privy to official information. It is fair to assume that his estimate was honestly arrived at with the information at hand, but might be grossly understated, nonetheless.

Apologists for the Turkish position dismiss modern suggestions of a much higher number of fatalities. Is this just another example of Melson's contention that regarding the dispute over the Armenian genocide, "those who would deny it tend to minimize the number"?[39] Or is there merit to their argument?

Stanford Shaw contended that claims of more than one million fatalities were the exaggerated product of "the Entente propaganda mills and Armenian nationalists."[40] Justin McCarthy further suggests that the population and mortality figures given by the Armenians were "intended for publication" and merely inflated to advance their cause after World War I.

His position seems to insinuate that the Armenians and other minority groups conspired to publish exaggerated estimates of their pre-war communities so as "to show that their populations had been massacred during the war. In this way they hoped to demonstrate that certain regions should not be awarded to a Turkish State, even though the regions now had a clear Turkish majority, for by doing so the Turks would be 'rewarded.'"[41]

Of course, Prof. McCarthy fails to acknowledge the obvious possibility that the Turks had actually ensured such numerical "majority" status by previously eliminating the non-Turks. On the other side, Vahakn Dadrian strongly disputes the findings of Justin McCarthy and questions his objectivity, charging that his work "is replete with...errors and fallacies." Dadrian, who subjectively argues for the Armenian position, suggests that McCarthy's bias is indicated by his own denial that a genocide ever occurred. "As far as he is concerned, the victims simply 'died or migrated.'"[42]

Not less reputable an observer than Arnold Toynbee (who was certainly no apologist for the Turks) declared in his contemporary report to the British government that 600,000 Armenians were killed.[43] Melson points out, however, that Toynbee only calculated the deaths that, "stop with the winter of 1915 and the spring of 1916," suggesting that any subsequent fatalities through 1922 would have obviously been excluded.[44]

It is also fair to assume that evidence regarding the enormity of the genocide was still far from being fully received in 1916. Dr. Johannes Lepsius, a key eyewitness to the genocide, posited that one million Armenians died.[45] Melson again concludes that due to the fact that Lepsius published his work in 1918, he would naturally have also understated the final tally.[46]

The position of most Armenian apologists, as well as many other scholars, asserts that the death total was much higher than 600,000, or even 1 million. For example, Peter Balakian recently posited that when including the years from 1915 to 1922, the Armenian death toll ranged "from over a million to a million and a half."[47]

Dadrian, Hovannisian and other Armenian-American scholars generally share that view.[48] Marxist historian Eric Hobsbawm, seemingly impartial in his published views on the Armenian genocide, suggests that "the most usual figure is 1.5 millions" of Armenians who perished.[49]

Needless to say, whether it was 600,000 or upwards of 1,500,000, the numbers of slain are horrendous in either case, representing between 40%-80% of the total pre-war Armenian population of the Ottoman Empire. To give a historical context to the enormity of the catastrophe, the Armenians lost *at a minimum*, as many citizens as the total combined fatalities suffered only fifty years previously by the Union and the Confederacy, during the American Civil War. That comparison is even more amazing when one remembers that the 1915 Armenian population was less than one-tenth that of the Northern States alone.

To quibble over the actual final death toll is fairly problematic and certainly obscures the real issue. Hovannisian argues that "the important point in understanding a tragedy of this magnitude is not the precise count of the number who died...but the fact that more than half the Armenian population perished and the rest were forcibly driven from their ancestral homeland."[50]

By comparison, Hobsbawm correctly asserts that the horror of the Jewish Holocaust would be no less ghastly if historians suddenly concluded that four or five million Jews perished instead of the usually stated number of six million. He asks, "Can we really *grasp* figures beyond the reality open to physical intuition? In any case, what does statistical exactitude mean, where the orders of magnitude are so astronomic?"[51]

A Grim Matter of Perspective

Most Americans today have little knowledge of the terrible plight of Turkey's Armenian population. Nonetheless, it is one of the most notable historical cases of mass genocide for one very important reason.

Somewhat obscured by the excessive civilian casualties of the Second World War, and the unspeakable horror of the Jewish Holocaust; the Armenian Genocide remains unique in that it had no modern precedent. Such a colossal crime had not been committed by a ruler against a people for more than five centuries.

The enormous scope of the number of victims is also difficult for an American to grasp. This nation lost barely one-tenth of one percent of its total pre-war population in World War I (117,000) and an additional third of one percent (420,000) in World War II. In both cases virtually the entire number of those that perished was comprised of military personnel. While the sacrifice of so many valiant men and women is terribly tragic (the author's own Grandfather being among those that gave his life) the past American experience is relatively guarded when compared to that of other nations and peoples. Thankfully, we cannot fully understand the abject horror of losing hundreds of thousands or even millions of American civilians. The senseless death of nearly 3,000 innocent victims on 9/11 is embedded in our national consciousness. How much more so must the enormous slaughter of the Armenians be remembered, regardless of the actual total numbers of those that perished? Perhaps a grim matter of perspective is in order.

To this observer, sitting in my quiet study in southeastern Wisconsin, the disparity between 600,000 and 1,500,000 deaths is tantamount to comparing the hypothetical extermination of the total population of the City of Milwaukee proper, with the fictional massacre of the entire surrounding metropolitan area. The relative figures are exactly the same and either result is inconceivable in the extreme!

My own belief is that the Armenians would not have needed to make their case by inflating the number of deceased victims. In the years following 1915, world opinion would have lamented no more loudly at the slaughter of 1.5 million Armenians than they would for half that number. Even the minimally agreed-to estimate of 600,000 slain Armenian civilians would have had no contemporary modern equivalent, the grisly horrors of the First World War notwithstanding.

There had been no comparable precedent since Tamerlane.

12

CRIMSON AFTERMATH

WITH THE FALL of the Tsarist government in Russia and the subsequent defeat of the Ottoman Empire, the Armenian survivors from both sides of the border believed that the victorious Allies would finally help them to realize their dream of a restored national homeland. Many in the West took up their cause both out of sympathy for the recent genocide victims and out of abject hatred for the Turks. For a brief time it appeared that the terrible suffering of the Armenians might not have been in vain.

Passionate advocates for the re-establishment of an independent Armenia were vocal in their demands. Some in the West desired not just the creation of a free nation, but also wished for the end of Turkey altogether.

The Rev. S. Ralph Harlow, who had maintained a mission in Smyrna during the genocide, wrote vehemently (and with the questionable parlance of the times) against any continued Turkish hegemony. "If we leave such a government over any portion of [Anatolia] we are betraying our trust and we are permitting an injustice to continue in the world which will be a canker sore in the heart of Asia Minor. Far better would it be to establish a Negro republic in the heart of the southern states than to leave a Turkish Regime bordering an autonomous Armenia."[1]

Dated vernacular notwithstanding, the righteously indignant anti-Turkish and pro-Armenian rhetoric expressed by the former missionary was initially shared by many concerned Christians on both sides of the Atlantic. It seemed a foregone conclusion that Turkey would be forced to suffer just punishment and that Armenia would be avenged and compensated.

As had so often previously been the case however, the Armenians would first be promised justice and then be quietly abandoned.

ARMENIA? YES! TURKEY? NO!

The war in the Caucasus had fueled Armenian hopes for independence. Early Tsarist victories against the Turks convinced many that their liberation from Ottoman oppression was at hand. The Russian advances into Eastern Anatolia continued even after the fall of the Tsar and the declaration of a republic in March 1917. For the exhausted Russian people the conflict had lasted far too long, however.

In October, Vladimir Lenin overthrew the Provisional Government of Alexander Kerensky and proclaimed a new Soviet state. The Russian defeat by the Central Powers, and the rise of the Bolsheviks prompted the signing of the Treaty of Brest-Litovsk which ceded back to the Ottoman Empire those lands that had been previously forfeited in the Russo-Turkish War of 1877-78. As part of the treaty, the Turks regained the provinces of Kars and Batumi despite local opposition from Georgian revolutionaries. The Armenian Revolutionary Federation (*Dashnaks*) also moved to create an independent state in defiance of the certain threat of Turkish military intervention.

Despite being hard-pressed on other fronts, the Ottoman army invaded the area in a spring campaign. Nonetheless, in the wake of the Russian withdrawal from the region, the First Republic of Armenia had been officially declared in late May, 1918, alongside the newly formed Democratic Republic of Georgia in the north, and the Azerbaijan Democratic Republic to the east.

After winning a series of initial engagements, the Armenians were finally forced into peace negotiations with the Turks and in June, 1918 agreed to the Treaty of Batum. Although harsh, the terms of the treaty at least recognized a small Armenian independent state in what was formerly Russian territory. In less than five months the situation changed again, however, with the final defeat of Turkey and the other Central Powers.

In the aftermath of the First World War and the Allied scramble for spoils that were being greedily handed out at the peace table, Turkey became something of a conundrum for the victorious powers. At first openly supportive of Armenian statehood, Allied concerns soon arose over the fear of a possible regional power vacuum that would likely be brought about by a full Turkish collapse. Those fears were further exacerbated by the ominous nearby presence of the emerging Soviet State. Franco-British designs over control of the newly mandated portions of the old Ottoman Empire, as well as the imperialist aspirations of Italy, and Greece soon tended to cloud the issue of Armenian sovereignty.

After the hurried flight of the defeated Young Turk leaders into foreign exile, the post-war Turkish government was initially pressured to agree to an Allied plan that would have effectively partitioned most of the remaining Ottoman Empire. Forced to sign the punitive Treaty of Sèvres in August 1920, the new Turkish Grand Vizier Damat Ferid Pasha effectively endorsed the virtual end of his own nation.

Carving out for themselves individual spheres of influence; the British, French, Italians, and Greeks each occupied extensive portions of Ottoman territory. In addition, Armenia was finally promised an independent national homeland that presumably bordered upon the shores of the Black Sea, and on paper encompassed nearly 70,000 square miles of Eastern Anatolia. The Kurds were similarly promised their own land by the victorious allies but the final borders were as yet ill-defined, and still remained to be fully determined.

The collapse of the Ottoman Empire created an opportunity for the Armenians to expand their borders. Unfortunately, the peoples of

Georgia and Azerbaijan had the same intention. Only one month after the armistice was signed ending the First World War, the Armenian Republic entered into armed hostilities first with Georgia, and later with Azerbaijan. The first conflict was a brief border dispute that was eventually ended by British mediation. The Georgian-Armenian relations remained strained, however.

The Armenian-Azerbaijani War (1918-1920) was more intense due to ongoing ethnic, religious, and cultural differences. Once again, due to ill-defined national borders the two new republics clashed in a series of bitter engagements. Azerbaijan and Armenia claimed much of the same territory, and the conflict was only concluded by the advance of the Red Army and eventual absorption of both republics into the Soviet Union. Ironically, after more than seventy years under Soviet rule, the two republics each re-gained independence in 1991 and promptly renewed fighting over the disputed territory of Nagorno-Karabakh. As of 2014, tensions remain high between the two adjoining nations.

In addition to the desultory regional warfare with its newly independent neighbors, Armenia's greatest adversary remained the Turks. In the aftermath of the First World War, one man arose from the Turkish ashes to secure the aspirations of his people, and also ensure the demise of the hopes of another.

ATATÜRK

In defeat the Ottoman Empire had been severely and mercilessly dealt with. Outraged at the final terms of the treaty that was forced upon them; many within Turkey rose-up against their own weak government. In April, 1920, the newly formed "Grand National Assembly" (GNA) met in Ankara and called for Turkish Independence and the establishment of a national army. The highly nationalistic opposition party was led by Mustafa Kemal, a World War I hero of the Ottoman army, and an ardent Pan-Turkist. Later known to posterity by the epithet of

Ataturk ("Father of the Turks") the head of the rising Turkish national movement struggled to preserve the remaining Anatolian homeland, and deny any further territorial encroachments by foreign powers.

Increasingly besieged at every corner of eroding Ottoman territory, the landing of Greek forces on the Mediterranean coast "seemed to complete a ring of enemies around the Turkish homeland." With the Royal Navy patrolling the Straits; the Greek army newly landed at Izmir; Italian, British and French troops stationed throughout the south; Russian Bolsheviks reentering the Caucasus; and a newly proclaimed independent Armenia in the east; the Turkish situation was extremely dire.[2] From the perspective of the GNA, it was imperative for Mustafa Kemal to act quickly for any chance of Turkish national survival.

The future leader of the Republic of Turkey was born in Salonica (Thessaloniki) in 1881, the son of a middle class Muslim family. As a student young Mustafa was given the title *Kemal* meaning "perfection" by an admiring mathematics teacher. Mustafa Kemal was a product of the Turkish military command in Macedonia where he too was strongly influenced by the Pan-Turanist dogma that was currently becoming vogue in the officers' mess.

Like Enver, Djemal and other rising officers stationed in Macedonia, Mustafa Kemal soon became obsessed with Young Turk politics. "Only when he perceived that factionalism based on military membership in political societies would undermine the discipline—and therefore the fighting capacity—of the armed forces did he advocate that the military disengage itself from partisan politics...thus allowing it to assume an autonomous position and hence a commanding role."[3]

For his stance, he soon fell into relative disfavor with the more ardent Young Turks who overshadowed him; most notably his later rival Enver Pasha, who was six months junior to him in age. Serving alongside the future CUP leader, whom he personally disliked, Mustafa Kemal distinguished himself during the Ottoman conflicts in Albania,

Libya, and again in the Second Balkan War. Staying clear of the political turmoil in Constantinople, Mustafa Kemal did not participate
in the 1913 coup that placed the Triumvirate of Enver, Talaat, and
Djemal into power. Instead, he was summarily stationed to faraway
Bulgaria as a military attaché in Sofia.

With Turkey's entrance into the First World War, Mustafa Kemal
was sent to command a division on the critical Gallipoli peninsula in
preparation for the imminent enemy assault. The subsequent allied
campaign was stymied due in no little part to the brilliant defense,
and tactical genius of Mustafa Kemal, who correctly anticipated the
exact site of a planned enemy thrust which he subsequently thwarted.

Due to his role in the Turkish victory at Gallipoli, the young officer emerged as a hero of the Ottoman army and was readily stationed
to other trouble spots. Later victorious against the Russians in the
Caucasus, Mustafa Kemal witnessed the final collapse of the enemy
front due to the Russian Revolution. He emerged from the war as one
of the few Ottoman army commanders with his reputation intact.

Following the proclamation of the Grand National Assembly,
Mustafa Kemal's forces dealt with the surrounding enemy armies
in successive detail. First defeating a joint command of French and
Armenians in Eastern Anatolia; the Turkish commander soon secured
an unofficial understanding of friendship with the Soviets who supplied him with arms, money, and other needed material support. The
combined Turkish and Soviet pressure all but doomed the fledgling
Armenian Republic.

After securing Turkey's eastern frontier, Ataturk next turned his
attention to the west, and eventually smashed the Greeks occupying
Smyrna (Izmir) on the Mediterranean coast. To the present time the
decisive Turkish triumph over the Greeks at the Battle of Dumlupinar
is annually commemorated each August 30th, as national "Victory
Day."

By early September, 1922, after nearly three years of hard cam-
paigning, Ataturk had effectively ended the foreign threat to Turkish

independence, and territorial integrity. The allies, tired of the seemingly endless conflict, and unable to persuade the Turks to cease offensive operations, finally decided to call it quits.

A second peace conference was convened in November, and the following year on July 24, 1923, a new treaty was signed at Lausanne that confirmed the establishment of the present day Republic of Turkey with Mustafa Kemal Ataturk as its first President.

In the years that followed, Ataturk took virtual dictatorial control of Turkey, and eventually ended all internal opposition. Strongly nationalistic and Pan-Turkic, the founder of modern Turkey established a secular state that was the antithesis of the former Pan-Ottoman, Pan-Islamic empire from which he came. His government was particularly harsh in its rejection of the former Young Turks whom Ataturk personally blamed for the disastrous national defeat of the First World War.

Ironically, in 1923 one of the new regime's most vocal internal opponents was forced to escape the country. Yet again, for the third and what would be the final time, the perennial royal Turkish "bride's-maid," Prince Sabahaddin fled into foreign exile to Switzerland.

Wilson's "Twelfth Point" and the Betrayal of a People

The end of the First World War witnessed the death of four great empires and the total demise of their royal houses.

Imperial Russia had collapsed in 1917 and the three hundred year Romanov dynasty ended with the murder of Tsar Nicholas and his family at the hands of the Bolsheviks. For the five years that followed the October Revolution of 1917, up until the final communist victory in October 1922; Red and White armies waged a brutal civil war that added another 750,000 military deaths to the more than two million that had already perished in the First World War.

In 1918, following the sixty-eight year reign of Franz Joseph I, the last Emperor of Austria-Hungary, Karl I abdicated after just two years on the throne. The multi-ethnic empire was dismembered, and from it was carved a small Austrian republic as well as a separate independent Hungary. In addition, the new nations of Czechoslovakia, Poland and Yugoslavia emerged either all or in part from the corpus of the dissolved Hapsburg monarchy. Portions of Austro-Hungarian territory were also ceded to victorious Italy and Romania. Ironically, the motto of the old Hapsburg Empire was "Indivisible and Inseparable."

The often bellicose and flamboyant German Kaiser Wilhelm II was forced into fleeing to neutral Holland following his abdication and removal from the throne in 1918. The Prussian House of Hohenzollern would never re-emerge despite the Kaiser's later hope that the ascendant Adolf Hitler would welcome him back to Germany. He died in the Nazi occupied Netherlands in 1941, just days before Hitler invaded the Kaiser's old Russian enemy, and having witnessed the German defeat of France and seemingly imminent victory over Great Britain.

Finally, the Ottoman Empire, whose official motto was "the eternal state," was effectively terminated by the 1923 Treaty of Lausanne, and the subsequent proclamation of the new Turkish Republic. As was the case with their Austro-Hungarian ally; the Turkish Empire was comprised of a number of ethnic minorities, each clamoring for autonomous statehood. It was not just the Christian Armenians that petitioned for an independent homeland, but the Jews along with the Muslim Arabs, and Kurds also demanded autonomy.

The victorious "Big Four" powers of Great Britain, France, Italy, and the United States convened the Paris Peace Conference in 1919 to set the terms of capitulation for the vanquished Central Powers and to address the territorial demands of the myriad of nationalities that sprang from the carcasses of the defeated empires.

In their race for post-war hegemony and colonial expansion, the victorious European powers were typically more concerned with their own national interests than the national aspirations of the have-not ethnic groups. Although England and France voiced sympathy for the rights of the minorities; their solution was often the imposition of a sponsored mandate over the lands in question.

As a result, the United States, under the direction of President Woodrow Wilson, emerged as the leading proponent of the rights of the ethnic minorities.

In the spirit of "Wilsonian" self-determination, the United States appeared to be in full support of an independent Armenia. Contrary to President Wilson's anti-imperialist sentiments, he was even seriously considering a United States mandate over Anatolia[4]which was being demanded by some as an American "right" in accordance with her sole war aim of making "the world safe for Democracy."[5]

The twelfth of Wilson's celebrated "Fourteen Points" for a program of world peace, idealistically promised that ethnic Turkey should be preserved, but also demanded that the tottering empire's subject nationalities be granted the opportunity for autonomous statehood.[6]

The President stated, "The Turkish portions of the present Ottoman Empire should be assured a secure sovereignty, but the other nationalities which are now under Turkish rule should be assured an undoubted security of life and an absolutely unmolested opportunity of autonomous development." Wilson's philosophy of nationhood was consistent with the aspirations of the Armenians. He wrote that, "... nations do not consist of governments but consist of people."[7]

The Armenians believed they had a champion in Washington, and could not foresee that American political competition and isolationism would eventually trump idealism. After the 1918 U. S. mid-term elections resulted in a clear Republican majority, Theodore Roosevelt observed that "Mr. Wilson has no authority whatever to speak for the American people at this time."[8] The greatly strengthened Republican Congress would nullify Wilson's international hopes and those of Armenia in the balance.

As previously discussed, Mustafa Kemal's bold military move against the French, and Greeks, combined with his non-aggression treaty with Soviet Russia, secured his flanks and enabled him to eventually crush Armenia militarily. The Armenians fought valiantly, particularly during the siege of Aintab, but were simply overwhelmed. At the same time the Allied powers prevaricated and failed to send meaningful assistance to the Armenian nationalists.

In Washington, Senator Henry Cabot Lodge led the isolationist Republican majority in defeating Wilson's international policies including U. S. admission to the League of Nations, and acceptance of an American mandate in Turkey.[9]   Some have argued that United States foreign policy was "bribed" by Turkish oil concessions.[10]

Whether correct or not, the simple fact is that the postwar United States electorate would have never supported the placement of American troops in Turkey. With a deep feeling of betrayal, the Armenian people once again saw their traditional homeland divided between Turkey and Russia.

BLOOD FEUDS AND BLOOD-BATHS

With all of the enduring Armenian claims of Turkish atrocities; the aftermath of the First World War witnessed a continuation of savage outrages that were being perpetrated by both sides. Muslims and Christians; Turks and Armenians continued to kill each other with barbaric savagery. The Blood Feud had lasted so long that it was now hard to remember when and why it all began. All that mattered was the continuing need for revenge and the never-ending "eye for an eye." The Armenians and the Turks had become a colossal Middle Eastern version of the Capulets and the Montagues; the Hatfields and McCoys. The matter of who started it all, or the question of who originally did what to whom; probably meant very little to the raped, maimed, and murdered victims that came later.

For those that blame only Turks for the depredations; the aftermath of the First World War should serve to prove that neither side is free from having blood-stained hands. In the summer of 1919, two American observers toured Eastern Anatolia in order to gauge the need for relief efforts. What they and others discovered was evidence of a terribly brutal and vengeful Armenian backlash.

Soon after, Capt. E. N. Niles and Mr. A. E. Sutherland reported that, "In this entire region we were informed that the damage and destruction had been done by the Armenians, who, after the Russians retired, remained in occupation of the country, and who, when the Turkish army advanced, destroyed everything belonging to the Musulmans.

"Moreover, the Armenians are accused of having committed murder, rape, arson and horrible atrocities of every description upon the Musulman population. At first we were incredulous of these stories, but we finally came to believe them, since the testimony was absolutely unanimous and was corroborated by material evidence...At every town and village at which we stopped the inhabitants' first desire was to tell us, not of their needs, but of horrors which the Armenians had committed upon them and their families, the details of which were almost exactly the same as those perpetrated by the Turks upon the Armenians.

"We believe that it is incontestable that the Armenians were guilty of crimes of the same nature against the Turks as those of which the Turks are guilty against the Armenians."[11]

It is not my intention to in any way excuse the horrible crimes that were perpetrated against the Armenians. The ghosts of one million martyrs would not permit it. Rather, I mention this report of alleged Armenian sponsored atrocities merely to illustrate that there is no doubt horrific crimes were inflicted upon innocent victims from both peoples.

It is important that the descendants from both opposing sides clearly understand that corporately, each of them likely has at least one ex-butcher perched well within the branches of their family tree.

COMING HOME TO ROOST...

After all was said and done, the three leaders who had actually overseen the final demise of the Ottoman Empire, and the near destruction of the Armenian people, initially seemed to escape any and all retribution.

In the aftermath of the genocide, the Young Turk Triumvirate of Enver, Talaat and Djemal were tried *in abstentia* by the new Turkish government on the charges of "massacres, and unlawful personal profiteering."[12] As material proof of Ottoman responsibility for the holocaust, all three were convicted by a *Turkish* court and subsequently sentenced to death on July 13, 1919.[13] Some have contended that the trial was merely a sham for Allied consumption and only intended to soften Western public opinion.[14]

What is important, however, is that even though they fully blamed the exiled Young Turks, the Turkish government publicly admitted that crimes were committed and therefore that the genocide actually happened.

Regarding the main Turkish leadership of the tragic affair; each individual player evaded government custody, but they did not avoid eventual punishment.

Mehmed Talaat Pasha, referred to as the "architect" of the Armenian genocide, was unrepentant and likely unaffected by his legacy of death. He never saw the demise of the Armenians as anything less than a calculated necessity. On the night of November 3, 1918, with the final collapse of Ottoman military resistance; Talaat escaped from Constantinople onboard a German submarine bound for Berlin. For the next two and one-half years, he resided fairly openly in the fashionable Charlottenburg District on the west side of the German capital which, by the 1920's was rapidly becoming a centre of arts, leisure, and a vibrant night life.

The British and Soviet governments, hardly on the friendliest of terms in 1921, both feared that Talaat might be plotting to incite a Pan-Turanist, and Pan-Islamic uprising in the east. Deciding that he must be put out of the way, the secret services of both countries agreed to secure the assistance of Armenian revolutionaries for a revenge killing. Interviewed in early spring, 1921, by an agent from British intelligence; Talaat allegedly revealed plans to return to Turkey and join the budding nationalist movement.[15]

In the interim, the Armenian Revolutionary Federation (Dashnaks) had created and implemented "Operation Nemesis." Named after the Greek goddess of vengeance, the plan was to find and execute all those responsible for the Armenian genocide.[16]

Nine days after his discussion with the British agent, Talaat was assassinated in Berlin by a young Armenian Dashnak who was recruited expressly for the mission. Soghomon Tehlirian, a twenty-four year old student had taken rooms near Talaat's residence and quietly bided his time while observing the former Grand Vizier's daily routine. Finally on March 15, Tehlirian shot Talaat Pasha in front of his home killing him in broad daylight.

Immediately arrested by German police, the Armenian revolutionary was held over for trial. The Armenians had hoped that the sensational court proceedings would put on world display the crimes committed by Talaat, and the Young Turks. The publicity was extensive with one German socialist newspaper describing the assassin as a modern day "William Tell" (the legendary Swiss hero who had later killed the man that had forced him to shoot an apple off of his son's head).[17]

For his defense, Tehlirian had a trio of lawyers led by University of Kiel legal professor, Dr. Theodor Niemeyer. During the trial, the defense did not attempt to proclaim Tehlirian's innocence, but merely tried to demonstrate that the genocide had such an appalling effect upon the young Armenian that it drove him to kill out of revenge for the murder of his own family. Expert witnesses that testified at the trial included such notable figures as Protestant missionary Johannes Lepsius; Armenian church bishop, and holocaust survivor Grigoris Balakian; and General Liman von Sanders, the Turkish-German commander at the Battle of Gallipoli.

After a sensational trial that lasted two days, the jury found the defendant, "not guilty" after deliberating barely an hour.[18] It was

reported that after the verdict was read in court the German attend-
ees broke out in applause.[19] That is all the more remarkable when one
considers that Germany was Turkey's ally in the First World War.

Operation Nemesis was also responsible for the execution of other
key leaders of the Young Turks. Djemal Pasha suffered a similar fate as
that of Talaat, also being shot to death by Armenian assassins.

Immediately following the collapse of the Ottoman government
Djemal fled to Central Asia lured by the quixotic dream of Pan-
Turanism. Hired as the military Chief of Staff for the Afghan Army;
Djemal was killed en route from Berlin to Kabul by two Armenian
gunmen as he stopped in the Georgian capital of Tiflis (Tbilisi).[20]

Dr. Behaeddin Shakir, the alleged leader of the infamous "Special
Organization," had read the eulogy at Talaat's funeral in 1921. He
was also assassinated in Berlin the following year along with the former Young Turk governor of Trabzon, Cemal Azmi. In reporting the
deaths, *The New York Times* recorded that German authorities were
investigating, "a secret murder organization whose headquarters, the
Berlin police say, is in America."[21]

The "Butcher of Diyarbakir," Dr. Mehmed Reshid did not escape
the country but was captured a week after the armistice by the post-
war Turkish government. He was charged and convicted of murder
and the responsibility for the massacre of Armenians within his province. He shot and killed himself less than three months later after
first escaping, and then realizing that his re-capture, and eventual execution was imminent.[22]

The reputed mastermind of the genocide, Dr. Nazim Bey escaped
Turkey in 1918, but eventually returned after the establishment of
the Republic of Turkey. Ironically, although he was never brought to
ground by agents from *Nemesis*, Dr. Nazim was later hanged in 1926 for
allegedly conspiring to assassinate President Mustafa Kemal Ataturk.

Meanwhile Germany's vainglorious ex-Kaiser Wilhelm II, the man
who might have stopped the genocide, vainly awaited an invitation
to return to Berlin. He abdicated the imperial throne in November,

1918, and now, languishing in comfortable exile in Holland; the deposed monarch later watched with keen interest as the rejuvenated German army easily smashed through Poland, Denmark, Norway, the Lowlands and finally, his hated enemy France, in 1940.

He believed that the resurgence of the Reich would mean his return to the imperial throne, or the succession of his eldest grandson at the very least. As was so often the case with him; the Kaiser was badly mistaken. The former army corporal who had once served in the Kaiser's 16th Bavarian Reserve Regiment felt no desire to share power with anyone, let alone the monarch whom he personally despised for the defeat of the Reich in the First World War.

Upon receiving a congratulatory telegram from the former emperor, following the swift conquest of Holland in 1940, the German Fuhrer was amazed by the absurdly naive tone. Wilhelm wrote to Hitler, "I congratulate you and hope that under your marvelous leadership the German monarchy will be restored completely." Military historian Antony Beevor wryly observed, "Hitler was amazed that the old Kaiser expected him to play Bismarck."[23] Upon his reading of the former emperor's self-serving message, Hitler reportedly commented aloud, "What an idiot."

Kaiser Wilhelm II died at the age of eight-two on June 3, 1941 without ever again seeing his native Germany.

The final member of the Young Turk leadership was never caught by vengeful Armenian executioners but he also died violently nonetheless.

Following the First World War a number of out of work warlords and ex-generals began raising personal armies in an attempt to carve out individual fiefdoms across central Asia. The Russian Civil War (1917-1922) was the backdrop for terrible devastation being wrought upon civilians by merciless perpetrators from both the "Red" and "White" armies.

Many of the Asiatic warlords were chasing Pan-Turanian "windmills." The mad "Bloody White Baron," Nikolai von Ungern-Sternberg, a former Russian military officer, proclaimed himself to be the heir of Genghis Khan. For nearly four years the crazed and sadistic warlord terrorized eastern Siberia and northern China in an attempt to create a Turanian realm before eventually being killed by the Soviet Red Army in Mongolia.[24]

Finally, the "Turkish Napoleon," held to his life-long aspirations of imperial greatness until the very end. In pursuit of his elusive dream of a Central Asian, Turkic empire; Enver Pasha was also killed in combat while leading a "Pan-Turanian" insurgency against the Red Army on the Russian border with Afghanistan.[25]

As has so often happened throughout history, violent men had suffered suitably violent ends. In the case of the Young Turk Triumvirate of Enver, Talaat, and Djemal; many understood that the bullets that felled them were leveled on behalf of the countless victims who were slain as a result of their ruthless regime.

All the architects of the holocaust were gone. The voracious birds that had feasted on the bodies of the Armenian dead had finally come home to roost.

13

"ENNUI"

PERHAPS THE STRANGEST part of the story of the Armenian Genocide is that after one hundred years, it still has no ending.

As I first discovered in 1999, during my visit to Jerusalem's celebrated Armenian Quarter, the terrible wrongs of 1915 have never been resolved. As a result, the hatred and anger on both sides is yet to be satiated.

There is truly something alarming about the fact that the Turks and Armenians remain so adamant about the events of a century ago. Each fully blames the other for the tragic episode and accepts virtually no responsibility, whatsoever. Armenians refuse to believe that revolutionary forces existed which threatened Turkish national security at the start of the First World War; even as Turks fully dismiss the notion that the Ottoman government's response was terribly excessive, resulting in the wanton murder of hundreds of thousands of innocent civilians.

The total lack of liability and indignation equally exhibited by both sides is all the more amazing when one considers that virtually all of the participants of the tragedy, both perpetrators and victims alike, have long since perished. It may be part of an eastern mindset.

When I was a young boy, my immigrant Greek grandfather assured me that there were no prisons in Greece. Asking him to explain why that was, he responded sincerely that there wasn't any need for prisons as there were "no bad Greeks."

Many years later, my wife and I toured Turkey. On the first day of our visit we were duly informed by our guide that there were "no bad Turks." The prisons, which she freely admitted <u>did</u> exist, were simply filled with foreigners.

Like my grandfather before her; she was totally serious.

CENTENNIAL MADNESS

Amazingly, for all of their continuous acrimony, the century-old dispute between Turk and Armenian is now being revisited in the violent ethnic and religious struggles that are currently being waged throughout the Near East.

Contemporary newspaper headlines daily illustrate that the underlying problems of the past century still remain. Ethnic, religious, and ideological hostilities are as virulent in the present as they were in 1915.

The State of Israel remains besieged by hostile Arab neighbors without and by angry Palestinians within. Seemingly never-ending warfare is still being waged in Afghanistan; Iraq remains in perpetual turmoil following the overthrow of Saddam Hussein, and the subsequent withdrawal of American led Coalition forces; Syria is embroiled in a lengthy civil war; and Iran continues to pursue the development of nuclear arms. Meanwhile, despite the death of Osama Ben Laden, the forces of Al Qaeda remain committed to fomenting a world-wide war of terror.

At the time of this writing *Jihadi* Sunni Muslim extremists dubbed the *State of Iraq and ash Sham* (ISIS) have stormed out of the desert sands and begun a wholesale onslaught upon Christians, and rival Muslims that is eerily reminiscent of the ride of the *Hamidye* more than a century ago. Once again Assyrian Christians, Zoroastrian Yazidis, and Shiite Arabs are being brutally targeted for extinction with grisly beheadings, crucifixions and mass murders. Oddly enough, in an ironic twist the fleeing refugees of today's depredations are being aided and rescued by *Kurdish* fighters.

As a result of the continuous strife in the Middle East, today's immediate threats have naturally overshadowed those of the past. With all else that is currently happening in the region; the world has either forgotten or become weary of what occurred in Anatolia so long ago. Nonetheless to many Armenians, the death and despair continues virtually unabated.

Prior to the fall of the Soviet Union age-old tensions in the Caucasus began to re-erupt. A vacuum created by Soviet decentralization provided the climate for ethnic cleansing and as a result Armenians were massacred in Azerbaijan.[1] In February 1988, the Caspian city of Sumgait in what was Soviet Azerbaijan was the scene of four days of brutal pogroms against the small Armenian population. It was a violent prelude of things to come.

In the continuation of their century old dispute that had been forcefully suppressed by decades of Soviet rule; Armenia and Azerbaijan resumed their unfinished war of 1918-1920, shortly after both nations regained independence in 1991. The disputed region of Nagorno-Karabakh was the focus of the conflict with Armenia gaining control of the Azerbaijani stronghold of Shusha in 1992. In classic *deja vu*, Turkish reaction was fully supportive of the Muslim Azeris, and Ankara sent material aid and military advisors to assist against the Armenians. Finally, a cease-fire was agreed-to in 1992 but the region is still contested being currently administered as a semi-autonomous republic. Armenia and Azerbaijan remain bitter, and sporadic fighting continues occasionally.

To illustrate how virulent the relations remain between these two neighboring peoples one need look no further than a currently popular video game. "Today, youngsters in Azerbaijan have the opportunity to alter history via a video game called 'Under Occupation.' The objective is to recapture Shusha from Armenian forces. Gamers assume the role of an Azerbaijani soldier who engages in virtual firefights with Armenian soldiers in house-to-house combat...Under Occupation is not for the faint of heart: there's lots of killing and computer-generated gore...including shooting lots of Armenian enemies."[2]

The provocative game apparently enjoyed the approval of the Azerbaijani government. A formal presentation of it was sponsored by the Ministry of Youth and Sports at a public event held in Baku in the summer of 2012.

The madness continues.

AN END WITHOUT A NEW BEGINNING

For a full century the Turks have officially denied any responsibility for the events of 1915. For this failure, the Armenians have perpetually fanned the flames of hatred, vengeance, and a demand for justice. The Armenian response has at times been ugly.

The violent demise of the three Turkish leaders, two of which were killed by Armenian gunmen, ultimately did nothing to heal the enduring bitterness and seething hatred that have followed through the ensuing decades. Since the 1970's Armenian operatives have allegedly assassinated hundreds of Turkish diplomats around the world. They have also been linked to terror bombings at airports in Paris and Ankara.[3]

Meanwhile the Turks have been insensitive in their handling of Armenian grievances often appearing to actually take lengths at further offending them. In 1996 the mortal remains of Enver Pasha were returned to Istanbul from his burial place in Tajikistan, for a "Heroes Funeral" seventy-four years after the former War Minister's death. The event was attended by the Turkish President, along with numerous government cabinet members, senior military leaders, and other Turkish dignitaries.

Ankara news media reported that, "After prayers, led by a group of turbaned imams, a group of soldiers representing the various branches of Turkey's armed forces shouldered the casket... and placed it on a gun carriage, which drove through the streets of Sisli [in central Istanbul], accompanied by a military band playing Chopin's 'Funeral March.'"[4]

The Turkish tribute given to Enver Pasha would certainly be disquieting to the living descendants of the Armenian victims of the 1915 holocaust, particularly with the General's final interment on Eternal Freedom Hill near to the grave of his one-time partner, Talaat Pasha.

Of perhaps even greater concern, and quite indicative of the passions that the tragic events of so long-ago still continue to incite; was the report of a disturbing demonstration that took place during the funeral procession.

"Hundreds of members of the neo-fascist Idealist's Club waved flags and chanted slogans as they marched behind the hearse. The idealists are youth members of the ultra-right Nationalist Action Party, the powerful political group that was blamed for most of the right wing bombings and political murders in the 1970s. 'Turkey will become the great Turan,' they chanted, referring to the imaginary Turkish state linking all the ethnic Turkish peoples in the vast area stretching from the Balkans to central China -- a state which Enver Pasha futilely tried to create."[5]

BITTER CROSSROADS

Aside from providing overdue fairness for the victims; the modern importance of the Armenian genocide is more germane to *where* it happened than *why*. Located at the crossroads of three continents, the strategic significance of the stage upon which the holocaust occurred cannot be overstated. Finally resolving a controversy that took place fully one hundred years in the past is actually paramount to helping achieve contemporary stability in this vital region.

Today Turkey desires to join the European Union, and is a valuable participant in the North Atlantic Treaty Organization (NATO)

as well as in the West's worldwide War on Terror. The newly independent Armenian Republic also aspires to having greater ties to Europe
and the West, while cautiously balancing its critical relationship with
neighboring Russia.

For modern Turkey and Armenia the current stakes are high yet
both nations continue to vehemently oppose the other on the matter
of the alleged genocide. Meanwhile, the rest of the world is typically
influenced by how the matter affects their own current affairs. It has
even appeared at times that both the European and the American
"court of opinion" have been unjustly influenced by modern political
expediency rather than the attempt to find a fair and just remedy of
the long-ago atrocity.

Instead of using the example of the past tragedy to help further
international cooperation into the twenty-first century; the European
Union has used the Armenian holocaust as a reason for excluding
the Turks from membership. With the real underlying concern that
Turkish inclusion would dilute the over-all economy of the rest of
Europe; the EU has rejected their application on the "convenient"
grounds of their failure to admit to any past responsibility for the
genocide.

In a "post 9/11" world, the exacerbation of tensions in western
Asia, and the strategic security of the region are as critical and
dangerous today as had ever existed during the Cold War. It is vital
to the future safety of the area that this long festering problem at
last be satisfactorily resolved. What is essential to the resolution of
this matter is a total willingness on the part of both sides to objec-
tively discuss and attempt to eliminate the bias and inflammatory
rhetoric.

Fears of forced reparations in land and money have fueled the
Turkish denials. The present lack of any living claimants, and the recent independence of the State of Armenia following the dissolution
of the Soviet Union, should finally serve to mollify any future Turkish
concerns.

With Armenian independence now a reality, world public opinion (to the extent that it actually exists) has been generally assuaged. In this country the topic has actually been somewhat avoided. The United States has never officially recognized the Armenian genocide beyond occasional readings into the U. S. Senate "minutes," or through various state and local proclamations.

Every past presidential administration, whether Republican or Democrat, has refrained from antagonizing our Turkish NATO ally, much to the chagrin of America's sizeable Armenian community. The present occupant of the White House is no exception.

Even now during the centennial commemoration of the tragedy, very little is heard or discussed. Surprisingly, the "United States Holocaust Memorial Museum" in Washington D.C. also fails to make any serious reference to the plight of the Armenians even though exhibits exist on the genocides in Rwanda (1994); in Bosnia-Herzegovina (1995); and in the Sudan (2003-2005).[6] In fairness, the story of the Armenian Holocaust is addressed in a small number of publications but very little else.

At the time of this writing it has been recently announced that, "In April 2015, on the 100th anniversary of the Armenian Genocide...the Armenian Apostolic Orthodox Church will take the momentous step to officially recognize as saints of the church the countless souls who perished during the Genocide in witness of their Christian faith."[7]

With the unprecedented church act of canonizing 1.5 million souls; the dead of Armenia will finally receive closure on their violent past. It is hoped that the descendants of both sides of the tragedy will also take this centennial opportunity to bury the deep animosity that has existed for far too long.

THE DEPRAVITY OF MEN

In the twentieth century, genocide has become a far too common reality. The Jewish Holocaust of the 1930's-40's so greatly overshadows the events of 1915 to such an extent that few in this country have even heard of the Anatolian tragedy outside of the Armenian-American community. In short, the subject of the century-old genocide is today virtually unknown and little regarded by anyone that is not of Armenian or Turkish descent.

The very notion that the public memory of a chapter so inhumane could be swallowed up and virtually forgotten in the years that followed is remarkable and testifies to how far we have fallen as a society. The subsequent decades of ever-escalating holocaust, and "ethnic cleansing," have become so terribly commonplace, as to finally overshadow the horrors that were visited upon the Armenians. That such a result could even transpire, loudly testifies to the never-ending violence of the 20th century and the depravity of man.

William Brustein posits that the Jewish genocide was unique in that it was driven by four separate root causes, and he enumerates them as religious, racial, economic, and political.[8] (In a brief conversation with Dr. Brustein following his lecture at my university, I suggested that the same four roots could be equally applied to the Armenian genocide, to which possibility he politely acquiesced).

The century-old tensions of Muslim versus Christian; Asian versus Caucasian; Poor against Affluent, and Turanist versus Dashnak, have strong parallels to Anti-Semitism in 1930's central Europe.

As modern society's first genocide, the events of 1915 set a diabolical precedent for the rest of the twentieth century. Jews, Cambodians, Rwandans, Sudanese, Bosnians, and other persecuted peoples would later follow the same blood-stained path that was initially paved by the bodies of the Armenians.

The fact that hundreds of thousands of Armenians, including innocent women and children, were slaughtered in Anatolia is not questioned. Even those that vehemently deny the charge of government orchestrated genocide, admit to the virtual destruction of Turkey's Armenian population. It is only the number of people that were actually slain, and the motivation of those responsible for their deaths that continues to be debated.

THE BALANCE SHEET

The intention of this book was not to become overly concerned with the infamous details of the holocaust itself, as numerous scholarly volumes already exist that describe, and certainly *prove* the tragic events. The brief but extremely grisly episodes that were recounted are rather intended to illustrate and confirm the proposed rationale for the genocide. My purpose in this thesis was an attempt to identify and explain the motives that led up to the events of 1915.

Research has suggested that there were as many as ten separate, but totally interdependent reasons that existed for the mandated mayhem. In summary, we discussed the following:

(1) Justifiable Turkish fears of a Russian supported Armenian "fifth-column" during the First World War;

(2) The real existence of the Armenian Revolutionary Federation and its avowed program of resistance to, and gaining independence from, Turkish rule;

(3) The violent release of feelings of pent-up rage and vengeance, that were poured out upon the easily persecuted Armenians, as the result of European military victories over the Turks;

(4) The centuries of blood-feuds and reprisals between Turks and Armenians that had seen the killing of innocent victims by both sides;

(5) The call for Muslim *Jihad* or Holy War declared by the advocates of Pan-Islam, against the Christian "infidels," not only for the will of Allah, but also as a unifying force in the Turkish Empire;

(6) The timeless desire for spoils and plunder, particularly in light of the low standard of living in the Turkish military. The

avarice ranged from the localized taking of plunder to the arrogant government demand for Armenian life insurance proceeds;

(7) The subjugation of the male population into forced labor and the female citizens into sexual bondage;

(8) The removal of a large physical geographic obstacle to the planned Pan-Turanian expansion into Central Asia;

(9) As backlash to the perceptions of European contempt for the "racially inferior" Asians; and

(10) As a direct result of the personal pride, perfidy, or paranoia of the Turkish leaders themselves.

Although the actions of the relatively small number of Armenian revolutionaries certainly contributed to the creation of the final tragedy, and some Turkish precautions were justifiable, it is the opinion of this observer that the Ottoman Government knowingly sanctioned, and orchestrated the violent solution to the "Armenian Question."

Historian Gwynne Dyer expressed it well. "The almost unanimous Turkish reaction has been to try to forget the whole episode, and when that becomes impossible to seek complete justification for the holocaust in allegations of wholesale disloyalty, treason and revolt by the Ottoman Armenians in the gravest crisis in the history of the Turkish nation — allegations wholly true as far as Armenian sentiment went, only partly true in terms of overt acts, and totally insufficient as a justification for what was done."[9]

At the start, the terrible course later adopted by the Turkish leadership was not premeditated, but rather was the result of cumulative years of growing frustrations, fears and fantasies that ultimately pervaded the thinking of the Young Turks. It was not, however, the product of any initially conceived program to uproot and destroy the Armenians.

It is the firm opinion of this observer that when the Young Turks first came to power in 1908, they clearly exhibited a uniform and sincere desire to improve the conditions of all national, ethnic and religious groups within the Ottoman Empire.

It was only after enduring numerous internal and external threats that the Young Turk leadership (ultimately dominated by the flawed "Triumvirate" of Enver, Djemal and Talaat) grew in paranoia; hardened in its attitudes; and finally descended into violent and prolonged depravity.

This does not in any way excuse the heinous crimes that the Turks committed against the Armenians, but it does help to explain how such a tragedy could happen.

"ENNUI"

Alas, after one hundred years, the time has certainly arrived to bring final closure to this single, sorrowful chapter in the never-ending and shameful saga of man's inhumanity.

During the passage of that same century, Americans have fought terrible and costly wars with Germany twice, Japan and Italy once, and even outlasted what at times was a very "hot" Cold War with Russia, China and Viet Nam. Yet despite the ubiquitous presence of American military gravesites found all over the world; we have somehow managed to come to terms and now have relatively peaceful, and in some cases even friendly relations with our former deadly adversaries. Frankly, the world should be growing a bit tired of the never-ending hatred between Turks and Armenians.

The ultimate goal of any student of the genocide should be to help enhance the development of a serious dialogue between the two contentious parties. More importantly, the lessons taught should help to prevent such a tragedy from ever happening again. Sadly, the great number of twentieth century genocides that have occurred since the Armenian holocaust, have proven that ultimately nothing has been learned. "Who today still speaks of the massacre of the Armenians?"[10]

This small contribution will hopefully add to the literature the observations of one who at the outset was completely dispassionate and virtually free of any personal prejudice or prior influence. Although I do not presume to believe that my humble efforts will materially alter the course of a debate that has angrily persisted for more than a century; I do fervently hope that it has helped to open the eyes of some who had not yet heard of the great Anatolian tragedy.

My only caution is that any further study be done with a warning about the high degree of subjectivity that is attached to most of what has been written on the subject. Little scholarship exists, out of the plethora of published material, which has not been somewhat tainted by subjectivity and preconception.

Nonetheless, it is high time that the Turks should finally admit to their national role in the tragedy, fully recognizing the fact that <u>no</u> <u>living</u> individual is personally responsible for the alleged crimes. The Germans do not deny the holocaust of 1933-1945, and it is now actually a crime in that country to do so. Rather than accept shame for the actions of their ancestors, it is important for modern Turks to finally acknowledge and actually examine *why* such events took place.

Equally, the Armenians should be willing to move on, and appreciate that all those who actually perpetrated the crimes now rest in death with the victims. A public apology from the Turkish government is merited and then should suffice to close the sad and grisly chapter once and for all. Everyone must understand that modern Turks are no more responsible for the century old genocide than contemporary living Americans are to blame for the sordid history of American slavery.

For the Turkish government, possibly fearful of any potential economic loss; the overdue admission of the genocide of 1915 will not likely force the forfeiture of any monetary reparations. After a century, there are simply no living survivors left to compensate. The West Germans agreed to pay reparations to Israel in the early 1950's but even that gesture waned with the passage of time. Oddly enough, in that particular instance many Jews were adamantly opposed to any

German payment of financial restitution as it might have given the appearance that they could purchase forgiveness for their crimes.

Just as importantly, the fear of a potential award of Turkish territory to the newly independent Armenian Republic is as fanciful as any notion that the United States Government, sorely penitent at the nineteenth century extermination of Native Americans, would ever willfully return Manhattan to the Indians.

For their part, Armenians must renounce terror and violent acts of revenge. The deadly extremists who, since the 1970's have willfully murdered Turkish citizens, more resemble the evil minions of Osama Bin Laden than the noble disciples of Elie Wiesel, and must be denounced and rejected by the Armenian community. After all, nobody that has been slain during the past few decades had anything to do with the crimes that were committed a century ago.

In addition, we must change the long-standing official "non-position" of this country. The United States needs to finally join with Uruguay (who was first to act in 1965), along with Canada, France, Germany, Italy, Argentina, Australia, and even Russia, with more than a dozen other countries, in formally recognizing and condemning the genocide of 1915.

Our own nation's presidential failure to formally recognize the Armenian Holocaust for fear of offending our Turkish NATO ally has curiously been the unanimous position of <u>both</u> Democrat and Republican occupants of the White House. The United States has equally strong ties to the Turks and the Armenians, however, and should make an effort to finally bring the opposing parties to the conference table.

The current American President might even take-on the role of mediator as had earlier been accepted by three of his predecessors: Theodore Roosevelt's arbitration of the Russo-Japanese War of 1905-06; Woodrow Wilson's work in ending the First World War and creating the League of Nations; and Jimmy Carter's hosting of the 1978 "Camp David Accords" between Egypt's Anwar Sadat and Israel's Menachem Begin. For their efforts each of the former presidents later received a Nobel Peace Prize.

The pursuit of peace has indeed been elusive. Nowhere has this been more so than between the Turks and Armenians. Woodrow Wilson presciently forecast in his 1920 Nobel acceptance speech, "It will be a continuing labor. In the indefinite course of [the] years before us there will be abundant opportunity for others to distinguish themselves in the crusade against hate and fear and war."[11] That crusade, that labor, that mantle need now be duly taken up again.

Eighty-nine years later to the exact same day, it was conceded at Oslo in an acceptance speech by President Obama himself, "...that for all the cruelty and hardship of our world, we are not mere prisoners of fate. Our actions matter, and can bend history in the direction of justice."[12] Already possessing his own Peace Prize, Barak Hussein Obama, by virtue of his name and dual Islamic and Christian upbringing, may have a unique and unprecedented opportunity to facilitate a long-overdue rapprochement. As Theodore Roosevelt concluded in yet another Nobel lecture, "The credit belongs to the man...who at the worst, if he fails, at least fails while daring greatly."[13]

Finally, subjective historians need to soberly and dispassionately reexamine the record and cease the biased rhetoric, and exaggerated claims that have often been exhibited by apologists from both camps. The current academic polemic is often as heated and vitriolic as that displayed by the descendants of the actual participants themselves. There is also the lingering suspicion of potential conflicts of interest and even charges and counter-charges of collusion. The desire for obtaining foundation research grants; or the currying of favor with special interests in order to obtain personal physical access to previously inaccessible archives, and other jealously guarded academic domains; have appeared at times to unfairly influence the otherwise respected scholarship emanating from *both* sides.

All that matters in the end, however, is that the historian composes his thesis without prejudice and faithfully presents it "before the only tribunal that matters to him—the tribunal of history."[14]

Regarding my own humble pronouncement upon the events of 1915, I believe that the truth about motive and responsibility exists somewhere between the two opposing extremes. That crimes were actually committed on a colossal scale is undeniable. Pre-meditation is harder to prove. At the very least the knowledge that unforeseen events got disastrously out of control in the years, and days leading up to the holocaust of 1915 (some exacerbated by the Armenians them-selves) may help to explain, but not exonerate the Turkish actions.

What is certain, however, is that after the passage of ten decades, all those who willfully perpetrated the horrendous acts of genocide, have since joined their victims in the deep finality of death. For the living descendents of both sides, it is now time to move on.

Unfortunately, for genocide scholars, "plaintiffs," and "defen-dants" alike, as of the time of this writing, the century-old court still remains in session.

It is high time that the denial is ended, and the Emperor is clothed.

LORD HAVE MERCY! LORD HAVE...!"

For those that survived, their lives were forever changed.

Never able to erase the horrible images that they had witnessed and endured, Armenian holocaust survivors lived with a fear and loathing of the Turks for the rest of their lives. Third generation Armenian-American Peter Balakian recounted his grandmother's fears that the "Turks" were bombing Pearl Harbor on December 7, 1941.[15]

In October 2014, a lady believed to be the oldest remaining holo-caust victim living in America, finally passed on at an advanced age variously reported as being between 108 and 116. A long-time resident of Chicago, Helen Paloian still visualized terrible images that no child should ever have witnessed. UCLA Professor Richard Hovannisian credited her as being, "one of the few survivors left in the world who could remember in detail all the horrors." The *Chicago Sun Times* reported that Mrs. Paloian vividly recalled as a young girl making a miraculous, solitary escape from incarceration shortly before likely being burned alive in a building about to be torched by the Turks. Afraid, orphaned and alone, "she said she begged on the streets for food, grubbed for roots and ate grass 'like a chicken.'"[16]

As the steadily diminishing roster of aged survivors finally disappears with the passage of time, their living descendants choose not to forget. Passed along to the victim's children and grandchildren, the horrifying stories of the Anatolian tragedy have been kept alive and perpetuated. To the Genocide survivors and their scions, "the special term of *medz yegherne* is now part of their language as a consecrated word for recalling the inhumanity of the period. Heavy sorrow has marked the lives of the descendants of the martyrs. To the new generations *medz yegherne* carries the concept of 'great crime' or 'great calamity,' and they meditate on this subject of survival with almost mystical sanctity."[17]

Dr. Charles Hajinian, a third generation Armenian-American still contemplates the vision of his maternal great-grandmother, diligently weaving her own burial shroud as she marched hopelessly through the Anatolian desert.[18] In his reverent solitude, he can almost hear her weakened voice continuously whispering through parched and swollen lips the words, *"Der Voorghmia, Der Voorghmia"* ("Lord have mercy, Lord have mercy") before finally stumbling to the ground, and being lifted unto Heaven.

<hr />

INDEX

NOTES:

CHAPTER ONE:

[1] *The New York Times* (17 September 1915).

[2] McCarthy, Justin A., <u>Death and Exile: The Ethnic Cleansing of Ottoman Muslims, 1821-1922</u> (Princeton, NJ: Darwin Press, 1995) 187.

[3] Kuper, Leo, <u>International Action Against Genocide</u> (London: Minority Rights Group Report, Number 53, 1982) 11.

[4] Lemkin, Raphael, <u>Axis Rule in Occupied Europe</u> (Washington, DC: Carnegie Endowment, 1944) 81.

[5] Weitz, Eric D., <u>A Century of Genocide: Utopias of Race and Nation</u> (Princeton, NJ: Princeton University Press, 2003) 8-9.

[6] Andreopoulos, George J., Ed. <u>Genocide: Conceptual and Historic Dimensions</u> (Philadelphia, PA: University of Pennsylvania Press, 1994) 2-7.

[7] Weitz, 8.

[8] Lewy, Guenter. "Were American Indians the Victims of Genocide?" *George Mason University's History News Network*, reprinted from *Commentary* (September, 2004) Retrieved 01-25-2013.

[9] Brown, Dee, <u>Bury My Heart At Wounded Knee: An Indian History of the American West</u> (New York: Bantam Books, 1970) 413-418.

[10] Lewy, Guenter. "Were American Indians the Victims of Genocide?" *George Mason University's History News Network*, reprinted from *Commentary* (September, 2004) Retrieved 01-25-2013.

[11] Kuper, Leo, "Theoretical Issues Relating to Genocide," in Andreopoulos, 33.

[12] Andreopoulos, 6.

[13] Weitz, 240.

[14] Chalk, Frank, and Kurt Jonassohn, The History and Sociology of Genocide: Analyses and Case Studies (New Haven, CT: Yale University Press, 1990) 249.

[15] Markusen, Eric, and David Kopf, The Holocaust and Strategic Bombing: Genocide and Total War in the Twentieth Century (Boulder, CO: Westview Press, 1995) 43.

[16] Weitz, 7.

[17] Toynbee, Arnold J., "A Summary of Armenian History Up to and Including 1915," in Viscount J. Bryce, The Treatment of Armenians in the Ottoman Empire: Documents Presented to Viscount Grey of Fallodon, Secretary of State for Foreign Affairs (London: H.M.S.O., 1916) 651.

[18] Hovannisian, Richard G., Ed., Remembrance and Denial: The Case of the Armenian Genocide (Detroit, MI: Wayne State University Press, 1998) 15.

[19] Auron, Yair, The Banality of Denial: Israel and the Armenian Genocide (New Brunswick: Transaction Publishers, 2003) 301.

[20] Chalk, 44.

[21] Bournoutian, George A., A History of the Armenian People, Volume II: 1500 A.D. to the Present (Costa Mesa, CA: Mazda Publishers, 1994) 102.

[22] Melson, Robert F., Revolution and Genocide: On the Origins of the Armenian Genocide and the Holocaust (Chicago: The University of Chicago Press, 1992) 247.

[23] President's Commission on the Holocaust (Washington, DC: Executive Order 12093, 1979) 3.

[24] Derogy, Jacques, Resistance and Revenge: The Armenian Assassination of the Turkish Leaders Responsible for the 1915 Massacres and Deportations (New Brunswick: Transaction Publishers, 1990) 195.

[25] Gulbekian, Edward V., "The Poles and Armenians in Hitler's Political Thinking," The Armenian Review 41, No.3 (Autumn, 1988) 3.

[26] Shirer, William L., <u>The Rise and Fall of the Third Reich: A History of Nazi Germany</u> (New York: Simon and Schuster, 1959, 1988) ff 529.

[27] Anderson, Margaret Lavinia, "Who Still Talked about the Extermination of the Armenians?" From <u>A Question Of Genocide: Armenians and Turks at the End of the Ottoman Empire</u>, Edited by Ronald Grigor Suny, Fatma Müge Göçek, and Norman M. Naimark (New York, NY: Oxford University Press, 2011) 199.

[28] Gulbekian, 11.

[29] Hitler, Adolf, <u>Mein Kampf</u> (Boston, MA: Houghton Mifflin Company, 1925, 1971) i.

[30] Dadrian, Vahakn N., <u>The History of the Armenian Genocide: Ethnic Conflict from the Balkans to Anatolia to the Caucasus</u> (Providence RI: Berghahn Books, 1995) 410-412.

[31] Bormann Martin, <u>The Bormann Letters</u>, Edited by H. R. Trevor Roper (London: 1954) 192-194.

[32] Dadrian, 256, 259.

[33] Weitz, 51.

[34] Power, Samantha, <u>A Problem From Hell: America and the Age of Genocide</u> (New York: Basic Books, 2002) 19.

[35] Smith, Roger W., "Genocide and Denial: The Armenian Case and Its Implications," *The Armenian Review* 42, No.1 (Spring, 1989) 4.

[36] Ibid., 4.

[37] Papazian Dennis, "Misplaced Credulity: Contemporary Turkish Attempts to Refute the Armenian Genocide," *The Armenian Review* 45, No.1-2 (Spring/Summer, 1992) 185.

[38] "The United States Holocaust Memorial Museum," website lists little information regarding the Armenian genocide citing a 1995 lecture as the principal reference (accessed 2 March 2013).

[39] <u>President's Commission on the Holocaust</u>, 3.

[40] McCarthy, Justin, <u>The Ottoman Peoples and the End Of Empire</u> (London: Arnold, 2001). 106.

[41] Lowry, Heath W. <u>The Nature of the Early Ottoman State</u> (Albany, NY: State University of New York Press, 2003) 99-100.

[42] MacFie, A. L., The End of the Ottoman Empire, 1908-1923 London: Longman, 1998) 133.

[43] Ibid., 134.

[44] Langer, William L., The Diplomacy of Imperialism, 1890-1902, Volumes I & II (New York: Alfred A Knopf, 1935, 1951) 157.

[45] Ibid., 321-350.

[46] Hovannisian, 242.

[47] Shaw, Stanford J., and Ezel Kural Shaw, History of the Ottoman Empire and Modern Turkey, Volume II: Reform, Revolution, and Republic: The Rise of Modern Turkey, 1808-1975 (Cambridge: Cambridge University Press, 1977) 315.

[48] Ibid., 315.

[49] The Armenian Allegations: Myth and Reality/ A Handbook of Facts and Documents, Second Edition (Washington, D.C.: Assembly of Turkish American Associations, 1987) 21-29.

[50] Hovannisian, 248.

[51] Bournoutian, 103.

[52] Ruggiero, Adriane, The Ottoman Empire (New York: Benchmark Books, 2003) 22.

[53] Hovannisian, 244.

[54] Ibid., 244.

[55] Gunter, Michael M. Pursuing the Just Cause of Their People: A Study of Contemporary Armenian Terrorism (New York: Greenwood Press, 1986) 3.

[56] Tall Armenian Tale: The Other Side of the Falsified Genocide, http://www.tallarmeniantale.com/GS-Manne.htm (accessed September 19, 2014).

[57] Horowitz, Irving Louis, "Government Responsibilities to Jews and Armenians: Nazi Holocaust and Turkish Genocide Reconsidered," The Armenian Review 39, No.1 (Spring, 1986) 3.

[58] Carzou, Jean Marie, Un Genocide Exemplaire: Armenie 1915 (Paris: Flammarion, 1975) Photographs following 128.

[59] Horowitz, 5.

[60] The Wall Street Journal, Editorial (12 August 1983).

[61] Fein, Helen, "Testing Theories Brutally: Armenia (1915), Bosnia (1992) and Rwanda (1994)," in Levon Chorbajian and George Shirinian, Eds., Studies in Comparative Genocide (London: MacMillan Press, Ltd., 1999) 158.

[62] Chalk, Frank and Kurt Jonassohn, The History and Sociology of Genocide: Analyses and Case Studies (New Haven, CT: Yale University Press, 1990) 15.

[63] Ibid., 158.

[64] Waller, James, Becoming Evil: How Ordinary People Commit Genocide and Mass Killing (Oxford: Oxford University Press, 2002) 51.

[65] Ibid., 51.

CHAPTER TWO:

[1] Ramsaur, Ernest Edmondson, Jr., The Young Turks: Prelude to the Revolution of 1908 (Princeton, NJ: Princeton University Press, 1957) 136.

[2] D---ian, Dikran, Autobiography of Dikran D---ian, and Political Events, 1852-1915 (Constantinople: [Family Records] 1915, 1963) 57.

[3] MacFie, 39.

[4] The London Times (10 August 1908).

[5] Ramsaur, 137.

[6] Haslip, Joan, The Sultan: The Life of Abdul Hamid II (New York, NY: Holt, Rinehart, and Winston, 1958) 221.

[7] The New York Times (12 September 1896).

[8] Kinross, 579.

[9] Haslip, 1-5, 19.

[10] Wheatcroft, Andrew, The Ottomans (London: Viking, 1993) 194.

[11] Ibid., 194.

[12] Fest, Joachim C., Hitler (New York: Harcourt Brace Jovanovich, Inc., 1973, 1974) 15.

[13] Shakespeare, William, Hamlet, Act III, Scene 2.

[14] *The Economist* (March 27, 2004) 52.

[15] Ramsaur, 9.

[16] Ibid., 9.

[17] 82 Weitz, Eric D., "Germany and the Young Turks:Revolutionaries into Statesmen," from Suny, Ronald Grigor, Fatma Müge Göçek, and Norman M. Naimark, Editors, A Question of Genocide (New York, NY: Oxford University Press, 2011) 181.

[18] *The Los Angeles Herald* (1 September 1890).

[19] Davis, William Stearns, "The Roots of the War," *The Century Illustrated Monthly Magazine*, Volume 98, May-October, 1919 (New York, NY: The Century Co., 1919) 247-248.

[20] Latimer, Elizabeth W., Russia and Turkey in the Nineteenth Century (Chicago, 1893) in Ramsaur, 9.

[21] Haslip, 265.

[22] Wheatcroft, 200.

[23] Ibid., 201.

[24] Ibid., 219.

[25] Davis, 248.

[26] Finkel, Caroline, Osman's Dream: The History of the Ottoman Empire (New York, NY: Basic Books, 2005) 491.

[27] Wheatcroft, 26.

[28] Ibid., 25.

[29] Davison, Roderic H., Turkey (Englewood Cliffs, NJ: Prentice-Hall, Inc., 1968) 78.

[30] Kushner, David, The Rise of Turkish Nationalism, 1876-1908 (London: Frank Case and Company, Ltd., 1977) 3.

[31] Ibid., 3.

[32] Ibid., 3.

[33] Ibid., 3.

[34] Davison, 80.

[35] Etmekjian, James, "Tanzimat Reforms and Their Effect on the Armenians in Turkey," *The Armenian Review* 25 (Spring, 1972) 10.

[36] Arai Masami, <u>Turkish Nationalism In the Young Turk Era</u> (Leiden: E. J. Brill, 1992).

[37] Etmekjian, 10.

[38] Kushner, 57.

[39] Davison, 80.

[40] Etmekjian, 10.

[41] Ibid., 10.

[42] Haddad, William W., and William Ochsenwald, Eds., <u>Nationalism In A Non-National State: The Dissolution of the Ottoman Empire</u> (Columbus, OH: Ohio State University Press, 1977) 33.

[43] Davison, 80-81.

[44] Ibid., 80.

[45] Ibid., 80.

[46] Etmekjian, Lillian, "Armenian Cultural and Political Contributions to Reform in Turkey," <i>The Armenian Review</i> 29 (Summer, 1976) 168.

[47] Ibid., 168.

[48] Ibid., 169.

[49] Wheatcroft, 87.

[50] Ibid., 97.

[51] Ibid., 89.

[52] Ibid., 124.

[53] Etmekjian, 169.

[54] Ibid., 169, 181.

[55] Davison, 84.

[56] National Congress of Turkey, <u>The Turco-Armenian Question: The Turkish Point of View</u> (Constantinople: The National Congress of Turkey, 1919) 14.

[57] Ibid., 15.

[58] Haddad, 41.

[59] Ibid., 41.

[60] <u>Ottoman Turkish 'Reform Rescripts' of the XIX Century</u> (Constantinople: The Firman and Hatt-I-Humayun of the Sultan

Relative to Privileges and Reforms in Turkey, 1856) *The Armenian Review* 28 (Spring, 1975) 71.

[61] Ibid., 71.

[62] Donabedian, Kevork, "The Eastern Question and the Armenian Case," *The Armenian Review* 25 (Spring, 1972) 52.

[63] Ibid., 51.

[64] Mardin, Serif, The Genesis of Young Ottoman Thought: A Study in the Modernization of Turkish Political Ideas (Syracuse, NY: Syracuse University Press, 1962, 2000) 19.

[65] Ibid., 19.

[66] Davison, 88.

[67] Ramsaur, 6.

[68] Davison, 85.

[69] Ibid., 85.

[70] Ibid., 85.

[71] Ibid., 86.

[72] Kushner, 51.

[73] Davison, 86.

[74] Ramsaur 6.

[75] Ibid., 6.

[76] Chalk, 252.

[77] Ibid., 252.

[78] Davison, 86-87.

[79] Ibid., 87.

[80] Ramsaur, 7-8.

[81] Etmekjian, L., 177.

[82] Davison, 87.

[83] Ibid., 87.

[84] Ramsaur, 8.

[85] Davison, 92.

[86] Ramsaur, 8.

[87] Etmekjian, L., 185.

[88] Davis, Fanny, The Palace of Topkapi in Istanbul (New York, NY: Charles Scribner's Sons, 1970) 222.

[89] McMeekin, Sean, <u>The Berlin-Baghdad Express: The Ottoman Empire and Germany's Bid For World Power</u> (Cambridge, MA: The Belknap Press of Harvard University Press, 2010) 55ff.

[90] Wheatcroft, 197.

[91] Davison, 92.

[92] Davis, W., "The Roots of the War," 248.

[93] Haslip, 248-249.

[94] Davis, 248-249.

[95] Haslip, 115.

[96] Davis, 248.

[97] Curtis, William Elroy, <u>To-Day in Syria and Palestine</u> (New York, NY: Fleming H. Revell Company, 1903) 46.

[98] *The Independent*, Volume LV, February 5, 1903 (New York, NY: The Independent, January-December, 1903) 293.

[99] Ibid., 293.

[100] Davis, 248.

[101] Jelavich, Charles, and Barbara Jelavich, <u>The Establishment of the Balkan National States: 1804-1920</u> (Seattle, WA: The University of Washington Press, 1977) 139.

[102] For an eyewitness account of the Bashi-Bazuks, see Money, Edward, <u>Twelve Months with the Bashi-Bazouks</u> (London: Chapman and Hall, 1857, reprinted by Elibon Classics, 2002).

[103] Shashko, Philip, "The Bulgarian Massacres of 1876 Reconsidered: Reaction to the April Uprising or Premeditated attack?" *Academie Bulgare Des Sciences Institut D'Etudes Balkaniques* 4 (1986) 19.

[104] *Encyclopaedia Britannica, Inc.* http://dictionary.reference.com/browse/bashi bazouk (accessed September 09, 2014).

[105] Ibid., 25.

[106] Davison, 88.

[107] Tuchman, Barbara W., <u>Bible and Sword: England and Palestine from the Bronze Age to Balfour</u> (New York: Ballantine Books, 1956, 1984) 261.

[108] Massie, Robert K., <u>Dreadnought: Britain, Germany and the Coming of the Great War</u> (New York: Random House, 1991) 197.

[109] Eyck, Erich, <u>Bismarck and the German Empire</u> (New York: W. W. Norton & Company, Inc., 1968) 190.

[110] Davison, 88-89.

[111] Bismarck, Otto von, <u>Reflections and Reminiscences</u>, Edited by T. S. Hamerow (New York: Harper and Row, Publishers, 1968) 227-228.

[112] Cirakman, Asli, <u>From the "Terror of the World" to the "Sick Man of Europe": European Images of Ottoman Empire and Society from the Sixteenth Century to the Nineteenth</u> (New York: Peter Lang, 2002) 164.

[113] Hanioglu, M. Sukru, <u>Young Turks in Opposition</u> (New York: Oxford University Press, 1995) 31.

[114] Kinross, Lord John Patrick Douglas Balfour, <u>The Ottoman Centuries: The Rise and Fall of the Turkish Empire</u> (New York: William Morrow and Company, Inc., 1977) 528.

[115] Astourian, Stephen, "Genocidal Process: Reflections on the Armeno-Turkish Polarization," in <u>The Armenian Genocide: History, Politics, Ethics</u>, Richard G. Hovannisian, Ed., (New York: St. Martin's Press, 1992) 58.

[116] Davis, 248.

[117] Hanioglu, 30.

[118] Missakian, J., <u>A Searchlight on the Armenian Question, 1878-1950</u> (Boston, MA: Hairenik Publishing Company, 1950) 24.

[119] Davison, 96.

[120] Haslip, 127, 238.

[121] Bryce, James, <u>Transcaucasia, and Ararat</u> (London: Macmillan and Co., Ltd., 1896, 1970) 460-461.

[122] Langer, 159.

[123] Ramsaur, 11.

[124] Krikorian, Robert O., Quoted from a lecture given at The University of Wisconsin, April 19, 2004.

CHAPTER THREE:

[1] Wheatcroft, 199.

[2] Lantz, Kenneth A., <u>The Dostoevsky Encyclopedia</u> (Westport, CT: Greenwood Press, 2004) 370.

[3] Wheatcroft, 199-200.

[4] Ibid., 199-200.

[5] Haslip, 244.

[6] Ibid., 244.

[7] Wheatcroft, 199.

[8] Kidwai, Shaikh Mushir Hosain, <u>Pan-Islamism</u> (London: Lusac and Company, 1908) 46.

[9] Ibid., 47.

[10] Bury, G. Wyman, <u>Pan Islam</u> (London: MacMillan and Company, Ltd., 1919) 14.

[11] Ibid., 14.

[12] Othman, Siyamend, "Kurdish Nationalism: Instigations and Historical Influences," *The Armenian Review* 42, No.1 (Spring, 1989) 48.

[13] Kinross, 557.

[14] Davison, 100.

[15] Nalbandian, Louise, <u>The Armenian Revolutionary Movement: The Development of Armenian Political Parties through the Nineteenth Century</u> (Berkeley, CC: University of California Press, 1963) 85.

[16] McCarthy, <u>Death and Exile</u>, 117.

[17] McKiernan, Kevin, <u>The Kurds: A People in Search of Their Homeland</u> (New York, NY: St. Martin's Press, 2006) 9-11.

[18] G. S. Reynolds, "A Reflection on Two Qurʾānic Words (Iblīs and Jūdī), with Attention to the Theories of A. Mingana," *Journal of the American Oriental Society*, Vol. 124, No. 4 (October –December, 2004), 683-684, 687. Cited in *Mamoste* website, retrieved 2 Feb 2013.

[19] Xenophon, <u>The Persian Expedition</u>, Translated by Rex Warner (New York, NY: Penguin Classics, 1950) 173.

[20] Grousset, René, <u>The Epic of the Crusades,</u> Translated by Noël Lindsay (New York, NY: Orion Press, 1970).

[21] "Iraqi Kurds Prepared For ISIS Offensive For A Year And Expanded Their Territory By 40% In Hours," *Reuters* (June 14, 2014) http://www.

businessinsider.com/iraqi-kurds-expand-territory-2014-6 (Accessed 09-22 -14).

[22] "Kurdish Leader: We Will Vote For Independence Soon, " *Agence France Press* (July 1,2014) http://www.businessinsider.com/kurdish-leader-vote-for-independence-2014-7 (Accessed 09-22-14).

[23] Langer, 160.

[24] Nalbandian, 161.

[25] "Still Critical," *Human Rights Watch*, March, 2005, 3. (Retrieved, August, 20, 2013).

[26] Kinross, 557.

[27] Nalbandian, 78-79.

[28] Ibid., 79.

[29] Astourian, Stephan H., "The Silence of the Land," from <u>A Question of Genocide</u>, Edited by R. G. Suny, F. M. Göçek, & N. M. Naimark (New York: Oxford University Press, 2011) 62-64.

[30] Ibid., 64.

[31] Ibid., 64.

[32] Nalbandian, 161.

[33] McCarthy, Justin A., <u>Death and Exile: The Ethnic Cleansing of Ottoman Muslims, 1821-1922</u> (Princeton, NJ: Darwin Press, 1995) 91, 339.

[34] Greene, Francis Vinton, <u>The Russian Army and Its Campaigns in Turkey in 1877-1878</u> (New York, NY: D. Appleton and Company, 1879) 360.

[35] Medlicott, William Norton, <u>The Congress of Berlin and After: A Diplomatic History of the Near Eastern Settlement 1878-1880</u>, Second Edition (London: Methuen/Routledge, 1938/1963) 157.

[36] Jelavich, 139.

[37] Grant, Ulysses S., *Letter dated March 09, 1878*, from Young, John Russell, <u>Around the World with General Grant</u> (New York, NY: American News Company, 1879) 346.

[38] 227 Libaridian, Gerard J., "What was Revolutionary about Armenian Revolutionary Parties in the Ottoman Empire?" from Suny, Ronald

Grigor, Fatma Müge Göçek, and Norman M. Naimark, Editors, _A Question of Genocide_ (New York, NY: Oxford University Press, 2011) 86.

[39] Ibid., 58.

[40] Nalbandian, 149.

[41] Shashko, Philip, "Gotse Delchev and G'orche Petrov on Permanent Internal War and General Uprising," (Sofia, 1983) 52.

[42] Perry, Duncan M., "The Macedonian Revolutionary Organization's Armenian Connection," _The Armenian Review_ 42 No.1 (Spring, 1989) 64-65.

[43] Ibid., 104.

[44] Ibid., 108.

[45] Libaridian, 86.

[46] Kinross, 557.

[47] Nalbandian, 159.

[48] Ibid., 162.

[49] Kinross, 563.

[50] Hopkirk, Peter, _The Great Game: The Struggle for Empire in Central Asia_ (New York: Kodanasha International, Ltd., 1990, 1992) 112.

[51] Langer, 160.

[52] Wheatcroft, 204.

[53] Ramsaur, 9.

[54] McCarthy, _Death and Exile_, 118.

[55] Langer, 160.

[56] Nalbandian, 181.

[57] Balakian, _Burning Tigris_, 57-58.

[58] Gürün, Kamuran, _The Armenian File: The Myth of Innocence Exposed_ (London: Palgrave MacMillan, 1986) 168.

[59] Chalk, 256.

[60] Kinross, 561.

[61] Ramsaur, 10.

[62] Langer, 323.

[63] Dadrian, Vahakn, N., <u>The History of the Armenian Genocide: Ethnic Conflict from the Balkans to Anatolia to the Caucasus</u> (Providence, RI: Berghahn Books, 1995) 139.

[64] Ramsaur, 10.

[65] Haslip, 223-224.

[66] Ramsaur, 10.

[67] Astourian, 59.

[68] Balakian, Peter, "Armenians in the Ottoman Empire," <u>Encyclopedia of Human Rights</u>, Volume I, Edited by David P. Forsythe, (New York, NY: Oxford University Press, 2009) 93.

[69] Dadrian, 143.

CHAPTER FOUR:

[1] Ramsaur, 10.

[2] Haslip, 221.

[3] Balakian, Peter, "Armenians in the Ottoman Empire," 93.

[4] Jackh, Ernest, <u>Der Aufsteigende Halbmond</u>, 6th Ed. (Berlin, 1916) 139, in Dadrian, 155.

[5] Dadrian, 155-156.

[6] Gates, Caleb, to William Peet, quoted in <u>Great Need Over the Water: The Letters of Theresa Huntington Ziegler, Missionary to Turkey, 1898-1905</u>, Stina Katchadourian, Ed., (Reading, England: Taderon Press, 1999) 73.

[7] Haslip, 226.

[8] Shaw, 205.

[9] Kinross, 555.

[10] Hochschild, Adam, <u>King Ludwig's Ghost</u> (New York, NY: Houghton Mifflin Company, 1998) 167-168.

[11] Oren, Michael B., <u>Power, Faith, and Fantasy: America in the Middle East, 1776 to the Present</u> (New York, NY: W. W. Norton and Company, Inc., 2007) 293.

[12] Ibid., 294-296.

[13] Ibid., 293.

[14] Ibid., 294.

[15] Akcam, Taner, <u>A Shameful Act: The Armenian Genocide and the Question of Turkish Responsibility</u> (New York, NY: Henry Holt and Company, 2006) 42.

[16] 274 Balakian, "Armenians in the Ottoman Empire," 93-94.

[17] National Congress of Turkey, 35.

[18] Dadrian, Vahakn, N. <u>Warrant For Genocide: Key Elements of Turko-Armenian Conflict</u> (New Brunswick: Transaction Publishers, 1999) 85.

[19] Ibid., 85.

[20] Haslip, 217.

[21] Ibid., 217.

[22] Weitz, 4.

[23] *The New York Times* (2 April 1903).

[24] Ferro, Marc, <u>Nicholas II: The Last of the Tsars</u>, Trans. by Brian Pearce (New York: Oxford University Press, 1993) 101.

[25] Ibid., 100.

[26] Radzinsky, Edvard, <u>The Last Tsar: The Life and Death of Nicholas II</u> (New York: Anchor Books, Doubleday, 1992) 69.

[27] Bobrick, Benson, <u>East of the Sun: The Epic Conquest and Tragic History of Siberia</u> (New York: Poseidon Press, 1992) 355.

[28] Lieven, Dominic, <u>Nicholas II: Twilight of the Empire</u> (New York: St. Martin's Griffin, 1993) 18-19.

[29] *The New York Times* (2 April 1903).

[30] Chirot, Daniel, and Clark McCauley, <u>Why Not Kill Them All?: The Logic and Prevention of Mass Political Murder</u> (Princeton, NJ: Princeton University Press, 2006) 23.

[31] Ibid., 23.

[32] Lewy, Guenter. "Were American Indians the Victims of Genocide?" *George Mason University's History News Network*, reprinted from *Commentary* (September, 2004) Retrieved 01-25-2013.

[33] Dadrian, 85.

[34] Langer, 328.

[35] Nassibian, Akaby, <u>Britain and the Armenian Question, 1915-1923</u> (New York: St. Martin's Press, 1984) 35.

[36] Cirakman, 80-81.

[37] Wheatcroft, 233.

[38] Gladstone, William Ewart, <u>Bulgarian Horrors and the Question of the East</u>, (London: John Murray, 1876) 9.

[39] Nicolson, Harold, <u>Peace Making 1919</u> (New York, NY: Grosset and Dunlap, 1933, 1965) 35.

[40] Gobineau, Arthur, <u>An Essay on the Inequality of the Human Races</u>, Translated by Adrian Collins (New York, NY: G. P. Putnam's Sons, 1915) 128.

[41] Hanioglu, 209.

[42] Darwin, Francis, <u>The Life and Letters of Charles Darwin, Vol. I</u> (New York: Elibron Classics Replica Edition, 2005, of original D. Appleton and Company, 1897) 285-286.

[43] Wheatcroft, 195, 240-247.

[44] Ibid., 244.

[45] Davison, 100.

[46] Ramsaur, 62.

[47] Davison, 102.

[48] Massie, 201.

[49] McMeekin, 7.

[50] Ibid., 10.

[51] Massie, 210-212.

[52] Davison, 95.

[53] Haslip, 199.

[54] Dadrian, Vahakn, N., <u>German Responsibility in the Armenian Genocide: A Review of the Historical Evidence of German Complicity</u> (Watertown, MA: Blue Crane Books, 1996) 8.

[55] McMeekin, 48.

[56] Dadrian, 8.

[57] Naltchayan, Nazaret, "Kaiser Wilhelm II's Visits to the Ottoman Empire: Rationale, Reaction, and the Meanings of Images," *The Armenian Review* 42, No. 2 (Summer, 1989) 61.

[58] Davison, 95.

[59] McMeekin, 22.

[60] Dadrian, 8.

[61] McMeekin, 43.

[62] Ibid., 15-16.

[63] Ibid., 16.

[64] Massie, Robert K., Nicholas and Alexandra (New York, NY: Dell Publishing Company, Inc., 1967) 89.

[65] Ibid., 89.

[66] Ibid., 89.

[67] McMeekin, 42.

[68] Ibid., 14.

[69] Ibid., 15.

[70] Langer, 369.

[71] Dupuy, R. Ernest, and Trevor Dupuy, The Harper Encyclopedia of Military History, Fourth Edition (New York: Harper Collins Publishers, 1993) 926.

[72] Haslip, 234.

[73] Dadrian, Warrant, 86.

[74] Bryce, Ararat, 455.

[75] "The Marquis of Salisbury to the Earl of Derby," (Pera, 1876), in *The Armenian Review* 29 (Summer, 1976) 209.

CHAPTER FIVE:

[1] Hayes, Carlton J. H., A Political and Social History of Modern Europe, Volume II (New York: The Macmillan Company, 1916, 1924) 525.

[2] Ramsaur, 4.

[3] Ibid., 25.

[4] Ibid., 4.

[5] Hanioglu, 8.

[6] Ibid., 8.

[7] Ibid., 74.

[8] Ramsaur, 44.

[9] Ibid., 44.

[10] Ibid., 43.

[11] Hanioglu, 84.

[12] Ibid., 85.

[13] Ramsaur, 30-33.

[14] Hanioglu, 86.

[15] Ramsaur 34.

[16] Ibid., 50.

[17] Ibid., 64.

[18] Hanioglu, 21.

[19] Davison, 86.

[20] Whyte, A. J., The Evolution of Modern Italy, (New York, NY: W. W. Norton & Company, Inc., 1959, 1965) 218.

[21] Kushner, 47.

[22] Ibid., 100.

[23] Stoddard, T. Lothrop, "Pan-Turanism," *The American Political Science Review*, Volume 11, Number 1 (1917) 16.

[24] Ibid., 19-20.

[25] Davison, 102.

[26] Kushner, 54

[27] Ersoy, Ahmet, Maciej Górny, Vangelis Kechriotis, Editors, Modernism: The Creation of Nation States (Budapest, Hungary: Central European University Press, 2010) 218-222.

[28] Balakian, Peter, Black Dog of Fate: A Memoir (New York: Basic Books, 1997) 156-157.

[29] Encyclopedia Britannica, *Encyclopedia Britannica, Inc.* 2014, www.britannica.com (Accessed September 8, 2014).

[30] Shaw, 302.

[31] Chalk, 281.

[32] Gokalp, Zia, The Principles of Turkism (Ankara & Leiden: E. J. Brill, 1920, 1968) 18-19.

[33] Ibid., 19-20.

[34] Ibid., 20.

[35] Djemal Pasha, Memoiries of a Turkish Statesman, 1913-1919, (New York: George H. Doran Company, 1922) 251.

[36] Ibid., 251.

[37] Kushner, 5.

[38] Ibid., 40.

[39] Gokalp, 14.

[40] Ibid., 12.

[41] Morgenthau, Henry, Murder of a Nation (New York: AGBU of America, 1918, 1974) 21.

[42] Ramsaur, 44.

[43] Ibid., 43.

[44] Ibid., 54.

[45] Ibid., 72-73.

[46] Ibid., 69.

[47] Ibid., 70.

[48] Hanioglu, 195.

[49] Ramsaur, 81.

[50] Ibid., 115.

[51] Ibid., 116.

[52] Macfie, 40.

[53] Morgenthau, 6-7.

[54] Ramsaur, 117-118.

[55] Ibid., 115.

[56] Warner, Denis, and Peggy Warner, The Tide at Sunrise: A History of the Russo-Japanese War, 1904-1905 (New York: Charterhouse, 1974) 25.

[57] Dupuy, R. Ernest, and Trevor N. Dupuy, The Harper Encyclopedia of Military History: From 3500 B.C. to the Present, Fourth Ed., (New York: Harper Collins Publishers, 1993) 1014.

[58] Hanioglu, 210.

[59] Me'yus Olmali Miyiz, quoted in Hanioglu, 210.

[60] **393** Dupuy, 1014.

[61] Davison, 103.

[62] Ibid., 104.

[63] MacKenzie, David, <u>Violent Solutions: Revolutions, Nationalism, and Secret Societies in Europe to 1918</u> (Lanham, MD: University Press of America, Inc., 1996) 265.

[64] Ibid., 260.

[65] Hanioglu, 40.

CHAPTER SIX:

[1] Davison, 105.

[2] Ramsaur, 133.

[3] Davison, 105.

[4] Ramsaur, 134.

[5] *The London Times* (16 July 1908).

[6] Davison, 105.

[7] Ramsaur, 135-136.

[8] Shaw, 267.

[9] *The New York Times* (19 July 1908).

[10] Ramsaur, 136.

[11] *The London Times* (27 July 1908).

[12] Ramsaur, 138.

[13] *The London Times* (19 August 1908).

[14] *The London Times* (27 July 1908).

[15] *The London Times* (29 July 1908).

[16] *The London Times* (25 July 1908).

[17] Ramsaur, 137.

[18] *The London Times* (27 July 1908)

[19] Haslip, 268.

[20] *The London Times* (22 December 1908).

[21] *The London Times* (26 July 1908).

[22] *The London Times* (8 August 1908).

[23] *The London Times* (10 August 1908).

[24] Shaw, 267.

[25] Ramsaur,129-130.

[26] Ibid., 137.

[27] *The London Times* (18 December 1908).

[28] *The London Times* (18 December 1908).

[29] Haslip, 268.

[30] Ibid., 91-92, 173, 244.

[31] Kaylan, Muammar, The Kemalists: Islamic Revival and the Fate of Secular Turkey (Amherst, NY: Prometheus Books, 2005) 74.

[32] Haslip, 277.

[33] Ibid., 287.

[34] McCarthy, Death and Exile, 117, 120, 136.

[35] Alkhateeb, Firas, "The Last Great Caliph: Abdülhamid II," *Lost Islamic History* (April, 2006) www.lostislamichistory.com/the-last-great-caliph-abdulhamid-ii. (accessed September 4, 2014).

[36] *The London Times* (16 December 1908).

[37] Lewy, 33.

[38] Ahmad, Feroz, The Young Turks: The Committee of Union and Progress in Turkish Politics, 1908-1914 (Oxford: Clarendon Press, 1969) 16.

[39] Ramsay, William M., The Revolution in Constantinople and Turkey: A Diary (London: Hodder, and Stoughton, 1909) 203.

[40] Shaw, 273.

[41] Ibid., 273.

[42] Morgenthau, 11.

[43] *The London Times* (15 August 1908).

[44] Lewy, Guenter, The Armenian Massacres in Ottoman Turkey: A Disputed Genocide (Salt Lake City, UT: The University of Utah Press, 2005) 34.

[45] *The London Times* (23 July 1908).

[46] *The London Times* (19 August 1908).

[47] *The London Times* (13 August 1908).

[48] *The London Times* (6 July 1908).

[49] Lewy, 34.

[50] *The London Times* (7 August 1908).

[51] Ibid., 34.

[52] *The London Times* (15 August 1908).

[53] Ibid., (8-C).

[54] Lewy, 33.

[55] *The Levant Herald,* obituary (13 April 1910)

[56] *The London Times* (3 August 1908).

[57] Langer, 147-148.

[58] Eliot, Sir Charles N., <u>Turkey in Europe</u> (London, 1900) 442, Quoted in Langer, 148.

[59] Hofman, Tessa, and Gerayer Koutcharian, "The History of Armenian-Kurdish Relations in the Ottoman Empire," *The Armenian Review* 39, No.4 (Winter, 1986) 23.

[60] Ramsay, 207.

[61] *The London Times* (15 August 1908).

[62] National Congress of Turkey, 35.

[63] Macfie, 50-51.

[64] Lawrence, T. E., <u>Seven Pillars of Wisdom: A Triumph</u> (London: Doubleday, 1926, 1935, 1991) 46.

[65] Wheatcroft, 206.

[66] Macfie, 61.

[67] *The London Times* (10 August 1908).

CHAPTER SEVEN:

[1] Ramsaur, 148.

[2] Ahmad, ff., 23.

[3] Shaw, 276.

[4] Ahmad, 152.

[5] Lewy, 35.

[6] Weitz, Eric D., "Germany and the Young Turks: Revolutionaries Into Statesmen," From A Question Of Genocide: Armenians and Turks at the End of the Ottoman Empire, Edited by Ronald Grigor Suny, Fatma Müge Göçek, and Norman M. Naimark (New York, NY: Oxford University Press, 2011) 191.

[7] Ibid., 191.

[8] Dadrian, German Responsibility, 183.

[9] McMeekin, 79.

[10] Arai, 62-63.

[11] Kazarian, Haigazn, "The Turkish Genocide of the Armenians: A Premeditated and Official Assault," The Armenian Review 30 (Spring, 1977) 5.

[12] Akcam, Taner, From Empire to Republic: Turkish Nationalism and the Armenian Genocide (London: Zed Books, 2004) 135.

[13] Gokalp, Zia, Turk Yurdu (Constantinople, 1913) in Taner, 136.

[14] Kayalı, Hasan, "Elections and the Electoral Process in the Ottoman Empire, 1876-1919," The International Journal of Middle East Studies, (1995) Volume 27, Number 3, 272-273.

[15] Ibid., 272-273.

[16] Ibid., 273-274.

[17] Bournoutian, 98.

[18] Ibid., 98.

[19] The New York Times (25 January 1912).

[20] Djemal Pasha, 13.

[21] Turkish Air Force, website, "First Establishment and the Early Years," http://www.hvkk.tsk.tr/EN/IcerikDetay. (accessed September 11, 2014).

[22] Lawrence, 47.

[23] Moorehead, Alan, Gallipoli (New York, Ballantine Books, 1956) 5.

[24] Kinross, 595.

[25] McMeekin, 109.

[26] Davis, Leslie A., The Slaughterhouse Province: An American Diplomat's Report on the Armenian Genocide, 1915-1917, From the

"Acknowledgements" by Editor Susan K. Blair (New Rochelle, NY: A. D. Caratzas, 1917, 1989) i.

[27] Tuchman, Barbara W., The Guns of August (New York: Macmillan Publishing Company, 1962) 138.

[28] Kinross, 595.

[29] Werfel, Franz, The Forty Days of Musa Dagh (New York: The Viking Press, 1934) 129.

[30] Firoozi, Edith, and Ira N. Klein, The Age of Great Kings, From The Universal History of the World, Volume, 9 (New York: Golden Press, 1966) 759-761.

[31] MacLean, Rory, Berlin: Portrait of a City Through the Centuries (New York, NY: Weidenfeld & Nicolson, 2014) 43-44.

[32] Kinross, 595.

[33] Morgenthau, Henry, Ambassador Morgenthau's Story (Garden City, NY: Doubleday, Page and Company, 1918) 21.

[34] Kinross., 595.

[35] Ibid., 595.

[36] Werfel, 144.

[37] Chandler, David G., The Campaigns of Napoleon (New York: The Macmillan Company, 1966) 1,011.

[38] Kinross, 595.

[39] Morgenthau, Ambassador, 21.

[40] Dadrian, Warrant, 114.

[41] Kinross, 595.

[42] Ibid., 595-596.

[43] Morgenthau, Ambassador, 108

[44] Ibid., 108.

[45] Shaw, 300.

[46] Djemal Pasha, 138-139.

[47] Ibid., 137-138.

[48] Ibid. 277.

[49] Kinross, 596.

[50] Shaw, 299.

[51] Kinross, 596.

[52] Shaw, 299.

[53] Kinross, 596.

[54] Hanioglu, 40.

[55] Kinross, 596.

[56] Morgenthau, <u>Ambassador</u>, 16.

[57] Werfel, 145.

[58] Tuchman, 138.

[59] Kinross, 596.

[60] Shaw, 287.

[61] Nalbandian, 185.

CHAPTER EIGHT:

[1] Chalk, 276-277.

[2] Graber, G. S., <u>Caravans to Oblivion: The Armenian Genocide, 1915</u> (New York: John Wiley & Sons, Inc., 1996) 94-95.

[3] Ibid., 93-94.

[4] Ibid., 96.

[5] Bryce, Viscount James, <u>Transcaucasia, and Ararat</u> (London: Macmillan and Co., Ltd., 1896, 1970) 117.

[6] Morgenthau, <u>Ambassador</u>, 21.

[7] Djemal, 104-107.

[8] Nassibian, Akaby, <u>Britain and the Armenian Question, 1915-1923</u> (New York: St. Martin's Press, 1984) 68.

[9] In actuality, Scliefffen's successor as Chief of the Imperial General Staff, Helmuth Von Moltke decided against invading Holland in 1914.

[10] Erickson, Edward J., <u>Ordered To Die: A History of the Ottoman Army in the First World War</u> (Westport, CT: Praeger Publishers, 2000) 20.

[11] Ibid., 27.

[12] Ibid., 28-30.

[13] Taylor, Alan J.P., <u>The Struggle for Mastery in Europe: 1848-1918</u>, (Oxford, UK: Oxford University Press, 1954, 1971) 534.

[14] Erickson, 28-29.

[15] Tuchman, 140.

[16] Kinross, 604.

[17] Tuchman, 160.

[18] Djemal, 118.

[19] Tuchman, 161.

[20] Djemal, 107-108.

[21] Kinross, 606.

[22] Moorehead, 19-20.

[23] Kinross, 606.

[24] Moorehead, 20.

[25] Erickson, 29.

[26] Kinross, 606.

[27] Tuchman, 159.

[28] Haskell, Edward B., "Bulgaria Points the Way," *Asia: Journal of the American Asiatic Association* 18, #11 (November 1918) 921.

[29] Fischer, Fritz, Germany's War Aims in the First World War, (New York: W. W. Norton & Company, Inc., 1961, 1967) 127-128.

[30] Djemal, 137-139.

[31] Dupuy, 1048.

[32] Dupuy, Trevor N., Curt Johnson, & David L. Bongard, The Harper Encyclopedia of Military Biography (New York: Harper Collins Publishers, 1992) 238.

[33] Dupuy, History, 1047.

[34] *The New York Times* (7 January 1915).

[35] Dadrian, Warrant, 114.

[36] Dupuy, History, 1047.

[37] Werfel, 144.

[38] *The New York Times* (7 January 1915).

[39] *The New York Times* (23 January 1915).

[40] Dupuy, History 1055.

[41] Adalian, R.P., "The Armenian Genocide," in Centuries of Genocide: Essays and Eyewitness Accounts, Edited by Samuel Totten, William S. Parsons, and Israel W. Charny (New York, NY: Routledge, 1997, 2013) 132.

[42] Mann, Michael, The Dark Side of Democracy: Explaining Ethnic Cleansing (Cambridge, NY: Cambridge University Press, 2005) 7.

[43] Ibid., 8.

[44] Ibid., 177.

[45] Ibid., 177.

[46] **Üngör, Uğur Ümit,** "Turkey For the Turks," From A Question Of Genocide: Armenians and Turks at the End of the Ottoman Empire, Edited by Ronald Grigor Suny, Fatma Müge Göçek, and Norman M. Naimark (New York, NY: Oxford University Press, 2011) 295.

[47] Shirer, 965.

[48] Dederichs, Mario R., Heydrich: The Face of Evil, (Drexel Hill, PA: Casemate, 2009) 92.

[49] Shirer, 434.

[50] Ibid., 519.

[51] Rifat, Mevlanzade, The Inner Aspects of the Turkish Revolution (Aleppo, 1929) quoted in Lewy, 51.

[52] Ibid., 51.

[53] Sarkisian, Ervand K., Ervand G. Sargsyan, and Ruben G. Sahakian, Vital Issues in Modern Armenian History (Watertown, MA: Armenian Studies, 1965) 22.

[54] Dyer, Gwynne, "Letter to the Editor," Middle Eastern Studies 9, (1973) 379-383, cited in Lewy, 52.

[55] Lewy, 52-53.

[56] Akcam, Taner, The Young Turks' Crime Against Humanity (Princeton, NJ: Princeton University Press, 2012) 412.

[57] Rausch, David A., A Legacy of Hatred (Chicago, IL: Moody Press, 1984) 123.

[58] Kaplan, Robert, "Long History of the Doctors of Doom," The Sydney Morning Herald, July 7, 2007, www.smh.com.au (Accessed September 5, 2014).

[59] Kieser, Hans-Lukas, "From Patriotism to Mass Murder," From A Question Of Genocide: Armenians and Turks at the End of the Ottoman Empire, Edited by Ronald Grigor Suny, Fatma Müge Göçek,

and Norman M. Naimark (New York, NY: Oxford University Press, 2011) 137.

[60] Kaplan, Robert, "Long History of the Doctors of Doom," *The Sidney Morning Herald*, July 7, 2007, www.smh.com.au (Accessed September 5, 2014).

[61] Remak, Joachim, "1914---The Third Balkan War: Origins Reconsidered," *The Journal of Modern History* 43 (September 1971) 365.

[62] Morgenthau, Murder,77.

CHAPTER NINE:

[1] Eliot, Sir Charles, Turkey In Europe (London: Edward Arnold, 1908) 382-383.

[2] Ibid., 383-384.

[3] Douglas, John M., The Armenians (New York: J. J. Winthrop Corporation, 1992) 9.

[4] *Genesis* 8:4

[5] Suny, Ronald Grigor, Armenia in the Twentieth Century (Chico: CA: Scholars Press, 1983) 6.

[6] Josephus, Flavius, Antiquities of the Jews (Book I, 3:5) Translated by William Whiston (Grand Rapids, MI: Kregel Publications 1960, 1980) 29.

[7] Uras, Esat, The Armenians in History and The Armenian Question (Istanbul: Documentary Publications, 1988) 245.

[8] Ibid., 245.

[9] Strabo, Book XI, Quoted in Bryce, 207.

[10] Douglas, 51.

[11] Uras, 266.

[12] Strabo, Geography, Book 11, Chapter 14:15, *The Loeb Classical Library*, Vol. V, Trans. by Horace Leonard Jones (Cambridge, MA: Harvard University Press, 1928) 338-341.

[13] Dupuy, History, 128.

[14] Redgate, A. E., The Armenians, (Malden, MA: Blackwell Publishing, 1998, 2000) 84.

[15] Boyajian, Zabelle C., and Aram Raffi, <u>The Anthology of Legends and Poems of Armenia</u> (New York, NY: Columbia University Press, 1st ed.,1916) 117.

[16] Cicero, <u>Political Speeches</u>, Trans. by D. H. Berry (Oxford, UK: Oxford University Press, 2006) 103.

[17] Dupuy, <u>History</u>, 104.

[18] Appian of Alexandria, <u>Roman History: The Mithridatic Wars</u>, 12:84, *The Loeb Classical Library*, Vol. II, Trans. by Horace White (Cambridge, MA: Harvard University Press, 1912).

[19] Plutarch, "The Life of Lucullus," 27:4, <u>The Parallel Lives</u>, *The Loeb Classical Library*, Vol. II, Trans. by Bernadotte Perrin (Cambridge, MA: Harvard University Press, 1914) 559.

[20] Gurzadyan, V.G, and R.Vardanyan, "Halley's comet of 87 BC on the coins of Armenian king Tigranes?" *Astronomy & Geophysics*, Volume 45, Issue 4 (August 2004) 4.6.

[21] Josephus, <u>Antiquities</u> (Book XV, 4:3) 319.

[22] Tacitus, <u>The Annals</u>, Book XIII, 37-41, Translated by A. J. Church and W. J. Brodribb (Chicago, IL: The University of Chicago, 1952, 1992) 134-138.

[23] Redgate, 116.

[24] Smith Anthony D., <u>Myths and Memories of the Nation</u>, (New York: Oxford University Press, 1999) 212-213.

[25] Nersessian, Sirarpie Der, <u>Armenian Art</u> (Paris: *Arts Et Metiers Graphiques*, Armenian General Benevolent Union, undated) 21.

[26] Eusebius, <u>The History of the Church</u>, Translated by G. A. Williamson, New York: Penguin Books, 1983) 67.

[27] Perhaps found in *Luke* 1:10.

[28] Wilson, Ian <u>The Blood and the Shroud</u> (New York: The Free Press, 1998) 266.

[29] Wilson, Ian, <u>The Shroud of Turin: The Burial Cloth of Jesus Christ?</u> (New York: Image Books. 1979) 128-129.

[30] Elgeria (Etheria), <u>The Pilgrimage of Etheria</u>, Translated by M. L. McClure & C. L. Feltoe (London: Society for Promoting Christian Knowledge, 1919) 33-35.

[31] Wilson, <u>Blood</u>, 263-313.

[32] Wilson, Ian, <u>Holy Faces, Secret Places:An Amazing Quest for the Face of Jesus</u> (New York: Doubleday, 1991) 126-127.

[33] Wilson, <u>Shroud</u>, 112-124.

[34] Nersessian, 21.

[35] Uras, 271-272, 315.

[36] Jones, W. R., "The Legend and Letters of Abgar, 'King of Armenia'," *The Armenian Review* 28 (Spring, 1975) 41-42.

[37] Garsoian, Nina, "The Arsakuni Dynasty (A.D. 12-[180?]-428)," published in <u>The Armenian People From Ancient to Modern Times, Volume I, The Dynastic Periods: From Antiquity to the Fourteenth Century</u>, Edited by Richard G. Hovannisian (New York: St. Martin's Press, 1997) 82-83.

[38] Ibid., 83.

[39] Delaney, John J., <u>Dictionary of Saints</u>, (Garden City, NY: Image Books, 1983) 225.

[40] Agathangelos, <u>History of the Armenians</u>, Translated by R. W. Thomson (Albany, NY: State University of New York Press, 1976) xxv.

[41] Ibid., 267-271.

[42] Ibid., 27, 401.

[43] Nersessian, 21.

[44] Sebeos, <u>The Armenian History</u>, Translated by R. W. Thomson (Liverpool, UK: Liverpool University Press, 1999) xlii.

[45] Ibid., 132.

[46] Ibid., lv.

[47] Zak'aria of K'anak'er, <u>The Chronicle of Zak'aria of K'anak'er</u>, Translated by George A. Bournoutian (Costa Mesa, CA: Mazda Publishers, Inc., 2004) 265ff.

[48] Ibid., 265.

[49] Douglas, 103.

[50] Nersessian, 23-46.

[51] Ibid., 42-43.

[52] McManners, John, Editor, <u>The Oxford Illustrated History of Christianity</u> (Oxford: Oxford University Press, 1990) 8.

[53] Suny, 18.

[54] Langer, 148.

[55] Barkley, Henry C., _A Ride Trough Asia Minor and Armenia_ (London, 1891) 87, quoted in Langer, 148.

[56] Bournoutian, George A. _A History of the Armenians, Volume II: 1500 A. D. to the Present_ (Costa Mesa, Ca: Mazda Publishers, 1994) 27.

[57] Dupuy, _History_, 425.

[58] _Revelation_ 6:8.

CHAPTER TEN:

[1] Balakian, _Burning Tigris_, (noted in caption to illustration following page 236).

[2] Moorehead, 84.

[3] Uras, 870.

[4] Mikassian, J., _A Searchlight on the Armenian Question, 1878-1950_ (Boston, MA: Hairenik Publishing Co., 1950) 56.

[5] Samouelian, Hrand, _The Armenian Question: A Memorandum_ (Boston, Ma: Hairenik Association, 1967) 6.

[6] Terzian, Aram, "1915: The Darkest Year," _The Armenian Review_ 28 (Summer, 1975) 159.

[7] Shaw, 314-315.

[8] Ibid., 315.

[9] Erickson, 98.

[10] Walker, Christopher J., _Armenia: The Survival of a Nation_ (London: Croom Helm Publishers, 1980) 206.

[11] Lewy, 99.

[12] Dupuy, _History_, 1047.

[13] _The New York Times_ (6 May 1915).

[14] Walker, Christopher J., "World War I and the Armenian Genocide," in Richard G. Hovannisian, _The Armenian People From Ancient To Modern Times_, Vol. II (New York, NY: Palgrave Macmillan, 2004) 251.

[15] Dupuy, _History_, 1047.

[16] Pasdermadjian, Garegin, <u>Why Armenia Should be Free: Armenia's Role in the Present War</u> (Boston, MA: Hairenick Publishing Company, 1918) 22.

[17] *The New York Times* (11 January 1915).

[18] *The New York Times* (1 February 1915).

[19] Moranian, Suzanne Elizabeth, "Bearing Witness: The Missionary Archives as Evidence of the Armenian Genocide," in Hovannisian, Richard G., <u>The Armenian Genocide: Histort, Politics, Ethics,</u> (New York: St. Martin's Press, 1992) 106.

[20] Missakian, quoting Arnold J. Toynbee, <u>Searchlight</u>, 40-42.

[21] Ibid., 40-42.

[22] Dadrian, <u>Warrant</u>, 116.

[23] Lewy, 99.

[24] Ibid., 228.

[25] Matosian, Khacher A., <u>Matosian Roots: Annals</u> (Athens, Greece: 1923) 48.

[26] Ibid., 48.

[27] Dadrian, <u>History</u>, 257.

[28] Lewy, 228.

[29] Ibid., 229.

[30] Dadrian, <u>History</u>, 258.

[31] Chaliand, Gerard, and Yves Ternon, <u>The Armenians: From Genocide to Resistance</u>, Translated by Tony Berret (London: Zed Press, 1983) 15.

[32] Atkinson, Dr. Tacy W., *Inquiry Document # 810* (Boston, MA, 1918) in James L. Barton, <u>"Turkish Atrocities": Statements of American Missionaries on the Destruction of Christian Communities in Ottoman Turkey, 1915-1917</u>, Edited by Ara Sarafian, (Ann Arbor, MI: Gomidas Institute, 1919, 1998) 41.

[33] Chaliand, 15.

[34] Dadrian, <u>Warrant</u>, 116

[35] Walker, "World War I," 251.

[36] Dadrian, <u>Warrant</u>, 116.

[37] Bournoutian, 101.

[38] Chaliand, 15.

[39] *The New York Times* (5 June 1915).

[40] *The New York Times* (17 September 1915).

[41] Hovannisian, <u>Armenian People</u>, Vol. II, 252.

[42] Moorehead, 83.

[43] Ibid., 83.

[44] Ibid., 84.

[45] Hosfeld, Rolf, "The Armenian Massacre and Its Avengers: The ramifications of the assassination of Talaat Pasha in Berlin," *IP – Transatlantic Edition* (Fall, 2005) 61.

[46] <u>Armenian Allegations: Myth and Reality, A Handbook of Facts and Documents</u> (Washington, DC: The Assembly of Turkish American Associations, 1987) xi.

[47] <u>The Turco-Armenian Question: The Turkish Point of View</u> (Constantinople: The National Congress of Turkey, 1919) 82.

[48] Djemal, 280.

[49] Alexander, Edward, <u>A Crime of Vengeance: An Armenian Struggle for Justice</u> (New York: The Free Press, 1991) 101.

[50] Ibid., 280.

[51] Kalfaian, Aris, <u>Chomaklou: The History of an Armenian Village</u>, Translated by Krikor Asadourian (New York: Chomaklou Compatriotic Society, 1930, 1982) 144.

[52] Matosian, 50.

[53] Longbridge, Stella H., *Inquiry Document* # 803(Boston, MA, 1918) in Barton, 116.

[54] Atkinson, Harriet H., "Mrs. Harriet H. Atkinson's Eyewitness Account of the Massacres at Harpoot," *The Armenian Review* 29 (Spring, 1976) 8.

[55] Hacobian, A. P., <u>Armenia and the War: An Armenian's Point of View with an Appeal to Britain and the Coming Peace Conference</u> (New York: George H. Doran Company, 1917) 51.

[56] *The New York Times* (11 January 1915).

[57] *The London Morning Post* (11 July 1915).

[58] *The New York Times* (4 August 1915).

[59] *The Reuters News Service* (20 August 1915).

[60] *The New York Times* (8 September 1915).

[61] *The New York Times* (14 September 1915).

[62] Dodd, Dr. William S., *Inquiry Document # 809* (Boston, MA, 1917) in Barton,145-146.

[63] Birge, Mr. And Mrs. Kingley, and Mr. And Mrs. S. R. Harlow, *Inquiry Document # 815* (Boston, MA, 1918) in Barton, 195-196.

[64] Emphasis added.

[65] *The London Times* (8 October 1915).

[66] Waller, James, <u>Becoming Evil: How Ordinary People Commit Genocide and Mass Killing</u> (Oxford: Oxford University Press, 2002) 18.

[67] Graber, 96.

[68] Suakian, Kevork Y., "The Preconditions of the Armeno-Turkish Case of Genocide," *The Armenian Review* 34 (December, 1981) 405.

[69] McMeekin, 123.

[70] Paice, Edward, <u>World War I: The African Front</u> (New York, NY: Pegasus Books, 2008) 213.

[71] Ibid., 213.

[72] 718 Sarkissian, Arshag O., "It Happened in 1915: The Massacre of the Armenians in the Ottoman Empire," *The Armenian Review* 30 (Spring, 1977) 27.

[73] MacCallum, Rev. Frederick W., *Inquiry Document # 805* (Boston, MA, 1918) in Barton, 177.

[74] Atkinson, 8

[75] Andrus, Rev. Alpheus N., *Inquiry Document # 825* (Boston, MA, 1917) in Barton, 98.

[76] White, George E., *Inquiry Document # 818* (Boston, Ma, 1918), in Barton, 82.

[77] Riggs, Henry H., <u>Days of Tragedy in Armenia: Personal Experiences in Harpoot, 1915-1917</u> (Ann Arbor, MI: Gomidas Institute, 1918, 1997) 179.

[78] Ryan, Rev. Arthur C., *Inquiry Document* 3 817 (Boston, MA, 1918) in Barton, 184-185.

[79] Bedoukian, Kerop, Some of Us Survived (New York: Farrar Straus Giroux, 1978) 38.

[80] Davis, 80.

[81] Parmelee, 57-58.

[82] Harley, Isabelle, *Inquiry Document* # 812 (Boston, MA, 1918) in Barton, 65.

[83] Smith, Dr. Floyd O., *Inquiry Document* # 822 (Boston, MA, 1919), in Barton, 90.

[84] Stapleton, Ida S., *Inquiry Document* # 821 (Boston, MA, 1918) in Barton, 23.

[85] Shane, Myrtle O., *Inquiry Document* # 804 (Boston, MA, 1918) in Barton, 10.

[86] Ibid., 10.

[87] Ibid., 10.

[88] Morgenthau, Murder,45.

[89] Phelps, Theda B., *Inquiry Document* # 824 (Boston, MA, 1918) in Barton, 136.

[90] Lewy, 188.

[91] Richmond, Clara Childs, *Inquiry Document* # 807 (Boston, MA, 1918) in Barton, 124.

[92] Parmelee, Dr. Ruth A., *Inquiry Document* # 811 (Boston, MA, 1918) in Barton, 59.

[93] Riggs, 32.

[94] Chaliand, 63.

[95] Riggs, 120.

[96] Webb, Elizabeth S., *Inquiry Document* # 819 (Boston, MA, 1918) in Barton, 172.

[97] Harley, 68.

[98] Riggs, 100.

[99] Richmond, 122.

[100] Aaronsohn, Aaron, "British War Office Memorandum" (London, 1916) in Auron, Yair, The Banality of Indifference: Zionism & the Armenian Genocide (New Brunswick, NJ: Transaction Publishers, 2000) 380.

[101] Riggs, Mary W., *Inquiry Document # 808* (Boston, MA, 1918) in Barton, 30.

[102] Hartunian, Abraham H., Neither To Laugh nor To Weep: A Memoir of the Armenian Genocide Translated by Vartan Hartunian (Boston, MA: Beacon Press, 1922, 1938, 1968) 86.

[103] Andrus, 98.

[104] Balakian, Black Dog of Fate, 216-217.

[105] Fischer, Harriet J., *Inquiry Document # 813* (Boston, MA, 1917) in Barton, 164.

[106] Miller, Donald E., and Lorna Touryan Miller, Survivors: An Oral History of the Armenian Genocide (Berkeley, CA: University of California Press, 1993) 178.

[107] Fischer, 164.

[108] Gaunt, David, "The Assyrian Genocide of 1915," *Assyrian Genocide Research Center*, 2009, www.seyfocenter.com (accessed October 3, 2014).

[109] Ibid.

[110] Ibid.

[111] Gaunt, David, Massacres, Resistance, Protectors: Muslim-Christian Relations in Eastern Anatolia During World War I (Piscataway, NJ: Gorgias Press, 2006) 299-315.

[112] Travis, Hannibal, "'Native Christians Massacred': The Ottoman Genocide of the Assyrians During World War I," *Genocide Studies and Prevention* 1, 3 (December 2006) 327-328.

[113] Ibid., 335.

[114] Ibid., 335-336.

[115] *The London Times* (7 October 1915).

[116] Moorehead, 86.

[117] Nassibian, Akaby, Britain and the Armenian Question, 1915-1923 (London: Croom Helm, 1984) 109.

[118] *The Reuters News Service* (12 October 1915).

[119] *The New York Times* (14 September 1915).

[120] *The New York Times* (25 September 1915).

[121] *The New York Times* (28 September 1915).

[122] *The New York Times* (29 September 1915).

[123] *The London Times* (13 October 1915).

[124] Post, Dr. Wilfred M., *Inquiry Document* # 823 (Boston, MA, 1918) in Barton, 155.

[125] Harley, 66.

[126] Riggs, 33.

[127] *The New York Times* (18 August 1915).

[128] Atkinson, Dr. Tacy W., *Inquiry Document* # 810 (Boston, MA, 1918) in Barton, 51.

[129] Barton, xii-xiii

[130] Webb, 170.

[131] *The New York Times* (18 September 1915).

[132] Davis, 90.

[133] Leslie, Elvesta T., *Inquiry Document* # 814 (Boston, 1917) in Barton, 108.

[134] Harley, 68.

[135] Smith, 92-93.

[136] Atkinson, 15-16.

[137] Riggs., 130.

[138] Sarkisian, ii.

CHAPTER ELEVEN:

[1] Uhrichsen, Kristian Coates, <u>The First World War in the Middle East</u> (London: Oxford University Press, 2014) 71, 99.

[2] Ibid., 99.

[3] Dupuy, <u>Military History</u>, 1066.

[4] Cline, Eric H., <u>Jerusalem Besieged: From Ancient Canaan to Modern Israel</u> (Ann Arbor, MI: University of Michigan Press, 2004) p. 2.

[5] Dupuy, <u>Military History</u>, 1080-1081.

[6] Hitler, 666.

[7] Oren, 333.

[8] Morgenthau, <u>Ambassador</u>, 3.

[9] Lewy, 140-142.

[10] Ibid., 142.

[11] Ibid., 142.

[12] Balakian, <u>Burning Tigris</u>, xx.

[13] *The New York Times* (16 January 1915).

[14] Halacoglu, Dr.Yusuf, <u>Facts Relating to the Armenian Displacement (1915)</u>, (Ankara, Turkey: TTK Publications, 2001) 128.

[15] Morgenthau, <u>Murder</u>, 80.

[16] Ibid., 81.

[17] Ibid., 68.

[18] Ibid., 71.

[19] *The New York Times* (11 January 1915).

[20] *The New York Times* (8 October 1915).

[21] Hosfeld, Rolf, "The Armenian Massacre and Its Avengers: The ramifications of the assassination of Talaat Pasha in Berlin," (Fall, 2005) 58.

[22] Djemal, 277.

[23] *The New York Times* (22 November 1915).

[24] Djemal, 97-98.

[25] Ibid., 73.

[26] Ibid., 302.

[27] Ibid., 280.

[28] Ibid., 281.

[29] Sarafian, Ara, <u>Talaat Pasha's Report On the Armenian Genocide, 1917</u> (London: Gomidas Institute, 2011) 9-10.

[30] Balakian, Grigoris, <u>Armenian Golgotha: A Memoir of the Armenian Genocide, 1915-1918</u>, Translated by Peter Balakian (New York, NY: Vintage Books, 2010) 78.

[31] Melson, Robert, "Provocation of Nationalism: A Critical Inquiry into the Armenian Genocide of 1915," in <u>The Armenian Genocide</u>

in Perspective Richard G. Hovannisian, Editor (New Brunswick, NJ: Transaction Books, 1986) 64.

[32] McCarthy, Justin, Muslims and Minorities: The Population of Ottoman Anatolia and the End of Empire (New York: New York University Press, 1983) 121.

[33] Shaw, 315-316.

[34] Patriarchate of Armenia, "Armenian Population of the Ottoman Empire in 1912," Population Armenienne (Paris, 1920) quoted in McCarthy, Minorities, 50.

[35] Karajian, Sarkis J., "An Inquiry Into the Statistics of the Turkish Genocide of the Armenians, 1915-1918," The Armenian Review 25 (Winter, 1972) 7.

[36] Morgan, Jacques de, Histoire des peuple armenien (Paris, 1919) 297., quoted in Sarkissian, E. K., and R. G. Sahakian, Vital Issues in Modern Armenien History: A Documented Expose of Misrepresentations in Turkish Historiography, Translated by Elisha B. Chrakian (Watertown, MA: Library of Armenian Studies, 1965) 24.

[37] Karajian, 18.

[38] Ibid., 18-19.

[39] Melson, 145-146.

[40] Shaw, 315.

[41] McCarthy, Handbook, 56.

[42] Dadrian, Warrant, 173, 177.

[43] Toynbee, Arnold, "A Summary of Armenian History Up to and Including 1915," in Viscount James Bryce, The Treatment of Armenians in the Ottoman Empire: Documents Presented to Viscount Grey of Fallodon, Secretary of State for Foreign Affairs (London: H. M. S. O., 1916) 651., quoted in Melson, 146.

[44] Melson, 147.

[45] Lepsius, Johannes, Le rapport secret sur les massacres d'Armenie (Paris: Payot, 1918) quoted in Melson, 147.

[46] Melson, 312ff.

[47] Balakian, Peter, <u>The Burning Tigris: The Armenian Genocide and America's Response</u> (New York: HarperCollins Publishers, Inc., 2003) 180.

[48] Hovannisian, Richard G., Editor <u>The Armenian Genocide in Perspective</u> (New Brunswick, NJ: Transaction Books, 1986) 87.

[49] Hobsbawm, Eric, <u>The Age of Extremes: A History of the World, 1914-1991</u> (New York: Vintage Books, 1996) 50.

[50] Hovannisian, Richard G., Editor, <u>Remembrance and Denial: The Case of the Armenian Genocide</u> (Detroit, MI: Wayne State University Press, 1998) 15.

[51] Hobsbawm, 43.

CHAPTER TWELVE:

[1] Harlow, Rev. S., Ralph, *Inquiry Document* # 815 (Boston, MA, 1918) in Barton, 191.

[2] Davison, 121-122.

[3] Turfan, M. Naim, "Atatürk, Mustafa Kemal," <u>The Oxford Encyclopedia of the Islamic World</u>, Edited by John L. Esposito (New York, NY: Oxford University Press, 2009) *Oxford Islamic Studies Online*, http://www.oxfordislamicstudies.com. (Accessed September 10, 2014).

[4] <u>The Armenian Section of the International Commission On Mandates in Turkey: Excerpts From the 'King-Crane' Report</u> (1919) 191-194.

[5] Main, Dr. John Hanson Thomas, "Maintenance of Peace in Armenia: Senatorial Subcommittee Debates SJR 106, 'The Williams Resolution'," (Washington, DC: September 29 & October 2, 1919) *The Armenian Review* 34 (March, 1981) 78-79.

[6] Nicolson, Harold, <u>Peacemaking, 1919</u> (New York: Grosset & Dunlap, 1933, 1965) 40.

[7] Wilson, Woodrow, <u>Selected Literary and Political Papers and Addresses of Woodrow Wilson</u>, Volume II (New York: Grosset & Dunlap, 1926) 364.

[8] Bemis, Samuel F., "The First World War and the Peace Settlement," in <u>Wilson at Versailles: Problems in American Civilization</u>, Edited by Theodore P. Greene (Boston, MA: D. C. Heath and Company, 1957) 10.

[9] Terzian, Sevan G., "Henry Cabot Lodge and the Armenian Mandate," *The Armenian Review* 44 (Autumn, 1991) 29.

[10] Gerard, James, "The Chester Oil Concession and the Lausanne Treaty," *The Armenian Review* 28 (Spring, 1975) 35-36.

[11] Johnson, Brian, "Americans Investigating Anatolia: The 1919 Field Notes of Emory Niles and Arthur Sutherland," *The Journal of Turkish Studies*, 34, II, 2010, 129-147, from http://courses.washington.edu/otap/archive/data/arch_20c/niles_suthr/bjohns.html (Accessed September 10, 2014).

[12] Dadrian, <u>History, 321.</u>

[13] Kamuran, Gurun, <u>The Armenian File: The Myth of Innocence Exposed (New York: St. Martin's Press, 1985) 232.</u>

[14] Hovannisian, <u>Armenian Genocide</u>, 208-209.

[15] Herbert, Aubrey, <u>Ben Kendim: A Record of Eastern Travel</u> (London: Hutchinson, 1924) 41.

[16] Derogy, Jacques, <u>Resistance and Revenge: The Armenian Assassination of the Turkish Leaders Responsible for the 1915 Massacres and Deportations</u> (New Brunswick, NJ: Transaction Publishers, 1990) xxvi, 72.

[17] Derogy, xxiv.

[18] <u>The Case of Soghomon Tehilirian</u>, Translated by Vartkes Yeghiayan (Los Angeles, CA: A. R. F. Varantian Gomideh, 1985) 15.

[19] Balakian, <u>Golgotha</u>, 401.

[20] Alexander, 131.

[21] *The New York Times* (19 April 1922).

[22] Kieser, 127.

[23] Beevor, Antony, The Second World War, (New York, NY: Little, Brown and Company, 2012) 93.

[24] Palmer, James, The Bloody White Baron, (New York, NY: Basic Books, 2009) 117.

[25] Alexander, 130.

CHAPTER THIRTEEN:

[1] Andreopolis, 115.

[2] Gojiashvili, Nino, "Azerbaijan: Video Game Revisits Nagorno-Karabakh War," *EurasiaNet* (21 August 2012) www.eurasianet.org. (Accessed September 10, 2014).

[3] Gunter, 4, 70.

[4] "Enver Pasha given hero's funeral 74 years after his death," *Hurriyet Daily News* (9 August, 1996) www.hurriyetdailynews.com, (Accessed September 10, 2014).

[5] Ibid.

[6] Despite the timeliness of the topic, the current web-site of the *United States Holocaust Memorial Museum* indicates the possession of a number of collected photos, and written archives but beyond occasional lectures, scant public exhibition or even mention regarding the Armenian genocide. http://www.ushmm.org/search/results.php?q=Armenians. (Accessed September 10, 2014).

[7] "The Canonization of the Armenian Martyrs of 1915. What Is Christian Martyrdom Anyway?" *The Zohrab Information Center,* (September 25, 2014) 20http://zohrabcenter.org/2014/09/25/the-canonization-of-the-armenian-martyrs-of-1915-what-is-christian-martyrdom-anyway/09 (accessed October 3, 2014).

[8] Brustein, William I., Roots of Hate: Anti-Semitism in Eurpe Before the Holocaust, (Cambridge: Cambridge University Press, 2003) 49, 95, 177, 265.

[9] Dyer, Gwynne, "Turkish 'Falsifiers' and Armenian 'Deceivers': Historiography and the Armenian Massacres," *Middle Eastern Studies* 12 (1976), 99.

[10] Derogy,195.

[11] Wilson, Woodrow, Nobel Acceptance Speech (10 December 1920) www.nobelprize.org. (Accessed October 10, 2014).

[12] Obama, Barack, Nobel Acceptance Speech (10 December 2009) www.nobelprize.org. (Accessed October 10, 2014).

[13] Miller, Nathan, Theodore Roosevelt: A Life (New York, NY: Quill, 1992) ff. 507.

[14] Chaliand, Gerard, and Yves Ternon, The Armenian Question: From Genocide to Resistance (London: Zed Press, 1981, 1983).

[15] Balakian, Black Dog of Fate, 178.

[16] O'Donnell, Maureen, "Chicago-area woman, one of oldest survivors of Armenian genocide, has died," *Chicago Sun Times* (17 November 2014) www.suntimes.com. (Accessed, November 18, 2014).

[17] Terzian, 158.

[18] Hajinian, Charles, A Brief History of My Grandfather Haji Sarkis Hajinian: The Sweetness of Memory (Delafield, WI: [Family Records], 1999) 6.

BIBLIOGRAPHY

PRIMARY SOURCES

OFFICIAL RECORDS:

The Armenian Allegations: Myth and Reality/ A Handbook of Facts and Documents, Second Edition (Washington, D.C.: Assembly of Turkish American Associations,1987).

The 'Armenian Papers' of the Conference of San Remo (London: Her Majesty's Stationary Office, 1958).

The Armenian Question: A Memorandum (Boston: The Delegation of The Republic of Armenia, 1919, 1967).

The Armenian Section of the International Commission On Mandates in Turkey: Excerpts From the 'King-Crane' Report (1919)

"British Papers of 1876," The Armenian Review 29 (Summer, 1976).

The Case Of Soghomon Tehlirian, Translated by Vartkes Yeghiayan (Los Angeles, CA: A. R. F. Varantian Gomideh, 1985).

Ottoman Turkish 'Reform Rescripts' of the XIX Century (Constantinople: The Firman and Hatt-I-Humayun of the Sultan Relative to Privileges and Reforms in Turkey, 1856).

The Report of the President's Commission on the Holocaust (Washington, DC: Executive Order Number 12093, 1979).

The Turco-Armenian Question: The Turkish Point of View (Constantinople: The National Congress of Turkey, 1919).

"The Wilson Resolution:" United States Senatorial Subcommittee Debates SJR 106, "Maintenance of Peace in Armenia" (Washington, DC: 29 September & 2 October 1919).

Two Memoranda To The United Nations (Beirut: The Central Committee to Commemorate the Sixtieth Anniversary of the Turkish Genocide of the Armenians, 1975).

MEMOIRS/ SELECTED WRITINGS:

Agathangelos, History of the Armenians Translated by R. W. Thomson (Albany, NY: State University of New York Press, 1709, 1914, 1976).

Appian of Alexandria, Roman History: The Mithridatic Wars, 12:84, *The Loeb Classical Library*, Vol. II, Trans. by Horace White (Cambridge, MA: Harvard University Press, 1912).

Atkinson, Harriet H., "Mrs. Harriet Atkinson's Eyewitness Account of the Massacres at Harpoot," Reprinted in *The Armenian Review* 29 (Spring, 1976).

Balakian, Grigoris, Armenian Golgotha: A Memoir of the Armenian Genocide, 1915-1918, Translated by Peter Balakian (New York, NY: Vintage Books, 1922, 2010).

Barton, James L., "Turkish Atrocities": Statements of Armenian Missionaries on the Destruction of Christian Communities in Ottoman Turkey, 1915-1917 (Ann Arbor, MI: Gomidas Institute, 1918, 1998).

Signed Affadavits to the American Board of Commissioners for Foreign Missions:

--Andrus, Rev. Alphaeus N., Inquiry Document # 825 (Boston, MA: April, 1918).

--Atkinson, Dr. Tacy, Inquiry Document # 810 (Boston, MA: April, 1918).

--Birge, Mr. & Mrs. Kingsley, and Mr. & Mrs. S. R. Harlow, Inquiry Document # 816 (Boston, MA: April, 1918).

--Dodd, Dr. William S., Inquiry Document # 809 (Boston, MA: December, 1917).

--Fischer, Harriet J., Inquiry Document # 813 (Boston, MA: April, 1917).

--Harley, Isabelle, Inquiry Document # 812 (Boston, MA: April, 1918).

--Harlow, Rev. S. Ralph, Inquiry Document # 815 (Boston, MA: January, 1918).

--Leslie, Elvesta T., Inquiry Document # 814 (Boston, MA: October, 1917).

--Longbridge, Stella H., Inquiry Document # 803 (Boston, MA: April, 1918).

--MacCallum, Rev. Frederick W., Inquiry Document # 805 (Boston, MA: April, 1918).

--Parmelee, Dr. Ruth A., Inquiry Document # 811 (Boston, MA: April, 1918).

--Phelps, Theda B., Inquiry Document # 824 (Boston, MA: April, 1918).

--Post, Dr. Wilfred M., Inquiry Document # 823 (Boston, MA: April, 1918).

--Richmond, Clara Childs, Inquiry Document # 807 (Boston, MA: May, 1918).

--Riggs, Mary W., Inquiry Document # 808 (Boston, MA: April, 1918).

--Ryan, Rev. Arthur C., Inquiry Document # 817 (Boston, MA: April, 1918).

--Shane, Myrtle O., Inquiry Document # 804 (Boston, MA: April, 1918).

--Smith, Dr. Floyd O., Inquiry Document #822 (Boston, MA: September, 1919).

--Stapleton, Ida S., Inquiry Document # 821 (Boston, MA: April, 1918).

--Webb, Elizabeth S., Inquiry Document # 819 (Boston, MA: June, 1918).

--White, George E., Inquiry Document # 818 (Boston, MA: April, 1918).

Bedoukian, Kerop, Some Of Us Survived (New York: Farrar Straus Giroux, 1978).

Bismarck, Otto von, Reflections and Reminiscences, Edited by T. S. Hamerow (New York: Harper and Row, Publishers, 1968).

Bormann, Martin, The Bormann Letters, Edited by H. R. Trevor Roper (London, 1954).

Boyajian, Zabelle C., and Aram Raffi, The Anthology of Legends and Poems of Armenia (New York, NY: Columbia University Press, 1st ed.,1916).

Bryce, Viscount James, The Treatment of Armenians in the Ottoman Empire: Documents Presented to Viscount Grey of Fallodon, Secretary of State for Foreign Affairs (London: H.M.S.O., 1916).

Bryce, Viscount James, Transcaucasia, and Ararat (London: Macmillan and Co., Ltd., 1896, 1970).

Bury, G. Wyman, Pan Islam (London: MacMillan and Company, Ltd., 1919).

Cicero, Political Speeches, Trans. by D. H. Berry (Oxford, UK: Oxford University Press, 2006).

Curtis, William Elroy, To-Day in Syria and Palestine (New York, NY: Fleming H. Revell Company, 1903).

Darwin, Francis, The Life and Letters of Charles Darwin, Vol. I (New York: Elibron Classics Replica Edition, 2005, of original D. Appleton and Company, 1897).

Davis, Leslie A., The Slaughterhouse Province: An American Diplomat's Report on the Armenian Genocide, 1915-1917, Edited by Susan K. Blair (New Rochelle, NY: A. D. Caratzas, 1917, 1989).

Davis, William Stearns, "The Roots of the War," *The Century Illustrated Monthly Magazine*, Volume 98, May-October, 1919 (New York, NY: The Century Co., 1919).

D---ian, Dikran, Autobiography of Dikran D---ian, and Political Events,1852-1915 (Constantinople: [Family records] 1915, 1963).

Eliot, Sir Charles, Turkey In Europe (London: Edward Arnold, 1908).

Elgeria (Etheria), The Pilgrimage of Etheria, Translated by M. L. McClure & C. L. Feltoe

(London: Society for Promoting Christian Knowledge, 1919).

Eusebius, The History of the Church (New York: Penguin, 1987).

Gates, Caleb, to William Peet, quoted in Great Need Over the Water: The Letters of Theresa Huntington Ziegler, Missionary to Turkey, 1898-1905, Stina Katchadourian, Ed., (Reading, England: Taderon Press, 1999)

Gesar, A. The Defense of Aintab (Boston, MA: Hairenik Press, 1945).

Gladstone, William Ewart, Bulgarian Horrors and the Question of the East, (London: John Murray, 1876).

Gobineau, Arthur, An Essay on the Inequality of the Human Races, Translated by Adrian Collins (New York, NY: G. P. Putnam's Sons, 1915).

Gokalp, Ziya, The Principles of Turkism (Ankara & Leiden: E. J. Brill, 1920, 1968).

Gorganian, General Gabriel, From Brest-Litovsk to Lausanne (Boston, MA: The Hairenik Association, 1976).

Grant, Ulysses S., *Letter dated March 09, 1878*, from Young, John Russell, Around the World with General Grant (New York, NY: American News Company, 1879) 346.

Greene, Francis Vinton, The Russian Army and its Campaigns in Turkey in 1877-1878 (New York, NY: D. Appleton and Company, 1879).

Hacobian, A. P., <u>Armenia and the War: An Armenian's Point of View with an Appeal to Britain and the Coming Peace Conference</u> (New York: George H. Doran Company, 1918).

Hajinian, Charles, <u>A Brief History of My Grandfather Haji Sarkis Hajinian: The Sweetness of Memory</u> (Delafield, WI: [Family records], 1999).

Hartunian, Abraham H., <u>Neither To Laugh nor To Weep: A Memoir of the Armenian Genocide</u> (Boston, MA: Beacon Press, 1922, 1968).

Haskell, Edward B., "Bulgaria Points the Way," *Asia: Journal of the American Asiatic Association* 18 (January-December 1918).

Hitler, Adolf, <u>Mein Kampf</u> (Boston, MA: Houghton Mifflin Company, 1925, 1971).

Jackh, Ernest, <u>Der Aufsteigende Halbmond</u>, 6th Ed. (Berlin, 1916).

Josephus, Flavius, <u>Antiquities of the Jews</u>, Translated by William Whiston (Grand Rapids, MI: Kregel Publications, 1960, 1980).

Kalfaian, Aris, <u>Chomaklou: The History of an Armenian Village</u> (New York: Chomaklou Compatriotic Society, 1930, 1982).

Kidwai, Shaikh Mushir Hosain, <u>Pan-Islamism</u> (London: Lusac and Company, 1908.

Kopoian, Sara, <u>God's Miracle In My Life</u> (Milwaukee, WI: [Family records], 1984).

Lawrence, T. E., <u>Seven Pillars of Wisdom: A Triumph</u> (London: Doubleday, 1926, 1935, 1991).

Lemkin, Raphael, <u>Axis Rule in Occupied Europe</u> (Washington, DC: Carnegie Endowment, 1944).

Lynch, H. F. B., <u>Armenia: Travels and Studies</u> In Two Volumes (Beirut: Khayats Booksellers & Publishers, 1898, 1965).

Matosian, Khacher A., <u>Matosian Roots: Annals</u> (Athens: [Family records], 1923).

Medlicott, William Norton, <u>The Congress of Berlin and After: A Diplomatic History of the Near Eastern Settlement 1878-1880</u>, Second Edition (London: Methuen/ Routledge, 1938/1963).

Miller, Donald E., and Lorna Touryan Miller, <u>Survivors: An Oral History of the Armenian Genocide</u> (Berkeley, CA: University of California Press, 1993).

Money, Edward, <u>Twelve Months with the Bashi-Bazouks</u> (London: Chapman & Hall, 1857, reprinted by Elibon Classics, 2002).

Morgan, Jacques de, <u>Histoire des peuple armenien</u> (Paris, 1919).

Morgenthau, Henry, <u>Ambassador Morgenthau's Story</u> (Garden City, NY: Doubleday, Page and Company, 1918).

Morgenthau, Henry, <u>Murder of a Nation</u> (New York, NY: Armenian General Benevolent Union of America, 1918, 1974).

Nicolson, Harold, <u>Peacemaking 1919</u> (New York, NY: Grosset and Dunlap, 1933, 1965).

Niles, Emory, and Arthur E. Sullivan, in Brian Johnson, "Americans Investigating Anatolia: The 1919 Field Notes of Emory Niles and Arthur Sutherland," *The Journal of Turkish Studies*, 34, II, (2010) 129-147.

Pasdermadjian, Garegin, <u>Why Armenia Should be Free: Armenia's Role in the Present War</u> (Boston, MA: Hairenick Publishing Company, 1918).

Pasha, Djemal, <u>Memoiries of a Turkish Statesman, 1913-1919</u> (New York: George H. Doran Company, 1922).

Pasha, Talaat, *Untitled Document*, Published as <u>Talaat Pasha's Report On The Armenian Genocide, 1917</u>, Edited by Ara Sarafian, (London: Gomidas Insitute, 2011).

Patriarchate of Armenia, "Armenian Population of the Ottoman Empire in 1912," <u>Population Armenienne</u> (Paris, 1920).

Plutarch, "The Life of Lucullus," 27:4, <u>The Parallel Lives</u>, *The Loeb Classical Library*, Vol. II, Translated by Bernadotte Perrin (Cambridge, MA: Harvard University Press, 1914).

Ramsay, William M., <u>The Revolution in Constantinople and Turkey: A Diary</u> (London: Hodder, and Stoughton, 1909).

Rifat, Mevlanzade, <u>The Inner Aspects of the Turkish Revolution</u> (Aleppo, 1929) quoted in Lewy, Guenter, <u>The Armenian</u>

Massacres in Ottoman Turkey: A Disputed Genocide (Salt Lake City, UT: The University of Utah Press, 2005).

Riggs, Henry H., Days of Tragedy in Armenia: Personal Experiences in Harpoot, 1915-1917 (Ann Arbor, MI: Gomidas Institute, 1918, 1997).

Sebeos, The Armenian History attributed to Sebeos, Translated by R. W. Thomson (Liverpool, UK: Liverpool University Press, 1999).

Shiragian Arshavir, The Legacy: Memoirs of an Armenian Patriot (Boston, MA: Hairenik Press, 1976).

Stoddard, T. Lothrop, "Pan-Turanism," The American Political Science Review, Volume 11, Number 1(1917).

Strabo, Geography, Book 11, Chapter 14:15, The Loeb Classical Library, Vol. V, Trans. by Horace Leonard Jones (Cambridge, MA: Harvard University Press, 1928).

Tacitus, The Annals, Translated by Alfred John Church, and William Jackson Brodribb (Chicago, IL: The University of Chicago, 1952, 1992).

Werfel, Franz, The Forty Days of Musa Dagh (New York: Viking Press, 1933, 1934).

Wilson, Woodrow, Selected Literary and Political Papers and Addresses, Volume II (New York: Grosset and Dunlap Publishers, 1926).

Zak'aria of K'anak'er, The Chronicle of Deacon Zak'aria of K'anak'er, Translated by George A. Bournoutian (Costa Mesa, CA: Mazda Publishers, 1699, 1870, 2004),

Ziegler, Theresa Huntington, Great Need Over the Water: The Letters of Theresa Huntington Ziegler, Missionary To Turkey, 1898-1905, Edited by Stina Katchadourian (Reading, England: Taderon Press, 1999).

NEWSPAPERS/ PERIODICALS

The Century Illustrated Monthly Magazine, Volume 98, May-October, 1919.
The Independent, Volume LV, January-December, 1903.

The Levant Herald (Contemporary Obituary)

The London Morning Post (Contemporary Dispatches).

The Los Angeles Herald (Contemporary Dispatches).

The New York Times (Contemporary Dispatches).

The Reuters News Service (Contemporary Dispatches).

The Times [of London] (Contemporary Dispatches).

The Wall Street Journal (Editorials).

SECONDARY SOURCES

Adalian, R. P., "The Armenian Genocide," in Centuries of Genocide: Essays and Eyewitness Accounts, Edited by Samuel Totten, William S. Parsons, and Israel W. Charny (New York, NY: Routledge, 1997, 2013).

Akcam, Taner, A Shameful Act: The Armenian Genocide and the Question of Turkish Responsibility (New York, NY: Henry Holt and Company, 2006).

Akcam, Taner, From Empire to Republic: Turkish Nationalism & The Armenian Genocide (London: Zed Books, 2004).

Akcam, Taner, The Young Turks' Crime Against Humanity (Princeton, NJ: Princeton University Press, 2012).

Ahmad, Feroz, The Young Turks: The Committee of Union and Progress in Turkish Politics, 1908-1914 (Oxford: Clarendon Press, 1969).

Alexander, Edward, A Crime of Vengeance: An Armenian Struggle for Justice (New York: The Free Press, 1991).

Alkhateeb, Firas, "The Last Great Caliph: Abdülhamid II," *Lost Islamic History* (April, 2006) .

Anderson, Margaret Lavinia, "Who Still Talked about the Extermination of the Armenians?" From A Question Of Genocide: Armenians and Turks at the End of the Ottoman Empire, Edited by Ronald Grigor Suny, Fatma Müge Göçek, and Norman M. Naimark (New York, NY: Oxford University Press, 2011).

Andreopoulos, George J., Ed., Genocide: Conceptual and Historical Dimensions (Philadelphia, PA: University of Pennsylvania Press, 1994).

Arai, Masami, Turkish Nationalism In the Young Turk Era (Leiden: E. J. Brill, 1992).

Artinian, Varian H., "The Formation of Catholic and Protestant Millets in the Ottoman Empire," The Armenian Review 28 (Spring, 1975).

Astourian, Stephan H., "The Silence of the Land," From A Question Of Genocide: Armenians and Turks at the End of the Ottoman Empire, Edited by Ronald Grigor Suny, Fatma Müge Göçek, and Norman M. Naimark (New York, NY: Oxford University Press, 2011).

Auron, Yair, The Banality of Denial: Israel and the Armenian Genocide (New Brunswick, NJ: Transaction Publishers, 2003).

Auron, Yair, The Banality of Indifference: Zionism & the Armenian Genocide (New Brunswick, NJ: Transaction Publishers, 2000).

Balakian, Peter, Black Dog of Fate: A Memoir (New York: Basic Books, 1997).

Balakian, Peter, The Burning Tigris: The Armenian Genocide and America's Response (New York: HarperCollins Publishers, Inc., 2003).

Bobrick, Benson, East of the Sun: The Epic Conquest and Tragic History of Siberia (New York: Poseidon Press, 1992).

Bournoutian, George A., A History of the Armenian People, Volume II: 1500 A.D. to the Present (Costa Mesa, CA: Mazda Publishers, 1994).

Brown, Dee, Bury My Heart at Wounded Knee: An Indian History of the American West (New York: Bantam Books, 1970).

Brustein, William I., Roots of Hate: Anti-Semitism in Europe before the Holocaust (Cambridge: Cambridge University Press, 2003).

Carzou, Jean-Marie, Armenie 1915 (Paris: Flammarion, 1975).

Chaliand, Gerard, and Yves Ternon, The Armenian Question: From Genocide to Resistance (London: Zed Press, 1981, 1983).

Chalk, Frank, and Kurt Jonassohn, The History and Sociology of Genocide: Analyses and Case Studies (New Haven, CT: Yale University Press, 1990).

Chandler, David G., The Campaigns of Napoleon (New York: The Macmillan Company, 1966).

Chirot, Daniel, and Clark McCauley, Why Not Kill Them All?: The Logic and Prevention of Mass Political Murder (Princeton, NJ: Princeton University Press, 2006).

Chorbajian, Levon, and George Shirinian, Eds., Studies In Comparative Genocide (London: MacMillan Press, Ltd., 1999).

Cirakman, Asli, From the "Terror of the World" to the "Sick Man of Europe": European Images of Ottoman Empire and Society from the Sixteenth Century to the Nineteenth (New York: Peter Lang, 2002).

Cline, Eric H., Jerusalem Besieged: From Ancient Canaan to Modern Israel (Ann Arbor, MI: University of Michigan Press, 2004).

Dadrian, Vahakn N., German Responsibility in the Armenian Genocide: A Review of the Historical Evidence of German Complicity (Watertown, MA: Blue Crane Books, 1996).

Dadrian, Vahakn N., The History of the Armenian Genocide: Ethnic Conflict from the Balkans to Anatolia to the Caucasus (Providence, RI: Berghahn Books, 1995).

Dadrian, Vahakn N., Warrant For Genocide: Key Elements of Turko-Armenian Conflict (New Brunswick, NJ: Transaction Publishers, 1999).

Davis, Fanny, The Palace of Topkapi in Istanbul (New York, NY: Charles Scribner's Sons, 1970).

Davison, Roderic H., Turkey (Englewood Cliffs, NJ: Prentice-Hall, Inc., 1968).

Delaney, John J., Dictionary of Saints (Garden City, NY: Image Books, 1983).

Derogy, Jacques, Resistance and Revenge: The Armenian Assassination of the Turkish Leaders Responsible for the 1915 Massacres and Deportations (New Brunswick, NJ: Transaction Publishers, 1990).

Donabedian, Kevork, "The Eastern Question and the Armenian Case," The Armenian Review 25 (Spring, 1972).

Douglas, John M., The Armenians (New York: J. J. Winthrop Corp., 1992).

Dupuy, R. Ernest, and Trevor N. Dupuy, The Harper Encyclopedia of Military History: From 3500 B.C. to the Present, Fourth Ed., (New York: Harper Collins Publishers, 1993).

Dyer, Gwynne, "Letter to the Editor," Middle Eastern Studies 9, (1973) 379-383, in Lewy, Guenter, The Armenian Massacres in Ottoman Turkey: A Disputed Genocide (Salt Lake City, UT: The University of Utah Press, 2005).

Dyer, Gwynne, "Turkish 'Falsifiers' and Armenian 'Deceivers': Historiography and the Armenian Massacres," Middle Eastern Studies 12 (1976).

Engholm, Christopher, The Armenian Earthquake (San Diego, CA: Lucent Books, 1989).

Erickson, Edward J., Ordered To Die: A History of the Ottoman Army in the First World War (Westport, CT: Praeger Publishers, 2000).

Ersoy, Ahmet, Maciej Górny, Vangelis Kechriotis, Editors, Modernism: The Creation of Nation States (Budapest, Hungary: Central European University Press, 2010).

Etmekjian, James, "The Tanzimat Reforms and Their Effect on the Armenians in Turkey," The Armenian Review 25 (Spring, 1972).

Etmekjian, Lillian, "Armenian Cultural and Political Contributions to Reform in Turkey," The Armenian Review 29 (Summer, 1976).

Eyck, Erich, Bismarck and the German Empire (New York: W. W. Norton & Company, Inc., 1968).

Ferro, Marc, <u>Nicholas II: The Last of the Tsars</u>, Trans. by Brian Pearce (New York: Oxford University Press, 1993).

Fest, Joachim C., <u>Hitler</u>, Translated by Richard and Clara Winston (New York: Harcourt Brace Jovanovich, Inc., 1973, 1974).

Finkel, Caroline, <u>Osman's Dream: The History of the Ottoman Empire</u> (New York, NY: Basic Books, 2005).

Fischer, Fritz, <u>Germany's Aims in the First World War</u> (New York: W. W. Norton & Company, Inc., 1961, 1967).

Firoozi, Edith, and Ira N. Klein, <u>The Age of Great Kings</u>, from, <u>The Universal History of the World</u> (New York: Golden Press, 1966).

Forsythe, David P., <u>Encyclopedia of Human Rights</u>, Volume I, (New York, NY: Oxford University Press, 2009).

Gaunt, David, "The Assyrian Genocide of 1915," *Assyrian Genocide Research Center*, 2009.

Gaunt, David, <u>Massacres, Resistance, Protectors: Muslim-Christian Relations in Eastern Anatolia During World War I</u> (Piscataway, NJ: Gorgias Press, 2006).

Gerard, James, "The Chester Oil Concession and the Lausanne Treaty," *The Armenian Review* 28 (Spring, 1975).

Graber, G. S., <u>Caravans to Oblivion: The Armenian Genocide, 1915</u> (New York: John Wiley & Sons, Inc., 1996).

Grousset, René, <u>The Epic of the Crusades,</u> trans. by Noël Lindsay (New York, NY: Orion Press, 1970).

Gulbekian, Edward V., "The Poles and Armenians in Hitler's Political Thinking," *The Armenian Review* 41, No. 3 (Autumn, 1988).

Gunter, Michael M., <u>"Pursuing the Just Cause of Their People": A Study of Contempory Armenian Terrorism</u> (New York: Greenwood Press, 1986).

Gürün, Kamuran, <u>The Armenian File: The Myth of Innocence Exposed</u> (New York: St. Martin's Press, 1985).

Gurzadyan, V.G, and R.Vardanyan, "Halley's comet of 87 BC on the coins of Armenian king Tigranes?" *Astronomy & Geophysics*, Volume 45, Issue 4 (August 2004).

Haddad, William W., and William Ochsenwald, Eds., Nationalism In A Non-National State: The Dissolution of the Ottoman Empire (Columbus, OH: Ohio State University Press, 1977).

Hanioglu, M. Sukru, The Young Turks In Opposition (New York: Oxford University Press, 1995).

Haslip, Joan, The Sultan: The Life of Abdul Hamid II (New York, NY: Holt, Rinehart, and Winston, 1958).

Hayes, Carlton J. H., A Political and Social History of Modern Europe, Volume II (New York: The Macmillan Company, 1916, 1924).

Hobsbawm, Eric, The Age of Extremes: A History of the World, 1914-1991 (New York: Vintage Books, 1996).

Hochschild, Adam, King Ludwig's Ghost (New York, NY: Houghton Mifflin Company, 1998).

Hofman, Tessa, and Gerayer Koutcharian, "The History of Armenian-Kurdish Relations in tne Ottoman Empire," *The Armenian Review* 39, No 4 (Winter, 1986).

Hoogasian Villa, Susie, and Mary Kilbourne Matossian, Armenian Village Life Before 1914 (Detroit, MI: Wayne State University Press, 1982).

Hopkirk, Peter The Great Game: The Struggle for Empire in Central Asia (New York: Kodanasha International, Ltd., 1990, 1992).

Horowitz, Irving Louis, "Government Responsibilities to the Jews and Armenians: Nazi Holocaust and Turkish Genocide Reconsidered," *The Armenian Review* 39, No. 1 (Spring, 1986).

Hosfeld, Rolf, "The Armenian Massacre and Its Avengers: The ramifications of the assassination of Talaat Pasha in Berlin," *IP – Transatlantic Edition* (Fall, 2005).

Hovannisian, Richard G., The Armenian Genocide: History, Politics, Ethics (New York: St. Martin's Press, 1992).

Hovannisian, Richard G., Ed., <u>The Armenian Genocide In Perspective</u> (New Brunswick, NJ: Transaction Books, 1986).

Hovannisian, Richard G., Ed., <u>The Armenian People From Ancient To Modern Times</u> Volume I (New York: St. Martin's Press, 1997).

Hovannisian, Richard G., <u>The Armenian People From Ancient To Modern Times</u>, Vol. II (New York, NY: Palgrave Macmillan, 2004).

Hovannisian, Richard G., Ed., <u>Looking Backward, Moving Forward: Confronting the Armenian Genocide</u> (New Brunswick, NJ: Transaction Publishers, 2003).

Hovannisian, Richard G., Ed., <u>Remembrance and Denial: The Case of the Armenian Genocide</u> (Detroit, MI: Wayne State University Press, 1998).

Jelavich, Charles, and Barbara Jelavich, <u>The Establishment of the Balkan National States: 1804-1920</u> (Seattle, WA: The University of Washington Press, 1977).

Johnson, Brian, "Americans Investigating Anatolia: The 1919 Field Notes of Emory Niles and Arthur Sutherland," *The Journal of Turkish Studies*, 34, II (2010) 129-147.

Jones, W. R., "The Legend and Letters of Abgar, 'King of Armenia'," *The Armenian Review* 28 (Spring, 1975).

Kaplan, Robert, "Long History of the Doctors of Doom," *The Sidney Morning Herald*, July 7, 2007, www.smh.com.au (Accessed September 5, 2014).

Karajian, Sarkis J., "An Inquiry Into the Stastistics of the Turkish Genocide of the Armenians, 1915-1918," *The Armenian Review* 25 (Winter, 1972).

Kayalı, Hasan, "Elections and the Electoral Process in the Ottoman Empire, 1876-1919," *The International Journal of Middle East Studies*, Volume 27, Number 3 (1995).

Kaylan, Muammar, <u>The Kemalists: Islamic Revival and the Fate of Secular Turkey</u> (Amherst, NY: Prometheus Books, 2005).

Kazarian, Haigazn, "The Turkish Genocide of the Armenians: A Premeditated and Official Assault," The Armenian Review 30 (Spring, 1977).

Kieser, Hans-Lukas, "From Patriotism to Mass Murder," From A Question Of Genocide: Armenians and Turks at the End of the Ottoman Empire, Edited by Ronald Grigor Suny, Fatma Müge Göçek, and Norman M. Naimark (New York, NY: Oxford University Press, 2011).

Kinross, Lord John Patrick Douglas Balfour, The Ottoman Centuries: The Rise and Fall of the Turkish Empire (New York: William Morrow and Co., Inc., 1977).

Kinzer, Stephen, Crescent And Star: Turkey Between Two Worlds (New York: Farrar, Straus and Giroux, 2001).

Kornberg, Jacques, "Theodore Herzl: A Reevaluation," The Journal of Modern History 52, No.2 (June, 1980).

Krikorian, Mesrob K., Armenians In the Service of The Ottoman Empire, 1860-1908 (Boston, MA: Routledge & Kegan Paul, 1978).

Kuper, Leo, International Action Against Genocide (London: Minority Rights Group Report, Number 53, 1982).

Kushner, David, The Rise of Turkish Nationalism, 1876-1908 (London: Frank Case and Company, Ltd., 1977).

Langer, William L., The Diplomacy of Imperialism, 1890-1902, Volumes I & II (New York, NY: Alfred A. Knopf, 1935, 1951).

Lantz, Kenneth A., The Dostoevsky Encyclopedia (Westport, CT: Greenwood Press, 2004).

Lewy, Guenter, The Armenian Massacres in Ottoman Turkey: A Disputed Genocide (Salt Lake City, UT: The University of Utah Press, 2005).

Libaridian, Gerard J., "What was Revolutionary about Armenian Revolutionary Parties in the Ottoman Empire?" from Suny, Ronald Grigor, Fatma Müge Göçek, and Norman M. Naimark,

Editors, A Question of Genocide (New York, NY: Oxford University Press, 2011).

Lieven, Dominic, Nicholas II: Twilight of the Empire (New York, NY: St. Martin's Griffin, 1993).

Lowry, Heath W., The Nature of the Early Ottoman State (Albany, NY: State University of New York Press, 2003).

MacFie, A. L., The End Of the Ottoman Empire, 1908-1923 (London: Longman, 1998).

MacKenzie, David, Violent Solutions: Revolutions, Nationalism, and Secret Societies in Europe to 1918 (Lanham, MD: University Press of America, Inc., 1996).

MacLean, Rory, Berlin: Portrait of a City Through the Centuries (New York, NY: Weidenfeld & Nicolson, 2014).

Mann, Michael, The Dark Side of Democracy: Explaining Ethnic Cleansing (Cambridge, NY: Cambridge University Press, 2005).

Markusen, Eric, and David Kopf, The Holocaust and Strategic Bombing: Genocide and Total War in the Twentieth Century (Boulder, CO: Westview Press, 1995).

Mardin, Serif, The Genesis of Young Ottoman Thought: A Study in the Modernization of Turkish Political Ideas (Syracuse, NY: Syracuse University Press, 1962, 2000).

Massie, Robert K., Dreadnought: Britain, Germany, and the Coming of The Great War (New York: Random House, 1991).

Massie, Robert K., Nicholas and Alexandra (New York, NY: Dell Publishing Company, Inc., 1967).

McCarthy, Justin A., Death and Exile: The Ethnic Cleansing of Ottoman Muslims, 1821-1922 (Princeton, NJ: Darwin Press, 1995).

McCarthy, Justin, Muslims and Minorities: The Population of Ottoman Anatolia and the End of the Empire (New York: New York University Press, 1983).

McCarthy, Justin, The Arab World, Turkey, and The Balkans (1878-1914): A Handbook of Historical Statistics (Boston, MA: G. K. Hall and Co., 1982).

McCarthy, Justin, The Ottoman Peoples and the End of Empire (London: Arnold, 2001).

McKiernan, Kevin, The Kurds: A People in Search of Their Homeland (New York, NY: St. Martin's Press, 2006).

McManners, John, Editor, The Oxford Illustrated History of Christianity (Oxford: Oxford University Press, 1990).

McMeekin, Sean, The Berlin-Baghdad Express: The Ottoman Empire and Germany's Bid For World Power (Cambridge, MA: The Belknap Press of Harvard University Press, 2010).

Melson, Robert F., "Provocation of Nationalism: A Critical Inquiry into the Armenian Genocide of 1915," in The Armenian Genocide in Perspective, Richard G. Hovannisian, Editor (New Brunswick, NJ: Transaction Books, 1986).

Melson, Robert F., Revolution and Genocide: On the Origins of the Armenian Genocide and the Holocaust (Chicago, IL: The University of Chicago Press, 1992).

Merani, Shambu T., The Turks of Istanbul (New York: Macmillan Publishing Co., Inc., 1980).

Miller, Nathan, Theodore Roosevelt: A Life (New York, NY: Quill, 1992).

Missakian, J., A Searchlight on the Armenian Question, 1878-1950 (Boston, MA: Hairenik Publishing Company, 1950).

Moorehead, Alan, Gallipoli (New York, Ballantine Books, 1956).

Nalbandian, Louise, The Armenian Revolutionary Movement: The Development of Armenian Political Parties through the Nineteenth Century (Berkeley, CA: University of California Press, 1963).

Naltchayan, Nazaret, "Kaiser Wilhelm II's Visits to the Ottoman Empire: Rationale, Reaction, and the Meanings of Images," The Armenian Review 42, No.2 (Summer, 1989).

Nassibian, Akaby, Britain and the Armenian Question, 1915-1923 (New York: St. Martin's Press, 1984).

Nazer, James, The Armenian Massacre (New York: T & T Publishing, Inc., 1968).

Nersessian, Sirarpie Der, Armenian Art (Paris: Armenian General Benevolent Fund, undated).

Oren, Michael B., Power, Faith, and Fantasy: America in the Middle East, 1776 to the Present (New York, NY: Sike, Inc., W. W. Norton and Company, Inc., 2007).

Othman, Siyamend, "Kurdish Nationalism: Instigators and Historical Influences," The Armenian Review 42, No.1 (Spring, 1989).

Paice, Edward, World War I: The African Front (New York, NY: Pegasus Books, 2008).

Papazian, Dennis, "Misplaced Credulity: Contemporary Turkish Attempts To Refute the Armenian Genocide," The Armenian Review 45, No.1-2 (Spring/Summer, 1992).

Perry, Duncan M., The Macedonian Revolutionary Organization's Armenian Connection," The Armenian Review 42, No.1 (Spring, 1989).

Peterson, Merrill D., Starving Armenians: America and the Armenian Genocide, 1915-1930 and After (Charlottesville, VA: University of Virginia Press, 2004).

Power, Samantha, "A Problem From Hell": America and The Age of Genocide (New York: Basic Books, 2002).

Radzinsky, Edvard, The Last Tsar: The Life and Death of Nicholas II (New York: Anchor Books, Doubleday, 1992).

Ramsaur, Ernest Edmondson, Jr., The Young Turks: Prelude to the Revolution of 1908 (Princeton, NJ: Princeton University Press, 1957).

Rausch, David A., A Legacy of Hatred (Chicago, IL: Moody Press, 1984).

Remak, Joachim, "1914--The Third Balkan War: Origins Reconsidered," The Journal of Modern History 43, No.3 (September, 1971).

Redgate, A. E., The Armenians, (Malden, MA: Blackwell Publishing, 1998, 2000).

Renzi, William A., "Great Britain, Russia, and the Straits," *The Journal of Modern History* 42, No.1 (March, 1970).

Ruggiero, Adriane, The Ottoman Empire (New York: Benchmark Books, 2003).

Salt, Jeremy, Imperialism, Evangelism and the Ottoman Armenians, 1878-1896 (Portland,OR: Frank Cass, 1995).

Sarkisian, E. K., and R. G. Sahakian, Vital Issues in Modern Armenian History: A Documented Expose of Misrepresentations in Turkish Historiography (Watertown, MA: Armenian Studies, 1965).

Sarkissian, Arshag O., "It Happened in 1915: The Massacre of the Armenians in the Ottoman Empire," *The Armenian Review* 30 (Spring, 1977).

Shashko, Philip, "The Bulgarian Massacres of 1876 Reconsidered: Reaction to the April Uprising or Premeditated Attack?" *Academie Bulgare Des Sciences: Institut D'Etudes Balkaniques* 4 (1986).

Shashko, Philip, "Gotse Delchev and G'orche Petrov on Permanent Internal War and General Uprising," (Sofia, 1983).

Shaw, Stanford J., and Ezel Kural Shaw, History of the Ottoman Empire and Modern Turkey, Volume II: Reform, Revolution, and Republic: The Rise of Modern Turkey, 1808-1975 (Cambridge: Cambridge University Press, 1977).

Shirer, William L., The Rise and Fall of the Third Reich: A History of Nazi Germany (New York: Simon and Schuster, 1959, 1988).

Smith, Anthony D., Myths and Memories of the Nation (Oxford: Oxford University Press, 1999).

Smith, Roger W., "Genocide and Denial: The Armenian Case and its Implications," *The Armenian Review* 42, No.1 (Spring, 1989).

Stone, Frank Andrews, "The Life and Death of Armenia or Euphrates College, Harpoot, Turkish Armenia," *The Armenian Review* 30 (Summer, 1977).

Suakian, Kevork Y., "The Preconditions of the Armeno-Turkish Case of Genocide," *The Armenian Review* 34, No. 4 (December, 1981).

Suny, Ronald Grigor, Armenia In the Twentieth Century (Chico, CA: Scholars Press, 1983).

Suny, Ronald Grigor, Fatma Müge Göçek, & Norman M. Naimark Editors, A Question of Genocide (New York, NY: Oxford University Press, 2011).

Taylor, Alan J.P., The Struggle for Mastery in Europe: 1848-1918, (Oxford, UK: Oxford University Press, 1954, 1971).

Terzian, Aram, "1915: The Darkest Years," *The Armenian Review* 28 (Summer, 1975).

Terzian, Sevan G., "Henry Cabot Lodge and the Armenian Mandate," *The Armenian Review* 44, No.3 (Autumn, 1991).

Travis, Hannibal, "'Native Christians Massacred': The Ottoman Genocide of the Assyrians During World War I," *Genocide Studies and Prevention* 1, 3 (December 2006).

Tuchman, Barbara W., Bible and Sword: England and Palestine from the Bronze Age to Balfour (New York: Ballantine Books, 1956, 1984).

Tuchman, Barbara W., The Guns of August (New York: Macmillan Publishing Company, 1962).

Uras, Esat, The Armenians In History And The Armenian Question (Istanbul: Documentary Publications, 1988).

Varandian, Michael, "A History of the Armenian Revolutionary Federation," *The Armenian Review* 25 (Winter, 1972).

Vratzian, Simon, "The Second World Congress of the Armenian Revolutionary Federation," *The Armenian Review* 32 (September, 1979).

Walker, Christopher J., Armenia: The Survival of a Nation (London: Croom Hem Publishers, 1980).

Walker, Christopher J., <u>Visions of Ararat: Writings on Armenia</u> (London: I. B. Tauris & Co. Ltd., 1997).

Walker, Christopher J., "World War I and the Armenian Genocide," in Richard G. Hovannisian, <u>The Armenian People From Ancient To Modern Times</u>, Vol. II (New York, NY: Palgrave Macmillan, 2004).

Waller, James, <u>Becoming Evil: How Ordinary People Commit Genocide and Mass Killing</u> (Oxford: Oxford University Press, 2002).

Warner, Denis, and Peggy Warner, <u>The Tide At Sunrise: A History of the Russo-Japanese War, 1904-1905</u> (New York: Charterhouse, 1974).

Weitz, Eric D., <u>A Century of Genocide: Utopias of Race and Nation</u> (Princeton, NJ: Princeton University Press, 2003).

Weitz, Eric D., "Germany and the Young Turks: Revolutionaries Into Statesmen," From <u>A Question Of Genocide: Armenians and Turks at the End of the Ottoman Empire</u>, Edited by Ronald Grigor Suny, Fatma Müge Göçek, and Norman M. Naimark (New York, NY: Oxford University Press, 2011).

Wheatcroft, Andrew, <u>The Ottomans</u> (London: Viking, 1993).

Whyte, A. J., <u>The Evolution of Modern Italy</u>, (New York, NY: W. W. Norton & Company, Inc., 1959, 1965).

Wilson, Ian, <u>Holy Faces, Secret Places: An Amazing Quest for the Face of Jesus</u> (New York: Doubleday, 1991).

Wilson, Ian, <u>The Blood and The Shroud</u> (New York: The Free Press, 1998).

Wilson, Ian, <u>The Shroud of Turin: The Burial Cloth of Jesus Christ?</u> (New York: Image Books, 1979).

ABOUT THE AUTHOR

William Colin Marris served as a commissioned officer in the United States Naval Reserve. He holds a Master's Degree in History *Summa Cum Laude* from the University of Wisconsin-Milwaukee, and is currently pursuing a Doctorate. Marris has also been accepted for membership in Mensa. His primary area of study is Biblical History which he has taught for more than a decade at a small Bible college, and he plans to publish a book on the Jewish roots of Christianity in 2016. W. Colin Marris has personally visited numerous Biblical sites throughout Israel, Palestine, Egypt, Greece, Turkey, Jordan and Italy. In addition, he has traveled to all fifty states, nearly seventy countries, and all seven continents. Marris and his artist wife Lynne seasonally commute between the "Lake Country" of Oconomowoc, Wisconsin and the Sonoran Desert of Anthem, Arizona. Together they have three adult married children, six grandchildren, and a Soft Coated Wheaten Terrier named Cosmo.

Made in the USA
San Bernardino, CA
17 April 2017